Non-Finiteness

'Non-finiteness' is a phenomenon that occurs in most natural languages, whereby a verb is not inflected by grammatical tense and does not possess the grammatical features of aspect, mood or voice. Various theories have been developed to explain their distribution and their role in clause structure, but many instances of non-finiteness remain unaccounted for. Taking a functional approach, this study proposes a 'process-relation framework' to explain the more complex, previously unaccounted for instances of non-finiteness in clause structure. It applies the framework comparatively to non-finiteness in English and Chinese, showing how it can be applied across typologically distinct languages. Drawing on corpus-based instances and observations, it introduces numerous thought-provoking cases, in which constructional (or combining) types and the predictability of non-finiteness co-occur. In terms of application, non-finiteness is decisive in categorizing language types, and it is critical in processing natural languages, text segmentation and annotation in particular.

BINGJUN YANG is Professor in Systemic Functional Linguistics at Shanghai Jiao Tong University. His publications include *Corpus-Based Investigations into Grammar, Media and Health Discourse* (Springer Nature, 2020), *Language Policy* (Routledge, 2017) and *Absolute Clauses in English from the Systemic Functional Perspective* (Springer, 2015).

Non-Finiteness
A Process-Relation Perspective

Bingjun Yang
Shanghai Jiao Tong University

Shaftesbury Road, Cambridge CB2 8EA, United Kingdom

One Liberty Plaza, 20th Floor, New York, NY 10006, USA

477 Williamstown Road, Port Melbourne, VIC 3207, Australia

314–321, 3rd Floor, Plot 3, Splendor Forum, Jasola District Centre, New Delhi – 110025, India

103 Penang Road, #05–06/07, Visioncrest Commercial, Singapore 238467

Cambridge University Press is part of Cambridge University Press & Assessment, a department of the University of Cambridge.

We share the University's mission to contribute to society through the pursuit of education, learning and research at the highest international levels of excellence.

www.cambridge.org
Information on this title: www.cambridge.org/9781009073691

DOI: 10.1017/9781009072502

© Bingjun Yang 2022

This publication is in copyright. Subject to statutory exception and to the provisions of relevant collective licensing agreements, no reproduction of any part may take place without the written permission of Cambridge University Press & Assessment.

First published 2022
First paperback edition 2025

A catalogue record for this publication is available from the British Library

ISBN   978-1-316-51341-5   Hardback
ISBN   978-1-009-07369-1   Paperback

Cambridge University Press & Assessment has no responsibility for the persistence or accuracy of URLs for external or third-party internet websites referred to in this publication and does not guarantee that any content on such websites is, or will remain, accurate or appropriate.

Contents

List of Figures	*page* viii
List of Tables	x
Preface	xiii
Acknowledgements	xvi
Symbols and Abbreviations	xviii
Leipzig Glossing Abbreviations	xx

1	**Introduction**		**1**
	1.1	Why This Study?	1
	1.2	The Finite/Non-finite Distinction	3
	1.3	Purpose of the Study	6
	1.4	Research Questions	7
	1.5	Methodology	7
	1.6	Organization of the Book	7
2	**Non-finiteness in the Literature**		**9**
	2.1	Non-finiteness in the Early History of English Grammar Writing	9
	2.2	Non-finiteness in Traditional Grammar: Morphology-Based	14
		2.2.1 The Property of the Verb	15
		2.2.2 The Categorization of Non-finite Clauses in English	16
		2.2.3 Sentence-Building Power and the Status of Tense	18
		2.2.4 Scale of Finiteness	20
	2.3	Non-finiteness from the Typological Perspective	21
		2.3.1 Category Space and the Continuum Hypothesis	21
		2.3.2 Obligatory and Asymmetry	25
		2.3.3 Root Infinitives in Children's Early Language	27
	2.4	Non-finiteness in Generative Grammar: Form-Based	29
		2.4.1 PRO as Subject of Non-finite Clauses	30
		2.4.2 Tense and the Finite/Non-finite Distinction	33
		2.4.3 Non-isomorphic Relation between Content and Form	36
		2.4.4 Gradient or Binary	37
	2.5	Non-finiteness in Cognitive Grammar: Meaning-Based	38
		2.5.1 Non-finiteness as Atemporal Construal	38
		2.5.2 The View of Scalarity	40
		2.5.3 Verbal and Finite versus Nominal and Non-finite	43
		2.5.4 Conceptual Motivation	44

		2.5.5 Non-finite Clauses as Constructions	45

    2.5.5 Non-finite Clauses as Constructions   45

2.6 Non-finiteness in Systemic Functional Grammar: Meaning- and Form-Based   46
    2.6.1 General Discussions on Non-finite Clauses   46
    2.6.2 Criteria of Non-finite Clause Identification   49
    2.6.3 Function-Specified Systems of Non-finite Clauses   51

2.7 Viewpoints from Other Theories and the Semantic Types   55
    2.7.1 Semiotic Grammar   55
    2.7.2 Role and Reference Grammar   56
    2.7.3 Functional Discourse Grammar   57
    2.7.4 Other Approaches and the Semantic Types   60

2.8 Some Special Types to Be Noted   62
2.9 A Summary of the Relevant Research   64

3 Theoretical Foundations   68

3.1 Prerequisite: Distinguishing Spoken and Written Language   68
    3.1.1 Differences between Spoken and Written Language   69
    3.1.2 Grammars for Speech and Writing   71

3.2 Cryptotype and Cline   73
3.3 Metafunctions as Universal Categories   75
3.4 Process as the Basic Semantic Unit   79
    3.4.1 Types of Situation and Types of Process   79
    3.4.2 Major, Median and Minor Processes   83

3.5 Clause as the Basic Syntactic Unit: Major, Median and Minor   84
3.6 Ideational Grammatical Metaphor   87
    3.6.1 A Sketch of Ideational Grammatical Metaphor   87
    3.6.2 Nominalization   89
    3.6.3 Adjectivization   91
    3.6.4 Verbalization   92
    3.6.5 Adverbialization   94

3.7 Embedding, Two Principles and Rankshifting   95
3.8 Defining Non-finiteness in Terms of Function   99

4 Basic Process Relations as One Solution to the Controversy   102

4.1 The Basic Construction and Its Functional Components   102
4.2 The Para-relation of Processes   104
4.3 The Hypo-relation of Processes   106
4.4 The Participant Conflated   108
4.5 Process as Primary Participant   111
4.6 Process as Secondary Participant   114
4.7 Process as Circumstance   117
4.8 The Triple Participant   119

5 Non-finiteness as the Bridge for Process Compression   122

5.1 Clause Combining   123
    5.1.1 Conjunctions in English and Chinese   123
    5.1.2 Reconsidering Coordination, Subordination and Embedding   125
    5.1.3 Non-finite Clauses as a Basic Category of Clause Combining   130

5.2 Basic Clause Relations and Non-finiteness   134
    5.2.1 Paratactic Relations   135

	5.2.2	Circumstantial Relations	136
	5.2.3	Participantial Relations	138
5.3		The Metaphoric Syndrome and Non-finite Clauses as the Bridge	140

6 Revisiting the Controversial English Constructions with Non-finiteness — 143

6.1	Controversial Constructions with Non-finiteness in English: A Sketch	144
6.2	Causatives and Non-causatives	144
6.3	COCA Distribution of Typical Verbs in (Non-)Causatives	146
6.4	Process Relations in Typical English Constructions with Non-finiteness	149
6.5	The Serial Verb Construction	151
6.6	The Existential Construction	154
6.7	The Absolute Construction	158
6.8	The Process Relation in Ambiguous Non-finite Constructions	159

7 Revisiting the Controversial Chinese Constructions with Non-finiteness — 163

7.1	The Serial Verb Construction	164
7.2	The Pivotal Construction	169
7.3	Pivotal Construction or Grammatical Metaphor?	179
7.4	The Existential Construction	183
7.5	Other Controversial Non-finite Constructions Revisited	190

8 Conclusion — 195

8.1	Overview of the Major Findings	195
8.2	Limitations and Further Study	197

References — 199
Index — 227

Figures

1.1	Google Ngram for 'finiteness' and 'nonfinite'	*page* 4
2.1	The finite and non-finite verbs in Kruisinga (1932 [1915])	12
2.2	Categories of non-finite clause in Quirk et al. (1985)	18
2.3	The continuum hypothesis (Wetzer 1996: 44)	22
2.4	Verbal system typology matrix (Lowe 2015: 322)	25
2.5	The scale of grammatical dependency (T. Payne 2011: 331)	40
2.6	Degrees of finiteness in English (Givón 2001: 26)	42
2.7	The scale of syntactic level (Lehmann 1988: 192)	42
2.8	Theme in non-finite dependent clauses (Halliday & Matthiessen 2014: 127)	48
2.9	System of non-finiteness in terms of Phenomenon: ideational (B. Yang 2003: 149)	53
2.10	System network of Mood in non-finite clauses: interpersonal (B. Yang 2003: 145)	53
2.11	System network of Theme in non-finite clauses: textual (B. Yang 2003: 146)	54
2.12	Logico-semantic system network of non-finite clauses (B. Yang 2003: 148)	54
2.13	Inter-clausal syntactic relations hierarchy (Van Valin & LaPolla 1997: 477)	57
2.14	The taxonomy of embedded constructions (Dik 1997: 143)	58
2.15	Predication and sentence (Hengeveld 1992: 27)	59
2.16	The distinction as a syntactic category of the clause (Huddleston & Pullum 2002: 89)	61
2.17	The scale of backgrounding (Leech et al. 1982: 187)	61
3.1	Grammatical categories in Whorf (1945)	74
3.2	The metafunctional framing of the grammar (Halliday 2004c [1998]: 50)	78
3.3	Types of situation (Mourelatos 1978: 423)	80
3.4	Process types in English (Halliday & Matthiessen 2014: 216)	82
3.5	The metaphoric syndrome: nominalization	91
3.6	The metaphoric syndrome: adjectivization	92

3.7	The metaphoric syndrome: verbalization	93
3.8	The metaphoric syndrome: adverbialization	94
4.1	Type I: the basic construction	103
4.2	Type II: the para-relation	104
4.3	Type III: the hypo-relation	106
4.4	Type IV: the participant conflated	108
4.5	Type V: process as primary participant	111
4.6	Type VI: process as secondary participant	115
4.7	Type VII: process as circumstance	117
4.8	Type VIII: the triple participant in a single process	119
5.1	The systems of clause complexing (Halliday & Matthiessen 2014: 438)	126
5.2	Parallelism of clause linkage continua (Lehmann 1988: 217)	129
5.3	The scale of verbalization in Chinese	141
6.1	Typical verbs used as VP_1 across genres in COCA	148

Tables

1.1	An overview of major corpora used in the present study	page 8
2.1	Disputes on the finite/non-finite distinction in Mandarin Chinese	24
2.2	Main clausehood, tense and agreement in non-finiteness	27
2.3	Proportions of optional infinitives (OIs) by age (Wexler 2004: 244)	28
2.4	Empty categories	33
2.5	The morphosyntax of the finite versus non-finite prototypes (Givón 2001: 352)	43
2.6	Non-finite tenses in English (Bache 2008: 17)	47
2.7	Semantic types of infinitive and gerund in English	62
2.8	Logical roles of absolute clauses (Q. He & Yang 2015: 16)	64
3.1	Cline between finite and non-finite clauses: morphological perspective (B. Yang 2015: 7)	75
5.1	Basic types of clause complex (Halliday & Matthiessen 2014: 447)	127
5.2	Types of embedding (Halliday & Matthiessen 2014: 492)	128
5.3	Inflections in Sino-Tibetan languages	133
5.4	Qualifiers realized by rankshifted median process in three different genres of the BCC corpus	139
6.1	Typical verbs for the six processes in COCA and causation	146
6.2	Query results of $NP_1 + VP_1 + NP_2 + VP_2$ in COCA	147
6.3	Major verbs used in the $NP_1 + VP_1 + NP_2 + VP_2$ construction in COCA	147
6.4	Major verbs used in the $NP_1 + VP_1 + NP_2 + VP_2$ construction in COCA (per million)	148
6.5	The hypo-relation of processes with non-finiteness	149
6.6	Participant conflation in mono-transitives	150
6.7	Participant conflation in complex transitives	150
6.8	Participant conflation and covert participant in complex transitives	151
6.9	The triple participant in a process with non-finiteness	151

6.10	Query results of the top five serial verbs in COCA	152
6.11	Process relation in paratactic SVC	153
6.12	Process in SVC of the hypo-relation	154
6.13	A combination of hypo-related SVC and conflated participants	154
6.14	Typical verbs used to realize existential constructions in COCA	156
6.15	Process relation in the event-type existential construction	157
6.16	Process relation in absolute construction with -ing clause	158
6.17	Process relation in absolute construction with -ed clause	159
6.18	Process relation in absolute construction with prepositional phrase	159
6.19	Process relation in multiple absolute clauses in a construction from COCA	159
6.20	Hypo-relation between major process and median process	160
6.21	Ambiguous hypo-relation between major and median processes	161
6.22	Process relation in *Flying planes can be dangerous*	161
6.23	Infinitive clause functioning as participant	162
6.24	Non-finite clause functioning as the participant in a minor process	162
7.1	A common Chinese expression with and without verb in the BCC corpus	163
7.2	Process relation in explicit SVC in Chinese	168
7.3	Process relation in implicit SVC in Chinese	168
7.4	Typical verbs used in pivotal construction in Chinese (Yóu 2002)	171
7.5	Typical verbs in pivotal constructions in Chinese	174
7.6	Process relation in pivotal construction of causative	175
7.7	Search query results for '派n做' in the BCC corpus	175
7.8	Process relation in non-causative material processes	176
7.9	Process relation in non-causative verbal processes	177
7.10	Triple participant in a single process	177
7.11	Process relation in pivotal construction of the mental process	178
7.12	Existential constructions with definite 这(zhè/this) in the BCC corpus	184
7.13	Chinese existential construction as ideational grammatical metaphor	186
7.14	Existential process combined with median process	187
7.15	Existential process embedded as participant	188
7.16	Typical ideational grammatical metaphors in existential constructions in the BCC corpus	189

Preface

With the help of Jianhui Xu, my English teacher in senior high school, I managed to write a letter in English to a potential pen pal in 1986. Fortunately, a girl named Julie Willson from Yorkshire wrote back to me and we became pen friends. While at college, I wrote to her asking if she could buy me a book on linguistics. She was generous and sent me the book entitled *Modern Linguistics: The Results of Chomsky's Revolution* by Neil Smith and Deirdre Wilson. That was my first impression of what linguistics looked like.

As a student of English at Southwest University, I was very much encouraged by many teachers, among whom are Fengying Zhang, who taught me comprehensive English, and Wenbiao Yang, who was a teacher of English at the senior high school from which I graduated and who was selected to be trained at the university under a programme by the British Council. During my undergraduate years, I was lucky to be taught and supervised by Professor Rijin Long, who earned a MA degree with Professor Michael Halliday at the University of Sydney in 1981, and Professor Jiarong Liu, who is a stylist and sociolinguist. I completed my MA thesis under the supervision of the systemicist Professor Zhi'an Chen. Professor Li Li, who earned his MEd in TESOL from the University of Manchester, taught me computer-assisted language learning in 1992, which elicited my passion for computers. These people helped me dive into the sea of linguistics.

At a national conference on functional linguistics in 1997, I became acquainted with the systemicist Guowen Huang, who was then a professor at Sun Yat-sen University. Professor Huang earned a PhD in applied linguistics from the University of Edinburgh and a second PhD in Systemic Functional Linguistics (SFL) from Cardiff University, and that was impressive in many ways. In 1999, I became a doctoral student under the supervision of Professor Huang. At an international conference held in Guangzhou that year, I met many leading systemicists, including Michael Halliday, Ruqaiya Hasan, Robin Fawcett, Christian Matthiessen and Peter H. Fries. For the purpose of learning the way of scientific observation better, I started a post-doctoral journey on narrative time in 2004 with the psychologist Professor Xiting Huang. With the help and guidance of these scholars, I learned to swim in SFL, which is a part of the linguistic sea.

After graduation with a PhD in June 2002, I received funding from the Freeman Foundation and went to the University of Illinois at Urbana-Champaign (UIUC) for further research. Professor Halliday once worked there, and it was quite by luck that I met him again at the World Englishes Conference held at UIUC. We talked a little about the relationship between theory and practice at tea break. There I also met Professor Carolyn G. Hartnett, who agreed to comment on the draft of my first book. She then wrote a foreword for me upon the acceptance for publication of the book. At UIUC, I attended classes taught by Adele Goldberg and several other professors. The whole class hoped that Professor Goldberg would teach us Construction Grammar, but she said she had to follow the requirements of the course, entitled 'Conceptual Semantics'. That year of visiting enriched my sense of a wider sea of linguistics.

In 2014 I transferred to Shanghai Jiao Tong University under the recommendation of Professor Feng Yang and with the support of Professor Jie Zhang, Professor Kaibao Hu and Professor Longgen Liu. Soon after the settlement, I was accepted by Miriam Locher and went to the University of Basel in Switzerland as a visiting professor. It was a privilege to be invited to attend all kinds of activities in the English department there during the whole academic year. I attended classes run by Professor Locher, and was very much enlightened by her and also by other linguists there, including Professor Heike Behrens, Dr Daria Dayter, Dr Catherine Diederich and Dr Thomas C. Messerli. During my stay, I was invited to deliver a lecture on interpersonal metaphors in online communication between doctors and patients. I also had an opportunity to have a long talk with Professor Wolfgang Teubert about topics of corpus linguistics in a pub in Basel. The year in Basel widened my vision further, and it seemed to me that I could swim better in the sea of linguistics.

My favourite sport is tennis, but doing research, as I have already hinted at, may be better compared to swimming. Without some teaching of the basics, you will never know how to swim; and without some advanced guidance, you will not be able to become a good swimmer. The sea of linguistics is so vast that it is impossible for me to swim across it. Yet, with the help of the people mentioned here, and many others, I think I am now able to swim towards a tiny destination: non-finiteness.

Tiny as it is, non-finiteness has been one of the most controversial topics in linguistics. It is a hard nut, which disturbs theoretical linguists, text annotators, typologists and many others. With numerous findings for this hard nut, there must have been some consensus on the 'cracking' of it, but quite unfortunately few people from distinctive perspectives may be ready to accept others' views on non-finiteness. This may not be akin to Plato's cave, where chained prisoners would not believe what a freed prisoner claimed to see outside of the cave. It is the real nature of academic pursuit. If we take the elephant as the truth, then scholars are indeed the blind men. It is not possible for any blind person to see the whole elephant, but it is still useful for a blind person to be able to tell others what the elephant is like in his/her perspective. What is important is that his/her way of investigating the part s/he feels or touches should be sound and convincing. What I present in this book is simply a perspective on the 'elephant' of non-finiteness, and I hope that my argument will be convincing. More importantly, I hope that the knowledge I add to the understanding of non-finiteness, if any, will be beneficial both in theory and in practice.

The year 2020 challenged human beings with COVID-19, and millions of people have suffered losses of their beloved ones, although numerous people in their professions rose to the challenges and helped others. At the time of this crisis, it is really tough for people to continue their work. Yet, in this period of time the commissioning editor at Cambridge University Press (CUP), Helen Barton, and the three anonymous reviewers helped me improve the book with their professional suggestions and insightful comments. Professor Akila Sellami Baklouti at the University of Sfax provided helpful and insightful comments at the stage of clearance reading. Isabel Collins and Joshua Penny from CUP helped a lot in preparing the documents. I am also grateful to Jayavel Radhakrishnan and Judy Napper for their professional work in copy-editing. Without their support and encouragement, this book would never have been completed in its present form. I am particularly grateful to Helen and the reviewers for their help.

Upon the publication of this book, I am thankful to my father, Canjin Yang, who loved me very much but who passed away in 2007. I am thankful to my mother, Zengyu Yang, and my siblings for their constant love. My family's warm support is always very much appreciated: my wife, Lijuan Wang, my elder son, Ziqing Yang, and my younger son, Zibai Yang. They are the indispensable meaning of life to me. It is with the help and love of the people mentioned here and many others that this book is possible. Sincere thanks go to them, and errors remain mine.

Acknowledgements

This research was supported by the National Social Science Fund of China (Project No.: 15BYY016). I am grateful to the original publishers for permission to use the following figures and tables.

 Figure 2.1 from *E. Kruisinga: A Chapter in the History of Linguistics in the Netherlands* (A. J. Van Essen, 1983), Springer.

 Figure 2.3 from *The Typology of Adjectival Predication* (Harrie Wetzer, 1996), Mouton de Gruyter.

 Figure 2.4 from *Participles in Rigvedic Sanskrit: The Syntax and Semantics of Adjectival Verb Forms* (John Jeffrey Lowe, 2015), Oxford University Press.

 Figure 2.5 from *Understanding English Grammar: A Linguistic Introduction* (Thomas E. Payne, 2011), Cambridge University Press.

 Figure 2.6, Table 2.5 from *Syntax: An Introduction* (Talmy Givón, 2001), John Benjamins.

 Figures 2.7, 5.2 from 'Towards a Typology of Clause Linkage' in *Clause Combining in Grammar and Discourse* (Christian Lehmann, edited by J. Haiman & S. A. Thompson, 1988: 181–225), John Benjamins.

 Figures 2.8, 3.4, 5.1; Tables 5.1, 5.2 from *Halliday's Introduction to Functional Grammar* (M. A. K. Halliday & Christian M. I. M. Matthiessen, 2014), Routledge.

 Figures 2.9, 2.10, 2.11, 2.12 from *A Study of Non-Finite Clauses in English: A Systemic Functional Approach* (Bingjun Yang, 2003), Foreign Language Teaching and Research Press.

 Figure 2.13 from *Syntax: Structure, Meaning & Function* (Robert Jr. Van Valin & Randy LaPolla, 1997), Cambridge University Press.

 Figure 2.14 from *The Theory of Functional Grammar: Complex and Derived Constructions* (Simon C. Dik, edited by K. Hengeveld, 1997), Mouton de Gruyter.

 Figure 2.15 from *Non-verbal Predication: Theory, Typology, Diachrony* (Kees Hengeveld, 1992), Mouton de Gruyter.

Figure 2.16 from *The Cambridge Grammar of the English Language* (Rodney Huddleston & Geoffrey K. Pullum, 2002), Cambridge University Press.

Figure 2.17 from *English Grammar for Today: A New Introduction* (Geoffrey Leech, Margaret Deuchar and Robert Hoogenraad, 1982), Macmillan.

Figure 3.2 from 'Things and Relations: Regrammaticizing Experience as Technical Knowledge' in *The Language of Science: The Collected Works of M. A. K. Halliday*, vol. 5 (M. A. K. Halliday, edited by J. Webster, 2004: 49–101), Continuum.

Figure 3.3 from 'Events, Processes, and States' in *Linguistics and Philosophy* (Alexander P. D. Mourelatos, 1978, 2: 415–34), Springer.

Table 2.3 from 'Lenneberg's Dream: Learning, Normal Language Development and Specific Language Impairment' in *Variation and Universals in Biolinguistics* (Ken Wexler, edited by L. Jenkins, 2004: 239–83), Elsevier.

Table 2.6 from *English Tense and Aspect in Halliday's Systemic Functional Grammar* (Carl Bache, 2008), Equinox.

Table 2.8 from *Absolute Clauses in English from the Systemic Functional Perspective: A Corpus-Based Study* (Qingshun He & Bingjun Yang, 2015), Springer.

Table 3.1 from 'On Finiteness in Chinese from the Perspective of Cryptotype and Cline' in *Contemporary Foreign Languages Studies* (Bingjun Yang, 2015, 22(8): 6–10), Shanghai Jiao Tong University.

Symbols and Abbreviations

α	dominant clause
β	dependent clause
‖‖	boundary symbol of a clause complex
‖	boundary symbol of a clause
^	followed by
+	extending
=	elaborating
×	enhancing
↘	realized by
AGR	agreement
ANC	action nominal construction
AUX	auxiliary
BCC	Beijing Language and Culture University Chinese Corpus
BNC	British National Corpus
CCL	Centre for Chinese Linguistics Corpus
CEC	Chinese existential construction
CG	Cognitive Grammar
COCA	Corpus of Contemporary American English
CP	complementizer phrase
DP	determiner phrase
EC	existential construction
EPP	Extended Projection Principle
FRP	Full Realization Principle
GG	Generative Grammar
GM	grammatical metaphor
IFG	*Introduction to Functional Grammar*
IGM	ideational grammatical metaphor
INFL	inflection
LFVP	Limit of Finite Verb Principle
LOB	Lancaster-Oslo/Bergen Corpus
MC	main clausehood
NOW	News on the Web corpus
NP	noun phrase
OI	optional infinitive
PRO	pronoun without phonological content
RRG	Role and Reference Grammar
SFG	Systemic Functional Grammar
SFL	Systemic Functional Linguistics
SG	Semiotic Grammar

SQ	search query
SVC	serial verb construction
T	tense
TAM	tense–aspect–modality
TP	tense phrase
VMC	verb-mediated construction
VP	verb phrase

Leipzig Glossing Abbreviations

ASP	aspect
CLF	classifier
COMP	complementizer
COMPL	completive aspect
CONJ	conjunction
EXCL	exclamative word
FUT	future tense indicator
JUSS	jussive mood
LNK	linking word
MOD	modal word
NEG	negation
PASS	passive voice indicator
PL	plural
POSS	possessive marker
PRS	present progressive tense indicator
PST	past tense indicator
Q	question particle/word

1 Introduction

1.1 Why This Study?

The issue of non-finiteness[1] is particularly important in the following areas: theoretical exploration, text[2] segmentation, text annotation and typological studies. By 'theoretical exploration', we mean that non-finiteness is a gateway to the fundamental questions in linguistic theories. For example, when it comes to the question of clause structure in English, some, such as Aarts (2011), may consider the italicized in (1.1) as non-finite clauses being subordinate.

(1.1)   a. I just want [*you to alter the scenario very slightly*].
           b. I suppose in a way that gave them something in common, and perhaps made him [*feel protective towards her*].
           c. We are [*training more of our young people*].
           d. I have [*benefitted from this*].

Aarts (2011: 28)

Others would not agree with Aarts, and consider 'want ... to do' and 'make ... do' as verbal group complexes (e.g. Halliday & Matthiessen 2014). This reflects the stances that different linguists take in treating non-finiteness in theory.

Aarts bases his classification in (1.1) on Generative Grammar (GG) proposed by Noam Chomsky, in which the issue of non-finiteness is particularly significant. In *Syntactic Structures* (Chomsky 1957), a sentence (S) is composed of noun phrase (NP) plus verb phrase (VP), and the VP may be decomposed into verb plus NP. Later, in *Government and Binding Theory* (Chomsky 1981), INFL(ection) is considered as a key component, and a sentence is composed of NP, INFL and VP. In non-inflectional languages,

---

[1] Note that 'non-finite' rather than 'nonfinite' will be used in the whole book, except for those in citations and quotations, or those in the Google Ngram viewer (see Figure 1.1).
[2] In the literature of linguistics, 'text' is often used to mean written language, and 'discourse' to mean spoken language, although either of them may refer to both written and spoken languages.

INFL as an indicator of being finite or non-finite may not be salient. In *The Minimalist Program* (Chomsky 1995), the X-bar-theoretic principle says S = I' (inflectional phrase). According to the X-bar perspective, the properties of a structure come from its head, and Inflection is the head. Thus, non-finite clauses can only be embedded. That explains why non-finite clauses in (1.1) are considered as subordinate (Aarts 2011). This stance is subject to change if we follow other approaches, for example, the way hypotaxis and parataxis are treated in Systemic Functional Grammar (Halliday 1985; Halliday & Matthiessen 2014).

In practice, non-finiteness is an unavoidable issue in natural language processing. Modern society has embraced automatic natural language processing in which text segmentation and text annotation play a decisive role. 'Text segmentation' refers to the process of dividing text into meaningful units (e.g. words, clauses or topics), and the segmentation is not only challenged by ambiguous signals (e.g. boundary markers), but also upset by disputes over syntactic features. Among the disputes, the finite/non-finite distinction is a prominent one which needs more consensus, particularly for languages with diverse morphological manifestations.

With proper segmentation of non-finiteness, texts will be better annotated. Let's take English, for example. One may annotate the verbal head (not auxiliaries), and clitics may be included in the verb form; one may also use an attribute which is responsible for distinguishing between non-finite and finite forms. The values may include: none (the default value which signals finite verb forms), infinitive, gerund and participle (e.g. Caselli & Sprugnoli 2017). Whatever techniques are used, the big challenge is how to deal with ambiguous constructions (see B. Yang 2004). In languages that do not show salient distinctions between finite and non-finite forms (e.g. Chinese), the ambiguity increases greatly and it is much more difficult to annotate the verbal elements.

Non-finiteness is also a key issue in typological research and application. 'Typology is concerned with similarities: defining universals and strong tendencies across languages', and at the same time 'it is concerned with differences, with identifying finer and finer distinctions in our understanding of linguistic categories and units as our knowledge of them increases' (Epps & Arkhipov 2009: 1). Current literature shows that the similarities and differences between English (inflectional language) and Chinese (non-inflectional language) in terms of non-finiteness have not been well addressed. Since 'linguistic typology and linguistic description are closely paired enterprises, each of which informs and enriches the other' (Epps & Arkhipov 2009: 1–2), the typological findings for finiteness will certainly enlighten the description of non-finiteness, and the description of non-finiteness will in turn be a good resource for typological studies of finiteness and other related topics.

A great number of linguists have recognized the significant role of non-finiteness. For example, Hudson thinks that non-finite clauses act as 'a bridge between the analysis of simple sentences and that of complex sentences' (Hudson 1971: 105). In the classification of clauses, '[t]he distinction between finite and non-finite verb phrases is important' (G. Nelson 2001: 92). In terms of language acquisition, the choice of finite or non-finite verbs helps answer whether children 'set the verb-second parameter correctly' (Wexler 2004: 243).

1.2 The Finite/Non-finite Distinction

The finite/non-finite distinction in English originates from Latin grammar writing. 'The year 1586 is the annus mirabilis of English grammar writing, the year it all started' (Linn 2006: 74). *Pamphlet for Grammar* by William Bullokar was published in that year, 'with the express intention of showing that English grammar was rule-governed like Latin' (Linn 2006: 74). In Bullokar's *Brief Grammar for English*, published in the same year of 1586, a verb is defined with mood, tense, number and person, and five moods are identified: the indicative, the imperative, the optative, the subjunctive and the infinitive (Bullokar 1906 [1586]). The influence of Latin on English began even before the Angles, Saxons and Jutes reached Britain (Freeborn 1992), and thus it is not surprising that 'grammars of English still tended to be written in Latin, Christopher Cooper's of 1685 being the last of the Latin ones' (Linn 2006: 74).

The term 'finite' in modern linguistics, as a consequence, goes back to the Latin *finitus*. In Latin, *finitus* in the sense of verb is used in three major ways in grammar: '(of pronouns) referring to a particular person (e.g. *ego*, *tu*, *ille*); (of space, time, etc.) having bounds or limits; (of sentences) carefully finished, rounded' (Glare et al. 1968: 705). Accordingly, 'finite' in the early years of research meant 'referring to a particular person', personal pronouns in particular, and later it came to refer to 'verbs expressing person and number' (Nikolaeva 2007b: 1). By contrast, 'non-finite' refers to those forms that do not express person or number. To be more exact, 'A finite ['fainait] verb is one expressing or implying tense, number, person, and mood. The non-finite forms are the infinitive, the participles, and the gerund' (Zandvoort 1975: 35).

There is far less research on non-finiteness than there is on finiteness, but the general trend is that there is a steady increase in the number of studies on non-finiteness (see Figure 1.1). More importantly, when research focuses on finiteness, in most cases non-finiteness is also discussed. Thus, the intellectual wisdom on non-finiteness is scattered among studies which focus on finiteness and/or non-finiteness.

'There is no useful or adequate definition of the term VERB. It is useful, however, to distinguish between finite and non-finite forms of verbs' (Hornby 1975 [1954]: 1). Useful as it is, the finite/non-finite distinction has remained

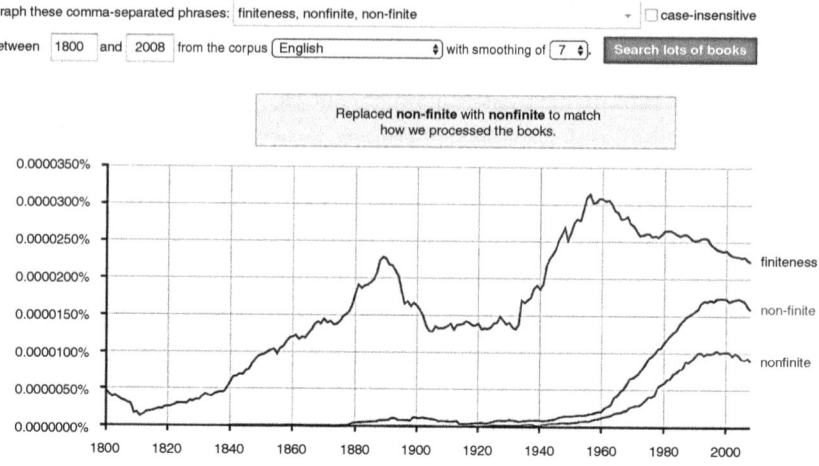

Figure 1.1 Google Ngram for 'finiteness' and 'nonfinite'[3]

highly controversial. The controversy results from little understanding of the phenomenon per se. As admitted in a recent study, 'The term "finite" has been used in the grammatical literature for centuries, but its meaning is difficult to pin down' (Cowper 2016: 47). The traditional notion of finiteness is ill-defined (see Joseph 1983; Nikolaeva 2007b), and it 'is used by everybody and understood by nobody' (Klein 2006: 245). 'Although standardly recognized by linguists of many diverse theoretical persuasions, finiteness continues to figure among [...] the most poorly understood concepts of linguistic theory' (Ledgeway 2007: 335). What is worse is that finiteness 'is not amenable to a theory-proof definition' (Koptjevskaja-Tamm 1994: 1245), and it 'remains one of the least understood concepts in linguistic theory' despite the increasing empirical research (McFadden & Sundaresan 2014: 1). Since non-finiteness goes hand in hand with finiteness, it is not difficult to imagine the consequences of the lack of understanding of finiteness in academia.

The finite/non-finite distinction, so far as the form is concerned, may not be prominent in some stages of language development in a specific language, and this may further hinder an understanding from the diachronic perspective. For example, non-finiteness in English has undergone a number of changes. In Old English, the finite verb is placed at the end of a subordinate clause, and the infinitive or the participle is placed at the end of a sentence (Classen 1919).

---

[3] Accessed on 27 Sept. 2018. See Michel et al. (2011) for more information on the Google Ngram viewer.

1.2 The Finite/Non-finite Distinction

The form-based distinction of 'finite' and 'non-finite' is problematic in the typological sense. Typological findings show that this distinction is not an issue that can be conveniently addressed by means of inflections. In derivational synthetic languages, morphemes of different types (affixes, nouns, verbs, etc.) are combined so as to form new words (e.g. German, Russian, English, Finnish). In relational synthetic languages, root words are joined to bound morphemes to represent grammatical function (e.g. Spanish, Latin, Japanese). In this manner, the parameters of finiteness (person, number, tense and gender) may differ even in synthetic languages where inflections are pervasive.

In analytic languages which do not have inflections on the verb, there seems to be no distinction between 'finite' and 'non-finite', and disputes over whether there is a distinction or not are fierce. Take modern Chinese, for example. While many linguists argue against a finite/non-finite distinction in modern Chinese (e.g. L. Wang 1984; Zhu 1985; L. Xu 1986, 1994, 1999; S. Lü 1990 [1882], 2002 [1979]; Y. Huang 1992a, 1992b, 1994, 2000; J. Hu et al. 2001; J.-W. Lin 2010; D. Liu 2010; J. Xu 2010), many others argue for the distinction (e.g. C. T. J. Huang 1982, 1983, 1984, 1987, 1989, 1991; Y. H. A. Li 1985, 1990; C.-C. Tang 1990; Yuzhi Shi 1995, 2001; Tan 1995; J. Hu 1997; Ma 1998 [1898]; Lee 2000; T.-C. Tang 2000; D. Wang 2001; X. Xing 2004; Jinglian Li & Liu 2005; Jinxi Li 2007 [1924]; Fang & Zhao 2008; Her 2008; Yiming Yang & Cai 2011; Guo 2011, 2013; T.-H. J. Lin 2012).

On morphological grounds, it seems reasonable to say that there is no finite/non-finite distinction in modern Chinese because of the lack of inflection and case marking. It is also reasonable to argue that there is a finite/non-finite distinction in Chinese because morphological features are not the sole criterion.[4] Semantic finiteness (the condition for an independent interpretation of an utterance) as well as morphological finiteness may also be identified (see Gretsch & Perdue 2007; Maas 2004). For example, if we take mood as the criterion of distinguishing finiteness from non-finiteness, Chinese may be considered as a typical language of non-finiteness. If we take tense as the criterion, Chinese may be considered as a typical language of finiteness.

Many linguists today believe that morphological features alone cannot help determine the status of being 'finite' or 'non-finite', so sentential aspect has been considered. A good many linguists, both functionalists and formalists,

---

[4] A number of linguists even argue that the grammatical category of Subject does not exist in modern Chinese. This view is still highly controversial. Many scholars in China today mix up spoken and written data, and some propose that there is no such distinction as 'noun' and 'verb' in modern Chinese, and nouns are verbs while verbs are nouns (e.g. Shen 2016). The data used in support of this view are mostly from spoken contexts, and thus we do not think this view holds water. Spoken instances are always extracted from wider social contexts – recall Wittgenstein's example of 'slab'. Without the contexts, the instances are meaningless. Moreover, studying the Chinese language without a degree of categorization is unimaginable. Parts of speech which have been used for hundreds of years fit quite well into the categories of modern Chinese.

6   Introduction

now consider the opposition of 'finite' and 'non-finite' as 'a property of the clause', and they believe that 'finiteness belongs to the grammar of inter-clausal connectivity' (Bisang 2001: 1400). However, theoretical construction and specific description from this perspective have not been well documented.

1.3   Purpose of the Study

The general purpose of this study is to provide a theoretical framework for the description of non-finiteness. For this general purpose, three specific purposes need to be fulfilled.

The first specific purpose is to find out the basic parameters of finite/non-finite identification. After confirming that the finite/non-finite distinction is necessary for both English and Chinese, a major question to be addressed will be whether there is a common criterion for the identification of non-finiteness in both languages. The hypothesis is that an event/state which is moodless in interpersonal meaning, dependent in clause structure and incomplete in ideational components, is non-finite. In other words, non-finite clauses are characteristic of moodlessness, clause dependency and incompleteness in ideation (participant, process, circumstance). The process-relation perspective provides a theoretical foundation for the criteria and the parameters concerned.

The second specific purpose is to find out how non-finiteness functions for inter-clausal connectivity. The hypothesis is that grammatical metaphor (GM) is an ideal starting point for understanding non-finiteness in inter-clausal connectivity. Non-finite clauses are intermediate between the metaphorical and the congruent in terms of ideational metaphor. Non-finite -ing forms may be nominalizations, non-finite to- forms may be verbalizations, and non-finite -ed forms may be adjectivizations. Without mood, non-finite clauses are intermediate between the metaphorical and the congruent.

The third specific purpose is to observe some controversial issues in English and Chinese. With the theoretical foundation drawn in the earlier chapters, controversial issues may be dealt with from the process-relation perspective.[5] It is hypothesized that some controversial constructions (e.g. serial verb construction, pivotal construction) may be well addressed from the process-relation perspective. Note that the object of the present study is written language for which the ideational dimension is prominent, but the interpersonal dimension will also be discussed when necessary.

---

[5] As one of the referees commented, non-finiteness in the present study is mainly explored from the perspective of ideational metafunction, but an interpersonal exploration may be more appropriate. We agree that the interpersonal exploration will be a good starting point for finiteness, but it may not be helpful for non-finiteness because no mood is involved. Mood is the core system in interpersonal metafunction, but as is found in this study, moodlessness is a determining parameter for non-finiteness.

1.4 Research Questions

Among numerous research questions on the issue of finiteness and non-finiteness, the following four are fundamental, and they need appropriate answers from a new perspective:

- In what way is the finite/non-finite distinction universal?
- In what context can non-finiteness be positioned and identified?
- How does non-finiteness function for inter-clausal connectivity?
- How will the controversial issues of non-finiteness in English and Chinese be dealt with?

1.5 Methodology

The present study first applies a top-down approach. Studies on non-finiteness by the major theories are reviewed, and those enlightening viewpoints serve as the basis. Applying Systemic Functional Linguistics (SFL), which considers meaning and form as an inseparable unity, we propose a process-relation framework to tackle the issue of non-finiteness. This approach is then examined for its power in explaining inter-clausal connectivity and controversial constructions in English and Chinese.

Similar issues in English and Chinese will be dealt with for the purpose of contrast and comparison, but the purpose is not to do a contrastive study. Those contrasts and comparisons are used to probe into the theoretical controversies.

In the course of demonstrating and examining the process-relation framework, case studies based on corpora will be carried out when necessary. In this sense, a bottom-up approach is also included. To ensure authenticity, examples except those quoted from other authors are taken from four corpora, listed in Table 1.1. Search queries specific to each corpus will be built up as comparisons and contrasts are carried out.

The corpora listed in Table 1.1 can be accessed for free on the Internet. Other corpora, such as the LOB (the Lancaster-Oslo/Bergen Corpus) and NOW (News on the Web) corpus, are also occasionally used. UAM Corpus Tool[6] (Version 3.3 g) and AntConc[7] (Version 3.5.7) will be used as corpus tools.

1.6 Organization of the Book

The book is composed of eight chapters. Chapter 1, the introduction, introduces the background, purpose, research questions and methodology of the study.

Chapter 2 is a review of the studies on non-finiteness. With enlightenments from the literature, Chapter 3 provides the theoretical basis according to which

---

[6] Source: www.corpustool.com/download.html
[7] Source: www.laurenceanthony.net/software.html

Table 1.1 *An overview of major corpora used in the present study*

Reference	Short description	Size
BCC	The BCC (Beijing Language and Culture University Chinese Corpus) is the largest genre-balanced corpus of Chinese, almost equally divided among news (14%), fiction (22%), blog (22%), science (22%), ancient Chinese (14%) and other (3%)	15,000 million Chinese characters
COCA	COCA (Corpus of Contemporary American English) is a genre-balanced corpus of American English, equally divided among spoken, fiction, popular magazines, newspapers and academic texts (20% for each).	560 million words
BNC	The BNC (British National Corpus) was originally created by Oxford University Press in the 1980s–early 1990s, and contains a wide range of genres.	100 million words
CCL	The CCL (Centre for Chinese Linguistics) Corpus contains multiple genres, such as spoken, history and biography, news, fiction, movie and TV, e-document, translated texts, etc. Most were produced after 1949.	700 million Chinese characters, 577 million in modern Chinese

the first research question (In what way is the finite/non-finite distinction universal?) will be answered. On this basis, the process-relation framework is proposed in Chapter 4 as the solution to the controversy of the finite/non-finite distinction. This is intended to answer the second research question (In what context can non-finiteness be positioned and identified?). Chapter 5 looks into the function of non-finiteness as a means of inter-clausal connectivity from the perspective of grammatical metaphor. Thus, the third research question (How does non-finiteness function for inter-clausal connectivity?) will be answered.

In Chapter 6 and Chapter 7, the process-relation framework is applied to the controversial constructions in English and Chinese respectively. Thus, answers will be provided for the fourth question: How will the controversial issues of non-finiteness in English and Chinese be dealt with by the process-relation perspective?

Chapter 8 summarizes the study with an overview of the findings. Limitations of the study and suggestions for further research are also pointed out.

2 Non-finiteness in the Literature

To outline the major viewpoints on non-finiteness, in this chapter we will take a quick look at the early history of 'non-finiteness' in English grammar writing, and then review the relevant studies of non-finiteness in traditional grammar, linguistic typology, Generative Grammar (GG), Cognitive Grammar (CG), Systemic Functional Grammar (SFG), Semiotic Grammar (SG), Role and Reference Grammar (RRG) and Functional Discourse Grammar (FDG) respectively. Relevant studies from other grammars will also be reviewed.

2.1 Non-finiteness in the Early History of English Grammar Writing

Grammars of English in the early 1600s were written in Latin. English grammar writing since the 1700s seems to have deliberately avoided the influence of Latin grammar, and it is interesting to find that scholars seem to ignore the term 'non-finite' intentionally. The most influential grammar book of English in the eighteenth century (more than 120 editions have been published including the abridgment), by Lindley Murray, said, 'A simple sentence has but one subject, and one finite verb' (Murray 1844 [1795]: 195). Yet, there is no mention of 'non-finite' in Murray's book. There is also no mention of 'non-finite' in Johnson's dictionary, which was designed as one illustrated by 'examples from the best writers' (Johnson 1785: title page). However, it does give an explanation of 'infinitive', as follows:

Finite adj. [finitus, Latin.]: limited; bounded; terminated

Infinitive, adj. [infinitif, Fr. infinivus, Latin]: In grammar, the infinitive affirms or intimates the intention of affirming, which is one uſe of the indicative; but then it does not do it abſolutely. [Note that there is no page number and 's' was written as 'ſ'.]

(Johnson 1785).

There is no term like 'nonfinite' or 'non-finite' in Webster's dictionary, which was published about thirty-three years later than Murray's (Webster 1828). In his grammar book published a few years later, non-finite as a term was still not mentioned, but four modes were identified: the infinitive, the indicative, the imperative and the subjunctive (Webster 1833: 55). Later, in a well-known grammar book on English by Harrison (1861), only participles were discussed (infinitives were mentioned), and there is no mention of a finite/non-finite distinction.

Like Webster, early English grammarians focused on moods, in which the infinitive is an important category. Murray's theory of moods is the most outstanding, in which a verb is defined as 'a word which signifies action, being, or suffering' and verbs 'are divided into three sorts, namely, Active, Neuter, and Passive' (Murray 1832: 65). Mood, or mode, 'is a particular form of the verb, showing the manner in which the being, action, or passion, is represented' and five moods of verbs are identified: the *indicative*, the *subjunctive*, the *potential*, the *infinitive* and the *imperative* (Murray 1832: 66). Though he didn't use the term 'non-finite', Murray did talk about the distinction by saying that '*Finite* verbs are those to which number and person appertain. Verbs in the *infinitive* mood have no respect to number or person' (Murray 1832: 87) (emphasis in original). What is illuminating is Murray's discussion of 'syntax', which is closely related to the finite/non-finite distinction itself: 'Syntax principally consists of two parts, CONCORD and GOVERNMENT. Concord is the agreement which one word has with another, in gender, number, case, or person. Government is that power which one part of speech has over another, in directing its mood, tense, or case' (Murray 1832: 88). Murray's categories of moods remain unchanged in his *English Grammar*, in which the infinitive is an important type. It is noteworthy that, though there is no mention of 'non-finite', he is probably the first grammarian who provided a definition of 'finite' in English grammar writing. See also Murray (1844 [1795]: 195).

Four modes (the infinitive, the indicative, the imperative and the subjunctive) were identified by Webster, but the 'potential' was not included (Webster 1833: 55). Cobbett and Ayres used the same types of modes as Webster (Cobbett & Ayres 1884). It is natural that scholars in the early years of grammar writing were very interested in talking about moods, because the verb which defines moods is the core category of language expression. The tradition of moods/modes, in fact, goes back to the earliest work on English grammar, by William Bullokar in 1586. Bullokar defined verbs as having mood, tense, number and person, and he identified five moods: the indicative, the imperative, the optative, the subjunctive and the infinitive (Bullokar 1906 [1586]: 353).

No grammarian in the nineteenth century, as far as we can find from the literature, proposed a distinction between finiteness and non-finiteness, except for Murray's distinction between 'finite verbs' and 'verbs in the infinitive mood'. What is significant is that, in the first volume of the three-volume English grammar by Maetzner, the middle forms of the verb are defined as 'those forms which border on the one hand on the substantive; (the infinitive and the gerund) on the other, on the adjective (participles)' (Maetzner 1874: 326). In the third volume, eighty-nine pages are devoted to the intermediate forms of the verb, such as adverbial determinations: that is, the infinitive, the pure infinitive, the participles, the compound participles and so on (Maetzner 1874). There is a similar treatment in Whitney (1886), in which a whole chapter (Chapter XV) is devoted to infinitive and participle constructions. Infinitive, present participle and past participle (except gerund) were also discussed in works from around the 1850s (e.g. Forbes 1848), but there was no mention of a finite/non-finite distinction in these works either.

Though with no finite/non-finite distinction, some grammarians in the late nineteenth century began to notice the importance of infinitive and participle constructions, and some focused on the difference between infinitives and participles. For example, in a very well-known book on English grammar published in 1851, Goold Brown wrote, 'the infinitive mood, a phrase, or a sentence, may in some instances be made the subject of a verb . . . . Many also will have participles, infinitives, phrases, and sentences, to be occasionally "in the objective case"' (G. Brown 1851: 281). When discussing spoken Swedish in 1879, Sweet (1913: 421) said, 'The substantival noun-forms are the infinitive; the adjectival, the present participle active and the past participle passive'.

Around 1900, scholars showed a good deal of interest in infinitives, participles and gerunds, but most of them focused on Latin or Greek. For example, Miller studied Vergil's use of the infinitive and made some enlightening claims: 'The infinitive is an abstract verbal noun. It gives us the verb in its most unlimited force. It has some marks that make it a noun, others that make it a verb' (D. Miller 1902: 5). Votaw (1896) examined the use of the infinitive in biblical Greek. Similarly, Williams examined the use of participles in the *Book of Acts* and categorized them into three groups: the ascriptive participle (including attributive, predicative and substantive), the adverbial participle and the complementary participle (Williams 1909). Sidey examined the use of participles in Plautus, Petronius and Apuleius, whose writings represent the three developmental stages of Latin (Sidey 1909).

As to English-related studies, Callaway proposed that the uses of the appositive participle in Anglo-Saxon are threefold: adjectival, adverbial and coordinate (Callaway 1901). The case of the absolute participle 'changed its form in Middle English from dative to nominative' (C. Ross 1893: 64). A very early piece of work on gerunds in English was completed as a doctoral dissertation by Rusteberg (1874), which claims that gerunds may be used to replace such secondary sentences as substantive sentences, adverbial sentences and attributive sentences.

It is surprising that well-known publications on grammar up until the early twentieth century still provided no distinction between the finite and non-finite (e.g. Onions 1904; Poutsma 1904; Wisely 1907). It seems that grammarians from 1586 to 1895 deliberately avoided the distinction of finite and non-finite for the purpose of foregrounding the distinctness of English from Latin.

It is in 1898 that 'non-finite' as a term first appeared in the literature on the English language. A finite verb is defined as 'any part of a verb that can be used for saying something about something else' (Nesfield 1908 [1898]: 3) and the 'non-finite parts of a verb' refer to 'those parts of a verb that are not limited to number or person, viz. the Infinitive, the Participle, and the Gerund' (Nesfield 1908 [1898]: 7).

In 1915, Kruisinga (1932 [1915]) argued that 'the non-finite verb in contemporary English is equal in importance to the finite verb' (cited in Van Essen 1983: 85). In the fourth edition of *A Handbook of Present-Day English*, Kruisinga distinguished finite verbs from non-finite verbs (see Figure 2.1, quoted from Van Essen 1983: 212).

In the first volume of Poutsma's *A Grammar of Late Modern English*, published in 1904, there are mentions of 'finite verb' here and there, but it is in the second volume published in 1926 that 'non-finite forms of the verb' are discussed. According to Poutsma, 'The non-finite forms of the verb, i.e. the infinitive, the gerund and the participles, stand without any indication of

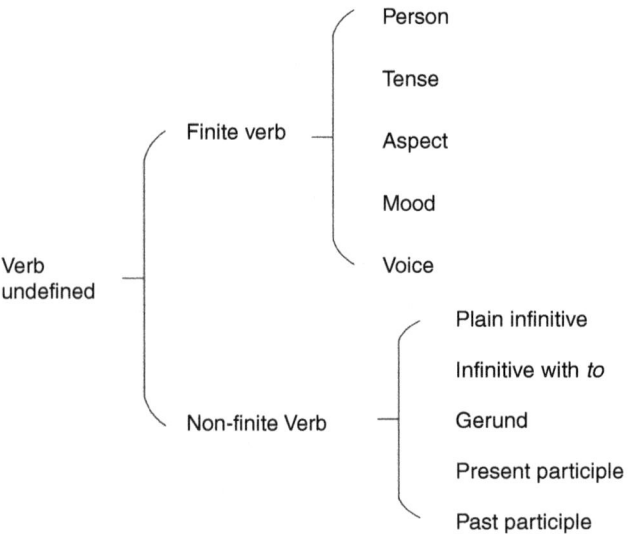

Figure 2.1 The finite and non-finite verbs in Kruisinga (1932 [1915])[1]

---

[1] Note that 'Finite verb' should be 'Finite Verb' so as to keep consistency in capitalisation. Here, we keep it as it is in Van Essen (1983: 212).

the originator of the predication they express' (Poutsma 1926: 8), and '(i)nfinitives, gerunds and present participles often have a passive meaning in the active voice, which is not shared by the finite forms of the verb' (Poutsma 1926: 67).

Poutsma may have been the first person to publish a monograph on non-finiteness in English: *The Infinitive, the Gerund and the Participles of the English Verb* (Poutsma 1923). He did not provide a distinction between finite and non-finite even in such a specialized monograph, but some ideas in the book are enlightening:

- Like the gerund, the infinitive is a substantival form of the verb, that is to say it has partly the character of a verb, partly that of a noun. (Poutsma 1923: 3)
- The gerund is a substantival form of the verb which is intermediate between the infinitive and the noun of action; i.e. it is of a less distinctly verbal nature than the infinitive, and of a more distinctly verbal nature than the noun of action . . . . All verbs have a gerund, only those which have no infinitive excepted. (Poutsma 1923: 101)
- Participles are those forms of the verb which partake of the nature of both verbs and adjectives . . . . There are two participles: the present and the past participle. (Poutsma 1923: 174)

The proposals on non-finiteness by Dutch scholars such as Etsko Kruisinga and Hendrik Poutsma are quite thought-provoking. Viewpoints on non-finiteness by the Danish linguist Otto Jespersen are also innovative; he pointed out that 'The sentence-building power is found in all those forms which are often called "finite" verb forms, but not in such forms as *barking* or *eaten* (participles), nor in infinitives like *to bark, to eat*' (Jespersen 1924: 87). In his thinking, participles are a kind of adjective formed from verbs, and infinitives may be similar with substantives.

From one point of view, therefore, we should be justified in restricting the name verb to those forms (the finite forms) that have the eminently verbal power of forming sentences, and in treating the 'verbids' (participles and infinitives) as a separate class intermediate between nouns and verbs (cf. the old name participium, i.e. what participates in the character of noun and verb) . . . and it is, therefore, preferable to recognize non-finite forms of verbs by the side of finite forms, as is done in most grammars. (Jespersen 1924: 87)

What distinguishes finite verbs from non-finite verbs is that a finite sentence 'is rounded off as a complete piece of communication' whereas a non-finite string 'lacks that peculiar finish' (Jespersen 1924: 87). Similar treatment of finite and non-finite forms is seen in Curme (1947), which first appeared in 1925:

The English verb has forms called voices, moods, tenses, aspects, numbers, and persons, which represent the action suggested by the verb as limited in various ways, such as in person, number, time, manner of conception, etc. A verb that can be limited in all these ways is called a finite verb: *I go, he goes, they go, he went, he may go, he might go*, etc. The infinite forms of the verb – the participle (§ 122), the infinitive (§ 123.A), and the gerund (§ 124) – are limited in fewer ways. (Curme 1947: 52)

The infinite (p. 52) forms of the verb – the participle, the infinitive, and the gerund – are forms which partake of the nature of verbs and have in addition the function of adjectives or nouns. (Curme 1947: 265)

Besides these, some insightful views on verbs can be seen in the discussions of verbs around 1900s that are relevant to non-finiteness. 'Verb' is defined as 'the part of speech by means of which we make assertions' (Daniel 1891: 62), and 'verbal noun' is proposed to refer to participles functioning as nouns (Daniel 1891: 67–9). 'A **Verb** is a word that asserts action, being, or state of being' (Reed & Kellogg 1900: 151, emphasis in original). A footnote on the same page states, '*Asserts* is here used to mean *declare* or *question* or *wish* or *command* or *exclaim* or to unite in any way the verbal sign of action, being, or state with that of the actor'. 'All verbs, but not all of their forms, assert. Of the forms that do not assert, one is THE PARTICIPLE' (Reed & Kellogg 1900: 152). 'Another form of the verb, expressing action or being without asserting it, is the **infinitive**' (Reed & Kellogg 1900: 154, emphasis in original). 'A nounal verb is a form of the verb partaking of the nature of a noun, and expressing action or being without asserting it' (Reed & Kellogg 1900: 158).

From what has been shown in this section, we can see that English grammarians since Christopher Cooper have tried every means not to be influenced by Latin, but the terms 'finite' and 'non-finite', which originated in Latin, seem to be inevitable in the prescription and description of the English language.

2.2 Non-finiteness in Traditional Grammar: Morphology-Based

It is important to note that 'traditional' here is used to mean both prescriptive approaches and descriptive approaches that do not adopt a single specific linguistic theory. For example, the work of Quirk et al. (1985) is descriptive, but it does not follow a specific theory, and thus we consider it to be traditional.

According to the traditional approach, a language of which the verb form can be marked for morphological categories (i.e. person agreement, number, tense) is a finite language (e.g. English), and one in which the verb form does not have to be marked for morphological categories is a non-finite language (e.g. Chinese). In this tradition, the property of the verb, the categorization of non-finite clauses, the sentence-building power, the status of tense and the scale of finiteness are the focal topics.

2.2.1 The Property of the Verb

Finite and non-finite in traditional grammar are distinguished on the basis of verb morphology. In this tradition, 'finite' refers to the situation in which verbal forms are limited by person, number and tense, and 'non-finite' to the situation in which verbal forms are not limited by person, number or tense. Thus, synthetic languages (e.g. Classical Arabic, Finnish, Japanese) that strictly express person, number and tense by means of inflections on the verb contain both 'finite' and 'non-finite' forms. Analytic languages (e.g. Chinese) that do not express person, number or tense by inflections on the verb are devoid of finite/non-finite distinction. Some typical analytic languages do not even have inflections at all (e.g. Vietnamese), and it is generally believed that these languages do not distinguish verbal forms in terms of 'finite' and 'non-finite'.

In other words, finiteness in traditional grammar is considered as the property of the verb, and it is defined according to the distribution and morphological features of the verb. The origin of this tradition goes back to the description of Indo-European languages. In describing Indo-European languages, a great many linguists argue that finite verbs are those that bear morphological inflections, while non-finite verbs are 'those which exhibit reduced morphology, manifested in the absence of both personal and objective inflection(s), and possibly a change of category' (Ledgeway 1998: 2).

Since the traditional perspective views finiteness as a morphological property of verbal forms, '[t]he question is then which verbal categories are absent from non-finite forms compared to finite ones' (Chamoreau & Estrada-Fernández 2016: 2). Many argue that tense and subject agreement are the standard categories that are absent from non-finite forms (e.g. D. Miller 2002). The finite verb is believed to be marked by tense, aspect, number, mood and person agreement, while the non-finite verb is not marked by these categories. Non-finite forms 'comprise action nominals (including infinitives and gerunds), participles, and converbs' (Nikolaeva 2010: 1177).

More recent grammarians take a very different stance, and their views on non-finiteness seem somewhat radical. For example, 'in a finite verb phrase the first or only verb is finite, and the other verbs (if any) are non-finite'; 'in a non-finite verb phrase all the verbs are non-finite' (Greenbaum & Nelson 2002: 61). Thus, in *We will play football later today*, *will* is the finite verb, whereas *play* is non-finite. Similarly, *played* in *We have played football every day this week* is non-finite because *have* is the finite verb.

A more radical view holds that a non-finite verb phrase is one that functions other than as a predicate: 'Verbs and verb phrases acting as adjectivals, adverbials, and nominals within the sentence are nonfinite' (Kolln & Funk 2012: 358).

2.2.2 The Categorization of Non-finite Clauses in English

In traditional English grammar, three main types of clauses are identified: the finite clause (a clause containing a finite verb), non-finite clause (a clause containing a non-finite verb) and verbless clause (a clause containing no verbal element at all) (Quirk et al. 1972: 590). According to Leech and Svartvik (2002 [1975]: 275), a main clause is almost always a finite clause, while a subclause can be finite, non-finite or verbless, all of which may have further subclauses inside them.

Quirk et al. (1985: 992) explained that the reason for recognizing non-finite clauses as clauses is that we could 'analyse their internal structure into the same functional elements that we distinguish in finite clauses'. The traditional approach to the study of non-finite clauses is much concerned with such classification. Hence, according to Quirk et al. (1985: 993), non-finite clauses are classified into four categories on the clause level:

(a) to- infinitive
Without subject: *The best thing would be to tell everybody.*
With subject: *The best thing would be for you to tell everybody.*

(b) bare infinitive
Without subject: *All I did was hit him on the head.*
With subject: *Rather than you do the job, I'd prefer to finish it myself.*

(c) -ing participle
Without subject: *Leaving the room, he tripped over the mat.*
With subject: *Her aunt having left the room, I asked Ann for some personal help.*

(d) -ed participle
Without subject: *Covered with confusion, they apologized abjectly.*
With subject: *The discussion completed, the chairman adjourned the meeting for half an hour.*

In addition, Quirk et al. (1985) noted that the infinitive clause led by *to* plus a subject is typically found in constructions with anticipatory *it*, and that without *to*, it can characteristically be found in pseudo-cleft sentences. The classification by Huddleston and Pullum (2002) is quite similar, except that verbless clauses and non-finite clauses are discussed in the same section.

As we can see, Quirk et al. (1985) and Huddleston and Pullum (2002) may be the most comprehensive English grammar books of the twentieth century. Detailed discussions on non-finiteness can be found in both books. Unfortunately, neither of them has much discussion on the absolute clause, which in the broad sense may be a type of non-finite clause. In Quirk et al. (1985: 1120), 'absolute clauses' refers to 'nonfinite and verbless adverbial

2.2 Non-finiteness in Traditional Grammar: Morphology-Based

clauses that have an overt subject but are not introduced by a subordinator and are not the complement of a preposition'. They argue that absolute clauses may be -ing, -ed or verbless clauses, but not infinitive clauses. For example (Quirk et al. 1985: 1120):

(2.1)   a. *No further discussion arising*, the meeting was brought to a close.
       b. *Lunch finished*, the guests retired to the lounge.
       c. *Christmas then only days away*, the family was pent up with excitement.

Similarly, Huddleston and Pullum (2002: 1265) list some special constructions in a supplement, as follows:

(2.2)   a. *His hands gripping the door*, he let out a volley of curses.
       b. *This done*, she walked off without another word.
       c. *Realising he no longer had the premier's support*, Ed submitted his resignation.
       d. *Born in Aberdeen*, Sue had never been further south than Edinburgh.
       e. *Whether working or relaxing*, he always has a scowl on his face.

They argue that the italicized in (2.2) are non-finites with the main clauses as anchor, (2.2a) and (2.2b) being absolute constructions (Huddleston & Pullum 2002: 1265). In the same manner, 'absolute clause' is defined as '[a] non-finite or verbless clause containing its own subject, attached to a sentence from which it is separated by a comma (or commas), and not introduced by a subordinator' (Aarts et al. 2014: 4). In other words, absolute clauses may be either non-finite clauses or verbless clauses.

Aspect and voice of non-finite clauses have also been dealt with in Quirk et al. (1985: 994). Non-finite clauses have been discussed under the following headings: nominal clauses, adverbial clauses, conditional clauses, conditional-concessive clauses, comment clauses, post-modification, complementation, nominalization, apposition, extra-position and punctuation. These discussions are claimed to focus on the grammatical functions of non-finite clauses, but little about grammatical functions is presented.

Quirk et al.'s (1985) grammar of English drew much from contemporary theories in the English language. As far as non-finite clauses are concerned, the descriptions in Quirk et al. (1985) are still form-oriented, as illustrated in the categorization shown in Figure 2.2.

As shown in Figure 2.2, non-finite clauses include to-clauses, -ing participle clauses and -ed participle clauses. A to-clause may be either a bare infinitive clause or an infinitive clause, and each of the two cases can be with or without subject. Similarly, both -ing and -ed participle clauses may be with or without subject.

Form and meaning (function) cannot be separately observed. A formal treatment cannot be said to be function-free, and a functional one cannot be said to be form-free. Categorization of non-finiteness, non-finite clauses in

18   Non-finiteness in the Literature

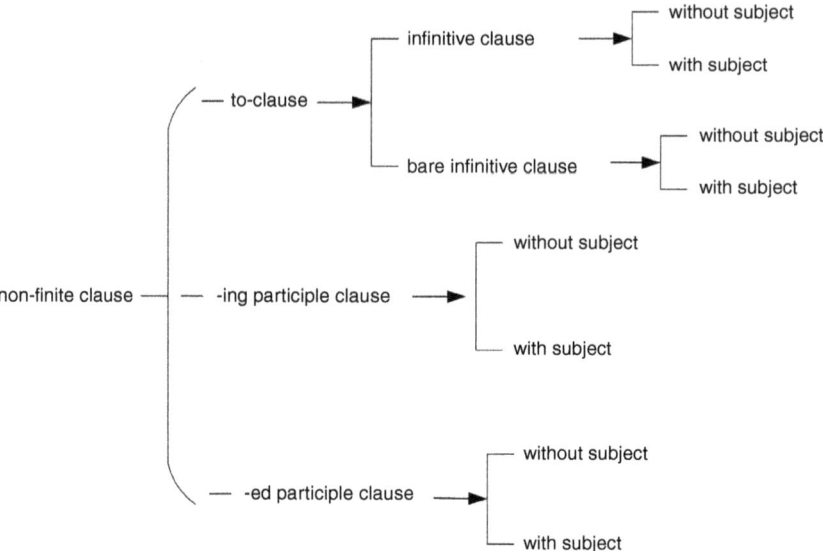

Figure 2.2 Categories of non-finite clause in Quirk et al. (1985)

particular, may be much more illuminating when both form and function are considered.

2.2.3   Sentence-Building Power and the Status of Tense

Defining finiteness and non-finiteness in terms of verbal inflections legitimizes the status of independent sentences. Grammarians thus focus on the verb, and a 'finite verb' is usually understood as 'one that is "limited" by properties of person, number and tense' (Huddleston 1988a: 44).

As such, a combination of words that contains a finite verb can form a sentence, while a combination with no finite verb usually cannot. 'The sentence-building power is found in all those forms which are often called "finite" verb forms', but not in non-finite verb forms (Jespersen 1924: 87). In other words, finite verb forms that are marked for morphological changes in person, number and tense can build independent sentences, while non-finite verb forms cannot.

This view is reflected in many works, among which some are very influential. For example, when discussing the actor–action construction in English, Bloomfield distinguishes nominative expressions from finite verb expressions, the former being 'words and phrases which can fill the actor position' and the latter being 'words and phrases which can fill the action position' (Bloomfield

2.2 Non-finiteness in Traditional Grammar: Morphology-Based

1933: 185). However, it should be noted that the actor–action construction is constituted by finite verb expressions, but non-finite expressions may also be used to fill the actor–action position (see 2.3).

(2.3)   a. *for you to say so ...*;
          b. *for me to have said so ...* (Firth 1968: 105)

In (2.3), the actors (i.e. *you*, *me*) and the actions (i.e. *to say*, *to have said*) constitute two constructions respectively, but the action positions are filled with non-finite verb expressions. That is to say, non-finite verbs can also build up actor–action constructions, but the constructions cannot operate as independent sentences in English.

In Trask's definition, 'finite' denotes 'a form of a verb or auxiliary which can in principle serve as the only verb form in a sentence and which typically carries the maximum in morphological marking' (Trask 1992: 103); 'non-finite' denotes 'any form of a verb which cannot serve as the only verb in a simple sentence' (Trask 1992: 185). This distinction can be found in 'many (not all) languages' where 'a single verb may exhibit a number of different forms serving different grammatical functions' (Trask 1999: 62). A similar definition is suggested in Matthews (1997), where a finite verb can be sufficient to form a simple sentence but a non-finite verb cannot. The role of non-finite forms (i.e. *to be* infinitive, participle, etc.) is either nominal or adjectival (Matthews 1997).

The claim that the dependent/independent status is determined by the finite/non-finite distinction runs into conflict in languages of the Nakh-Daghestanian (East Caucasian) group. Forms that express presuppositions in Daghestanian lack finite categories, but these forms can occur in both dependent and independent clauses (Kalinina & Sumbatova 2007). Usually, the 'finite' forms are used to express the assertive part in a proposition, and the 'non-finite' forms are more often used in declarative and interrogative sentences with narrow focus (Kalinina & Sumbatova 2007). Thus, the sentence-building power of 'finiteness' is much weakened in some languages where there is no strict contrast between the verbal forms used in independent clauses and those used in dependent contexts.

Finite and non-finite forms also differ in the status of tense if non-inflectional languages are taken into consideration. Finite verbs in English show tense, mood, aspect and voice, while non-finite verbs do not show tense or mood but are 'still capable of indicating aspect and voice' (Quirk et al. 1972: 40–1). As pointed out by Comrie, finite verb forms in English have absolute tense, while non-finite verb forms have relative tense; by contrast, 'in written Arabic and (Mandarin) Chinese there are verb forms that express relative, rather than absolute, tense' (Comrie 1976a: 2). This indicates that non-finite verb forms in Chinese, if there are any, cannot be distinguished from finite verbs by means of tense.

Typological studies (see Section 2.3 for more examples) show that in most European languages the categories correlate, but in many Asian languages the categories may not do so. For example, finite verbs in Kannada (a language of South India) inflect in declarative clauses, but the optative verb does not inflect for person or number; infinitives in Kannada are uninflected, but gerunds, participles and dependent conditionals take tense (Sridhar 1990). Moreover, neither tense nor person, nor number, nor agreement is a universal category. Verbs inflect for tense in many European languages, but they do not inflect for tense in Punjabi (Bhatia 1993), Nakh-Daghestanian (Kalinina & Sumbatova 2007) or Lango (Noonan 1992). Verbs (including infinitives; see Joseph 1983) may be marked for agreement (e.g. in Portuguese), or not marked for agreement (e.g. in Kannada; see Sridhar 1990).

To sum up, the sentence-building power of finiteness varies from language to language, and there is no causal relation between the status of tense and the finite/non-finite distinction.

2.2.4 Scale of Finiteness

Within the same language, finiteness may be described in a scale, with graded categories. To distinguish finite verb phrases from non-finite phrases in English, for example, Quirk et al. (1985: 149) proposed five criteria:
- Finite verb phrases can occur as the verb phrase of independent clauses.
- Finite verb phrases have tense contrast.
- There is person concord and number concord between the subject of a clause and the finite verb phrase.
- Finite verb phrases contain, as their first or only word, a finite verb form which may be either an operator or a simple present or past form.
- Finite verb phrases have mood, which indicates the factual, nonfactual, or counterfactual status of the predication.

Based on the criteria, Quirk et al. (1985: 150) represented the finite/non-finite distinction in English in a scale of finiteness ranging from the most finite (i.e. indicative) to the least finite (i.e. infinitive verb phrase). This scale emphasizes finiteness only, and non-finiteness has not been included in the graded categories. For scales of non-finiteness proposed by functionalists, see Section 2.4.

As commented by Binnick, there are two main criteria underlying the finite/non-finite distinction in traditional grammar: the ability of the verb to be the main verb of a full, independent clause, and its ability to take personal endings (Binnick 1991). Traditional approaches have inherited much knowledge from the long history of grammar writing, and the relevant viewpoints in traditional grammar are more accessible to the majority of readers.

Most of the viewpoints we have described are pervasive in modern grammar textbooks of the English language. They have exerted a strong impact on the grammar writing of other languages in the world.

2.3 Non-finiteness from the Typological Perspective

'The traditional approach has no principled grounds for establishing which feature is responsible for finiteness' (Nikolaeva 2007b: 2). The inflectional categories have raised conflicts found in a number of languages, and those conflicts confirm the view that the traditional notion of finiteness is ill-defined (Joseph 1983; Nikolaeva 2007b). This was also noticed in the 1960s by typologists like Greenberg, who in discussing 'verbal subordination to verb', speculates that 'conjunctions are more frequent in prepositional languages, nonfinite verb forms in postpositional languages, and that finite verb forms are found in both'(Greenberg 1963: 83).

The major purpose of typological study is to figure out the common properties and the structural similarity of the world's languages. Language-specific features have been accepted as the by-products of typological studies. As time has gone on, typological views on the universal features have become more comprehensive. Since non-finiteness has not so far been the focus of typological studies, we will review the literature on finiteness, which is scattered across articles and books. A great number of studies claim that languages depend on overt agreement or tense features for finiteness, but other studies show that finiteness may depend on 'mood' (e.g. Holmberg et al. 1993), negation markers (e.g. Amritavalli 2014), or spatial markers or participant markers (e.g. Ritter & Wiltschko 2014). Among various typological views, the following are the most relevant to the present research.

2.3.1 Category Space and the Continuum Hypothesis

Morphology-based studies classify languages into isolating/analytic languages (e.g. almost full correspondence between a single word and a single aspect of meaning in modern Chinese), fusional languages (e.g. several meanings being fused into a single morpheme in Latin), agglutinative languages (e.g. each morpheme being a discrete semantic unit in Turkish) and polysynthetic languages (e.g. relying mostly on morphology in Persian).

Since the 1960s, typologists have shifted the focus from morphology to word order (e.g. Greenberg 1963), and six fundamental types of word order have been identified in world languages: Subject ^ Verb ^ Object (SVO), Subject ^ Object ^ Verb (SOV), Object ^ Subject ^ Verb (OSV), Object ^ Verb ^ Subject (OVS), Verb ^ Subject ^ Object (VSO), Verb ^ Object ^ Subject (VOS). Languages of a certain word order may favour or disfavour the use of non-finiteness. For example, Jeffers (1976) considers Old Irish, Ancient Egyptian, Squamish and Tahitian, and concludes that VSO languages are sparse in non-finite verbal forms, and that these languages favour embedding by nominalization.

In recent years, word class has again become the focus of linguistic typology. Categorization of word classes is fundamental in linguistic research, and it has a long history. The traditional view puts word classes into discrete and unrelated categories. Many modern linguists disagree with this view, especially those who base their theories on Wittgenstein's 'family resemblance' in categorization (Wittgenstein 1953). Among these theories, the 'continuum hypothesis' (J. Ross 1972) was put forward to distinguish word classes on the basis of clusters of properties which typically are non-discrete. The clusters more or less overlap, and gradual differences can be observed between word classes. For example, 'adjectival words occupy an intermediate position in a language-independent lexical continuum or "category space" from Verb to Noun' (Wetzer 1996: 44); see Figure 2.3.

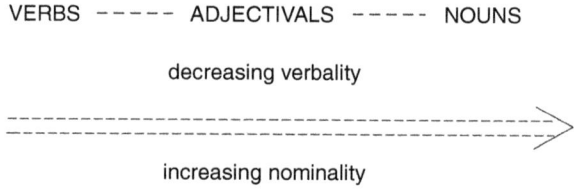

Figure 2.3 The continuum hypothesis (Wetzer 1996: 44)

With the continuum hypothesis as the background, and with data from a number of languages, it is argued that the selection of either verby or nouny adjectivals 'is strongly related to and can largely be predicted by the absence or presence of morphological tense marking in the language at issue' (Wetzer 1996: 268). Cross-linguistic evidence in favour of this hypothesis can also be found in Comrie (1975).

Among the typical word classes, adjectives are regarded as a separate word class which tend to display morphological and syntactic similarities with nouns or with verbs (see Thompson 1988). Many linguists tend to consider adjectives as an intermediate lexical category in the continuum of 'verb–noun'. This status 'leaves open the possibility for adjectives to behave in some languages more like one terminal category (Verb) and in other languages more like the other terminal category (Noun)' (Wetzer 1996: 46). A typical example is that adjectivals in Chinese can be directly used as predicates.

This overlapping of word class has its impact on linguists who work with diverse theories of language. A number of those linguists believe that the relation of grammar to meaning is indirect and arbitrary, and in linguistic

2.3 Non-finiteness from the Typological Perspective

analysis, they stick to the model of 'surface x is really deep y' (Halliday & Matthiessen 1999: 446). Thus, views such as the following have been popular:
- Nouns are really verbs (Clark & Clark 1979).
- Pronouns are really articles (Postal 2014 [1966]).
- Adjectives are really verbs (Chafe 1970).
- Quantifiers are really higher verbs (Carden 1967).
- Auxiliaries are really full verbs (J. Ross 1969; Borsley 1996).
- Reduced auxiliaries are really simple clitics (Anderson 2008).
- Negation is really a higher verb (J. Payne 1985).
- Negated adjunct phrases are really partitive (Franks & Dziwirek 1993).
- Tense is an adverb (Kiparsky 1968).
- Tense is really a [higher] verb (Huddleston 1969).
- Tense is an obligatory expansion of the node auxiliary (Chomsky 1965).

These views reflect the behaviour of word class or other grammatical categories on the basis of individual languages. A cross-linguistic perspective or a language-specific perspective may result in different views. Adjectives, which is 'a notorious swing-category in languages' (Givón 1979: 13), may be a good example.

'Object-dominated languages' and 'event-dominated languages' are distinguished according to features of their nouns and verbs (Capell 1965). An object-dominated language has an elaborate system of nouns, but verbs remain uninflected. By contrast, an event-dominated language has a simple noun system, but verbs are marked for tense, aspect and mood. Some linguists hypothesize that the selection of verby or nouny adjectivals in a particular language is not form-based but reflects a way of looking at the world. For example, the presence of verby adjectivals reflects an 'event-dominated' view of the world, while that of nouny adjectivals may reflect an 'object-dominated' world view (Wetzer 1996: 59).

The understanding of word classes and the related typological claims determine, to a great extent, the categorization of non-finiteness. If we simply follow the traditional classification of words, then non-finiteness will be a feature of some languages but not of others. In this tradition, 'finiteness is defined as the property of the verbal form which has to do with (i) tense marking, (ii) subject agreement, and (iii) the ability of the form to be used exclusively or predominantly in independent/main contexts' (Nikolaeva 2010: 1176).

If, however, we follow the continuum hypothesis for the classification of words, then non-finiteness may not be a significant feature of languages. Since verbs and nouns in many cases cannot be distinguished from each other, and other categories such as adjectivals may be either nouny or verby, markings in tense, person/number, mood and aspect will not be significant in distinguishing finite constructions from non-finite ones.

Table 2.1 *Disputes on the finite/non-finite distinction in Mandarin Chinese*

Views	Major supporters
There are only finite clauses in Mandarin Chinese	Y. Huang (1989, 1991a, 1991b, 1992a, 1992b, 1994)
There is a finite/non-finite distinction in Mandarin Chinese	C. T. J. Huang (1982, 1983, 1984, 1987, 1989, 1991); Y. H. A. Li (1985, 1990); C.-C. Tang (1990); Yuzhi Shi (1995, 2001); Tan (1995); J. Hu (1997); N. Zhang (1997); Ma (1998 [1898]); Lee (2000); T.-C. Tang (2000); D. Wang (2001); X. Xing (2004); Jinglian Li & Liu (2005); Jinxi Li (2007 [1924]); Fang & Zhao (2008); Her (2008); Yiming Yang & Cai (2011); T.-H. J. Lin (2012); Guo (2011, 2013); Grano (2015); Ussery et al. (2016)
There is no finite/non-finite distinction in Mandarin Chinese	L. Wang (1984); Zhu (1985); L. Xu (1986, 1994, 1999); S. Lü (1990 [1982], 2002 [1979]); Y. Huang (1992a, 1992b, 1994, 2000); J. Hu et al. (2001); J. Xu (2010); J.-W. Lin (2010); Liu (2010)
There are only non-finite clauses in Mandarin Chinese	R. Li (2003)

With distinct traditions, the issue of whether there is a finite/non-finite distinction in Mandarin Chinese is still under heated discussion. At least four major viewpoints are popular, and two of them are supported by the majority (see Table 2.1).

A number of linguists insist that the finite/non-finite distinction 'does not exist in Chinese' (J. Hu et al. 2001: 1144). At the same time, others insist that there is a covert distinction of finiteness and non-finiteness in Chinese (e.g. C. T. J. Huang 1982, 1983, 1989; Y. H. A. Li 1985, 1990), for the overt morphological marking is not the sole way to identify finiteness in a language, and the distinction can be manifested in the distribution of overt NPs and empty categories. Some generativists take this assumption to be a basic fact in Chinese syntax (e.g. Ernst 1994; Gasde & Paul 1996; Ting 1998; C. T. J. Huang 1999; C. Liu 1999). Table 2.1 shows that the general trend is for a distinction between finite and non-finite in Chinese, but the criteria should not be based on form.

More important than proper criteria is an unbiased treatment. Particularly, the bias towards English as a language substantially diverse from Chinese should be discarded. A very important reason is that, even in English, which has long been considered as a language with clear categories, flexibility is apparent: 'The potentialities of "objectifying" include functioning as a participant in transitivity, as subject interpersonally, and as theme textually . . . . It is not that some things are nominal and some things are verbal, the English language is highly flexible' (Fontaine 2015: 185–6).

2.3 Non-finiteness from the Typological Perspective

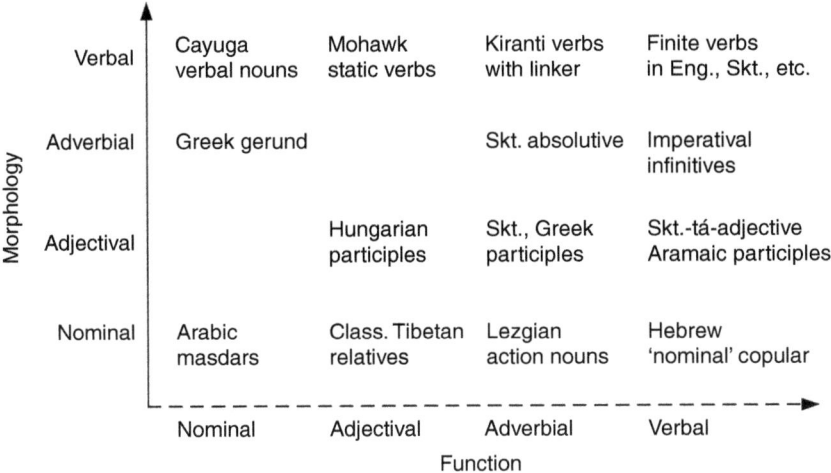

Figure 2.4 Verbal system typology matrix (Lowe 2015: 322)
Key: Skt. = Sanskrit

With typological findings, we can see from the matrix in Figure 2.4 that languages are more or less nominal or verbal. Some of the features (e.g. Arabic masdars), both functional and morphological, may be very close to being nominal. However, these features are still within the matrix, and being verbal is still inevitable. Some features, converbs, for example, which are 'nonfinite verb form[s] whose main function is to mark adverbial subordination', are found to be 'cross-linguistically valid' (Haspelmath 1995: 3).

Inspired by the continuum hypothesis and Whorf's grammatical categories (cryptotype, in particular) (Whorf 1945), B. Yang (2015) proposes a recategorization of non-finiteness in Chinese, in which pseudo-nonfiniteness is the focus (see Section 2.6; cf. pseudofiniteness in Cowper (2016)). Similar to the continuum hypothesis, Givón (2001: 26–9) distinguishes between extreme nominalizing and extreme finite languages. In extreme nominalizing languages, 'all subordinate clauses are (at least historically) nominalized' and in extreme finite languages, 'no clause-type is nominalized, and thus all clause-types are fully finite' (Givón 2001: 26). The extreme nominalizing languages include Carib, Quechuan, Tibeto-Burman and Turkic, while the finite languages include Athabaskan, Iroquois, South Arawak and others.

2.3.2 Obligatoriness and Asymmetry

To better illustrate the finite/non-finite distinction, Bisang (1995, 1998) employs obligatoriness and asymmetry to cover all aspects of the distinction across different languages. This idea is more adequate cross-linguistically, but it is mainly based on the morphology of verbs. According to Bisang (1995, 1998), East and Southeast Asian languages (e.g. Chinese, Vietnamese and Thai) do not have obligatory categories such as tense-aspect and number and they are characterized as indeterminate, and these languages cannot develop any asymmetry between finite and non-finite clauses.

'A central notion of the structuralist tradition is that the primary functional categories are the obligatory ones in a sentence' (Muysken 2008: 14). It is generally believed that some categories are optional, but some other categories (e.g. aspect in Nootka) are obligatory. The obligatory status of functional categories suggests peculiarity rather than universality (Sapir & Swadesh 1946). Functional categories lead to the fact that each language makes its own distinctions in terms of obligatory choices (Boas 1938).

The difference in obligatoriness between some languages has been verified through experiments. For example, non-obligatory imperfective aspectual morphemes in Thai and obligatory grammaticized imperfective aspectual marking on the verb in English have been found to affect 'the expression of co-occurring temporal events and actions depicted in three different short animations' (Winskel & Luksaneeyanawin 2009: 355).

In the view of Bisang (2007), cognitive domains such as tense, person, illocutionary force and politeness require obligatory linguistic expressions. The reason for this is that a category represented by a paradigm is obligatory, if the speaker has no choice but to express a certain value or subcategory of that paradigm. Thus, finiteness is obligatory for independent sentences in many languages while non-finiteness is not. In other words, the finite/non-finite distinction depends on the obligatoriness of some linguistic expressions.

According to Bisang (2007), languages create asymmetries between independent and dependent clauses, and an asymmetry arises if the obligatorily expressed domain in an independent clause cannot occur or if it occurs with a reduced set of subcategories. In this sense, the finite/non-finite distinction is only relevant for those languages that show a morphological asymmetry. Some languages are without obligatory categories, and asymmetries of this kind are far from being universal. In Bisang's view, finiteness can be considered as a device that humans use to recognize 'sentences as maximal syntactic units' (Bisang 2007: 137).

Let us see some specific facts. Among eight possible combinations of three finiteness features (i.e. main clausehood (MC), tense (T) and agreement (AGR) marking), at least four are associated with the term 'non-finite' in descriptive practice (Johns & Smallwood 1999; see Table 2.2).

In addition, asymmetry is apparent in some features for a number of languages. For example, 'in Kannada infinitives are uninflected, but participles, gerunds and dependent conditional take tense' (Nikolaeva 2007b: 1).

2.3 Non-finiteness from the Typological Perspective

Table 2.2 *Main clausehood, tense and agreement in non-finiteness*

	MC	T	AGR
English infinitives	−	−	−
European Portuguese infinitives	−	−	+
Tamil and Lezgian participles	−	+	−
Russian and Middle Welsh infinitives	+	−	−

In Northern Khanty and Mansi, 'clausal nominalizations inflect for agreement in complement and adverbial clauses, but not in relative clauses' (Nikolaeva 2007b: 2). In Lango, verbs do not inflect for tense (Noonan 1992). By contrast, verbs in Japanese 'inflect for tense but not agreement' (Nikolaeva 2007b: 2). In Daghestanian, finite categories are associated with the focus constituent which expresses tense, mood and agreement (Kalinina & Sumbatova 2007). Non-finite verb forms in European Portuguese occur only in dependent contexts, but they could carry overt agreement markers (Raposo 1987). In Russian, there is a syntactic requirement that the subjects of finite clauses be nominative, and those of non-finite clauses be dative (Perlmutter 2007). In Turkish, both the nominative and the genitive subject case can be an expression of finiteness (Kornfilt 2007).

These facts show that the obligatoriness of features of non-finiteness depends on the specific languages and contexts of language use. Asymmetry is pervasive, and the features are characteristic of 'family resemblance' (Wittgenstein 1953).

2.3.3 Root Infinitives in Children's Early Language

As the studies reviewed show, '[f]inite and nonfinite verbs behave very differently in many languages' (Wexler 2004: 242). More than this, they behave differently within the same language if learners of different age or learning background are brought into focus. Research has found that children and second-language adult learners develop forms of linguistic organization from which finite verbs are absent.

One of the major breakthroughs in this respect is the discovery of the Optional Infinitive (OI) stage (Wexler 1994, 1998), which is typical of root infinitives and lasts in normal children from birth to around three years old in learning languages. The term 'root infinitive' refers to main clauses in which the verb carries no inflection. As early as 1917, Van Ginneken commented on the existence of root infinitives in Dutch child language, 'noting that such utterances had a modal reference' (quoted in Hoekstra & Hyams 1998: 83). See Table 2.3 for the use of root infinitives by children.

Table 2.3 *Proportions of optional infinitives (OIs) by age (Wexler 2004: 244)*

Age group	% OIs
1;07–2;00	83% (126/152)
2;01–2;06	64% (126/198)
2;07–3;00	23% (57/253)
3;01–3;07	7% (29/415)

Children do not distinguish between finiteness and non-finiteness before two years old, and they continue to use root infinitives very often around two and a half years. The distinction between finite and non-finite gradually shows up and becomes prominent at about three. As found by Wexler (2004) and many others, the properties of the OI stage are:
- Root infinitives (non-finite verbs) are used by children as grammatical sentences.
- The infinitives and the finite forms co-exist.
- The children know the underlying relevant grammatical principles and they are able to set their parameters correctly.

It is significant that in English, which is an inflectional language, non-finite forms also show all the properties of OIs: the proportion of non-finite English forms increases as the child ages. In fact, it has been well known since R. Brown (1973) that children often produce what sounds like the stem form (e.g. *eat* instead of *eats*).

OIs have been found not only in English, but also in many other languages, such as Cypriot Greek (Georgiou et al. 2016), Dutch (Blom et al. 2001), German, French and Russian (see Hyams 2011). These languages usually carry salient inflections. The question is whether the OI phenomenon is universal. At least, we may ask if this can be found in languages that lack inflections. The answer to this question is positive. OIs has also been found in Chinese children before about two years old (Yiming Yang & Cai 2011: 171):

(2.4)   a. 爸爸不睡了,[2] 天亮了, 起来了! (1;09–10)
   bàba bù-   shuì-le,   tiānliàng-liǎo, qǐlái-le
   Daddy not-NEG sleep-JUSS day break-ASP get up-JUSS
   'Don't sleep, Daddy. The day breaks and you get up now.'

---

[2] '了', pronounced either as 'le' or 'liǎo' in modern Chinese, is extremely complicated. It may be used as a verb, an adverb or a particle. According to 现代汉语词典 (*Modern Chinese Dictionary*, 7th ed., The Commercial Press, 2020), 了 (le) is a particle which suggests the completion or initiation of an activity, or it may be simply an exclamative word. 了 (liǎo) may be used as a verb or a jussive mood indicator, or an aspect marker. Recent discussions on the function of 了 as an aspect marker can be seen in Youwei Shi (2017).

b. 爸爸不去! (2;01)
   bàba   bù-   qù
   Daddy   not-NEG go.
   'Don't go, Daddy.'
c. 爸爸不看书! (2;01)
   bàba   bù-   kàn   shū
   Daddy   not-NEG read   book.
   'Don't read now, Daddy.'

These expressions mean to prohibit or dissuade. Without the use of a modal verb, they are ungrammatical in adult Mandarin Chinese. Most often, a modal verb 'yào' and/or an aspect marker 'le' or 'liǎo' are obligatory. See (2.5) from Yang and Cai (2011: 171) for an example.

(2.5)   爸爸不要走! vs. 爸爸不走! (2;03)
        bàba   bú-   yào   zǒu   vs.   bàba   bù-   zǒu
        Daddy not-NEG should-MOD go   vs.   Daddy not-NEG go
        'Don't go, Daddy' (by adult) vs. 'Daddy not go' (2;03)

Further research shows that root infinitives are restricted to event-denoting predicates (e.g. Wijnen 1997, 1998; Hoekstra & Hyams 1998). Recent research has found that it is not only root infinitives that are restricted to eventive predicates; other non-finite forms are also similarly restricted (Hyams 2011). The consensus is that OIs are cross-linguistically valid: children acquiring different languages pass through a stage in which they use root infinitives (Hoekstra & Hyams 1998).

As a general analogy in linguistics, language development in children may be compared to language evolution in human history. The OIs may indicate that non-finiteness is a universal feature of language in terms of language evolution. As time has gone on, languages have developed distinct means of expressing tense, aspect, mood, person and number. That is why the disparities in non-finiteness between languages are apparent, but similarities can be found here and there, either synchronic or diachronic.

Most studies on OIs start from the perspective of GG. However, their significance is more in their typological implication than as evidence of a generative grammar. Specific studies of non-finiteness from the perspective of generative linguistics are described in the next section.

2.4 Non-finiteness in Generative Grammar: Form-Based

In formal literature, the term 'finiteness' has been used to refer primarily to syntactic domains, usually phrases headed by morphologically finite predicates. '[T]o date the most widespread diagnostic for finiteness (especially within formal approaches) is the presence of morphologically expressed tense and agreement features on the verb' (Eide 2016: 2). 'Non-finiteness' accordingly refers to phrases headed by non-finite forms, which do not express tense or agreement. For example, Börjars and Burridge (2010: 202) said that one difference between finite and non-finite clauses is that 'a complementizer is never optional' in non-finite clauses, and another major difference is that 'non-finite clauses need not have a subject and hence they look like simple VPs'.

Universality of non-finiteness is the major concern in this tradition. For example, '[I]nfinitival clauses are found only in embedded position, never as free-standing matrix clauses … it holds across all natural languages' (Hornstein 1990: 146). The following topics are much concerned with non-finiteness in the generative tradition.

2.4.1 PRO as Subject of Non-finite Clauses

In GG, *'pro'* as an empty category refers to a pronoun without phonetic properties, and it can be specified as [+pronominal, −anaphoric] by the Binding Theory. PRO (big pro) is a pronominal determiner phrase without phonological content. They are both part of the set of empty categories, the difference being that the null pronoun PRO is postulated in the subject position. When occurring in a non-finite complement clause, PRO can be bound by the main clause subject ('subject control') or the main clause object ('object control').

The Extended Projection Principle (EPP) proposed by Chomsky (1982) requires that all clauses should have a subject. As a consequence, clauses that lack an overt subject must have a covert subject. In non-finite clauses, the covert subject is called PRO (Camacho 2013). In other words, a PRO subject is required to make the sentence grammatical. A finite clause allows its subject to have independent reference, while a non-finite clause requires its covert subject (PRO) to be controlled by a noun phrase in the matrix clause. See (2.6) for an example.

(2.6)   a. We promised domain experts to describe their approach.
        b. We asked domain experts to describe their approach (COCA_ACAD)

In these sentences, the subjects of the to-clauses are not overtly expressed but can be understood to be controlled by an argument of the main clauses. In (2.6a), the PRO subject of the non-finite clause (i.e. *to describe their approach*) co-refers with *We*. By contrast, the subject of *describe* in (2.6b) is understood to be the same people who were asked (i.e. *domain experts*). Here, the PRO subject of $[_{TP}to\ describe]$ co-refers with *domain experts* (note that TP means tense phrase), which is the object of the main clause. As we can see, the argument that controls PRO in (2.6a) is the subject, and this is called subject control, for PRO is co-indexed with its antecedent *we* which is the subject of the main clause. When the argument that controls PRO is the object of the main

2.4 Non-finiteness in Generative Grammar: Form-Based

clause, we have object control (2.6b). In such sentences with non-finite clauses, the null pronominal subject PRO can be co-indexed with different DP (Determiner Phrase) arguments, so subject and object control are observed in terms of EPP.

According to the theta criterion, every verb has theta roles and every theta role must be present in the structure of the sentence (Camacho 2013). This means that theta roles must be present even if there is no overt argument. In the absence of an overt subject, the null category PRO has to be there so as to satisfy the theta criterion. Recent research into the theta-role information which takes Chinese into account can be found in X. Hu (2018).

The claim that non-finite clauses have a phonologically null PRO subject is motivated by the Binding Theory (Chomsky 1982), according to which an anaphor requires a local antecedent to be present. For example, reflexive pronouns in non-finite clauses (e.g. *myself*) require local antecedents, which may be present (2.7a) or replaced by PRO (2.7b).

(2.7)   a. It is difficult for me to ask myself about the class.
          b. It is difficult [PRO$_i$ to ask myself$_i$ about the class]. (NOW corpus)

Nominal agreement is another reason for the existence of a phonologically null PRO subject. In principle, predicate nominals must agree with the subject of a copular clause (Radford 2004). See (2.8) and (2.9) from Radford (2004: 110).

(2.8)   a. They want [**their son** to become **a millionaire / *millionaires**]
          b. He wants [**his sons** to become ***a millionaire / millionaires**]

(2.9)   a. He wants [PRO to become **a millionaire / *millionaires**]
          b. They want [PRO to become ***a millionaire / millionaires**]

The examples in (2.8) suggest that the number of predicate nominals must agree with that of the overt subject. Such nominal agreement holds true to PRO subjects in (2.9). If PRO is controlled by a singular antecedent (2.9a), then the predicate nominal must be singular. If PRO is controlled by a plural antecedent (2.9b), then the predicate nominal must be plural.

Research since the 1980s has tried to derive the existence of PRO from the PRO Theorem (i.e. PRO must be ungoverned). If PRO is ungoverned, then it must not be case marked. The problem is that research has shown that in some languages PRO does appear to be case marked (e.g. Icelandic), and PRO is thus governed. Later research focuses on the connection of PRO with weak case. It has been argued that PRO has case, which is checked by non-finite T (Chomsky & Lasnik 1993). See (2.10) from R. Martin (2001: 141).

(2.10)   a. *Kerry attempted [Bill [$_T$ to] study physics].
           b. *Kerry persuaded Sarah [Bill [$_T$ to] study physics].
           c. *It is not easy [Bill [$_T$ to] study physics].

(2.11) a. Kerry$_i$ attempted [PRO$_i$ [$_T$ to] to study physics.
b. Kerry persuaded Sarah$_j$ [PRO$_j$ [$_T$ to] study physics.
c. It is not easy [PRO$_k$ [$_T$ to] study physics.

The examples in (2.10) are contexts where an overt DP subject is ungrammatical in the specifier position of the TP. The contrasting examples in (2.11) show that a null PRO subject is grammatical in exactly the same contexts. Thus, PRO is grammatical as the subject of non-finite clauses, but it is not grammatical in corresponding finite clauses. The subject of the non-finite T must satisfy the case checked by T, and this case cannot be satisfied by a pronounced (i.e. overt) DP. For this reason, it is argued that null case is the only case assignable to PRO (R. Martin 2001). Hornstein (1999) argued that control verbs can be explained without resorting to PRO, and PRO can be done away with: obligatory control is explained with movement while non-obligatory control is explained with *pro*.

In the study by Plag (1993), the finite/non-finite distinction in Sranan (English-based Creole spoken in Surinam) is visible only from the perspective of syntax. Employing the standard assumption of Principles and Parameters that empty subjects can be either *pro* or PRO, Plag observed *pro*, the subject of a final clause licensed by a finite INFL, and PRO, an ungoverned position which must be the subject of a non-finite clause. Plag's analysis shows that finite and non-finite languages can be meaningfully distinguished regardless of the absence of morphological indications.

However, it needs to be noted that 'the area of well-formedness for null subjects (distinct from controlled PRO and trace of raising) must be broadened to include certain non-finite clauses which have a peculiar process of nominative assignment' (Rizzi 1982: 130). 'In non-finite clauses in which no case is available for the subject, a (*pro*) nominal inflection would never give rise to a well-formed structure' (Rizzi 1982: 142).

C. T. J. Huang (1984, 1989) also discussed the finite/non-finite distinction in Chinese in terms of *pro*/PRO. In his research, *pro*/PRO is defined as an empty category in which *pro* and PRO are two variants: in a finite clause, a zero anaphor occurring in subject position can be interpreted as a *pro*; in a non-finite clause, the zero anaphor occurring in subject position is a PRO. Some opposite views were provided by Y. Huang (1994) on this topic. In Huang's view, PRO as defined by Chomsky cannot occur in Chinese because there are only finite clauses in Chinese; *pro* as defined by Chomsky cannot occur in Chinese either because *pro* cannot be 'locally identified' in the language (Y. Huang 1994: 57).

Actually, both *pro* and PRO are empty categories (Chomsky 1982); the categories are illustrated in Table 2.4.

Of the categories, variable and NP trace come from movement while *pro* and PRO are generated. Non-finite clauses in Chinese may be explained as a result

2.4 Non-finiteness in Generative Grammar: Form-Based

Table 2.4 *Empty categories*

	empty categories
+anaphor, −pronominal	NP trace
−anaphor, +pronominal	*pro*
+anaphor, +pronominal	PRO
−anaphor, −pronominal	variable

of interaction of EPP, PRO Theorem and Case Theory. EPP requires that a sentence should have a subject; PRO Theorem requires that PRO should not be governed; and Case Theory requires that lexical NP should be case marked. Following these principles, J. Hu (1997) proposed the criterion of non-finite clause identification in Chinese as follows:

A clause in Chinese can be a non-finite clause if the subject is simultaneously:
- in the θ-position
- in a position that cannot be lexicalized.

Therefore, the clauses in brackets in (2.12) are non-finite clauses because they occupy the θ-position and cannot be lexicalized.

(2.12) a. 张三设法 [不抽烟] (J. Hu 1997: 39)
    Zhāng Sān shèfǎ   [bù   chōuyān]
    Zhang San tried   [not-NEG smoke].
    'Zhang San tried not to smoke.'

  b. 张三决心 [戒烟]
    Zhāng Sān juéxīn [jiè   yān]
    Zhang San decided [quit smoke].
    'Zhang San decided to quit smoking.'

  c. 她逼丈夫 [戒了烟]
    tā   bī   zhàngfu [jiè-le yān]
    She forced husband quit-ASP smoking.
    'She forced her husband to quit smoking.'

It should be noted that Hu later modified his viewpoint, and he and his colleagues argued that there is no such a distinction as finite and non-finite in Chinese (J. Hu et al. 2001).

2.4.2 Tense and the Finite/Non-finite Distinction

A non-finite clause is syntactically transparent (Chomsky 1973), and in the classical Binding Theory the non-finite INFL does not define a binding domain (Chomsky 1981). Thus, the anaphors in non-finite clauses are bound by the next binder available (i.e. the main subject). Other grammatical phenomena (e.g. control of PRO, NP-movement, pronominal binding and wh-movement) are responsible for the distribution of bound anaphors.

By assigning finiteness the status of a clausal head, generativists hold that finiteness somehow represents the whole clause. Finiteness thus corresponds to a position on a tree from where it dominates the rest of the clause. It is represented as the AUX(iliary) node in early transformational grammar, and later replaced by INFL(ection) or I. In the framework of Principles and Parameters it is a carrier of information about tense and agreement (Chomsky 1981, 1995). As to the distinction between the finite and non-finite I, it is held that finiteness is positively specified for tense or agreement, but non-finiteness is not.

Tense thus plays a crucial role in the finite/non-finite distinction in formal linguistics. Many authors in the past few decades have implicitly equated *finite* with *tensed*. Languages that show explicit tense with tense marking are considered as finite. For example, Shlonsky assumes that a full clause must contain a TP in Semitic languages and there is a dependence between TP and CP, the essential difference between full and small (or reduced) clauses being that 'the former are CPs, and are hence endowed with a TP projection, while the latter are clausal chunks that may vary in size' (Shlonsky 1997: 6).

An underlyingly finite clause takes on infinitival form if the subject is removed, either by subject raising or by Equi-NP deletion; a finite verb requires an overt subject, and an overt subject requires a finite verb (Soames & Perlmutter 1979). Finiteness is even equated with the presence of person agreement (George & Kornfilt 1981). Since nominative case and subject–verb agreement are regarded as two manifestations of a single AGREE relation (e.g. Chomsky 1995, 2000), some consider finiteness to be equal to nominative case and subject agreement, even in languages that lack overt agreement marking.

Finiteness together with case and agreement are crucial in the Theory of Government and Binding, according to which nominative case is assigned to subject position by an INFL. In finite clauses there is an INFL [+TENSE], and it usually contains a nominal element to carry person and number features. Thus, the values that the elements of INFL take determine whether there is a finite/non-finite distinction. Since INFL is composed of tense and agreement (AGR), finite clauses are characterized as [+Tense] and [+AGR], and non-finite clauses as [−Tense] and [−AGR].

This distinction based on the [+/−Tense] features of the node INFL is sufficient to distinguish finite and non-finite clauses in inflectional languages (Luraghi & Parodi 2008). In languages that are not inflectional, it may not be suitable. A typical case is modern Chinese. It has been widely agreed that modern Chinese does not have AGR, but controversies on Tense in Chinese are still unsettled.

Y. H. A. Li (1990) claims that it is necessary to distinguish tensed clauses from infinitives in Chinese even if it is not possible to distinguish between finite and non-finite clauses. In Li's view, finite clauses but not infinitives can have tense; future markers, that is, real tense markers, cannot occur in non-finite clauses (e.g. clauses whose matrix verb is a verb for persuasion, like 劝(*quàn*)).

According to Stassen, a typological distinction between tensed and non-tensed languages can be made on the basis of a tensedness parameter: 'If a language has a grammatical category which is morphologically bound on verbs and minimally involves a distinction between past and non-past time reference, then that language is tensed. In all other cases, a language is non-tensed' (Stassen 1997: 350–1). In other words, a tensed language should have 'grammaticalised location in time' (Comrie 1985: 9). The location in time may include 'temporal adverbs or adverbial phrases, auxiliaries, particles, and morphological markings' (Stassen 1997: 351).

Another criterion proposed by Stassen (1997: 357) is the tensedness universals of adjective encoding: if a language is tensed, it will have nouny adjectives, and vice versa. If a language is non-tensed, it will have verby adjectives, and vice versa. Since the predicative adjectives in Chinese side with verbs (e.g. C. N. Li & Thompson 1981), Chinese can be considered as a non-tensed language in this sense.

Other criteria may also be applied to the discussion. Some argue that in Chinese non-finite clauses do not have tense in INFL but finite clauses do (e.g. Y. H. A. Li 1985). Thus, a tensed analysis is necessary in terms of control constructions, the distribution of modal auxiliaries, aspect markers and adverbs (e.g. C. T. J. Huang 1982; C.-C. Tang 1990; T.-C. Tang 2000; Sybesma 2007; T.-H. J. Lin 2012). Others believe that Chinese is a non-tensed language for the reason that there is no morphological marking of a past/non-past distinction in the language (e.g. J. Hu et al. 2001; C. Smith & Erbaugh 2005; J.-W. Lin 2006, 2010).

The obligatoriness of tense has been found in many languages (Comrie 1985; Dahl 1985; Bybee & Dahl 1989). However, this does not appear to be the case in modern Chinese, which seems to be strong evidence for the non-tensedness of Chinese. However, 将(*jiāng*) is found to be a future tense morpheme, not a modal auxiliary, nor a time adverb nor irrealis marker, which shows that modern Chinese has syntactic tense (Z. Huang 2015).

Since the essence of finiteness is the ability to assign nominative case to a subject and to agree in person and number with that subject (Cowper 2016: 49), recent studies no longer focus on tense. To the extent that the term 'tense' has to do with the semantic relationship between the time associated with a clause and some other time, such as the moment of speech, 'finiteness and tense should not be equated' (Cowper 2016: 49). This debate is ongoing, and it needs time to arrive at good consensus.

2.4.3 Non-isomorphic Relation between Content and Form

As we know, the Chomskyan theory was developed into the Principles and Parameters approach in the 1980s, which in the 1990s gave way to the Minimalist Programme, aimed at finding simpler but more universal grammatical features. In the Minimalist Programme, syntactic operations are said to be morphologically driven, but morphological features should be interpreted to mean abstract, formal features. Considerable evidence suggests that finiteness will always be morphologically marked and non-finiteness morphologically unmarked (Joseph 1983; Vincent 1998).

A pervasive assumption in the early days of GG is that categories of morphology (inflectional morphology, in particular) are isomorphic to those of syntax. It was generally believed that there is an isomorphic relationship between content paradigms of a language and its form paradigms. Thus, if there are no inflections for finiteness in a language, this has been taken to suggest that there is no distinction between finite and non-finite.

According to Anderson (2002: 273), observations such as the following were quite popular: 'case morphology allows for greater freedom of word order; rich verbal agreement makes it possible to omit overt pronominal subjects; ergative case marking reflects an underlying "passive" organization of grammatical structure within the clause'. A number of linguists have attempted to find some property of a language's verbal agreement morphology that can be correlated with syntactic movement of the Verb to the **I**(nflection) position: '[this] tends to be extremely legalistic, relying on conditions like "if and only if at least one number in at least one tense of the regular verb paradigm distinguishes first from second person, then **V** moves to **I**" or "if and only if there is person morphology in all tenses, then **V** moves to **I**," and so on' (Anderson 2002: 272; emphasis in original).

Syntactic and morphological structure may be non-isomorphic. Morphological features do not necessarily imply syntactic features. If finiteness is determined by inflection, then languages without inflectional morphology will not be distinguished in terms of finiteness and non-finiteness. However, a number of languages without inflectional morphology are found to present relevant syntactic effects. For example, it is found in modern Chinese that clauses embedded under verbs of saying (e.g. *ask*, *promise*, *advise*) can have an overt subject, but clauses embedded under volitional verbs cannot (C.-T. J. Huang 1984; Y. H. A. Li 1990; T.-C. Tang 2000). This means that the morphological form of the verb cannot be regarded as a universal criterion for distinguishing finite from non-finite clauses (Ledgeway 1998; Vincent 1998).

2.4 Non-finiteness in Generative Grammar: Form-Based

For some languages, some morphological features may be related to syntactic features. For example, non-finiteness in modern Neapolitan does not morphologically inflect for such categories as person/number and tense, but personal infinitives behave like finite tensed verb forms, which licenses a nominative subject 'with independent reference not to be controlled by an argument of the matrix clause' (Ledgeway 2007: 352).

'Recent versions of generative syntax have given up the strong isomorphism between syntactic structure and morphology' (Nikolaeva 2007b: 8). Generativists today treat the finite/non-finite distinction on a language-specific basis (e.g. Adger 2007). This to some extent defies the fundamental assumption of GG: to look for the universal features.

2.4.4 Gradient or Binary

'[T]he two-way distinction between "finite" and "non-finite" employed in traditional and also within early GG is much to [sic] coarse grained, and ... we need to appeal to notions that take an intermediate position between the two' (Eide 2016: 19). Though insisting on the purely syntactic property of finiteness, Cowper (2016) argues that the intermediate notions can be given principled and consistent analyses.

Regardless of the isomorphic controversy, a view of taking finite and non-finite clauses as a gradient phenomenon can indeed be seen in earlier formal literature as well. As pointed out by Ledgeway (1998), the traditional definitions of non-finiteness prove insufficient, and a conception of finiteness as a spectrum should be recognized. In this conception, non-finiteness may be broken down into a number of variable features. Subtle shifts, such as the development from inflected infinitive (a relatively finite form) to non-inflecting infinitive (a thoroughly non-finite form), suggest that it is necessary to regard non-finiteness as a linguistic phenomenon that is on a spectrum (Ledgeway 2007).

As a morphosyntactic category of the clause, finiteness controls the realization of the subject argument, and regulates tense and agreement on the verb, in the formalist literature. By contrast, non-finiteness is considered as the other end on a scale, thus creating a binary view. However, many cases do not support this view if non-finiteness is considered. For example, all infinitives in Welsh agree with pronominal subjects, and infinitives embedded under different verbs differ in terms of binding (Tallerman 1998).

In the early days, a number of generativists shifted from analysing finiteness as an inflectional feature of the verb to viewing it as a more abstract category. The feature belongs to 'the clause as a whole; a category occupying a specific position in a clausal structure originally dubbed AUX and later renamed I(NFL)' (Eide 2016: 3). This is supported by other relevant studies. Mensching (2000), for example, found that case assignment by infinitival

AGR is a marginal phenomenon. More and more studies in the generative tradition today suggest that finiteness should be a gradient phenomenon.

As is well known, the aim of the GG initiated by Noam Chomsky is to identify the universal rules for generating grammatical sentences in languages. After many years of effort, some linguists in this tradition began to consider finiteness as a clausal category, which has an important impact on the analysis of non-finiteness. The significant conceptual move from verb to clause seems to make it 'possible to maintain the universality of the finite/non-finite distinction' (Nikolaeva 2007b: 4).

2.5 Non-finiteness in Cognitive Grammar: Meaning-Based

The distinction of finiteness and non-finiteness, which is based on morphosyntactic criteria and which refers primarily to the verbal systems of European languages, 'turns out to be of limited cross-linguistic applicability' (Cristofaro 2003: 53). The distinction 'involves the same problems as the one between coordination and subordination .... In the case of coordination and subordination, the solution was to abandon the distinction altogether, and classify clause types on the basis of functional criteria' (Cristofaro 2003: 54). Abandoning the distinction seems to be an impossible mission, because it is deep-rooted in linguistics. A feasible approach is to shift perspectives so that we can observe the phenomenon better.

Cognitive approaches, in general shifted the perspective from morphosyntax to semantics and pragmatics, dealing with non-finiteness as a property of the clause. Moreover, cognitive approaches consider finiteness to be a scalar, or gradient, phenomenon not reducible to tense-aspect marking and agreement. It is signalled by such features as 'tense, modality, aspect markers, agreement, case markings on the subject and object, articles, determiners, and topic markers .... The more visible features of this sort, the "more finite" the clause' (Eide 2016: 12). Non-finiteness, as a consequence, is not the opposite to finiteness as a binary category, but a phenomenon on one side of the pole.

2.5.1 Non-finiteness as Atemporal Construal

In his CG, Langacker (1987, 1991a, 1991b, 1999, 2008, 2013) has not given much space to non-finiteness. In a short discussion in the book published in 2009, Langacker (2009: 221) wrote, 'the most basic shortcoming of Chomsky's original account is the absence of any attempt to deal with meaning ... [T]ense and modality are precisely the elements characterized semantically as serving the function of clausal grounding', while 'grounding is a defining property of finite clauses', so 'tense and modals are naturally excluded from non-finite complements'. In Langacker's view, the elements such as 'have + -en', 'be + -ing' and ' be + -ed' are meaningful, and 'the perfect, progressive, and passive meanings are largely compositional with respect to their parts' (Langacker 2009: 221).

2.5 Non-finiteness in Cognitive Grammar: Meaning-Based

Infinitival clauses in a number of expressions are considered to be the result of raising in the GG. See (2.13), from Langacker (2009: 302), for an example.

(2.13) a. They expect that she will be late.
b. **They** expect **her** to be late.
c. It is likely that she will be late.
d. **She** is likely to be late.

Generativists consider the use of *her to be late* in (2.13b) as a result of raising of *that she will be late*: the complement clause has raised its status to be a nominal complement. Similar treatment can be applied to (2.13d), in which the complement clause has raised to be a nominal subject (i.e. *she*). The so-called raised nominal specifies the topic to which an assessment is made, which may be characterized as epistemic.

By contrast, cognitivists consider this to be variants making different choices of trajector or landmark (Langacker 1995). 'Trajector' (tr) refers to 'the entity the expression is concerned with tracking, locating, assessing, or characterizing', and 'a second relational participant is accorded the status of secondary figure and it is called a Landmark (lm)' (Langacker 1995: 11). 'A verb profiles a process, as do modals, tense markers, and certain higher-order structures (notably finite clauses)', and the categories such as adjectives, adverbs and prepositions 'profile different sorts of atemporal relations' (Langacker 1995: 13). 'Infinitives and participles are derived from verbs', but 'they impose an atemporal construal' (Langacker 1995: 14). This atemporalizing function is part of the meaning of *to, -ing* and *-ed*.

'Relational predications are divided into those that profile "processes", and those that designate "atemporal relations"': The former is 'coextensive with the class of verbs' while the latter corresponds 'to such traditional categories as prepositions, adjectives, adverbs, infinitives, and participles' (Langacker 1991a: 78).

To observe categories, Langacker (1991a: 78) distinguishes conceived time (time as an Object of conceptualization) from processing time (time as the Medium of conceptualization). Non-finite forms are called verb forms, but they are not verbs by Langacker's definition. They 'designate atemporal relations' (Langacker 1991a: 82): each derivational morpheme (*to, -ing, -ed*) 'profiles a schematically characterized atemporal relation, and imposes its atemporal profile on the processual base provided by the stem' (Langacker 1991a: 82). The conclusion is as follows:

a. A finite clause always profiles a process.

b. A nonfinite noun modifier is always atemporal. (Langacker 1991a: 132) With infinitives and participles being atemporal, both temporality and atemporality can be construed. Thus, '[t]he noun and verb categories are universal and fundamental to grammatical structure' (Langacker 1991a: 100).

2.5.2 The View of Scalarity

Cognitivists advocate a scalar view of finiteness and non-finiteness. For example, Thomas E. Payne proposes the scale of grammatical dependency (Figure 2.5), in which degrees of grammatical dependency and types of clauses have been drawn on a scale.

High degree of grammatical dependency			Low degree of grammatical dependency
Non-finite clauses:	Semi-finite clauses:		Finite clauses
• Bare form infinitives • '"to" infinitives'	• Present participles • Past participles	• Present subjunctive • Past subjunctive	

Figure 2.5 The scale of grammatical dependency (T. Payne 2011: 331)

In his early research, Givón pointed out there may be a universal phenomenon in which 'the lexical categories VERB, ADJECTIVE, and NOUN occupy different areas of a *continuum*, and the scalar property of that continuum seems to be *time-stability*' (Givón 1979: 14; emphasis in original). Before discussing the continuum, it is necessary to explain the view of finiteness as the property of the clause. As we know, finiteness/non-finiteness was considered by traditional grammarians to be a property of verbs. In Givón's view, this distinction is concerned with other parts of the clause. See (2.14) for an example.

(2.14)   a. **Finite**: They categorically reject the offer
          b. **Non-finite**: The**ir** categori**cal** rejec**tion of** the offer (Givón 1995: 33; emphasis in original)

With adjustments, the finite (2.14a) has been changed into the nominalized non-finite expression (2.14b), and such change from finite to non-finite usages indicates that finiteness may be concerned not with the verb, but the clause (Givón 1995: 33). In his earlier research, Givón (1990: 852–91) proposed four characteristics for the finite/non-finite distinction:

- Clausal domain: Finiteness is a property of the clause (rather than of the verb in a clause).
- Complexity and scalarity: Finiteness is a complex, multifeatured, scalar grammatical meta-phenomenon (rather than a single, discrete, binary feature).
- Coding function: Finiteness is the systematic grammatical means used to express the degree of integration of a clause into its immediate clausal environment.
- Scope of dependency: While some clause dependencies may be expressed in terms of purely syntactic relations, clausal dependency is ultimately

2.5 Non-finiteness in Cognitive Grammar: Meaning-Based

a matter of discourse coherence. Syntactic dependencies are but a restricted subset of discourse-pragmatic dependency.

In his discussion of these characteristics, Givón (1990: 853) considers the first five 'main syntactic features' listed below to determine the degree of finiteness of a given clause, and Bisang (2001) adds the sixth feature (topic marker) for dealing with pragmatics:

- tense–aspect–modality (TAM)
- pronominal ('grammatical') agreement
- nominalizing affixes
- case marking of the subject and object
- articles, determiners
- topic marker.

Changes in these features will result in changes in degree of finiteness. With regard to the degree of finiteness in terms of major verb-form categories, Givón (1990: 854) presents the following hierarchical scale:

most finite
indicative
subjunctive/modal
participial
infinitive
nominal
least finite

TAM seems to be the most widely discussed feature as far as the finite/non-finite distinction is concerned. Givón (1990: 854) presents a scale of finiteness of TAM in which being 'more finite' has such features as 'terminated, realis, punctual, and in-sequence', while being 'less finite' has such features as 'non-terminated, irrealis, durative, and anterior'. Givón (1990) also gives a scale of finiteness ranking of TAM per se, in which tense is most finite and negation is least finite, while modality and aspect are in between, but modality is more finite than aspect. Note that Noonan (1985: 57) provided an inflection-based scale which is not limited to TAM, and negation is not included. An example from the English language may help understand Givón's insightful views. See Figure 2.6 for his scale of non-finiteness in English. In the gradation from the main clause to nominalization in English, most types are well exemplified as non-finite.

As we can see from Givón's scales, nominals and finite verbs are the two pole ends of the scale of finiteness. This may explain why nominalization and finiteness attract much more attention from linguists than non-finiteness does.

Bisang (1998) looked at clause combining in three different language types: European; Eurasian or converb; and Far Eastern or verb serialization. The parametric techniques of clause combining include the following: converbs and adverbial subordinators, which are morphological; verb serialization,

least finite

a. (lexical nominal) Her good *knowledge* of math helped

b. (-ing infinitive) *Her knowing* math well helped

c. (to-infinitive) For her *to know* math so well surely...

d. (verb complex) She wanted *to know* math well

e. (perfect participle) *Having known* math well since high school, she...

f. (finite verb form) She *should have known* math well

most finite

Figure 2.6 Degrees of finiteness in English (Givón 2001: 26)

which is both morphological and syntactic; and relativization/nominalization, which is syntactic.

In addition to Bisang's categories of clause combining, Lehmann (1988: 182–3) proposed several scales, the first of which is the scale of clause linkage across languages:
(a) the hierarchical downgrading of the subordinate clause
(b) the main clause syntactic level of the subordinate clause
(c) the desententialization of the subordinate clause
(d) the grammaticalization of the main verb
(e) the interlacing of the two clauses
(f) the explicitness of the linking.

'Hierarchical downgrading is not only an important parameter in the typology of clause linkage, but is also a central criterion for the traditional notion of subordination' (Lehmann 1988: 189). Another scale proposed by Lehmann (1988: 192) is the scale of syntactic level, as shown in Figure 2.7.

sentence < ──────────────────────── > word

subordinate clause is				complex predicate formation		
outside main clause	at margin of main clause	inside main clause	inside VP	verb serial- ization	auxiliary peri- phrasis	verbal deriva- tion

Figure 2.7 The scale of syntactic level (Lehmann 1988: 192)

2.5 Non-finiteness in Cognitive Grammar: Meaning-Based

According to cognitivists, finite forms prototypically function as the only predicate of an independent clause, participles as nominal attributes, infinitives as sentential arguments, and verbal nouns as arguments (Nedjalkov 1995). 'Finiteness is thus fundamentally an aggregate grammatical feature of clauses. Its converse, non-finiteness, is thus an aggregate grammatical feature of nominals, i.e. noun phrases' (Givón 2001: 25). In a word, non-finiteness is considered as a phenomenon to be observed on specific scales.

2.5.3 Verbal and Finite versus Nominal and Non-finite

As we can see from the literature, a number of cognitivists link finiteness with verbs, and non-finiteness with nouns. For example, Noonan defines infinitives as 'verb-like entities that do not bear syntactic relations to their notional subjects' (Noonan 1985: 57). Givón argues that finiteness as a clausal phenomenon can be 'discussed in terms of two extreme prototypes – the verbal (finite) vs. nominal (non-finite)' (Givón 2001: 352). The morphosyntax of these prototypes is shown in Table 2.5.

Table 2.5 *The morphosyntax of the finite versus non-finite prototypes (Givón 2001: 352)*

	Finite (verbal)	Non-finite (nominal)
a. Verbal inflections		
• tense-aspect-modality	+	–
• pronominal affixes	+	–
• nominalizers	–	+
• determiners	–	+
• classifiers, number	–	+
b. Nominal inflections		
• case markers	Nom/Acc	Gen
• obligatory zero-anaphors	–	+

Key: Nom = nominative; Acc = accusative; Gen = genitive

This categorization is semantic and cognitive, but it is still inflection-based. Moreover, it may not be applied cross-linguistically. In Turkish, for example, there are both verbal finite and nominalized finite clauses, and nominal embeddings can be finite (Kornfilt 2007). The purpose of cognitivism is not to search for universality, but it is possible that some categories may be universal. For example, the frequent occurrence of analytical forms with the light verbs 'be', 'become' or 'do' in heritage speech 'supports the notion that aspectual distinctions are universal, belonging with the conceptual representation of events' (Polinsky 2008: 263).

2.5.4 Conceptual Motivation

Finiteness in terms of cognitive linguistics is considered to have various morphosyntactic realizations across languages (e.g. Noonan 1985, 1992), and the conceptual motivation behind this has been a focal topic. According to Givón (1990, 2001), dependent events cannot be conceptualized as independent processes, but as components of main events. In other words, a dependent event/state may be integrated into a higher clause, which can be iconically reflected at the morphosyntactic level. The semantic bond corresponds well with the degree of integration of the clauses. Finiteness, as a consequence, is the 'systematic grammatical means used to express the degree of integration of a clause into its immediate clausal environment' (Givón 1990: 853).

In terms of CG, 'finite' and 'non-finite' are two poles of the functionally motivated scale of desententialization. Between the two poles there are many intermediate situations, which may be observed through verbal and nominal properties. The loss of verbal properties (e.g. tense, aspect, mood, person/number marking), and the gaining of nominal properties (e.g. case, omission of verbal arguments), are manifestations of non-finiteness. '[S]emantic finiteness and syntactic finiteness, while coinciding in many instances, do not always go hand in hand' (Kornfilt 2007: 307). The conceptual motivation, as a consequence, may only be true of prototypical categories. For the categories, the iconicity meta-principle proposed by Givón (1985: 189) is a useful guideline:

The iconicity meta-principle: All other things being equal, a coded experience is easier to *store*, *retrieve* and *communicate* if the code is maximally isomorphic to the experience. (emphasis in original)

Why do speakers of a language conceptualize finiteness and non-finiteness as they do? To answer this question from the cognitive perspective, cognitive linguists would say that humans share similar physical properties (e.g. vocal organs), but the societal and environmental communities are different, an important reason for disparity in conceptualization. The linguistic facts also indicate that the same state/event may be conceptualized in distinct ways. Even in the same language, many ways are possible for diachronic conceptualization of the same state/event. In other words, finiteness and non-finiteness are just alternative ways for conceptualizing states/events. This is universally true of human languages.

2.5.5 Non-finite Clauses as Constructions

Construction Grammar, generally speaking, is part of cognitive linguistics. It is a family of theories rather than a unified theory, and includes Lakovian Construction Grammar (Lakoff 1987), Berkeley Construction Grammar (Fillmore et al. 1988), Goldberg's (1995) Construction Grammar, Sign Based Construction Grammar (Michaelis & Lambrecht 1996), Radical Construction Grammar (Croft 2001) and Embodied Construction Grammar (Bergen & Chang 2005). Many construction-oriented studies of non-finiteness are based on Goldberg (1995, 2003), though some of the studies may be more specific in terms of construction. For example, Waldenfels (2012) deals with the grammaticalization of 'give + infinitive' in Polish, Czech and Russian, and the constructions include the causative, the modal and the imperative. The findings in this study confirm the definition of grammaticalization 'as a change whereby lexical items and constructions come in certain linguistic contexts to serve grammatical functions and, once grammaticalized, continue to develop new grammatical functions' (Hopper & Traugott 2003: xv).

Some studies pursue more general questions. For example, Ungerer in a recent study aims to answer 'whether infinitive constructions show a different constructional meaning from parallel finite clauses' (Ungerer 2017: 2). Ungerer thus proposes a non-finite interface, that is, 'a special way of adding a second verbal element to a construction (either as a participant or circumstance) or of modifying a nominal head in a VMC [verb-mediated construction]', and in each case, 'a specific form/meaning pairing is established, which differs from subordinate clause constructions' (Ungerer 2017: 203).

Ungerer argues that, in terms of perspectivizing, 'to-infinitives perspectivize volitional, deontic and epistemic modality, gerunds perspectivize factuality', and participles perspectivize the progressive aspect or the perfective aspect (Ungerer 2017: 203). Ungerer's study is concerned with not only typical non-finite constructions but also non-finite constructions with notional subjects, that is, for + noun + infinitive constructions, with + noun + participle/infinitive constructions and noun + genitive/possessive determiner + gerund constructions.

In a study of non-finite complementation, Egan (2008) puts complement constructions into different-subject constructions and same-subject constructions according to the numbers of subjects they contain. With data from the BNC, Egan (2008: 22–3) identifies six types of different-subject constructions: perception constructions (e.g. *You noticed me watching you, I shouldn't wonder*); mental process constructions (e.g. *Most scientists believe the infill to be lava ...*); attitude constructions (e.g. *I dread mine reaching their teens*); communication constructions (e.g. *The master commands you to stay*); enablement constructions (e.g. *Outside he allowed her to examine the bird*); causation constructions (e.g. *He halted, forcing the rest of the field to bunch up behind him*). Same-subject constructions are also identified: positive attitude constructions, negative attitude constructions, comparative attitude constructions and aspect constructions. In addition to these types, forward-looking constructions and backward-looking constructions are identified. The problem that remains is that how the specific constructions can reveal the use of non-finiteness.

Research into the acquisition of non-finite constructions has produced interesting results. For example, drawing on observational data, Holger Diessel examined the acquisition of infinitival and participial complement clauses, which shows that simple, non-embedded sentences gradually evolve into bi-clausal constructions (Diessel 2004).

2.6 Non-finiteness in Systemic Functional Grammar: Meaning- and Form-Based

Functional grammars are basically usage-oriented and are meaning- and form-based, and SFG is of no exception. SFG, developed by M. A. K. Halliday, describes language in terms of meaning potentials by various meaning-form choices in communication. As a typical approach which considers meaning and form as an inseparable unity, SFG provides us with illuminating insights on language as a whole.

SFG was first proposed by M. A. K. Halliday in the 1950s, and it became well developed in the 1980s. Being 'one of the major breakthroughs in twentieth-century theoretical linguistics' (Matthiessen 2014a: xvii), a core idea of SFG is that meaning is realized through various forms, and a single form of language of whatever length may have more than one meaning potential. Choices of form are determined by the meaning to be realized, and meanings of forms are determined by the context. According to SFG, '[n]on-finite realizations are typically associated with act clauses' (Hita 2018: 229). The significant views in Halliday's works about non-finite clauses and other relevant views by systemicists are summarized in Sections 2.6.1–2.6.3.

2.6.1 *General Discussions on Non-finite Clauses*

Not only finite verbal groups but also non-finite ones in English can be tensed. Thus, thirty-six finite tenses, twenty-four finite tenses in projected clauses, and twelve non-finite tenses have been identified for English (Halliday 1985, 1994). See Table 2.6 for a summary of non-finite tenses in English by Bache (2008).

The frequent mention of non-finite clauses in Halliday's publications can be found in the illustration of hypotactic relations in clause complexes. The grammatical marking of the hypotactic clause combination essentially includes two types of marking: *connective*, which is usually a conjunction or

2.6 Non-finiteness in Systemic Functional Grammar

Table 2.6 *Non-finite tenses in English (Bache 2008: 17)*

	Tense	Example
1.	(none)	*to take, taking; can take*
2.	past	*to have, having; can have + taken*
3.	present	*to be, being; can be + taking*
4.	future	*to be, being; can be + going to take*
5.	past in future	*to be, being; can be + going to have taken*
6.	present in past	*to have, having; can have + been taking*
7.	present in future	*to be, being; can be + going to be taking*
8.	future in past	*to have, having; can have + been going to take*
9.	past in future in past	*to have, having; can have + been going to have taken*
10.	present in past in future	*to be, being; can be + going to have been taking*
11.	present in future in past	*to have, having; can have + been going to be taking*
12.	present in past in future in past	*to have, having; can have + been going to have been taking*

a preposition, and *finiteness*, which may be 'marked with respect to finiteness by being non-finite (infinitival or participial)' (Matthiessen and Thompson 1988: 304).

In the view of Halliday (1994), a non-finite clause usually occurs in one of the two types of logico-semantic relation: expansion and projection. Within expansion, a non-finite clause may be employed to elaborate (2.15a), extend (2.15b), or enhance (2.15 c) a finite clause, or it may be embedded in another element (2.15d); while within projection, it may be projected by the finite clause (2.15e) (Halliday 1994: 221–73).

(2.15)   a. ||| I worked for a local firm at that time, || selling office equipment. |||
                     α   =β

         b. ||| Besides missing the wedding, ||she spent the whole week in hospital. |||
                     +β   α

         c. ||| They must be crazy, || throwing all that good stuff away. |||
                     α   ×β

         d. || the house [being built by Jack] || (embedded as Postmodifier)

         e. ||| Mary hopes || to go to Sweden next year. |||
                     α   'β

Another treatment of non-finite clauses by systemicists can be found in Hudson (1971), who was one of the leading systemicists in his early years of research. Hudson's treatment of non-finite clauses is based on SFG, but to a great extent it is a summary of the tense/aspect and voice features of non-finite elements in clauses, with generalizations of the feature-realization rules. This, strictly speaking, is not systemic functional but systemic formal, for 'the facts are complex, but can be handled without too much difficulty in a systemic formalization' (Hudson 1971: 157).

When analysing the lexicogrammatical features of the text *Zero Population Growth*, Halliday (2002a [1992]) found that in terms of taxis and interdependency (logical-semantic relation), the favoured type is hypotactic enhancement with a number of non-finite clauses. In the systemic grammar of English, all major clauses in principle 'choose for polarity, whether finite or non-finite; whereas only finite clauses have primary tense' (Halliday 2005 [1993]: 147). Imperatives belong to non-finite verbal groups, but they are special in that they have no primary tense but realize finite clauses.

As to the thematic structure, many non-finite clauses consist of Rheme only (d. in Figure 2.8), but it is still possible for them to include other components: structural and topical Themes (a. and b. in Figure 2.8) and structural Theme (c. in Figure 2.8).

a. with	all the doors	being locked	[we have no way in]
b. for	that printer	to work off your machine	[you need a cable]
c. while		not blaming them	[I'm still disappointed]
d.		to avoid delay	[have your money ready]
structural	**topical**		
Theme		**Rheme**	

Figure 2.8 Theme in non-finite dependent clauses (Halliday & Matthiessen 2014: 127)

Fontaine (2012: 116) proposed that a clause may be considered finite if at least one of the following conditions is met, and non-finite if none of them is met.

- The clause includes a Finite verbal element that can be shown as an inflection for past or present tense (e.g. *he walks* vs. *he walked*).
- The clause includes a Finite verbal element in the form of a modal auxiliary verb (e.g. *I can swim*).
- The clause includes a verbal operator that can be shown to be inflected for grammatical mood (e.g. *you are happy* vs. *be happy*).

In addition to these conditions, Fontaine (2012: 119) proposed three characteristics for determining the finite status of a clause: (a) Finiteness: 'if a clause is finite then the Finite element must be identifiable and can be revealed by re-expressing the clause'; (b) Auxiliary morphology: 'non-finite clauses display unexpected verb forms since they appear in what is a recognizable form (progressive, perfective or infinitive) but without a finite precedent trigger (e.g. specific auxiliary forms)'; (c) Pronoun replacement: all 'embedded non-finite clauses fill a particular function in a higher unit within the clause (e.g. participant, circumstance or qualifier)'.

The major characteristics of non-finite clauses, according to Downing (2015: 101), are being 'loosely integrated into' the main clause, and analysable as 'a chain-like structure'. Besides, Downing (2015) holds that non-finite clauses tend to evoke different situations: to infinitives for potential situations, -ing clauses for factual situations, and bare infinitive for events.

In the work of Downing (2015: 108), non-finiteness (e.g. the italicized text in 'They believe him *to be a genius*', 'He made them *stand up*', 'She saw two men *enter the shop*', 'He kept us *waiting*' and 'I heard two shots *fired*') is treated as non-finite clauses. This is different from the view of 'verbal group complex' by Halliday and Matthiessen (2014). The criteria of non-finite clause identification provided by B. Yang (2003, 2004) may be helpful in this respect: see Section 2.6.2.

Usage-based approaches or corpus linguistic approaches may belong to function-based research. Among others, five types of non-finite clauses are identified in Biber et al. (1999: 201): infinitive clauses, -ing clauses, -ed clauses, supplementive clauses and verbless clauses. 'Supplementive clause' refers to 'the loosely integrated clauses' (e.g. *She gazed down at the floor, biting her lip, face clouded*). Verbless clauses are also considered as non-finite in Biber et al. (1999), for example, *when in difficulty* in *She had also been taught, when in difficulty, to think of a good life to imitate*.

Biber et al. (1999: 601) also categorize the use of non-finite clauses as postmodifiers across several registers: -ing clauses are moderately common in all three written registers but most frequent in academic prose; -ed clauses and appositive noun phrases are considerably more common in written non-fiction than in other registers, and more common in academic prose than in any other register; to-clauses are relatively rare in all registers. 'The non-finite complement clauses – *to*-clauses as well as *ing*-clauses – are predominantly a feature of written language' (Biber et al. 1999: 749). They are most common in fiction but 'relatively rare in conversation' (Biber et al. 1999: 754).

2.6.2 Criteria of Non-finite Clause Identification

Non-finites in some constructions, catenatives in particular, are believed to be clauses. For example, the infinitives in (2.16) are said to be clauses (Huddleston & Pullum 2002: 65).

(2.16) a. Max seemed *to like them*.
        b. Jill intended *to join the army*.
        c. Everyone believed *Kim to be guilty*.
        d. She asked me *to second her motion*.

The status of non-finiteness in the constructions in (2.16), as we have reviewed, is controversial. B. Yang (2004) proposed the criteria of non-finite clause identification in English, according to which a non-finite component may or may not form into a clause on its own. The first is process-oriented, and includes 'number of processes' and 'order of processes' as criteria. Following the idea that the relation between clauses in a clause complex is 'a relation between processes' (Halliday 1994: 216), Yang argued that 'A construction which consists of a finite clause plus a non-finite component is a clause complex containing a dependent non-finite clause when the number of processes in the construction is more than one so long as embedding is excluded' (B. Yang 2004: 240). Another process-oriented criterion considers the order of processes: 'Where a finite verb is directly followed by a non-finite component, a clause complex is set up if the process expressed by the non-finite component can precede the process expressed by the finite verb; if not, the finite verb and the non-finite component together tend to form a verbal group complex' (B. Yang 2004: 241).

Since the process-oriented method 'does not suffice to explain all constructions that contain non-finite components' (B. Yang 2004: 242), the participant-oriented method is also used to identify the status of a non-finite component: Thus, 'a clause is a clause only when there is a participant and a Predicator which expresses the process', except for minor clauses (exclamations, calls, greetings and alarms) which lack modal choices, and 'the generally applicable rule is that there must be a process and a participant at least' (B. Yang 2004: 242).

The two criteria proposed by Yang are useful in identifying the status of many ambiguous clauses. The third criterion is 'relator-oriented'. A relator is a category of function on the ideational level which is 'typically realized by conjunctions' (Halliday & Matthiessen 1999: 178). The status of a construction as a clause complex becomes apparent when a relator can be inserted between two clauses. Thus, the criterion goes as follows: 'If a relator can be inserted between a finite clause and a non-finite component, the construction is likely to be a clause complex containing a non-finite clause' (B. Yang 2004: 245).

The criteria have been shown useful in identifying non-finiteness in constructions such as the following:

(2.17) a. Frank sat reading the newspaper (Quirk et al. 1985: 1126).
        b. She telephoned hoping for a job (Quirk et al. 1985: 489).
        c. I hate lying (LOB).

(2.18) a. He agreed to marry Jimena Diaz (LOB).
        b. Pardao will be easy to beat (LOB).

(2.19) a. I got the watch repaired (Quirk et al. 1985: 1171).
        b. Mary considered John to be responsible (Halliday 1994: 286).

The criteria also work for absolute clauses (Q. He & Yang 2015: 45–50). As a special type of non-finiteness, absolute clauses have been observed in corpora from the systemic functional perspective by Q. He and Yang (2015). In this study, issues such as the meaning potential of absolute clauses according to the identification criteria, the relationships realized by absolute clauses in the network of clause complex, types of absolute clauses in terms of independence, and the relations of elaboration, extension and enhancement realized by absolute clauses have been discussed, involving such aspects as function types, genre distribution, historical distribution and case choice.

2.6.3 Function-Specified Systems of Non-finite Clauses

As we can see from the description of non-finite clauses in English in Quirk et al. (1985), the system of non-finite clauses is function-targeted, but it is in fact form-based, because they are categories identified via the structure of non-finite clauses (see Figure 2.2).

As a formerly devoted systemicist, Hudson provided readers with a system network of non-finiteness in one of his early works, which was claimed to be systemic. In Hudson's category, non-finiteness may be observed either from the word level in which 'infinitive, ing-form and en-form' are identified, or from the clause level in which participial and nominal are the major categories (Hudson 1971: 138).

A closer observation reveals that Hudson's system of non-finite clauses is similar to Quirk et al.'s (1985: 993) classification. The difference lies in the fact that Hudson's non-finite clauses consist of two subcategories: participial and nominal. The 'participial' category includes 'bare' and 'inflected', and we can infer that the 'inflected' is composed of the present and the past participles. The 'nominal' category includes the 'infinitive' and the 'gerundial'. What is unique here is the inclusion of the infinitival clause into the 'nominal' category.

Halliday's first system network of finiteness was proposed in 1964, in a paper that wasn't published until 1976 (see Halliday 1976: 125). This network does not change in his later writings, and non-finiteness is observed from the perspective of aspect and put into three further categories: imperfective, perfective and neutral (Halliday 2003b [1995]: 408). The system networks of non-finite clauses have been specified as systems of specific functions in B. Yang (2003). These systems include the ideational (Phenomenon), the interpersonal (Mood), the textual (Theme) and the logic-semantic relation.

The system in terms of Phenomenon is a good example of functional description of non-finite clauses. Phenomenon is set up as a participant role in the transitivity structure of a mental clause where there are two participants: Senser and Phenomenon, either implicit or explicit. If the participant role as Phenomenon is more than an ordinary 'thing', Macro-phenomenon and

Meta-phenomenon are employed to make the distinction. 'Macro-phenomenon' refers to 'an act', while 'Meta-phenomenon' refers to 'a fact'.

In the general sense, the Phenomenon 'can be phenomenal (an ordinary "thing"), macro-phenomenal (an act or macro-thing, i.e. process configuration) or meta-phenomenal (a fact or meta-thing, i.e. a projected process configuration)' (Matthiessen et al. 2010: 67, 158). See (2.20) and (2.21) for the difference (Halliday & Hasan 1976: 52–6; see also Halliday & Matthiessen 1999: 102–3).

(2.20) They broke a Chinese vase.
    a. That was valuable. (Phenomenon: thing – vase)
    b. That was careless. (Macro-phenomenon: the act of their breaking the vase)

(2.21) It rained day and night for two weeks. The basement flooded and everything was under water.
    a. It spoilt our calculations. (Meta-phenomenon – the fact that it rained so much upset our predictions)
    b. It spoilt our calculations. (Macro-phenomenon – the act of raining destroyed physical records)

In other words, Phenomenon in the general sense is not confined to mental processes. More importantly, the fact and the act can be frequently realized by non-finiteness. See (2.22) from Matthiessen et al. (2010: 67). Note that (2.22d) is added here for comparison.

(2.22)   a. *visiting relatives* are hungry (thing)
      b. *visiting relatives* is possible (Macro-thing, act)
      c. *for us to visit relatives* is possible (Macro-thing, act)
      d. *the time for visiting relatives* is suitable (Meta-thing, fact)
      e. *that we visit relatives* is obvious (Meta-thing, fact)

Non-finite clauses that are macro-phenomenal or meta-phenomenal can be any of the six basic processes. The system of non-finiteness in terms of Phenomenon, thus, can be illustrated as in Figure 2.9.

In terms of SFG, meaning is simultaneously represented by ideational, interpersonal and textual dimensions. The interpersonal meaning of non-finite clauses may be determined by the status of Mood; the system of Mood in non-finite clauses in English is shown in Figure 2.10.

Textual meaning is typically realized by the thematic structure, and the system network of Theme in non-finite clauses in English has been provided in B. Yang (2003); see Figure 2.11.

According to B. Yang (2003), non-finite clauses in English, if not rank-shifted, are usually combined with finite clauses to form clause complexes. Hypotactic relations are thus set up between finite and non-finite clauses.

2.6 Non-finiteness in Systemic Functional Grammar

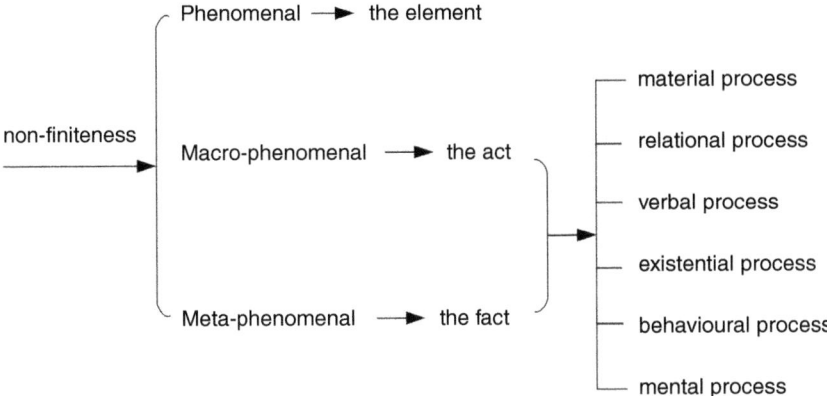

Figure 2.9 System of non-finiteness in terms of Phenomenon: ideational (B. Yang 2003: 149)

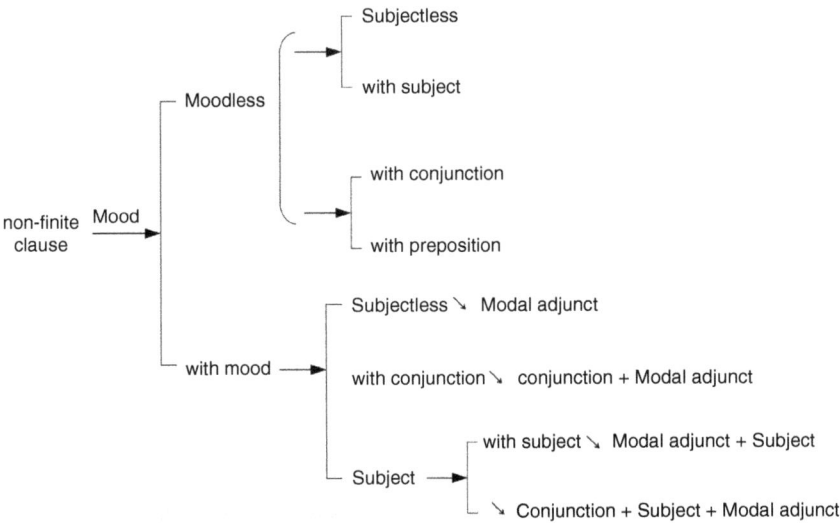

Figure 2.10 System network of Mood in non-finite clauses: interpersonal (B. Yang 2003: 145)

Paratactic relations may also be possible when several non-finite clauses come together. See Figure 2.12.

As we can see, the systemic functional approach to non-finiteness has produced a number of illuminating ideas, the problem being the lack of

54   Non-finiteness in the Literature

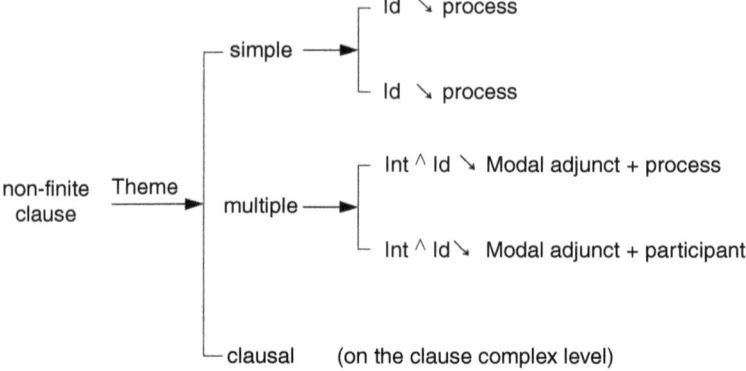

Figure 2.11 System network of Theme in non-finite clauses: textual (B. Yang 2003: 146)

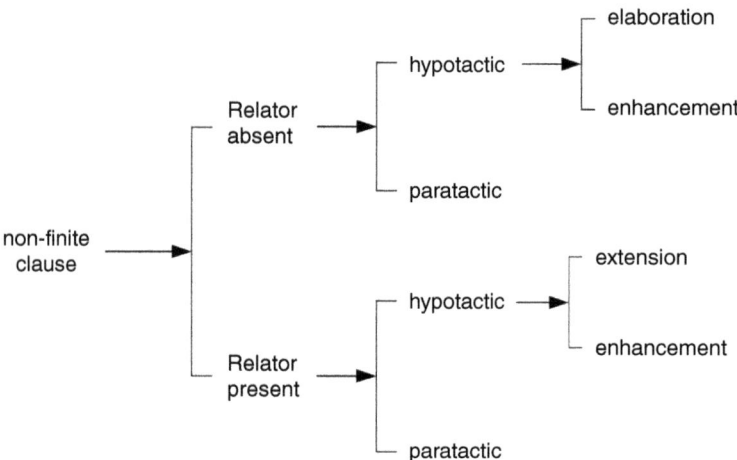

Figure 2.12 Logico-semantic system network of non-finite clauses (B. Yang 2003: 148)

relevant research in languages other than English. Many issues, research questions raised in the present study in particular, need to be addressed with different language facts and data. Moreover, meaning beyond clause (J. Martin 2002) has not been much studied, although it is an important area for considering non-finiteness.

2.7   Viewpoints from Other Theories and the Semantic Types

In addition to the viewpoints already reviewed in this chapter, linguistic wisdom on the issue of non-finiteness can be found in SG, RRG, FDG and a few other theories. We will review the most relevant views here. The semantic types of non-finiteness, one of the most heated topics, will also be summarized in this section.

2.7.1   Semiotic Grammar

Similar to SFG, SG, proposed by William B. McGregor, holds that form and meaning are inseparable. SG takes the sign as the fundamental unit of grammatical analysis, with the stance that neither a purely functional nor a purely formal account of language is adequate. Four types of grammatical signs (experiential, logical, interpersonal and textural) are distinguished, and four syntagmatic relationships (constituency, dependency, conjugational and linking) are considered for linguistic analysis (McGregor 1997). Closely related to SFG as it is, differences are apparent.

Having studied languages in Australia, McGregor proposed that verb category systems in Australia prototypically involve 'two verbal elements forming a compound: an inflecting verb (IV) that is inflected for verbal categories such as tense, mood, and aspect, as well as (in many languages) person and number of the subject and/or object; and an *uninflecting verb* (UV) that takes no inflections' (McGregor 2002: 25; emphasis in original). This may apply to both inflectional languages and non-inflectional languages.

What is more relevant to the present study in SG is that, both in typically popular languages such as English and typically endangered languages such as Gooniyandi (an Australian Aboriginal language mostly spoken by people who live in or near Fitzroy Crossing in Western Australia), non-finite clauses are found to be able to appear as rankshifted clauses, but they do not permit tense marking (McGregor 1997). 'Rankshifting refers to the process whereby a unit of a given rank is as it were demoted in size, and reclassified as a unit of lower rank' (McGregor 1997: 127). Rankshifting is different from embedding.[3] 'In embedding, a unit of a given rank serves as a constituent of a unit of the same or lower rank, and thus discharges an experiential role in it', while 'rankshifting does not imply that the rankshifted unit serves as a constituent of another unit' (McGregor 1997: 128).

---

[3] Rankshifting and embedding are confusing in many ways. In this research, we observe the phenomenon from the perspective of degree of realization, and three types are distinguished, in which the full realizations are rankshifted to function as IGMs. See Chapter 3, especially Section 3.7, for details.

In the theory of SG, a necessary (but not sufficient) 'requirement for a clause to be rankshifted is that it be non-finite', for finite clauses 'express propositions about them which may be true or false', but non-finite clauses 'do not express propositions and are not directly amenable to argumentation' (McGregor 1997: 135). Thus, it may be assumed that non-finite clauses in any language will be 'closely associated with rankshifting' while finite clauses 'will preclude it' (McGregor 1997: 136).

The principle is as follows: A unit cannot consist of a unit of higher rank, unless that unit has been 'demoted' in size (McGregor 1997: 83). Thus, 'clauses may (in many languages) be rankshifted to word status by making them non-finite'. Non-finite clauses may then be embedded in finite clauses, or they may relate to them by the dependency relationship of hypotaxis, but never parataxis' (McGregor 1997: 189–90).

'The non-finiteness of a clause which occurs in combination with a finite clause may serve as an indicator, albeit imperfect, of the syntagmatic relationship between the clauses' (McGregor 1997: 190). By rankshifting it, 'the clause no longer expresses a proposition, and represents a situation as though it were an entity or quality' (McGregor 1997: 192).

Since major clauses are considered to be of two types: 'finite (having an inherent conjugational relationship) and non-finite (without an inherent conjugational relationship, but agnating with a finite clause)', *They followed his dripping blood until nightfall* is a finite clause whereas *(They wanted to) follow his dripping blood until nightfall* is non-finite (McGregor 1997: 236). This explains why non-finite clauses are frequently 'subordinated to' finite clauses: they are out of the range of questions of truth or falsity. Thus, non-finite clauses in many languages are 'normally found either embedded in, dependent on, or enclosed within, finite clauses' (McGregor 1997: 239).

In a word, clauses have to be rankshifted to become non-finite in the theory of SG. This view, with evidence from languages in Australia in particular, confirms the dependency of non-finite clauses. Moreover, the difference between embedding and rankshifting drawn in SG is thought-provoking. The problem to solve is whether non-finite clauses are 'demoted' in size and embedded at the same time. The dependency of non-finite clauses seems to indicate embedding, while their incompleteness in ideation tends to imply 'demoting' or 'rankshifting'.

2.7.2 Role and Reference Grammar

RRG, developed by Robert Van Valin (see Van Valin 1992), describes language in terms of semantic structure, communicative function, and the grammatical procedures used to express meanings. It is 'a linguistic framework that combines insights from cross-linguistic syntactic analysis, lexical semantics and

2.7 Viewpoints from Other Theories and the Semantic Types

formal pragmatics', and it is believed to be 'equally attractive for theoretical linguists, field linguists and psycholinguists' (Fleischhauer et al. 2016: 7). Few specific discussions on non-finiteness can be found in the major literature of RRG, but the inter-clausal relations drawn in RRG are helpful in understanding the nature of non-finite clauses.

In RRG, three layers of linkage are distinguished (nucleus, core and clause). The nucleus is the predicate, the core is the nucleus plus obligatory arguments, and the clause is the core plus the peripheral or non-obligatory adjuncts. According to RRG, 'form and meaning are closely interwoven in the historical development of clause linkage, whose path is typicaly [sic] from lower to higher clause integration' (Ohori 1992: 1). Nine possible juncture-nexus types have been identified in RRG as a hierarchy in which the tightness of the syntactic link or bond lines up in degrees. Figure 2.13 shows the inter-clausal syntactic relations hierarchy.

Nuclear cosubordination
Nuclear subordination
Nuclear coordination
Core cosubordination
Core subordination
Core coordination
Clausal cosubordination
Clausal subordination
Clausal coordination

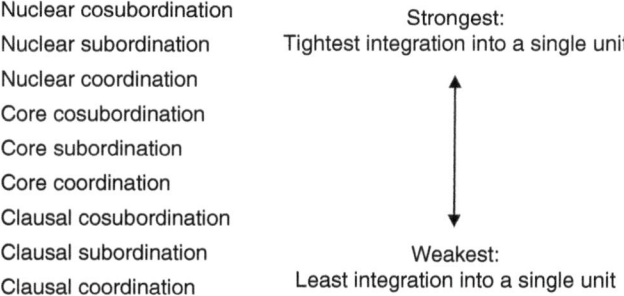

Figure 2.13 Inter-clausal syntactic relations hierarchy (Van Valin & LaPolla 1997: 477)

The juncture-nexus types shown in Figure 2.13 are purely syntactic, but a wide variety of semantic relations between units can be expressed. These semantic units have been identified and categorized into thirteen types (Van Valin & LaPolla 1997: 480). Non-finiteness is in between the tightest and the least integration. This view confirms the intermediateness of non-finite clauses in terms of integration.

2.7.3 Functional Discourse Grammar

Functional Grammar has been developed by Simon C. Dik (1980, 1981), and has most recently been revised by Kees Hengeveld and Lachlan Mackenzie (Hengeveld & Mackenzie 2008, 2010). It is now called Functional Discourse Grammar (FDG), by which constituents (parts of speech) of a linguistic utterance are assigned three functions (semantic function, syntactic function and pragmatic function).

According to Simon C. Dik, the taxonomy of embedded constructions illustrated in Figure 2.14 has quite general cross-linguistic validity (Dik 1997). In this taxonomy, embedded constructions may be finite or non-finite. Thus, non-finite clauses are in the first place embedded. Regardless of embedding or rankshifting, the dependency of non-finite clauses is apparent in Dik's theory.

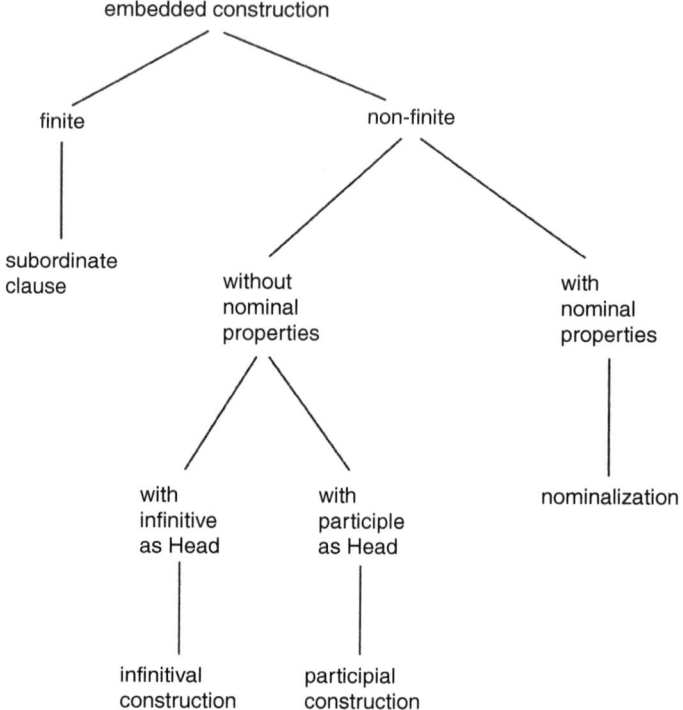

Figure 2.14 The taxonomy of embedded constructions (Dik 1997: 143)

'In probably all languages, however, there are also non-verbal constituents which can be used in predicative function' (Dik 1997: 193). Such non-verbal predicates generally include the five types shown in (2.23).

(2.23) a. John (is) intelligent. [adjective]
        b. John (is) president. ['bare' nominal]
        c. John (is) a nice boy. [indefinite term]
        d. John (is) the winner. [definite term]
        e. John (is) in the garden. [adpositional phrase] (Dik 1997: 193).

2.7 Viewpoints from Other Theories and the Semantic Types

The function of a copula is defined as a supportive one: enabling a non-verbal predicate to act as a main predicate (Hengeveld 1992). The lack of copula in (2.23), it seems, is a typical feature of spoken English. This is also pervasive in spoken Chinese, but not in written Chinese. The question is how to locate non-finiteness among the verbal and non-verbal predication.

One approach is to consider the semantic categories. In terms of semantic function, the semantic categories of component units have been assigned the following properties: zero-place (e.g. *It rained*), one-place (e.g. *The boy is swimming*), two-place (e.g. *Charles lives in Antwerp*), three-place (e.g. *The woman forced the man to leave*), four-place (e.g. *I made Hasan put the pitcher into the cupboard*), relational (*This tea is from Sri Lanka*), classification (e.g. *That man is a painter*), identification (e.g. My teacher is Peter) and existence (e.g. *There are courses that help you become more assertive*) (Hengeveld & Mackenzie 2008: 186–94). Now it is apparent that non-finiteness may appear in such categories as three-place, four-place and existence. Since the issues of embedding and rankshifting are not included in these semantic categories, other possibilities of non-finiteness have not been observed.

These functional categories 'can be applied crosslinguistically' (Hengeveld & Mackenzie 2008: 356). See Figure 2.15 for the distinction between verbal sentences and nominal sentences in terms of 'predication'.

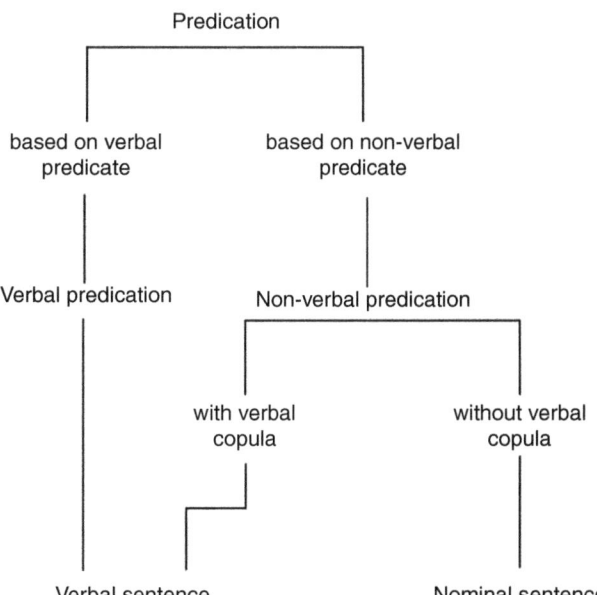

Figure 2.15 Predication and sentence (Hengeveld 1992: 27)

With the relationship between predication and sentence shown in Figure 2.15, FDG makes it clear that verbal sentences and nominal sentences are different in terms of predicates. This has been proven cross-linguistically valid, but spoken language is not distinguished from written language in the observation. What is significant to the present research is that sentences are observed in terms of predication frames, which is evidence for the appropriateness of considering process relations in discussing finiteness and non-finiteness.

2.7.4 Other Approaches and the Semantic Types

A number of viewpoints from other theories are also illuminating. For example, Sells (2007) employs Head-Driven Phrase Structure Grammar and Lexical-Functional Grammar to address finiteness. He argues that there should be a distinction between finiteness as a property of the clause and overt morphosyntactic features of a finite verbal form. By observing Japanese and Swedish, Sells shows that grammatical phenomena can be sensitive to clausal finiteness or morphological finiteness.

Nikolaeva (2007a) presents evidence that some independent clauses tend to contain non-finite patterns while other do not. She suggests that the reduction of finiteness in independent clauses should be understood as a cross-linguistic tendency for economic expression. She follows the Construction Grammar of Goldberg (1995) and others, and proposes the Principle of Constructional Economy, which prevents the doubling of constructional meaning by inflectional or phrasal meaning within the same construction.

The Principle of Constructional Economy: If two syntactic patterns are inherently associated with the same constructional meaning, the pattern that has less phrasal or morphological material expressing this meaning is to be chosen. (Nikolaeva 2007a: 136)

Huddleston and Pullum (2002) adopt an integrational approach, and some of their views on non-finiteness are helpful. For example, they regard the finite/non-finite distinction 'as a syntactic category of the clause, rather than as an inflectional category of the verb' (see Figure 2.16). Thus, '[c]lauses whose verb is a primary form are finite, those whose verb is a past participle or gerund-participle are non-finite, but those with a plain form verb can be either, depending on the construction' (Huddleston & Pullum 2002: 88–9).

According to Huddleston and Pullum (2002: 89), non-finite clauses 'are characteristically subordinate, and non-finiteness can be seen as an instance

2.7 Viewpoints from Other Theories and the Semantic Types 61

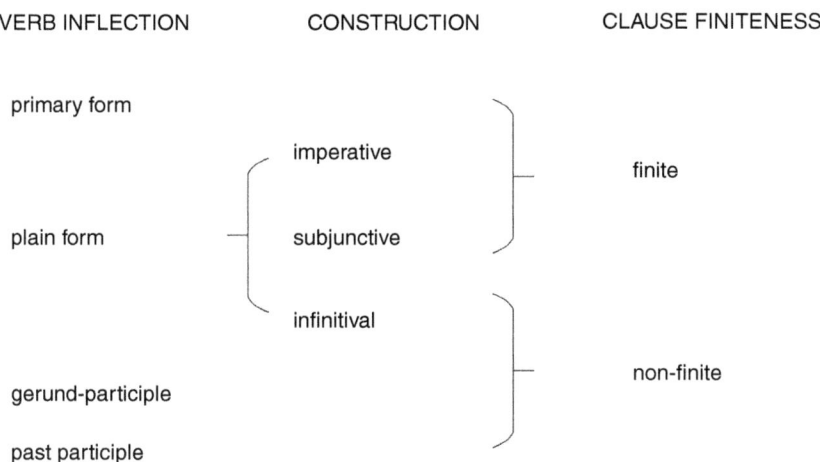

Figure 2.16 The distinction as a syntactic category of the clause (Huddleston & Pullum 2002: 89)

of the phenomenon known as "desententialization", the loss of properties that are associated with a clause standing alone as a full sentence'.

A similar view is that 'Putting an idea in a main clause is like shining a spotlight on it; and putting it in a subordinate clause, by the same simile, is like a [sic] placing it in the shadow' (Leech et al. 1982: 186). In coordination, equal importance is given to the clauses and there is no backgrounding. By contrast, a phrase is most backgrounded. Non-finite subordinate clauses are more backgrounded than finite subordinate clauses; see Figure 2.17.

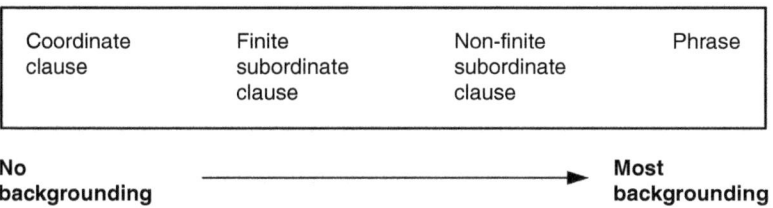

Figure 2.17 The scale of backgrounding (Leech et al. 1982: 187)

Corpus-based studies (e.g. Biber et al. 1999) have provided persuasive evidence for a number of viewpoints on non-finiteness. 'Infinitive clauses and ing-clauses are the most versatile grammatically', and non-finite clauses may be 'loosely integrated into the main clause' (i.e. supplementive clauses), and they may not take a verb at all (i.e. verbless clauses) (Biber et al. 1999: 198).

Table 2.7 *Semantic types of infinitive and gerund in English*

Infinitive	Gerund	Authors
specific	general	Jespersen (1949); Wood (1956)
non-factive	factive	Kiparsky & Kiparsky (1971); Givón (1990)
non-fulfilment	fulfilment	Bolinger (1968); Kempson & Quirk (1971)
potentiality	performance	Quirk et al. (1985)
future; vague futurity	actual; vague simultaneity	Wierzbicka (1988, 2006)
non-referring	referring	Conrad (1982); Dirven (1989)
potentiality	activity extended in time	Dixon (1991, 2005)
less immediate	more immediate	Verspoor (1990, 1996, 2000)
holistic construal	immediate scope	Langacker (1991a)
conceptual distance	conceptual overlap	M. Smith & Escobedo (2001)
future	interior	Duffley (2003, 2006)
targeted alternative	extended in domain	Egan (2008)
similar to VPs	similar to DPs	Veselovská & Emonds (2015)
non-entailment	entailment	Rudanko (2015)
[+Choice] context	[-Choice] context	Rudanko (2010); Rickman & Rudanko (2018)

Numerous studies focus not on the finite/non-finite distinction but on *to* infinitive and gerund, many exploring the semantic types. Table 2.7 gives a brief overview of some typical studies on the semantic types.

An interesting view is on the use of 'Trigger', which is used to refer to 'the grammatical role of the obligatory argument of the clause' (Cumming 1991: 3). Finite clauses are those with triggers (an Agent, Subject or Patient), and non-finite clauses are triggerless ones (Cumming 1991: 45). Thus, three clause types in Malay are distinguished: the intransitive clause, the agent-trigger clause and the patient-trigger clause (Cumming 1991: 29). This adds to the exploration of non-finite clauses in terms of both syntactic and semantic roles.

To sum up, some studies are function-oriented, while others are form-oriented. '[A] difference in syntactic form always spells a difference in meaning' (Bolinger 1968: 127), and meaning and form are inseparable (e.g. Firth 1957; Halliday 1975, 1978; Sinclair 1991; Stubbs 1996). Even 'in morphology form should not be studied independently of meaning' (Bybee 1985: v).

2.8 Some Special Types to Be Noted

Some linguists propose a quite different categorization for non-finiteness. For example, a whole chapter of *A Critical Account of English Syntax* by K. Brown and Miller (2016) is devoted to non-finite clauses, and eight types are recognized

2.8 Some Special Types to Be Noted

in English: infinitives, free participles, gerunds (Type 1), gerunds (Type 2), reduced adverbials, reduced relatives, verb stem, and with + NP. Brown and Miller (2016: 71) argue that these types play two roles in the organization of text: bringing together two or more events that are presented as part of a larger event, and aiding 'the production of dense, well-integrated text'. See (2.24) from K. Brown and Miller (2016: 128–40).

(2.24) a. I want for you *to be happy*. (infinitive)
       b. *Having locked the door*, he opened the parcel. (free participle)
       c. *Steeping grounds* by filtering extracts more caffeine. (Type 1 Gerund)
       d. I found Cordelia *sitting on the terrace*. (Type 2 Gerund)
       e. *While waiting for the train*, James lost his smartphone. (reduced adverbial)
       f. The woman *reading a book* is the person you're looking for. (reduced relative)
       g. The firm made the employees *sign this agreement*. (verb stem)
       h. Jane strode up the hill *with her setter loping along behind*. (with + NP)

In this classification, 'with + NP' is traditionally taken as an absolute clause, which may not even require forms of verbs at all. 'Absolute clause' is defined as 'an independent expression consisting of a substantive with modifying participle', and it is usually understood as an adverb clause (House & Harman 1950 [1931]: 293). See (2.25) for an example.

(2.25) a. *Hope lost*, all is lost. (House & Harman 1950 [1931]: 293)
       b. *There being no objection*, we may continue. (House & Harman 1950 [1931]: 294)

Absolute clauses include 'nonfinite and verbless adverbial clauses that have an overt subject but are not introduced by a subordinator and are not the complement of a preposition' (Quirk et al. 1985: 1120). In other words, an absolute clause is a non-finite or verbless clause 'containing its own subject, attached to a sentence from which it is separated by a comma' (Aarts et al. 2014: 4). Three major types of absolute construction can thus be identified (see Q. He & Yang 2015: 10–14).

Type 1: Free adjunct construction
e.g. *Unable to meet his eyes*, she stared at the garden, wondering vaguely why it looked the same when she felt so very different. (BNC_FIC)
In his teens, he learned to drink and swore an allegiance to the pint. (BNC_FIC)

Type 2: Nominative absolute construction
Exhausted and confused, I came, *cap in hand*, busking for help and half sang, half cried. (BNC_MISC)
Episode over, put it out of your mind. (BNC_FIC)

Type 3: Augmented absolute construction
With time running out, they desperately need points to avoid relegation. (BNC_NEWS)

They gave us some time back afterward, *because of the brain having an operation*. (BNC_NA)

Some argue that an absolute construction 'is so called because it has no grammatical bonds with the rest of the sentence. It is "free" ("absolute")' (Burton 1984: 128). This is true in the sense of form, but the logical roles of absolute clause can be various: see Table 2.8.

Table 2.8 *Logical roles of absolute clauses (Q. He & Yang 2015: 16)*

	Time	Cause	Circumstance	Condition	Concession	Manner
Curme	✓	✓	✓	✓	✓	✓
Kruisinga	✓	✓	✓		✓	
Jespersen	✓	✓	✓	✓		
Visser	✓	✓	✓	✓		
Quirk et al.	✓	✓	✓			

If finiteness is considered as the property of the clause, then verb forms will not be the decisive factor in determining finiteness and non-finiteness. Following this logic, the verbless constructions that are called absolute clauses may be non-finite as well.

Another special type in English is the serial verb construction (SVC). With serial verbs functioning as the predicates, SVC attracts much attention. 'Some speakers find these marginal, but they are well attested in both the BNC and the COCA' (T. Payne 2011: 330).

(2.26).   a.   You don't just *run go play* this music ... (COCA_MAG)
          b.   She's the professor I want to *go see* (T. Payne 2011: 330)
          c.   Don't make me *come get* you! (T. Payne 2011: 330)

As a construction whereby two or more verbs function as predicate, SVC 'allows the speaker to express various aspects of a situation as a single cognitive package within one clause and with one predicate' (Aikhenvald 2006: 56).

These special constructions may also be found in modern Chinese and other languages. They are highly involved with non-finiteness. See Chapters 6 and 7 for details.

2.9   A Summary of the Relevant Research

Non-finiteness did not receive much attention from linguists until 1900, when verbs were categorized into those that assert and those that do not. The major enlightening views on non-finiteness can be summarized as follows.

2.9 A Summary of the Relevant Research

The determining factors for a finite/non-finite distinction vary from theory to theory, but the general trend today foregrounds the view of the distinction to be a gradient phenomenon and regards finiteness as the property of the clause. Some consider tense, person, number and gender as the parameters of finiteness, while others argue that there is no causal relation between these parameters and the finite/non-finite distinction. Morphological features do not necessarily imply syntactic features, so no determinate relation can be assured between morphology and syntax. A radical view holds that 'non-finite verb phrase' refers to a phrase that functions other than as a predicate: '[v]erbs and verb phrases acting as adjectivals, adverbials, and nominals within the sentence are nonfinite' (Kolln & Funk 2012: 358). Thus, finite and non-finite languages can be meaningfully distinguished regardless of the absence of morphological indications (Plag 1993).

The 'continuum hypothesis' (J. Ross 1972) distinguishes word classes on the basis of clusters of properties which are typically non-discrete. For example, adjectival words occupy an intermediate position in a language-independent lexical continuum or 'category space' from verb to noun (Wetzer 1996). Views such as 'nouns are really verbs', 'adjectives are really verbs', 'tense is an adverb', and so on, reflect the behaviour of word class or other grammatical categories on the basis of individual languages. Since verbs and nouns in many cases cannot be distinguished from each other, and other categories such as adjectivals may be either nouny or verby, markings in tense, person/number, mood and aspect will not be significant in identifying certain constructions.

Thus, 'finite' and 'non-finite' are two poles of the functionally motivated scale of de(sententialization). Between the two poles, there are intermediate realizations. The realizations may be observed by verbal and nominal properties. The loss of verbal properties (e.g. tense, aspect, mood, person/number marking) and the gaining of nominal properties (e.g. case, omission of verbal arguments) are manifestations of non-finiteness.

Categories such as adjectives, adverbs and prepositions 'profile different sorts of atemporal relations' (Langacker 1995: 13). 'Infinitives and participles are derived from verbs', but 'they impose an atemporal construal' (Langacker 1995: 14). With these features, both temporality and atemporality can be construed. Thus, '[t]he noun and verb categories are universal and fundamental to grammatical structure' (Langacker 1991a: 100). Universal as they are, finiteness is not a property of the verb, but of the clause.

The universality of the finite/non-finite distinction is still debatable, but children prior to the OI stage present similarity in their use of non-finiteness cross-linguistically. Typological studies show that finiteness may depend on 'mood' (e.g. Holmberg et al. 1993), or negation markers (e.g. Amritavalli 2014), or spatial markers or participant markers (e.g. Ritter &

Wiltschko 2014). VSO languages are sparse in non-finite verbal forms, and these languages favour rankshifting by nominalization. According to Bisang (1995, 1998), East and Southeast Asian languages (e.g. Chinese, Vietnamese and Thai) do not have obligatory categories such as tense-aspect and number, are characterized as indeterminate, and cannot develop any asymmetry between finite and non-finite clauses.

What has been proven to be universal is that children from various language backgrounds do not distinguish between finiteness and non-finiteness before two years of age, and they continue to use root infinitives very often at around two and a half years. This use of OIs may indicate that non-finiteness is a universal feature in terms of language evolution.

The finite/non-finite distinction may be better construed from a functional perspective. The selection of verby or nouny adjectivals in a particular language is not form-based, but reflects a way of looking at the world. The presence of verby adjectivals reflects an 'event-dominated' view of the world, while that of nouny adjectivals may reflect an 'object-dominated' world view (Wetzer 1996: 59). Finiteness is the 'systematic grammatical means used to express the degree of integration of a clause into its immediate clausal environment' (Givón 1990: 853). Humans share similar physical properties (e.g. vocal organs), but their societal and environmental communities are different, an important reason for disparity in conceptualization. These facts indicate that the same state/event may be conceptualized in distinct ways. Even in the same language, many ways are possible for diachronic conceptualization of the same state/event. In other words, there is a physical foundation for the universality of the finite/non-finite distinction, but cultural and societal environments bring disparities.

Chinese and English, for example, share many common features in their histories, but there are far-reaching differences as well. 'The two belong, obviously, to different ends of that cultural continuum, and were located within very different material environments' (Halliday & Matthiessen 1999: 297). In both languages, polarity, person and nominal deixis, and so on, are grammatical while 'the vast thesaurus of experiential categories of processes, things and qualities are clearly lexical', and 'the two languages locate the various semantic domains at roughly equivalent points along the lexicogrammatical continuum' (Halliday & Matthiessen 1999: 299).

Another perspective is the notion of non-finite interface, that is, 'a special way of adding a second verbal element to a construction (either as participant or circumstance) or of modifying a nominal head in a VMC', and in each case, 'a specific form/meaning pairing is established, which differs from subordinate clause constructions' (Ungerer 2017: 203). This is expected to be cross-linguistically valid and may be used to explore non-finiteness.

The reduction of finiteness in independent clauses can be understood as a cross-linguistic tendency for economic expression (Nikolaeva 2007a). According to the Principle of Constructional Economy (Nikolaeva 2007a: 163), the doubling of constructional meaning by inflectional or phrasal meaning is not allowed within the same construction.

The controversy needs to be reduced by a higher abstraction of the phenomenon. Some linguists hold that '[m]ost languages of the world probably do not have anything like the difference between finite verbs and non-finite verbs' (Chelliah & de Reuse 2011: 330). Others argue that finiteness is both gradual and binary in nature (e.g. Nikolaeva 2007b: 13). Still others believe that the presence of tense, aspect, mood and agreement distinctions on the verb, the expression of these distinctions, and the presence of nominal morphology on the verb follow predictable patterns, but the individual combinations of morphosyntactic properties for finiteness are language-specific (e.g. Cristofaro 2007).

To address the validity of the finite/non-finite distinction, we need a higher abstraction of the phenomenon. The versatility of non-finite clauses (Biber et al. 1999) and desententialization (Huddleston & Pullum 2002) are a good basis for such abstraction. The formal properties of finiteness and non-finiteness shall be considered as the background, and the semantic/functional properties should be the focus of research. The assumption is that there must be some semantic/functional criteria which help reveal some universality for the finite/non-finite distinction. The distinction is both necessary and important.

3 Theoretical Foundations

Embracing the enlightening viewpoints from current literature such as 'finiteness as the property of clause', 'cross-linguistic similarity in OIs stage' and 'the finite/non-finite distinction to be construed functionally with higher abstraction', we will in this chapter consider the theoretical issues underlying non-finiteness. These issues include the basic semantic and syntactic units, the mechanism of form variations for meaning (i.e. GM), the principles to follow, and the definition of non-finiteness in terms of function. These are intended for answering the first research question: In what way is the finite/non-finite distinction universal?

3.1 Prerequisite: Distinguishing Spoken and Written Language

Many early scholars argued that written language is used to represent both sounds and meaning (e.g. Bradley 1913). A consequent problem in linguistic research is that linguists use the grammars of written language to observe spoken discourses. Another problem is that linguists use outputs from spoken language, which is characterised by repetition, error and disfluency, to make judgements on the correctness of utterances in their written form.

These problems originated in the bias towards writing since Sapir, who claims that writing is 'visual speech symbolism' (Sapir 1921: 19). Bloomfield's claim is more surprising to us: 'writing is not language, but merely a way of recording language by visible marks' (Bloomfield 1933: 21). A more recent claim is: 'spoken language is "true" language, while written language is an artifact' (Aronoff 1985: 28).

Agreeing with Hymes on the difference between grammatical competence and communicative performance according to which neither speech nor writing should be biased, Biber argues that 'it might well be the case that neither speech nor writing is primary; that they are rather different systems, both deserving careful analysis' (Biber 1988: 7).

As is admitted by many leading linguists today, spoken language is sharply different from written language in many ways. Such difference suggests that it is inappropriate to explore spoken discourses using grammars of the written

3.1 Prerequisite: Distinguishing Spoken and Written Language   69

language. It is also not appropriate to look at written language using examples of typical spoken language. For example, in Huddleston and Pullum (2002: 1176), it is said that non-finite clauses occur in a wide range of constructions, including minor main clause constructions such as polar echoes in (3.1):

(3.1)   A: Kim has resigned.
        B: Kim resign? (Huddleston and Pullum 2002: 890)

It is obvious that the non-finite clause (*Kim resign*) in (3.1) can be understood only in the context of conversation. It would be misleading to observe conversations using grammars designed for written language.[1]

Spoken language developed far earlier in human history than written language, and many languages today still have no written forms. Radical changes have taken place in the history of many languages, and the forms of writing today are quite different from those centuries ago. For example, radical language changes occurred in the whole Nordic area in the seventh and eighth centuries, and 'the old futhark was gradually replaced by the new futhark and the number of phonemes was reduced to only sixteen characters' (Larsson 2013: 75). The differences between written and spoken language in this sense can be expected, but this issue has been long neglected.

3.1.1   Differences between Spoken and Written Language

What differences are there between written and spoken language? 'Previous studies have relied on the sentence as a syntactic unit, but the difficulties of objectively identifying a sentence in speech are obvious' (O'Donnell 1974: 109). Thanks to efforts by a number of linguists, many morphological, lexical and syntactic differences between written and spoken language have been identified (e.g. Drieman 1962). An innovative idea in early 1900s was that writing requires a double abstraction: 'abstraction from the sound of speech and abstraction from the interlocutor' (Vygotsky 1986 [1934]: 181). As to speech, Vygotsky argues that 'the syntax of inner speech is the exact opposite of the syntax of written speech, with oral speech standing in the middle' (Vygotsky 1986 [1934]: 182). Inner speech is condensed, abbreviated and predicative, while written speech usually aims be detailed and intelligible; and thus '[t]he change from maximally compact inner speech to maximally detailed written speech requires what might be called deliberate semantics – deliberate structuring of the web of meaning' (Vygotsky 1986 [1934]: 182).

---

[1] It is true that spoken and written language are in many cases inseparable, but without a good grammar designed for spoken language and the features of spoken language, it is necessary to work on them separately.

In the collected volume on spoken and written language edited by Tannen, Chafe (1982) suggests two differences between spoken and written productions in English: involvement (spoken) against detachment (written), and fragmentation (spoken) against integration (written). These features have been found to be powerful indicators of the differences between spoken and written language (Redeker 1984).

Many other studies claim that speech is characteristic of hesitations, slips of tongue, false starts and repeating words, and that these features are not found in writing. However, Halliday recorded spontaneous spoken discourse and 'was struck by its fluency, well-formedness, and richness of grammatical pattern' (Halliday 2002c [1987]: 338; see also Halliday 1989). By comparing the recordings with the earlier drafts of writing, which are full of crossings out, revisions, change of directions, misspellings and re-draftings, Halliday concludes that spoken and written language are 'equally highly organized, regular, and productive of coherent discourse' (Halliday 2002c [1987]: 340).

Though being 'equally highly organized', spoken language is quite different from written language. For example, spoken English in terms of clause rank is marked by intricacy in the clause complex, whereas written English is marked by 'complexity in the nominal group' (Halliday 2002c [1987]: 343). This is because 'the written describes, explains and argues by nouns (as products) whereas the spoken tells by verbs (as processes)' (Halliday 2002c [1987]: 344).

Prepared speech (language that was written in order to be spoken) is also different from 'natural spoken language which is spontaneous and unselfconscious' (Halliday 2002c [1987]: 323). A characteristic of language is its degree of consciousness (Boas 1911). Generally, in natural spontaneous discourse, people are unconscious of what they themselves are saying (Halliday 2002c [1987]). Such discourses contain patterns of parataxis (clauses combined for equal status) and hypotaxis (clauses combined for unequal status), and they are 'remarkably well formed' (Halliday 2002c [1987]: 327). By contrast, written language is consciously produced for specific purposes.

In terms of lexical density and grammatical complexity, written language tends to be higher in density but simpler in structure; spoken language tends to be lower in density but more complex in structure. That being said, written/spoken is not a simple dichotomy, for there are 'many mixed and intermediate types' (Halliday 2002c [1987]: 328). '[W]riting is in essence a more conscious process than speaking' (Halliday 2002c [1987]: 336), and '[t]he more natural, un-self-monitored the discourse, the more intricate the grammatical patterns that can be woven' (Halliday 2002c [1987]: 335). In terms of GM, written language 'tends to display a high degree of grammatical metaphor, and this is perhaps its single most distinctive characteristic' (Halliday 2002c [1987]: 347). In spoken language, 'there is a loss of ideational information, but a gain in textual information' (Halliday 2002c [1987]: 348).

Disputes over the complicated relationship between spoken and written language are very strong. Some argue that speech is an innate human capability, and written language is a cultural invention (e.g. Chomsky 1965; Chomsky & Lasnik 1993; Pinker & Bloom 1990), while others believe that written and spoken language are equally intricate, with distinct qualities (e.g. Biber 1988; Halliday 1989). It is fortunate that some consensus has been achieved. Most linguists now agree that no act of communication is contextless, and every act of communication is uniquely contextualized (Harris 1998). 'Each word when used in a new context is a new word' (Firth 1957: 190).

Overlapping is unavoidable. For example, a comparative analysis of spoken and written versions of a narrative shows that typical features of oral discourse are also found in written discourse, and the written short story combines complexity in writing with features of speech (Tannen 1982). Thus, spoken and written language 'tend to display different **kinds** of complexity; each of them is more complex in its own way' (Halliday 2002c [1987]: 336; emphasis in original). 'The complexity of spoken language is choreographic' because 'each figure provides a context for the next one' (Halliday 2002c [1987]: 336). By contrast, 'the complexity of written language is crystalline' (Halliday 2002c [1987]: 336) because there is solidarity among the components. Written discourse is believed not to be dependent on its environment, but 'it would be more accurate to say that it creates an environment for itself' (Halliday 2002c [1987]: 348).

3.1.2 Grammars for Speech and Writing

Speech is paid increasing attention today, but no suitable grammar specifically for spoken language has been developed. Speech or spoken language, in fact, attracted much attention from linguists and educators in the middle of twentieth century, but '[l]anguage, in school, as in the community at large, meant written language' (Halliday 2002c [1987]: 323).

Written language has gained a dominant status since the advent of printing. 'For many centuries dictionaries and grammars of the English language have taken the written language as a benchmark for what is proper and standard in the language', and 'the spoken language has been downgraded and has come to be regarded as relatively inferior to written manifestations' (Carter & McCarthy 2006: 9). Given the significance of spoken language in the electronic era, it is quite natural that it is foregrounded in research, rather than written language.

The problem is that numerous linguistic studies that lay emphasis on spoken language simply use typical spoken instances to argue against theories of written language, while numerous other studies use typical written instances to argue against theories of spoken language. 'The linguists' professional commitment to the primacy of speech did not, however, arise from or carry with it an awareness of the properties of spoken discourse' (Halliday 2002c [1987]: 324). The interpretations 'did not involve any attempt to study the grammar and semantics of spoken as distinct from written language' (Halliday 2002c [1987]: 324).

Spoken language 'is as process, not as product' (Halliday 2002c [1987]: 336). Since studies in grammar develop from written text, 'our grammars are grammars of the written language', and '[w]e look at spoken language through the lens of a grammar designed for writing' (Halliday 2002c [1987]: 336). For example, Chafe (1982) 'has described both speech and writing using a grammar of writing' (Halliday 2002c [1987]: 337). This has been confirmed by Linell, for linguists today routinely emphasize the primacy of speech over writing while simply applying theories and methods that are best suited for written language (Linell 2005). Besides the lack in a grammar for spoken language, there is the lack of 'conventions for observing spoken language' (Halliday 2002c [1987]: 337).

Halliday's view has its echo: '[I]n some cases appropriate terms for describing particular features of spoken grammar are not available within existing grammatical frameworks' (Carter & McCarthy 2006: 9). For example:

(3.2) *Her friend, Jill, the one we met in Portsmouth,* **she** *said they'd moved house.* **He** *always makes a lot of noise and fuss, Charlie.*

This is typical spoken English and it is described by the way words are arranged in space (e.g. dislocation). Dislocation, however, is inappropriate because spoken language is concerned more with time than with space (Carter & McCarthy 2006). See (3.3) from the BNC for an example.

(3.3) ... and **she**'ll get all worked up. **They**'ll get all worked up because they're supposed to be fetching her. **There**'s all (unclear) not somebody else. (SP: PS6R8) (unclear) 2. (SP:PS6RC) **I** mean I know (unclear) **we**'ve had a car and we know. And (unclear) **we**'ve been all over the place haven't we Arthur (unclear). And then when it's been our turn to come, **we** broke down. **I I** won't forget (unclear). **I** gave them (unclear) the afternoon and **she** said, Oh that was lovely Mrs (–). And then **she** came to me and she said, (unclear) take four of us away and **I** just said, No I'm sorry he won't. And **she** said, Oh. Well weeks went by and then a a a few weeks after she came to me and **she** said, (unclear) ... (BNC)

Reading the passage without further context, nobody could properly understand what is being talked about. By contrast, a typical written text of this length will be very clear in conveying some message. That explains why Firbas discusses functional sentence perspective (see Section 3.3) in written communication and spoken communication respectively: the former is concerned with the sentence and the carriers of communicative dynamism, the contextual

3.2 Cryptotype and Cline

factor, the semantic factor, the theme and the non-theme, and word order; the latter with non-prosodic distribution of degrees of communicative dynamism and degrees of prosodic prominence, intonation and emotiveness (Firbas 1992).

To sum up, both spoken language and written language have distinctive features of their own, each being well formed and complicated in its ways. In linguistic studies, thus, **it may be more constructive to avoid spoken examples as evidence in the discussion of written texts, and more productive to avoid written examples as evidence in the discussion of spoken discourses.** The borderline categories (e.g. written speech) and the interface may involve intermediate examples, but these cases would require individual research. The difficulty is that a number of instances are simultaneously used in both spoken and written contexts.

Non-finiteness is used differently in spoken and written language, so it is necessary to discuss non-finiteness in spoken and written contexts respectively. In the present study, we focus on written language, but instances typically used in spoken language or frequently discussed in the literature may also be considered so long as they are acceptable in written language. The basic idea is that, regardless of the disparities, there is no fixed boundary between spoken and written language, and what we will focus on in this book is typical usage, usages in written language, in particular.

3.2 Cryptotype and Cline

In his landmark article, which first appeared in 1937, Whorf admits that 'The very natural tendency to use terms derived from traditional grammar, like verb, noun, adjective, passive voice, in describing languages outside of Indo-European, is fraught with grave possibilities of misunderstanding' (Whorf 1945: 1). To overcome this problem, Whorf suggests that we consider grammatical categories from a new perspective.

Whorf distinguishes overt category from covert category. The former is a category 'having a formal mark which is present (with only infrequent exceptions) in every sentence containing a member of the category' (Whorf 1945: 2); the latter is marked, 'whether morphemically or by sentence-pattern', 'only in certain types of sentence' (Whorf 1945: 2). The overt categories (i.e. phenotypes) 'find their realization via a specific formal marking or syntactic patterning', while the covert categories (i.e. cryptotypes) 'make themselves felt via their correlation with patterns of syntactic behaviour' (Lemmens 1998: 29).

The covert category is termed 'cryptotype' to reveal 'the rather hidden, cryptic nature of such word-groups' (Whorf 1945: 4). For example, '[n]ames of countries and cities in English form a cryptotype with the reactance that they

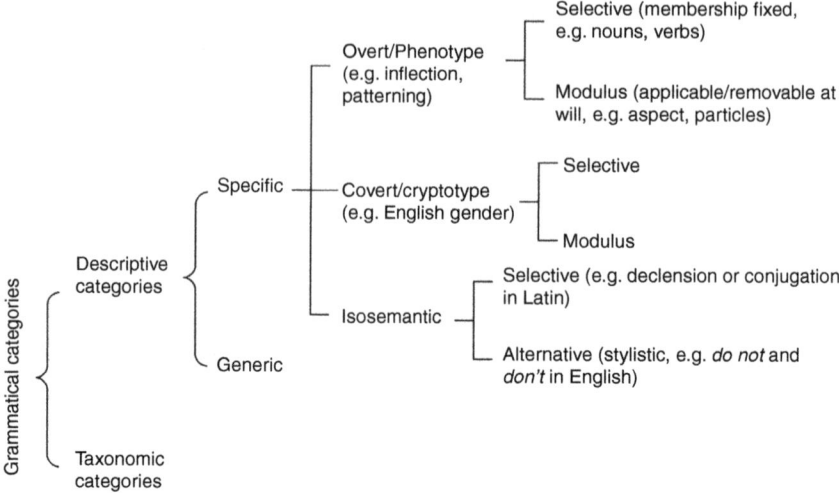

Figure 3.1 Grammatical categories in Whorf (1945)

are not referred to by personal pronouns as object of the prepositions *in, at, to, from*' (Whorf 1945: 4). Figure 3.1 illustrates Whorf's grammatical categories.

Among the grammatical categories proposed by Whorf, that of cryptotype is essential, but it has been long neglected. For example, when 'tea' appears in front of a reader or a listener, some properties of typical tea (green, brown in colour, healthy for drinking, etc.) will be automatically activated. These 'unnoticed' features can be retrieved by the reader without a second thought, and can be grouped under the cryptotype category.

Whorf's thinking suggests that inflections may be the overt features for the realization of 'non-finiteness' in some languages, but in some other languages, covert features operate so that moodless, tenseless, personless, subjectless situations can be realized.

Another useful term is 'cline', which is inherent in all categories. A cline involves 'relation along a single dimension', and 'instead of being made up of a number of discrete terms a cline is a continuum carrying potentially infinite gradation' (Halliday 1961: 249). Thus, boundaries are drawn within or between categories for the sake of observation, because intermediate (even blurring) types exist in every category or between categories. For example, even if we regard morphological inflections as the determining factors for the finite/non-finite distinction, there will be intermediate types, as shown in Table 3.1.

Linguistic concepts are experiential, and non-finiteness as a linguistic concept is no exception. Experiential concepts by nature form into clines.

3.3 Metafunctions as Universal Categories

Table 3.1 *Cline between finite and non-finite clauses: morphological perspective (B. Yang 2015: 7)*

	Subject	Verb as predicate	Person/number agreement
Non-finite	−	−	−
	+	+	−
Pseudo-non-finite	+	−	−
	−	+	−
	+	−	+
Pseudo-finite	−	+	+
	−	−	+
Finite	+	+	+

Key: + = plus feature; − = minus feature

Yet, a linguistic theory requires that categories be distinctive, because language phenomena cannot be properly described and explained without distinctions. For example, in discussing categories in the theory of grammar, Halliday said, 'The distinction between closed system patterns and open set patterns in language is in fact a cline; but the theory has to treat them as two distinct types of pattern requiring different categories' (Halliday 1961: 247). For this reason, we shall be aware of both 'cline' and 'distinct types' in linguistic categorization.

3.3 Metafunctions as Universal Categories

'[T]he absence of inflection does not exclude the existence of other means to express the same function' (Klein 2006: 246). Issue 4 in Volume 40 of *Linguistics* focused on how semantic aspects of finiteness relate to finite expressions. One of the findings is '[E]ven in languages where the expression of finiteness typically involves morphosyntactic means (such as verb placement or inflectional morphology), other elements may contribute to the expression of finiteness, or it may remain unexpressed' (Dimroth & Lasser 2002: 647). The implication is that, in languages that do not employ salient inflections, we need to consider other means for expressing finiteness.

'Familiar categories such as perfect, passive, subject, direct object ... are so fuzzy and ... should not be seen as theoretical notions' (Klein 2006: 246). Other theoretical notions need to be pursued, and among others, the syntactic effects should be considered:

(a) Finiteness is not just verb inflection; it clearly serves syntactic functions.
(b) These functions can apparently not be explained in terms of tense or mood.

(c) They rather seem to be connected to assertion and topichood, or, more generally speaking, with information structure. (Klein 2006: 256)

Categories that are not determined by inflections or explained in terms of tense or mood include metafunctions proposed in SFL, which are the ideational function, the interpersonal function and the textual function (Halliday 1985, 1994; Halliday & Matthiessen 2004, 2014). This functional perspective of language may be traced back to the early 1920s. In 1923, three uses (functions) of language were distinguished from an ethnographic point of view: Active, Narrative and Ritual (Malinowski 1946 [1923]). Later, two more uses were added: Magical and Pragmatic (Malinowski 1935).

Mathesius, from the Prague School, proposed 'functional sentence perspective' (FSP) (Mathesius 1983 [1927]: 126), which focuses on the utterance from the point of view of the information conveyed by it. Mathesius used the term 'function' to 'refer to functioning internal to the system' (Newmeyer 2001: 103). Later, Bühler, from a psychological point of view, distinguished three functions of language: the Expressive (*Ausdruck*), the Appealing (*Appell*) and the Representational (Bühler 2011 [1934]: 35). He regards these as semantic concepts.

With a focus on language context, Firth (1957) distinguished minor function (Phonetic) from major function (Lexical, Morphological and Syntactical). In his thinking, meaning is composed of the major and minor functions, the locution in context, and the province of semantics.

Unlike Firth, Jakobson (1960: 353) argues that six factors are 'inalienably involved in verbal communication' (addresser, context, message, contact, code and addressee), and '[e]ach of the six factors determines a different function of language'. The functions include Referential, Poetic, Emotive, Conative, Phatic and Metalingual.

František Daneš and Jan Firbas from the Prague School later advocated a view of the interaction of form and meaning they termed a 'three-level approach to syntax', which includes three levels: the grammatical structure of the sentence; the semantic structure of the sentence; and the organization of an utterance (Daneš 1964; Firbas 1964a, 1964b).

Functional sentence perspective was later improved by Firbas (1992: 66), in which Sett(ing) corresponds to a temporal or locative adverbial, Pr(esentation) to a verb of appearance, Ph(enomenon) to the entity, Q(uality) to a verb, B(earer) to the subject, Sp to specification, and FSp to further specifications. Thus, the combination will look like:

Set – Pr – Ph – B – Q – Sp – FSp

All these viewpoints and other similar discussions suggest that there are general functions underlying human language. As Halliday (1970: 140) wrote:

3.3 Metafunctions as Universal Categories

The nature of language is closely related to the demands that we make on it, the functions it has to serve. In the most concrete terms, these functions are specific to a culture: the use of language to organize fishing expeditions in the Trobriand Islands, described half a century ago by Malinowski, has no parallel in our own society. But underlying such specific instances of language use are more general functions which are common to all cultures.

Halliday's metafunctions were initiated as early as 1956 (Halliday 1956). The basic concepts for the theory were published in *Word* (Halliday 1961) and *Journal of Linguistics* (Halliday 1966a, 1966b). Soon after these publications, the outline and the major ideas were published as three parts in three issues of *Journal of Linguistics* (Halliday 1967a, 1967b, 1968). In his article published in 1969, he said, 'Let us then suggest four generalized components in the organization of the grammar of a language, and refer to them as the components of extralinguistic experience, of speech function, of discourse organization and of logical structure' (Halliday 1969: 81–2). The components are then called functions of language: ideational, interpersonal and textual (Halliday 1970).

This categorization also comes from Halliday's observation of his son's language development. In discussing linguistic ontogeny, Halliday recognized seven micro-functions (uses) in children's use of language (Halliday 1975: 244):

- instrumental: *I want*
- regulatory: *do as I tell you*
- interactional: *me and you*
- personal: *here I come*
- heuristic: *tell me why*
- imaginative: *let's pretend*
- representational: *I've got something to tell you.*

These micro-functions were then generalized into mathetic (observation and learning) and pragmatic (response-demanding and participatory) uses of language. To mean more than one thing at once, and, more importantly, to allow the different functions to be mapped on to one another, these are configured into three meta-functions: ideational, interpersonal and textual.

When discussing the functional components of the system, Halliday (1978: 130–1) reminds readers of the importance of perspectives when looking at the components. The logical component that is realized through recursive structures is the one that stands out if observed 'from below' (realization in the lexicogrammatical system). If to be observed 'from above' (functions of the linguistic system in relation to higher-level semiotic), the textual component will be distinct from others because it enables other components to operate. If observed from the same level (organization within the semantic system itself), 'the experiential and the logical go together because there is greater systemic interdependence between these two than between other pairs' (Halliday 1978: 131). According to Halliday's observation, '[t]his shows up in various places throughout the English semantic system (the general pattern may well be the same in all languages though the specifics are different)' (Halliday 1978: 131).

'[T]he grammar of every (natural) language is a theory of human experience' (the reflective function) and 'an enactment of interpersonal relationships' (the active function), which 'are actualized by a third function, that of creating discourse' (the discursive) (Halliday 2004c [1998]: 50). 'All languages are organized around two main kinds of meaning, the "ideational" or reflective, and the "interpersonal" or active' (Halliday 1994: viii). These are called metafunctions; see Figure 3.2.

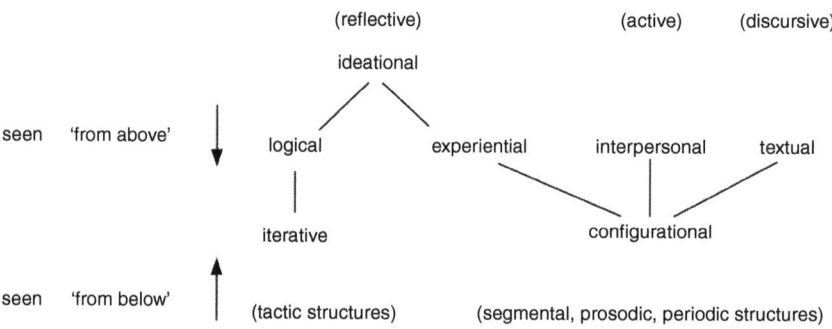

Figure 3.2 The metafunctional framing of the grammar (Halliday 2004c [1998]: 50)

Linguistics in the twentieth century is characterised by structure, system and function (Dirven & Fried 1987: x). Typological studies have revealed both similarities and disparities in structure between languages. A number of linguists, for example, Newmeyer (1999), call for dialogue and convergence between functionalism and formalism. However, metafunctions proposed by Halliday have largely been ignored by linguists from other backgrounds. As categories that are suitable to all languages, metafunctions can be used to describe language, and they point to new directions in understanding tough and pending issues in linguistics.

'A functional grammar is essentially a "natural" grammar, in the sense that everything in it can be explained, ultimately, by reference to how language is used' (Halliday 1994: xii). SFG has been used in the descriptions of major languages such as German, French, Danish, Spanish, Arabic, Vietnamese, Mandarin Chinese and Japanese. Linguists also use SFG in the description of languages or dialects spoken by far smaller populations: Telugu, Pitjantjatjara, Cantonese, Òkó and Bajjika (Halliday & Matthiessen 2014: 54). Such crosslinguistic applicability has proven the ubiquity of metafunctions, which serves as the foundation for the present exploration into non-finiteness.

3.4 Process as the Basic Semantic Unit

'Process' as a semantic term must be understood against the background of events and states. Events, processes and states have long been under heated discussion in both philosophy and linguistics. Some philosophers use 'event' as an umbrella term and distinguish four sorts of event: activities, accomplishments, achievements and states. An activity (e.g. *John's walking uphill*) has no natural finishing point or culmination; an accomplishment (e.g. *John's climbing the mountain*) may have a culmination; an achievement (e.g. *John's reaching the top*) is a culminating event; and a state (e.g. *John's knowing the shortest way*) may extend over time without being culminated (Vendler 1957).

In Vendler's view, 'persons or objects cannot be caused, while events, processes, and states of affairs can be' (Vendler 1967: 30). Thus, verbs are distinguished from one another in terms of their suggesting of processes, states, dispositions, occurrences, tasks or achievements (Vendler 1967).

Events may be contrasted with facts, one expressed by perfect nominals and the other by imperfect nominals. The process of nominalization in a perfect nominal (e.g. *Caesar's death*) is complete, and the expression can only be modified by adjectival phrases (e.g. *Caesar's violent death*). Thus, we have a fact. By contrast, the imperfect nominals such as that-clause (e.g. *that Caesar died*) or gerundive (e.g. *Caesar's dying*) are not complete, and they can tolerate auxiliaries and tenses (e.g. *That Caesar could die*), adverbs (e.g. *Caesar's dying violently*) and negation (e.g. *Caesar's not dying*) (Vendler 1967). In order to identify the differences between events, we first need to clarify the types of process.

3.4.1 Types of Situation and Types of Process

In Comrie's view, 'states are static ... whereas events and processes are dynamic ... events are dynamic situations viewed as a complete whole ... whereas processes are dynamic situations viewed in progress' (Comrie 1976a: 13).[2] Events, processes and states can be subsumed into the term 'situation' (Comrie 1985: 5).

With 'situation' as the umbrella term, Mourelatos (1978: 423) provides a categorization of states, processes and events, as depicted in Figure 3.3.

---

[2] Please note that the term 'processes' in this quote is used in the general sense.

80   Theoretical Foundations

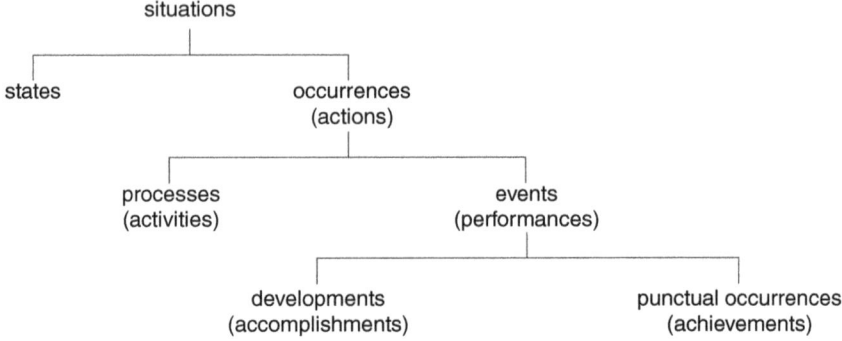

Figure 3.3 Types of situation (Mourelatos 1978: 423)

Mourelatos considers Vendler's scheme of verb types (i.e. performances, activities and states) too narrow both linguistically and ontologically, and he argues that different verbs describe different types of events. For example, verbs with no continuous form (e.g. *know*) correspond to states (Mourelatos 1978). Thus, the verb predications 'refer to purely physical situations' (Mourelatos 1978: 423):

State: The air smells of jasmine.
Process: It's snowing.
Development: The sun went down.
Punctual occurrence: The cable snapped. He blinked. The pebble hit the water.

We can see from these categories that process in linguistic philosophy is concerned with the progressive meaning of the verb predication.

Process in SFG, if taken as a general term, may be used in the analysis of both speech and writing. A text is naturally considered as a thing (i.e. a product). Halliday agrees with Hjelmslev in thinking of text as process and in referring to language as system and process, but he admits that 'to represent a process' is much more difficult than 'to represent a product' (Halliday 1994: xvii). The process/product distinction 'corresponds to that between our experience of speech and our experience of writing: writing exists, whereas speech happens' (Halliday 1994: xvii).

Process, in its specific sense in SFG, is therefore defined as happening, and all verbs may be grouped into different process types.

[P]henomena are interpreted clausally, in a kind of dynamic equilibrium of happenings and things. The prototypical thing is a concrete object which can be related by similarity to certain other objects, such that taken together they form a class, like engines. The prototypical happening is a change in the environment that is perceptible to the senses,

3.4 Process as the Basic Semantic Unit

or a change in the senser's own consciousness. A process is a happening involving one or two such objects, or one object and a conscious being. (Halliday & Matthiessen 1999: 537)

Here a process is much broader in scope than that in Vendler and others, because it is used to refer to a happening that involves one or more participants. A process together with the participants is represented by a clause. The clause, in its role as a representation, 'sets up a model of human experience, in terms of processes that take place around us and inside us'; thus, 'processes are construed by the grammar in terms of three components: the process itself; the participants in that process ... and any circumstantial factors' (Halliday 1994: 52).

Language enables human beings to construe experience and to make sense of the outer and inner worlds. In this process of enabling, 'the clause plays a central role, because it embodies a general principle of modelling experience – namely, the principle that reality is made up of PROCESSES' (Halliday 1994: 106).

'Our most powerful impression of experience is that it consists of "goings-on" – happening, doing, sensing, meaning, and being and becoming'. As a mode of action 'of giving and demanding goods-&-services and information', and as a mode of reflection 'of imposing order on the endless variation and flow of events', the clause helps construe 'the world of experience into a manageable set of PROCESS TYPES' (Halliday 1994: 106).

Thus, 'process' in SFG refers to the basic functional role in a typical clause. Process is by default realized by verbs or verbal groups. As a core term in understanding ideational function, typical process types in English can be portrayed as in Figure 3.4.

The central participants in the core process types are Actor and Goal for material processes, Senser and Phenomenon for mental processes, and Carrier/Identified/Token and Attribute/Identifier/Value for relational processes.[3] The central participants in other process types are Sayer and Verbiage for verbal processes, Behaver for behavioural processes, and Existent for existential processes.

Metafunctions are universal categories, and process types at the core of ideational function are also considered universal. Six types of process have been found to be typologically valid, as least in such major languages as French (Caffarel 2006; Banks 2017), Spanish (Lavid et al. 2010), Chinese (E. S.-H. Li 2007) and Japanese (Teruya 2007; Thomson & Armour 2008), and

---

[3] Note that more delicate process types have been described in SFL, particularly by Matthiessen (2014a), but we will focus on the typical types described by Halliday in the present research. That's why only central participants and typical process types are presented here.

82   Theoretical Foundations

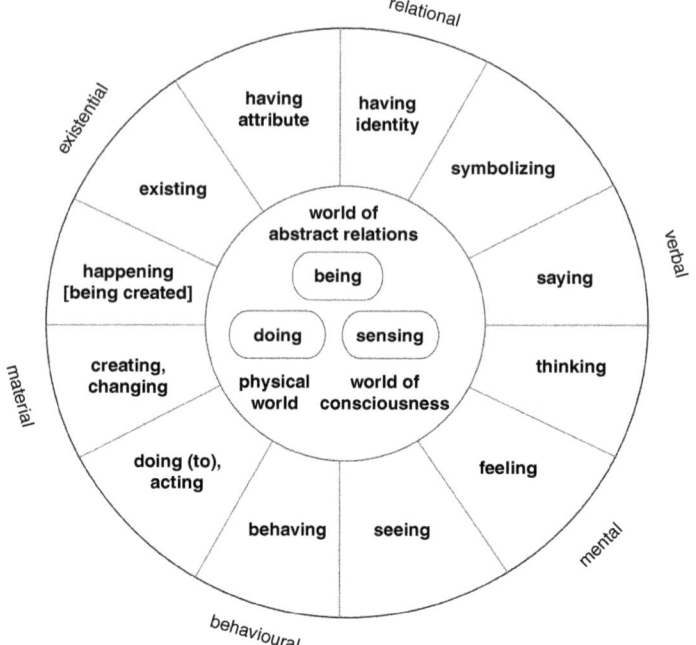

Figure 3.4 Process types in English (Halliday & Matthiessen 2014: 216)

in such less-used languages as Telugu, Pitjantjatjara, Cantonese, Òkó and Bajjika (Halliday & Matthiessen 2014: 54).

To consider process as the basic semantic unit has important implications for non-finiteness in English and Chinese, because process relations rather than morphological or syntactic parameters will be foregrounded. This is consistent with the approach of regarding finiteness as a property of the clause.

With three basic functional roles (i.e. participant, process and circumstance), various combinations may be formed. There may be one or more than one participant, and the participant may be realized by either things or persons, or nominalizations. Likewise, one or more than one circumstance may appear in a clause, and the circumstance may be realized by Adjuncts (adverbializations) or prepositional phrases.

What is special here is that there will be only one major process in a single clause. Several median processes may appear in a clause, and it is among these

3.4 Process as the Basic Semantic Unit   83

median processes that non-finiteness plays its role. Process realized by two or more verbs in English will most likely be involved with non-finiteness. For example:

(3.4) a. We must *continue to develop and grow* our people (NOW_14201243)
   b. As we *design, develop and switch* on the next generation of radio telescopes (NOW_ 4321243)

In (3.4a), the verbal group complex is composed of a major verb (*continue*) and a non-finite group (*to develop and grow*). The major verb and the non-finite is in the hypotactic relation. In (3.4b), the three verbs are in paratactic relation, and they form a verbal group complex. Thus, process is the basic semantic unit, and three levels of process should be distinguished.

3.4.2 Major, Median and Minor Processes

To account for the nature of clauses, two types of process are identified by Halliday: major and minor. Participant, process and circumstance are configured into one of the process types shown in Figure 3.4. Circumstances are usually realized by prepositional phrase, which 'can be interpreted as a shrunken clause, in which the preposition serves as a "minor process", interpreted as a kind of mini-verb' (Halliday 1994: 158; see also Halliday & Matthiessen 2014: 329). This classification is more meaning-oriented, although meaning and form are inseparable in the theory of SFG.

 The similarity between verb and preposition can be compared to that between a prepositional phrase and a non-finite dependent clause (Halliday 1994: 158; Halliday & Matthiessen 2014: 329). For example, *with a mop* in the clause *he cleaned the floor with a mop* can be understood as *using a mop*.

 It is enlightening to consider prepositional phrases as 'minor processes', in which the preposition is interpreted as a mini-verb, because prepositions in prepositional phrases take the role of processes in these phrases. However, they are different from non-finite verbs both in form and meaning. Prepositions are comparatively scarce in languages, but verbs (and thus non-finite verbs) are numerous.

 Prepositional phrases and non-finite clauses are comparable to some extent, but they are not the same thing. Here we would suggest identifying a third category of process in terms of structure: the median process. Thus, we have three types of process in terms of structure: major process, median process and minor process. Median process are processes realized by non-finite clauses. The prepositions in the form of non-finite verbs (e.g. *concerning, given, excepting, according to*) may be either median or minor process, depending on their specific function in the clause.

Process, participant and circumstance are first-level functions. Quality, qualifier and so on are delicate functions, because these functions are used to refine the first-level functions. Of the first-level functions, process is the minimal semantic unit for communication. 'The most fundamental unit for semantic typology is the sign' (Evans 2010: 506). However, the minimal semantic unit for actual communication cannot be a sign, because a sign without a context is meaningless in terms of communication. 'The unit with which we are associating the meaning is no longer a given sign with a given form, but a class of signs sharing the same combinatoric' (Evans 2010: 528).

A class of signs as well as a certain combinatoric are required so as to be complete in meaning, and a process realized by a verbal element may meet this requirement. A nominal word like *Park* displayed in a place that is not a park at all does not convey meaningful information (unless in a situation where vocabulary is being taught). By contrast, a nominalization that is intermediate between the verbal and the nominal (e.g. *Parking*, shortened to *P* on signs) is a median process. In this sense, a process can be considered as the minimal semantic unit for communication in the minimal context. This is also true of minor processes. For example, a sign like 'on sale' on a certain product is complete in meaning.

A number of linguists tend to use spoken instances that can only be fully understood in specific contexts, and such tendency is highly biased. For example, L. Wang (1984: 50) argued that the verb component is necessary only for those languages in which a sentence is an actor–action construction, and not necessary for languages like Chinese. Wang quoted Jespersen's example 'Waiter, another bottle' (Jespersen 1924: 302) to support his view. Jespersen's example is, in fact, an utterance with omission for specific contexts. In a bar or a restaurant, the customer may say to the waiter, 'Waiter, please give me another bottle' or 'Waiter, another bottle'. This utterance with omission is highly context-dependent. If spoken in a library where no waiter is around for the purpose of getting more drinks, then the utterance will be either meaningless or simply a joke. In other words, the recoverability of the verb in similar omissions suggests that the verb for expressing process is a component we cannot do without.

3.5 Clause as the Basic Syntactic Unit: Major, Median and Minor

A typical expression that is complete in meaning in a minimal context is usually represented as a clause. A sign like 'Entrance' on a wall is complete in meaning, but a wall and a place to get into are the necessary contextual elements. By contrast, a complete clause like 'I name this ship the *Queen Elizabeth*' (Austin 1962: 5) is meaningful without a context. Statements require less contextual factors, and a statement like 'Flying planes can be dangerous' (Chomsky 1965: 21) is ambiguous but meaningful, requiring no more context.

Psycholinguistic research has shown that prelinguistic infants are able to detect important units such as clauses in motherese (e.g. Hirsh-Pasek et al. 1987; D. Nelson et al. 1989). Other studies in language acquisition find that the clause plays a central role. 'Across the spectrum of positions ranging from nativism to empiricism, one finds that the clause occupies a central role in the language acquisition process' (Hirsh-Pasek et al. 1987: 270).

It is not only in language acquisition that researchers find the central role of the clause; those who work on speech find that the clause is fundamental in speech production and understanding. 'There is abundant evidence from the speech production literature that indicates that the clause is a salient organizing unit in speech processing', and 'Many of the prosodic changes at clause boundaries have obvious acoustic consequences' (Hirsh-Pasek et al. 1987: 270).

One consensus today is that human speech is multimodal. Three channels (the verbal component, prosody and kinetic-visual behaviour) play an important role in the overall process of language communication (Kibrik & Molchanova 2013). The modalities are all significant, but the verbal component is essential for writing, while prosody is essential for speech, and the kinetic-visual channel (i.e. gesticulation) is essential for sign languages. To study these channels, we need different grammars.

For both spoken and written language, the verbal component cannot be done without. Whatever grammar is used, the basic unit for analysis needs to be made clear. In written language, the basic unit is the clause, and it is fundamental in reporting events and states (Kibrik & Molchanova 2013).

If we think of a typical substantive intonation unit as having the form of a clause, and if we think of a clause as verbalizing the idea of an event or state, we can conclude that each such idea is active, or occupies a focus of consciousness, for only a brief time, each being replaced by another idea at roughly one- to two-second intervals. (Chafe 1994: 66)

Chafe links the concept of a clause to 'a focus of consciousness', which is reasonable, but more experimental evidence is needed to support this view. What has been demonstrated in numerous studies is that 'Languages have developed a universal syntactic structure for packaging events and states: the clause'; 'Clauses may report events of various complexity and with various amount of detail, and they may include additional elements' (Kibrik et al. 2015: 662).

In Halliday's view, a clause functions simultaneously as a message (the ideational function), an exchange (the interpersonal function) and a representation (the textual function) (Halliday 1961, 1985; see also

Halliday & Matthiessen 2014). In the first edition of Halliday's *An Introduction to Functional Grammar* (IFG), the overall meaning of a clause may be described and interpreted as follows:

- The Theme is a function in the *clause as a message*. It is what the message is concerned with: the point of departure for what the speaker is going to say.
- The Subject is a function in the *clause as an exchange*. It is the element that is held responsible: in which is vested the success of the clause in whatever is its particular speech function.
- The Actor is a function in the *clause as a representation* (of a process). It is the active participant in the process: the one that does the deed. (Halliday 1985: 36)

Thus, a clause is embodied with three distinct kinds of meaning (clause as a message, clause as an exchange, and clause as a representation). Theme, Subject and Actor occur simultaneously in a clause for the exact communicative purpose.

The three strands of meaning in a clause function as a unity. As 'a multiply structured concept', the clause is simultaneously a representation, interaction and message (Halliday [2002b] 1979]: 216). This again suggests the rationale for considering the clause as a basic syntactic unit. Halliday uses English instances as examples, but the theory has been found to be cross-linguistically valid.

A good number of linguists argue that multifunctionality is a characteristic of modern Chinese, and they believe that 'sentence' and 'group' are too similar to be distinguished from one another in Chinese (e.g. Zhu 1985). This view results from failure to identify the finiteness of the verb, and also from neglecting to distinguish spoken language from written language. For example, while some linguists criticize Chao for saying that 'The grammatical meaning of subject and predicate in a Chinese sentence is topic and comment, rather than actor and action' (Chao 2011 [1968]: 92–3), they ignore the fact that Chao's grammar is for spoken Chinese only. As we have discussed, spoken and written languages require different grammars.

As a language that is distinct from English in terms of inflection, tense and agreement, sharp disputes have been witnessed over the status of 'sentence' and 'clause' in Chinese (e.g. S. Lü 1990 [1982]; C. Qu 1996; Luke 2006; W. He & Wang 2018). Some even argue that 'text' should be the basic unit of grammatical analysis in Chinese (e.g. X. Peng 2011, 2017). Mandarin Chinese is considered by many Chinese linguists today as a language in which the clause is the pivot, being the basic unit of grammatical analysis (e.g. Xiao 1995; F. Xing 1995, 2017; Yuming Li 1997). This view corresponds well with the approach of taking 'clause' to be the basic syntactic unit for cross-linguistic purposes.

Corresponding with the three types of process in terms of structure, clause as the basic syntactic unit can be put into three categories: major, median and minor clauses.[4] The major clause usually corresponds with a major process which is typically realized by a finite verb, the median clause with a median process which is typically realized by a non-finite verb, and the minor clause with a minor process which is typically realized by a prepositional phrase. The categories of clause here lay more emphasis on the form, but meaning is what is focused on here.

3.6 Ideational Grammatical Metaphor

Ideational grammatical metaphor (IGM) serves as a window through which we can observe the continuum of language structures ranging from full clauses to entities. This 'window' helps us to better understand the nature of non-finiteness in languages.

3.6.1 A Sketch of Ideational Grammatical Metaphor

Metaphor has been popular since the publication of Aristotle's *Rhetoric*, and the theory of conceptual metaphor presented in *Metaphors We Live By* (Lakoff & Johnson 1980) is widely known. By contrast, GM is still unknown to many linguists. It was seeded in Halliday's article 'Grammar, Society and the Noun' (Halliday [2003a] 1966), and the term 'grammatical metaphor' first appeared in an article that compares English with Chinese (Halliday 1984). One year later, a comprehensive version of GM was published in the first edition of IFG (Halliday 1985). With further illustrations and improvements, GM has now become an illuminating approach to the configurational mechanism of linguistic components.

To understand GM, it is necessary to begin with correspondence between meaning and form. 'The phenomena of experience are of three orders of complexity: elementary (a single element), configurational (configuration of elements, i.e. a figure) and complex (a complex of figures, i.e. a sequence)' (Halliday and Matthiessen 1999: 48). When an element in semantics is realized by a group in lexicogrammar, a figure by a clause, and a sequence by a clause nexus, we have a direct correspondence between meaning and form, and no GM is involved (B. Yang 2020). Halliday makes this point clearer:

---

[4] 'Clause' is a typical syntactic term, while 'process' is a semantic term. As discussed elsewhere (see Section 3.4.2), meaning and form are inseparable. The reason for employing these categories is to better observe the phenomena with different focal points.

The grammar of every natural language is a theory of human experience .... The grammar breaks down the continuum of experience into *figures*, each figure representing a 'happening' of some kind; and it does this by means of the clause: you will hear small children saying things like (from my own records) *tiny bird flew away, that tree got no leaf on, put butter on toast*, and so on. It also analyses each figure into different types of **elements**: the happening itself, like *flew, got, put* and so on; and the various participating entities and circumstantial elements that surround it: *tiny bird, that tree, butter, away, on toast* .... And thirdly it joins the figures into **sequences** by means of various logical semantic relations such as time and cause; e.g. *but* in *That tree got leaf on but that tree got no leaf on* (Halliday 2004a [1995]: 9; emphasis in original)

This natural directness in realization as described by Halliday in this quote can be taken as an important manifestation of congruence in ideational meaning (Steiner 2002b). IGM occurs when the realization is as follows: a sequence is realized by a clause; a figure is realized by a group. Here the grammatical form becomes indirect and a tension rises between semantics and lexicogrammar. This indirect form (i.e. the incongruent form) in lexicogrammar is called IGM (Halliday & Matthiessen 1999: 227). See (3.5) from Halliday (2004b [1998]: 34).

(3.5)   a. Glass cracks more quickly the harder you press on it.
           b. The rate of glass crack growth depends on the magnitude of the applied stress.
           c. Glass crack growth rate is associated with applied stress magnitude.

Instances (3.5a) and (3.5c) are variations of (3.5b), which was taken from an article entitled 'The Fracturing of Glass' in *Scientific American* by Michalske and Bunker. They are different ways of expressing the same meaning. Instance (3.5a) is a sequence in semantics and is realized by two clauses. Two doing figures (*glass cracks quickly, you press on it*) were mapped onto two material processes (*crack, press*), and the relationship between semantics and lexicogrammar is natural and direct. Thus (3.5a) shows a direct realization (i.e. the congruent form).

The clause nexus in (3.5a) realized by a sequence is then rankshifted (downwards into two groups (*the rate of glass crack, the magnitude of the applied stress*) respectively in (3.5b).[5] In other words, the sequence has been compressed into a figure. Such downward rankshifting (transcategorization) results in incongruent expressions, which are usually IGMs. Thus, (3.5b) is an IGM here. The clause in (3.5b) is rankshifted downwards further, and we have nominalized groups in (3.5c). The clause in (3.5c) is thus a typical IGM as well. Here, 'some element other than a noun ... has nominal status assigned'

---

[5] 'Rank' in SFL refers to 'the hierarchy of units according to their constituency potential' (Halliday & Matthiessen 1999: 4), and the units include clause, group/phrase, word and morpheme.

(Halliday 2003a [1966]: 58). In a word, both (3.5b) and (3.5c) concern metaphoricity in two senses: nominalization, and clause nexus transcategorized into clause. Note that nominalizations may not necessarily be IGMs.

The theory of GM is 'an important step forward in systemic functional linguistics' (Ravelli 2003: 38). Compared with the incongruent forms, the congruent forms evolve 'earlier in the language'; they are 'learnt earlier by children' and they 'come earlier in the text' (Halliday & Matthiessen 1999: 235). In other words, the incongruent forms reflect certain advancement in language complexity. Among other implications, GM 'underpins linguistic creativity (ontogenesis), human language development (phylogenesis) and concept formation (logogenesis)' (B. Yang 2020: 163).

Literature on GM is comparatively rich in the following topics: theoretical pondering (e.g. Davidse 1999 [1991]; Steiner 2002a; Simon-Vandenbergen et al. 2003; Lassen 2003a, 2003b; Christie & Martin 2007; Q. He & Yang 2014; B. Yang 2018, 2019a, 2020); clarification and explanation (e.g. Taverniers 2002; Devrim 2015; Liardét 2016a); ontological observations (e.g. Derewianka 1995, 2003; Painter 2003); cross-linguistic studies (e.g. Yanning Yang 2008, 2014; Byrnes 2009; Magnusson 2013); applications and the use of GM in English as second/foreign-language-learner writing or language development (e.g. Bateman 1990; O'Halloran 1996; Steiner 2002b; Schleppegrell 2008; Ryshina-Pankova 2010, 2015; Liardét 2013, 2016b). As an economical means of packing up information (Halliday 2004b [1998]), GM has been found to be a common feature of scientific writing (e.g. J. R. Martin 1993; Banks 2005; Colombi 2006; Biber & Gray 2016). These studies have greatly enhanced the development of GM, but the status of embedded clauses has not been made clear. Readers, non-systemicists in particular, may get confused if embedding is not well explained in the theory of GM.

The overwhelming problem and subsequent misunderstandings may be overcome if we put IGM into four broad groups: nominalization, adjectivization, verbalization and adverbialization. Please note that nominalization does not mean a verb (or other parts of speech) being used as a noun. Nominalization has nothing to do with conversion in traditional grammar. The same is true of adjectivization, verbalization and adverbialization. The specific categories can be consequently arranged with clear-cut boundaries, as described in Sections 3.6.2–3.6.5.

3.6.2 Nominalization

As mentioned, not all nominalizations are IGMs. Four typical nominalizations contribute to the formation of IGM (Halliday & Matthiessen 1999), all of which are involved with rankshifting: either from clause to group or from clause complex to clause. The specific categories, with examples (see also B. Yang 2020: 167–8), are:

Nom1: quality → thing (clause → group)
e.g. the price is *unstable* = *instability* of price

Nom2: process → thing (clause → group)
e.g. a tadpole *transforms* into a frog = *the transformation* of a tadpole
she'll *try to* call him again = her *attempt* of calling him again
they're *going to* be massive = their *prospect* to be massive
they *can* run fast = the *possibility* of fast running
they *could* be right = the *potential* to be right

Nom3: circumstance → thing (clause → group)
e.g. Jane stays *with* her = Jane's *accompaniment*
we went *to* Prague last year = Prague as our *destination* last year
dust is *on the surface* = *surface* dust

Nom4: relator → thing (clause complex → clause)
e.g. I stayed behind *so* I could see you = the *cause* of my staying behind is to see you
if you try hard, it might work = the *condition* for it to work is to try hard

Every functional role in a clause can be nominalized. This can be exemplified by *we watched ivy carefully descending the Hörnli Ridge* (Fawcett, forthcoming). This instance may be expressed in various forms with similar meanings. The difference is that specific roles have been nominalized differently. See the variations in (3.6)–(3.8) (see also B. Yang 2020: 168):

(3.6) a. Ivy **is careful** when she descends the Hörnli Ridge.
       b. Ivy descends the Hörnli Ridge **with care**. (quality nominalized)

(3.7) a. Ivy acts **in a careful way** when she descends the Hörnli Ridge.
       b. Ivy's **care** in descending the Hörnli Ridge (circumstance nominalized).

(3.8) a. Ivy is careful **when** she descends the Hörnli Ridge.
       b. Ivy is careful at **the time** of descending the Hörnli Ridge (relator nominalized).

Examples (3.6)–(3.8) show that every functional role in a clause (i.e. participant, process, circumstance, relator and quality) can be nominalized. It is usual for a high-ranked component to shift to become a low-ranked component, and this brings forth the metaphoric syndrome, which is prevalent in IGM. We may take an example and portray the syndrome for nominalization as in Figure 3.5. Only the full realizations (see Section 3.7 for more explanations) can be regarded as metaphorical.[6]

---

[6] 'Syndrome' as a term is used by Halliday to differentiate the shift in lexical metaphor from that in grammatical metaphor. In lexical metaphor, a simple opposition is set up between two terms where no degrees may be drawn between. By contrast, the shift between categories in grammatical metaphor is usually more than one degree of metaphoric displacement. A congruent instance may proceed step by step towards the metaphorical, and the intermediate realizations may be more or less metaphorical. This phenomenon is called the metaphoric syndrome (Halliday 2004c [1998]: 79).

3.6 Ideational Grammatical Metaphor   91

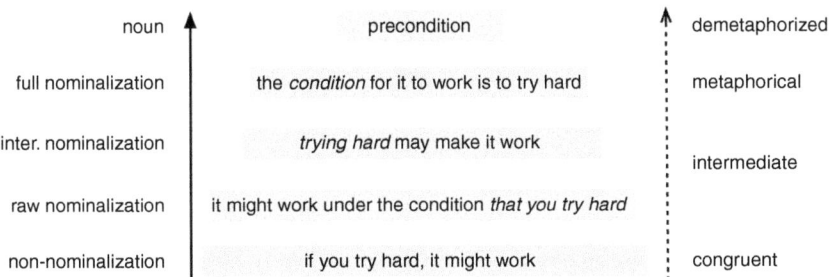

Figure 3.5 The metaphoric syndrome: nominalization
Key: inter. = intermediate; *italicized* clauses are those that have been nominalized

3.6.3   Adjectivization

IGM occurs when a clause complex is rankshifted into a clause and the meaning of the relator is realized by an adjective functioning as quality; or a clause is rankshifted into a group in which the meaning of the process (or the circumstance) is realized by an adjective functioning as a quality. Again, when a group is rankshifted downwards into a word functioning as quality, IGM also occurs. Thus, we have four basic categories for adjectivization.

Adj1: relator → quality (clause complex → clause)
e.g. I was planning to walk around *so* I bought a street map = the *resultant* street map of planning to walk around

Adj2: process → quality (clause → group)
e.g. property *increases* in mass = large *increasing* property
the road *used to be* a dirt track = the *previous* dirt track
their product *will always* sell better = the *constant* better sale of their product
the weeds *begin to* sprout = the *initial* sprouts of the weeds

Adj3: circumstance → quality (clause → group)
e.g. He lives *with* his grandmother = *accompanying* grandmother
marks are *on the surface* = *superficial* marks

Adj4: circumstance → quality (group → word)
e.g. *as cold as ice* = *ice-cold*
as solid as rock = *rock-solid*

These four categories are the basic ones, and the metaphoric syndrome can also be conveniently observed in adjectivization. Taking the clause *I met Betty, angry with me as always, at the luncheon* from (Quirk et al. 1985: 1125) as the anchoring example, we may portray the syndrome for adjectivization as in Figure 3.6.

92   Theoretical Foundations

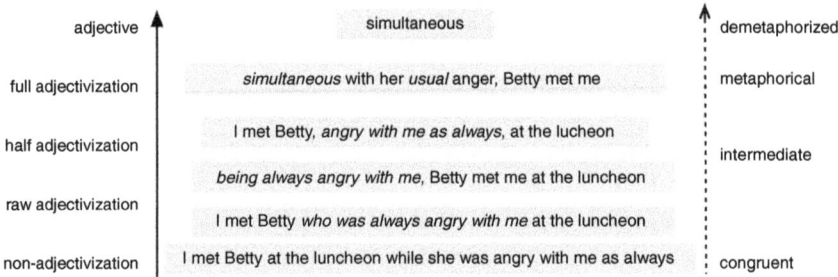

Figure 3.6 The metaphoric syndrome: adjectivization
Key: *italicized* clauses are those that have been adjectivized

Some expressions created out of *I met Betty, angry with me as always, at the luncheon* as variations in meaning may sound unnatural to native speakers (e.g. *simultaneous with her usual anger*). However, we cannot reject them as mere unacceptable coinages. IGM itself is a mechanism through which many ways of meaning are possible, and these expressions are possible in special contexts (novel writing, for example).

Raw adjectivization contains embedding where finite clauses (e.g. *who was always angry with me*) or non-finite clauses (e.g. *being always angry with me*) are adjectivized, but they are adjectivized only in meaning. These forms shall not be considered as IGMs (see Section 3.7).

3.6.4   Verbalization

Nominalization may be determined in a comparatively small context, but the judgement of verbalization depends on a larger context. As we have shown, Ravelli provided two categories of verbalization while Halliday provided three. Ravelli's examples (*the arms race CONTAINS the threat* and *night FOLLOWS day*) are considered metaphorical, but no context was provided (Ravelli 1988, 2003). Without a specific context and without following the principle of rankshifting, the examples would be misleading to readers outside SFL and they may take the capitalized verbs (CONTAIN and FOLLOW) as IGMs. It is not the capitalized verbs here that are IGMs, but the transcategorization resulted from rankshifting that forms IGM. Take (3.9) as an example.

(3.9)   a. They shredded the documents before they departed for the airport.
          b. Their shredding of the documents **preceded** their departure for the airport.
              (Halliday & Matthiessen 1999: 253)
          c. the fish **preceded** the reptile (BNC)

3.6 Ideational Grammatical Metaphor   93

Both (3.9b) and (3.9c) contain the verb 'precede', but it does not mean they are all IGMs. (3.9c), if used in the context of describing aquatic animals in a pond, does not involve rankshifting and is non-metaphorical. By contrast, (3.9b) is rankshifted from a clause complex (3.9a). Thus, only (3.9b) involves verbalization of the clause relations realized by the relator 'before', and 'preceded' here is verbalized both in form and in meaning. Please note that (3.9c) may be metaphorical in certain context. In a restaurant where both fish and reptiles (e.g. snakes in some Eastern countries) are served, the clause complex *The fish is served before the reptile is served* may be verbalized as *The fish preceded the reptile*. In this case, (3.9c) is verbalized both in meaning and form, and IGM occurs. In other words, context is the determining factor for making judgements for IGMs.

Following this approach, we may identify three basic categories of verbalization that are verbalized both in meaning and in form.

Verb1: relator → process (clause complex → clause)
e.g. give her the letter, *then* she'll understand = her understanding *follows* reading the letter
I stayed behind *so* I could see you = the wish to see you *causes* my staying behind
the music is good, *and* her voice is perfect with it = the music *complements* her voice perfectly

Verb2: process → process (projection/expansion → clause)
e.g. they all *think that* she's very kind = they *credit her with* kindness
she *made her ideas accepted* by the group = she *imposed her ideas* on the group

Verb3: circumstance → process (group → word)
e.g. wine *instead of* beer is served with dinner = beer *replaces* wine for dinner
put it in *a box* = *box* it

The metaphoric syndrome for verbalization can be portrayed as in Figure 3.7 (The anchoring example, *I think to put it in a box keeps it longer*, is from the BNC).

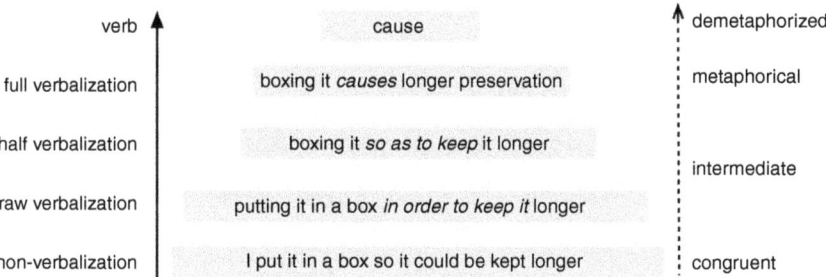

Figure 3.7 The metaphoric syndrome: verbalization
Key: *italicized* clauses are those that have been verbalized

94 Theoretical Foundations

Here, in this example, two verbalizations are realized at the same time (i.e. *box* and *cause*).

3.6.5 Adverbialization

Suffixation or derivation in traditional grammar (e.g. using -ly after adjectives) should not be confused with adverbialization in IGM. The focus of the traditional view is on the lexical aspect, while IGM is concerned with the grammatical aspect. More importantly, rankshifting, or transcategorization, is also the principle behind adverbialization in IGM. Thus, the three basic categories of adverbialization are:

Adv1: relator → circumstance (clause complex → group)
there was heavy fog, *so* the flight was delayed = for the flight delay *as a result of fog*
a whole day passed *before* the police arrived = with a whole day *until the police's arrival*

Adv2: circumstance → circumstance (clause → group)
e.g. *when you are successful* = *in times of* success
if [it snows] = *under/in* [snow(y) conditions]

Adv3: minor process → circumstance (minor clause → group)
e.g. the shop will close *on the same day* = the shop will close *the same day*
we fix it *in every possible way* = we will fix it *every possible way*
they work *on all days and in all nights* = they work *days and nights*

The metaphoric syndrome for adverbialization can be portrayed as in Figure 3.8 (the anchoring example, *this may seem unimportant if you are successful*, is from COCA).

We have now provided an improved taxonomy of IGM on the basis of Halliday and Matthiessen's typology, which we believe is easier to understand

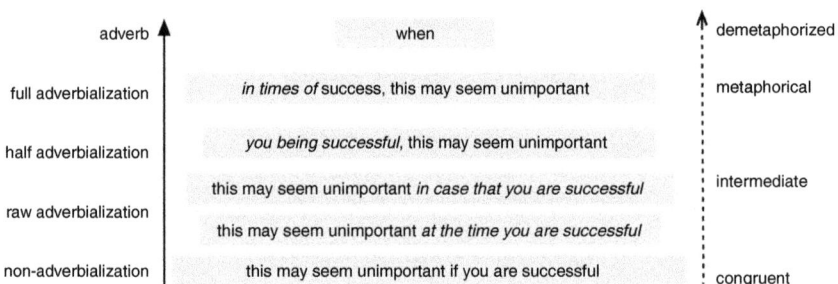

Figure 3.8 The metaphoric syndrome: adverbialization
Key: *italicized* clauses are those that have been adverbialized

and more accessible for readers. A principle of IGM is that no IGM occurs without downward rankshifting (Q. He & Yang 2014). Embedding may, however, function at a lower rank without the occurrence of IGM. This needs to be explained.

3.7 Embedding, Two Principles and Rankshifting

When reviewing the first edition of IFG (Halliday 1985), Huddleston (1988b) raised a number of problems, one of which was that viewing a clause as Head of a nominal group is considered problematic (e.g. *the man who came to dinner stole the silver*; *why she did it remains a mystery*). Another problem is Halliday's example, *the fifth day saw them at the summit*. Huddleston said that treating such examples as metaphorical 'is very plausible' (Huddleston 1988b: 168). The core reason behind Huddleston's criticism of GM lies in the vague status of the so-called embedded clauses (B. Yang 2020: 164).

In Halliday's illustration, *the evening the guests ate ice cream and then swam gently* is a congruent sequence, and its variation *the guests' supper of ice cream was followed by a gentle swim* is the metaphorical. Halliday (1994: 344) states that the participants 'the guests' and 'ice cream' here have been **embedded** as Modifiers. Later, embedded clauses are discussed in the section on interpersonal metaphor: embedded 'fact' clauses (e.g. *the strongest belief of all is that there is no trace.*). Apart from this, embedding is not mentioned in the discussions of IGM (see Halliday 2004a [1995], 2004b [1998], 2004c [1998], 2004d [1999]).

As mentioned, one remaining problem with the typology of IGM in Halliday (2004b [1998]: 24–48) and Halliday and Matthiessen (1999: 246–8) concerns the unclear status of embedding. For example, category 11 in the typology is involved with embedding. One interpretation may be that a 'covert' clause has been embedded as a modifier of *fact/phenomenon*. That is to say, a clause is embedded as a nominalization to modify *fact/phenomenon*. The embedded clause still keeps its original form, and nothing has been compressed, so it cannot be an IGM. Otherwise, numerous such antecedents in English and other languages will be IGMs.

Thus, the status of embedded clauses needs to be explained in the theory of GM. Embedded clause (or phrase) functioning as Head 'does not affect the status of the embedded element as a nominalization' (Halliday & Matthiessen 2014: 491). Thus, it is reasonable to say that embedded clauses that function as subjects (or objects or complements) may all be nominalizations. Appositives may also be regarded as nominalizations. See examples (3.10)–(3.12) from Quirk et al. (1985).

96   Theoretical Foundations

(3.10)   Nominal that-clauses function as subject, object or appositive:
    a. *That the invading troops have been withdrawn* has not affected our government's trade sanctions.
    b. I noticed *that he spoke English with an Australian accent.*
    c. Your criticism, *that no account has been taken of psychological factors*, is fully justified. (Quirk et al. 1985: 1049)

(3.11)   Wh- clauses function as subject, object, complement or appositive:
    a. *What I want* is a cup of hot cocoa.
    b. You should see *whoever deals with complaints.*
    c. April is *when the lilacs bloom.*
    d. I'll pay you the whole debt: *what I originally borrowed and what I owe you in interest.* (Quirk et al. 1985: 1058)

(3.12)   Nominal non-finite clauses function as subject or appositive:
    a. *Watching television* keeps them out of mischief.
    b. His current research, *investigating attitudes to racial stereotypes*, takes up most of his time. (Quirk et al. 1985: 1061–3)

In the current theory of SFL, the italicized clauses in these examples are all embedded, functioning as participants, which according to Halliday and Matthiessen (2014: 492) are all nominalized. However, it is not convincing to consider these nominalizations as IGMs. As is known, numerous embedded clauses may occur in a very short passage, in spoken language in particular (cf. Halliday 1989), and we cannot say the passage is full of IGMs.

As a leading systemicist, Fawcett (2008) questions the concept of GM for the reason that it 'requires enormous extensions to the descriptive apparatus of the Sydney Grammar' (Fawcett 2008: 164). To illustrate his viewpoint, he identifies three types of nominalization (Fawcett forthcoming)):

(3.13)   a. We watched *Ivy's careful descent of the Hörnli Ridge* (Type 1 nominalization)
    b. We watched *Ivy's careful descending of the Hörnli Ridge* (Type 2 nominalization)
    c. We watched *Ivy's carefully descending the Hörnli Ridge* (Type 3 nominalization)

Nominalization is used to refer to an event or an entity. According to Fawcett (forthcoming), we can also use a clause to refer to an entity (i.e. clausalization). See (3.14) from Fawcett (forthcoming).

(3.14)   a. *What you saw* wasn't *what I saw.*
    b. It was because he overslept *that he was late.*
    c. *Why he was late* was because he overslept.

Fawcett's 'clausalization' suggests that clauses such as those in (3.13) and (3.14) should be nominalizations, but they cannot be taken as IGMs. In other

3.7 Embedding, Two Principles and Rankshifting

words, the issue of embedding seems to uproot the theory of GM. A good approach to address the issue of embedding is to consider the functional roles of a clause and its variations. No matter how many embedded clauses are involved, a typical clause is composed of participant, process and circumstance in terms of SFL (see Figure 4.1, and also B. Yang 2020).

The number of embedded clauses does not change the status of the clause, because embedded clauses are modifiers which are used to restrict the functional roles (participant, process or circumstance) in various ways. The modifiers (finite or non-finite) restrict either participant or circumstance. That is to say, the embedded clauses can do nothing but restrict the functional roles, and they are raw realizations.

Let us illustrate this with (3.15). Instance (3.15a) contains the so-called embedded clause (*who rides a horse*). It is embedded to a Head and it becomes a nominalization (*the man who rides a horse*). With very frequent use of this in context, people may pack it up by compression (*the man's riding a horse*). Here, rankshifting takes place. If participants (e.g. *man*) do not need to be specified in certain contexts, then a more contracted form (*riding a horse*) may be used. The activity may be nominalized further and referred to as a phenomenon (*horse riding*). When people use a single term (*ride*) to refer to the activity, a noun occurs. This term may then be extended to cover similar activities (e.g. *bike ride, car ride*).

(3.15) a. a man who rides a horse is called a horseman (COCA, FIC)
        b. a man who rides a horse
        c. riding a horse
        d. a man's riding a horse
        e. horse riding
        f. ride

The instances in (3.15) are all involved with nominalization, but the embedded clauses in (3.15a) and (3.15b) are in the form of a clause. In other words, these embedded clauses are only compressed in meaning, not in form. By contrast, (3.15d) and (3.15e) are compressed both in meaning and form. (3.15c) is partly compressed in meaning and form, and (3.15f) is demetaphorized and becomes a noun. Accordingly, we can identify three basic types of nominalization (see also B. Yang 2020: 166):

- **full nominalization**: *horse riding* (compressed both in meaning and form)
- **intermediate nominalization**: *riding a horse* (compressed partly in meaning and partly in form)
- **raw nominalization**: a man *who rides a horse* (compressed only in meaning).

Among the three types of nominalizations, only full nominalization, which is compressed both in meaning and form, can be regarded as IGM. Intermediate nominalization, which is usually non-finite, is partly metaphorical. Raw nominalization is not metaphorical at all. This is called the **Full Realization Principle (FRP)**, according to which only full nominalizations are compressed both in meaning and form, and they can be regarded as IGMs (B. Yang 2020). Embedded clauses will no longer be a problem under this principle, because they are usually raw nominalizations, and they cannot be IGMs. It should be noted that raw nominalizations are not necessarily 'congruent' either, because 'congruence' refers to the most natural and direct expressions (see Steiner 2002b).

This can be generalized further, and we will have three basic realizations in dealing with other manifestations of IGM (B. Yang 2020: 167).

- **full realization** (compressed both in meaning and form)
- **intermediate realization** (compressed partly in meaning, partly in form)
- **raw realization** (compressed only in meaning).

By saying 'compressed both in meaning and form', we mean that a clause nexus has been rankshifted into a clause, or a clause to a group, or a group to a word, with the basic meaning being retained. By 'compressed only in meaning', we mean that no transcategorization takes place and the form is still in its original form. It is in the latter case that embedding is involved.

It is now very clear that embedded clauses are not IGMs, because they are not fully realized/compressed. Under FRP, only the fully compressed can be IGMs. FRP can be applied to nominalization, verbalization and other manifestations of IGM.

With the proposal for dealing with embedding illustrated in this section, and the wisdom on non-finiteness reviewed in Chapter 2, we may come back to the issue of finite verbs in clauses. We assume that a single clause contains only one finite verb, apart from paratactic relations conjoined either with or without conjunctions. In other words, the number of finite verbs in a single clause cannot exceed two, and other verbs if present (with the exception of paratactic relations) will function as non-finite verbs. This is called the **Limit of Finite Verb Principle (LFVP)**. On the one hand, 'a finite verb alone' 'constitutes a minimal sentence' (Nowak 1996: 75), and on the other, a clause contains only one finite verb excepting paratactic relations or embedding.

The LFVP echoes Klein's findings. According to Klein, there exists 'one finite element constraint' in many languages: a syntactically complex verb form can contain several infinite forms but maximally one finite form (Klein 2006: 250). The reason for this is that a single clause is limited to expressing an event or a state.

We agree with McGregor (1997) in treating embedding and rankshifting as different phenomena, because they should not be used interchangeably, Moreover, non-finite clauses should not be simply treated as a kind of rankshifting. According to the three types of realizations described in this section (raw, intermediate and full), 'embedding' refers to the situation in which grammatical units still keep their original forms but function as components of other units, and thus it is raw realization. By contrast, 'rankshifting' refers to those units that have been compressed. Since no upward rankshifting is allowed in IGM, clause complex will turn into clause, clause into group, group into word, and word into morpheme. That is to say, rankshifting is concerned with full realizations and IGM occurs. Non-finite clauses are in between and, in most cases, they are intermediate realizations. Their non-detachability from constructions in which they appear seems to imply that they must be embedded (cf. Hornstein 1990), but being half realized (i.e. intermediate realization) means that they may be either embedded to modify other components or rankshifted to lower units as IGMs. When non-finite clauses appear in constructions in their full forms (i.e. non-finite forms and participants come together), they are most likely embeddings; when they are nominalized, adjectivized or adverbialized to some degree, they tend to be compressed, and IGMs may occur.

To sum up briefly, inflectional indicators, those in English for instance, help determine which are the non-finite verbs, but more effortful observation for other parameters has to be carried out to decide the status of non-finite verbs in a number of non-inflectional languages such as modern Chinese.

3.8 Defining Non-finiteness in Terms of Function

'The traditional approach has no principled grounds for establishing which feature is responsible for finiteness ... neither tense nor agreement is a universal category, so whichever is chosen will be absent in a number of languages' (Nikolaeva 2007b: 2). The consensus in functionalism as well as in formalism today is that the finite/non-finite distinction is a property of the clause; that finiteness belongs to the grammar of inter-clausal connectivity. Thus, the finite/non-finite distinction shall be observed from the perspective of clause rather than morpheme.

Whatever language it is, there must be ways to express tense, person, subject, mood and so on, and there must be ways to express tenseless, personless, subjectless and moodless situations as well. It would be absurd to say that one language has devices to express the tensed situation but not the tenseless situation. Some devices are more prominent in some languages, but few devices are absolutely absent. Some are covert and others are overt. For example, a tensed language should have 'grammaticalised location in time' (Comrie 1985: 9), but 'temporal adverbs or adverbial phrases, auxiliaries, particles, and morphological markings' can also be devices to express the location in time (Stassen 1997: 351). Modern Chinese is a language that uses adverbials to express tense. Likewise, different languages have different ways for expressing non-finiteness.

Synchronically, some languages show salient manifestations of a number of features, and other languages do not show manifestations of those features. Diachronically, features of one language may be manifest in one period but not in all periods of its development. Just as Givón points out, 'today's micro-variation within the species/language engenders, at least potentially, tomorrow's macro-variation across species/languages' (Givón 2009: 41). Over a certain period of time, those micro-variations may gradually yield 'stark and seemingly unbridgeable gaps of macro-variation among extant species or languages' (Givón 2009: 42). The gaps are 'unbridgeable' because the linguistic changes are distinct in terms of form. They are 'seemingly unbridgeable' because some underlying principle may be used to reveal the universal features.

Thus, non-finiteness may be better defined in terms of function. 'All languages appear to have a constituent identifiable as a clause' (Chelliah & Reuse 2011: 330), and a typical clause is composed of four basic functional components (see Chapter 4). When a secondary part in a construction containing a primary finite clause keeps its status as clause but becomes embedded to modify any of these functional components, non-finiteness does not occur (see the Full Realization Principle described in Section 3.7). Non-finiteness occurs if the secondary part functions intermediately between a typical clause and a typical group (usually a nominal group). Thus, non-finiteness is a component that is intermediate between a typical clause and a typical group, functioning as a specific functional component in the typical clause. **An event/state that is moodless in interpersonal meaning, dependent in clause structure, and incomplete in ideational components tends to be non-finite (i.e. moodlessness, clause dependency and incompleteness).** We assume that the three parameters work simultaneously for modern Chinese, a typical language void of inflections; and the first two parameters work simultaneously for English, a language with typical inflection indicators. With inflection indicators, being moodless and clause dependent is sufficient for determining non-finiteness. For example, some absolute clauses in English that are complete in ideation may also be non-finite because of their moodlessness and clause dependency. An important principle is LFVP: **except for those in paratactic relation, a single clause contains only one finite verb, and the other verbs are non-finite**.

Since a non-finite clause is an expression intermediate between a clause and a group in status, it should contain fewer functional components than a typical clause, but more components (either covert or overt) than a group. A non-finite element is intermediate between a group and a word, and it usually functions either as a qualifier or an entity. When a non-finite element functions as an entity, nominalization may occur. When a non-finite element functions as a qualifier, adjectivization may occur. Adverbialization is more likely related to minor processes realized by prepositional phrases.

Now we come to a new definition of non-finiteness, which has been developed out of insightful views in the literature as well as our view from the functional perspective. The status of non-finite components has also been briefly described. The new definition and the sketchy status pave the way for further research into the phenomenon. With the focus on written language, the cryptotype nature of categorization, the cline view, the universality of metafunctions, ideational grammatical metaphor as the mechanism, and the FRP and LFVP, we are well equipped for the process-relation investigation into non-finiteness in Chapter 4.

4 Basic Process Relations as One Solution to the Controversy

As was discussed in Chapter 3, cryptotype and cline are universal properties not to be ignored in the categorization of non-finiteness. Metafunctions are also universal as linguistic categories for human languages, and are critical in observing non-finiteness. Process as an essential component of functional analysis is a basic semantic unit, and clause is a basic syntactic unit; these units are fundamental in the linguistic analysis. As to controversial constructions containing non-finiteness, the FRP and the LFVP may help reveal the underlying mechanism.

Having established the theoretical foundations in Chapter 3, we can now observe the phenomenon of non-finiteness in morphologically diverse languages such as English and Chinese. Our aim is to figure out in what contexts non-finiteness can be positioned and identified. To achieve this, we adopt the process-relation perspective to categorize constructions in English and Chinese.

4.1 The Basic Construction and Its Functional Components

As was discussed in the previous chapter, the unit of 'clause' has been found to be a universal category in human languages. Thus, the first step is to consider the functional components of a clause. In terms of function, a typical clause is composed of, at least, a participant (either covert or overt) and a process. Most often, a second participant and a circumstance are also involved, especially in written language. Note that a clause in spoken English such as 'Help!' is composed of two covert participants and a process: '(You) help (me) please'. Figure 4.1 shows the basic functional components of a typical construction in both written English and Chinese.[1]

---

[1] Note that, when more than one functional role occurs on the same level, superscripts in capital letters A, B, C and so on, are used for first-level processes, and those in lower-case letters (a, b, c) for lower-level processes. Similarly, the superscripts L, M, N and so on, are used for first-level participants, and those in lower case (l, m, n) for lower-level participants. Circumstances are distinguished by the superscripts X, Y and Z (x, y and z for lower levels) when necessary.

4.1 The Basic Construction and Its Functional Components

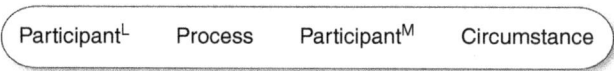

Figure 4.1 Type I: the basic construction

The basic construction is composed of a process, two participants and a circumstance. The participant may be a conscious being or an entity. The process may be realized by any verb that is used to express being, doing or sensing. The circumstance usually tells readers/listeners about time, place, manner and other situations. This is the most frequently used type of construction in English and Chinese, both in spoken and written registers, and it can be illustrated in (4.1).

(4.1)   a. You tell us about breakfast. (COCA_SPOK)
        b. 我赞成爸爸的想法 (BCC_FICTION)
           wǒ   zànchéng   bàba-de   xiǎngfǎ
           I   agree   Father-POSS   idea
           'I agree with Father's idea.'

In (4.1a), a Sayer (*you*) and a Receiver (*us*) are the participants. The verbal process (*tell*) links the participants with the Verbiage (*about breakfast*). This is a typical verbal process. As to (4.1b), a Senser (我 *I*) and a Phenomenon (爸爸的想法 *Father's idea*) are the participants, and the mental process (赞成 *agree*) links them together.

As shown in Figure 3.4, six types of process are involved in the representation of the world of abstract relations, the physical world and the world of consciousness. The typical processes in these 'worlds' are 'being', 'doing' and 'sensing' respectively. Thus, a relational process (realized by 'having identity') is used to represent the world of abstract relations; a material process (realized by 'changing' or 'creating') is used to represent the physical world; and a mental process (realized by 'thinking' or 'feeling') is used to represent the world of consciousness.

There is another process between 'being' ('having identity') and 'doing' ('changing or creating'). This process is neither about creating nor about having identity, but it is in between 'having attribute' and 'being created'. This process is called the existential process.

Similarly, there is a process between 'being' ('having identity') and 'sensing' ('feeling'). It is neither about 'having identity' nor about 'sensing', but it is in between 'symbolizing' and 'thinking'. This process is called the verbal process. And again, between 'acting', which is a material process, and 'seeing', which is a mental process, is the process of 'behaving'. This process is called the behavioural process.

Almost all verbs can be grouped under the six process types.[2] Some verbs may be on the borderline of the typical process, and no clear-cut boundaries can be drawn. This is quite natural, because categorization always follows the principle of 'family resemblance' (Wittgenstein 1953: §67). The participants and the circumstance may vary in different realizations, but six process types remain constant in both English and Chinese. Typically, a process is realized by a verbal group, a participant by a nominal group and a circumstance by an adverbial group or a prepositional phrase. This serves as a robust starting point for the observation of non-finiteness in clauses. Whether non-finiteness is involved in a construction can be predicted from the specific types of configurations. In other words, the contexts for positioning non-finiteness can be framed out of constructional configurations, as described in Sections 4.2–4.8.

4.2 The Para-relation of Processes

The typical construction with one process is very commonly used in languages. However, more than one process may be used in a single clause to indicate several possible 'doings', 'beings' and 'sensings' in relation to the participant. Here the processes are linked by paratactic relators, which include the 'and' type (e.g. *then, as well as, not only ... but also ...* in English; 并(bìng), 又(yòu), 和(hé), 与(yǔ) in Chinese), the 'or' type (e.g. *or, either ... or ...* in English; 或(huò), 又或(yòu huò), 还是(háishì), 要么(yàome) ...... 要么(yàome) ...... in Chinese) and the 'but' type (e.g. *but, rather, rather than* in English; 而(ér), 而是(érshì), 但(dàn), 但是(dànshì) in Chinese). These relators usually link components of equal grammatical status. With the paratactic relators, the clause may be composed of more than one process.[3] In this type of construction, non-finiteness will not be involved; see Figure 4.2.

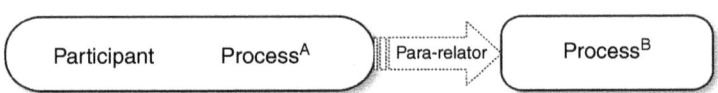

Figure 4.2 Type II: the para-relation

---

[2] Note that the six process types are the most typical types. As argued by Gwilliams and Fontaine (2015), process distinction can be unclear, and much indeterminacy can be found on the borderline of specific types. For practical purposes, we focus on the six typical types here.

[3] Note that in orthodox SFG, verbal group complexes rather than processes are used for these cases. We treat them differently here because 'complex' does not help in explain non-finiteness.

4.2 The Para-relation of Processes

The relators may help link words, groups and clauses. When clauses are linked by relators, clause complexes may be set up. However, components in a clause linked by the paratactic relators are in para-relation, and the processes linked are parallel in status. See (4.2) for examples.

(4.2) a. ... go ahead and dig in any time of day ... (NOW, 11243)
    b. This text ... may be updated or revised in the future (NOW, 31242)
    c. ... giving live birth rather than laying eggs (NOW, 131242)
    d. ...... 以提高或深入(CCL)

... yǐ	tígāo	huò	shēnrù
... to	enhance	or	deepen

      'to enhance or deepen'
    e. 他们既有独立性又有依赖性, 既有自觉性又有幼稚性 (CCL)

tāmen	jì-	yǒu	dúlìxìng	yòu-	yǒu
they	as well-CONJ	have	independence	as-CONJ	have

yīlàixìng,	jì-	yǒu	zìjuéxìng	yòu-	yǒu	yòuzhìxìng
dependence	as well-CONJ	have	consciousness	as-CONJ	have	naivety

      'They are both dependent and independent, both self-conscious and naïve'

Two material processes (*go ahead*, *dig*) are involved in (4.2a), while two other material processes (*be updated*, *be revised*) are involved in (4.2b). These processes share the same participants in each clause, and only single clauses occur, no matter how many processes are involved. The relator 'rather than' in (4.2c) links two processes. Since the components the relators link have parallel status, we shall consider them as clauses conjoined in the paratactic sense. The relator 'but', just like 'and' and 'or', may also be used to link groups (e.g. ... *not very good looks but a perfectly nice guy* ... from the NOW corpus, item 2931241).

Likewise, the two processes 提高(*enhance*) and 深入(*deepen*) in (4.2d) are linked by the typical relator 或(*or*). By contrast, (4.2e) is special in carrying four processes with the relator complex 既 ... ... 又 ... ... (*both ... and ...*). This suggests that more than one process may occur, but the participant remains the same. The processes are in para-relation and they share the same participant, so the construction should be considered as a single clause. Non-finiteness does not usually occur in this type of construction.

Again, please note that processes here and hereafter in some cases function on different levels, for example, embedding. We focus on process relations and distinguish between major, median and minor processes, and we treat projection and expansion with the process-relation view, which is quite different from orthodox SFG.

4.3 The Hypo-relation of Processes

Relators may also be realized by conjunctions (e.g. *so, if, because* ...), conjunctions with adverbs (e.g. *even if, just because* ...), prepositional phrases (e.g. *in addition, for fear that* ...), nominal groups remaining from earlier prepositional phrases (e.g. [*at*] *the moment* [*that*], [*on*] *the day* [*that*] ...), and expressions involving non-finite verbs (e.g. *supposing that, provided that* ...) (Halliday & Matthiessen 1999: 178). These we may call hypotactic relators because the components they link are in unequal grammatical status. See Figure 4.3 for this type of construction.

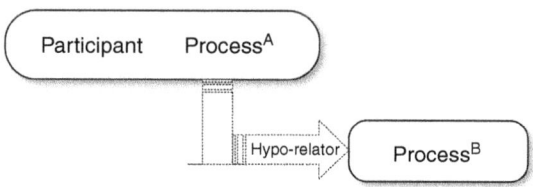

Figure 4.3 Type III: the hypo-relation

Clause complexes will occur if two or more clauses are linked by hypotactic relators and this will be discussed in Chapter 5. Here we will focus on the processes linked by hypotactic relators in a single clause. It is in this type of construction that non-finite verbal groups occur. See (4.3).

(4.3)   a. The exchanges were chosen so as to assure ... (COCA_NEWS)
       b. ... the Rabbit raised his right hand as if to indicate ... (COCA_FIC)

In the instances of (4.3), the processes are linked by hypotactic relators (*so as to, as if*). Hypotactic relators that are present to help link processes are good indicators for the process relations. A comparison of *to* in English and 去(qù) in Chinese is shown in (4.4).

(4.4)   a. I don't have money to buy her more baby food (NOW, 121244)
       b. 我常常邀请教师去察看我的上课情况 (BCC_NEWS)
         wǒ   chángcháng   yāoqǐng   jiàoshī   qù-   chákàn   wǒ-de
         I   often   invite   teacher   to-LNK   observe   I
         shàngkè   qíngkuàng
         teaching   situation
         'I often invite faculty members to observe my teaching'

The two processes in (4.4a) are linked by 'to', which may be replaced by 'in order to'. In this case, the focus is on the to-clause, that is, the secondary process. The two processes in (4.4b) are linked by 去(qù) in Chinese. Both constructions here involve non-finiteness. Most often, the secondary process is

4.3 The Hypo-relation of Processes

realized by a non-finite clause. In some cases, the relators may not appear in the clauses. See (4.5) for an example.

(4.5) a. Little Miss Muffet sat on a tuffet, eating her curds and whey (Halliday & Matthiessen 2014: 151)
b. 那两个当兵的也忍着笑使劲按他的头皮 (BCC_FICTION)
nà liǎnggè dāngbīngde yě rěn-zhe xiào shǐjìn àn tāde tóupí
that two soldiers also refrain-ASP laughter hard push his head
'The two soldiers tried not to laugh so that they could push his head hard'

In (4.5), no relators are used, but the relation between the processes is hypotactic: one is primary and the other secondary. The difference is that an inflectional form (-ing) in (4.5a) indicates the relation, while no relators are used between the two processes in (4.5b). The processes in (4.5b) cannot be in a para-relation because their order is fixed. The primary process is in its finite form while the secondary is in its non-finite form. This is in agreement with the LFVP (see Section 3.7).

When no relators are used between processes, the processes are usually verbal group complexes. '[A] hypotactic verbal group complex of the "expansion" type represented a single happening' (Halliday & Matthiessen 2014: 584). This can be put into three categories. See (4.6).

(4.6) a. phase: *he'll start to do it tomorrow*
b. conation: *he'll try to do it tomorrow*
c. modulation: *he'll help to do it tomorrow* (Halliday & Matthiessen 2014: 584)

In a verbal group complex, the primary group may be finite or non-finite, while the secondary group is always non-finite (Halliday & Matthiessen 2014: 568). The finiteness here belongs to the verbal group complex, not the whole clause. In other words, no non-finiteness occurs on the clause level in Type III construction. See (4.7) for examples.

(4.7) a. she <u>tried to be accepted</u> by people (Halliday 1994: 284)
b. I <u>keep getting bitten</u> by ants (Halliday 1994: 283)
c. 我想去问父亲 (CCL)
wǒ xiǎng qù wèn fùqīn
I want to ask ask father
'I want to ask Father'
d. 小李躺着看书 (CCL)
Xiǎo Lǐ tang-zhe kànshū
Xiao Li lie-ASP read
'Xiao Li lies down in order to read'

  e. 就会企图抹去那些不理智的部分 (CCL)
   jiù huì- qǐtú mǒqù nàxiē bùlǐzhìde bùfen
   just will-MOD try to erase those irrational part
   'will try to erase those irrational parts'

A verbal group complex may be quite complicated, but it is still a single process containing multiple elaborations. See (4.8) for more illustration.

(4.8) a. couldn't have been going to be being eaten (Halliday 1994: 197)
   b. 这种作法将来可能会产生重大的政治影响 (CCL)
    zhèzhǒng zuòfǎ jiānglái- kěnéng huì- chǎnshēng
    this action future-FUT probably will-MOD result in
    zhòngdàde zhèngzhì yǐngxiǎng
    great political impact
    'Such action probably will have great impact on politics in the future'

The verbal complex in (4.8a) contains components for expressing modality, tense and aspect, but 'eaten' is the primary and the only process. Non-finiteness has been conflated with other components. Similarly, the underlined text in (4.8b) consists of indicators of tense (将来jiānglái) and modality (可能kěnéng and 会huì), but '产生chǎnshēng' is the only process.

  Another type of verbal group complex, the projection type, 'is always, in fact, a relationship between processes – between a mental or verbal process ... and another process (of any kind)' (Halliday & Matthiessen 2014: 585). Verbal group complexes of the expansion type and the projection type are frequently used in both English and Chinese. They belong to construction Type VI, and we will discuss them in Section 4.6.

4.4 The Participant Conflated

Like the hypo-relation, Type IV is a construction that contains at least two processes in a single clause. The big difference is that the primary participant for the secondary process is always the secondary participant for the primary process. In other words, one participant is conflated. See Figure 4.4.

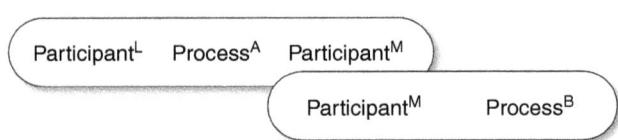

Figure 4.4 Type IV: the participant conflated

4.4 The Participant Conflated

In this type of construction, two processes are linked by a conflated participant. This participant serves as the secondary participant in the primary clause, and it is simultaneously the primary participant for the secondary clause. When two different processes share the same participant and are linked together by participant conflating, the secondary clause tends to be non-finite in both English and Chinese. See (4.9) for examples.

(4.9)   a. I humbly request **you** to peruse my study (COCA_FIC)
        b. John kept **the ball** rolling (Halliday 1994: 286)
        c. 我们已经在告诉人们应该做什么 (CCL)
           women   yǐjīng-   zài-   gàosù rénmen yīnggāi-   zuò   shénme
           we   already-PST being-PRS   tell   people should-MOD do   what
           'We have already told people what should be done.'
        d. 他还送他们去读EMBA (CCL)
           tā   hái   sòng   tāmen qù   dú   EMBA
           he   also   send   them   to   study   EMBA
           'He also sent them to study for EMBA.'

The participant 'you' in (4.9a) is a conflation of the participants for the primary process realized by 'request' and the secondary process realized by 'to peruse'. Similar conflation can be found in (4.9b). Different choices of non-finiteness in the secondary clauses suggest differences in tense potential. The secondary clauses in (4.9c) and (4.9d) are also non-finite. The reason for this is that two processes are involved, with one process primary and the other secondary, and these processes share a common participant. Since they are not in a paratactic relation, the processes are unequal in status. In this case, the primary clause is usually in its finite form and the secondary in its non-finite form.

The non-finiteness may be enhanced if more processes follow and create chains of action. This phenomenon is called 'chain pivots' by Chao (2011 [1968]: 150). See (4.10) for examples.[4]

(4.10) a. 我请你叫他找人寄这封信 (Chao 2011 [1968]: 150)
           wǒ   qǐng   nǐ   jiào   tā   zhǎo   rén   jì   zhè-fēng   xìn
           I   ask   you   let   he   find   someone   post   this-CLF   letter
        b. 东家叫掌柜的托人请个大师傅教徒弟们做菜 (Chao 2011 [1968]: 150)
           dōngjia   jiào   zhǎngguìde tuōrén   qǐng   gè   dàshīfu
           proprietor   order   manager   let someone request one   chef
           jiāo   túdì-men   zuò   cài
           teach   pupil-PL   cook   dishes

In (4.10a), three participants are conflated: '你(nǐ)' is the participant for the processes realized by '请(qǐng)' and '叫(jiào)'; '他(tā)' is the participant for both processes realized by '叫(jiào)' and '找(zhǎo)'; and '人(rén)' is the

---

[4] Note that these examples can be found in both spoken and written Chinese.

participant for both processes realized by '找(zhǎo)' and '寄(jì)'. The primary clauses in (4.10a) and (4.10b) are in their finite forms, and the other clauses are non-finite. The English translations provided by Chao himself are constructions that contain similar non-finite clauses. See (4.11).

(4.11)   a. I request you to tell him to find someone to mail this letter.
         b. The proprietor tells the manager to entrust someone to engage a chef to teach apprentices to cook. (Chao 2011 [1968]: 150)

In many cases, Type III may be used together with Type IV in a single clause, and more than two processes may appear in such constructions. For example:

(4.12)   a. 校领导抓住机遇请求他给孩子们做场报告 (CCL)
            xiào   lǐngdǎo   zhuāzhù jīyù   qǐngqiú   tā   gěi   háizi-men
            school   leader   seize   opportunity request   he   give   child-PL
            zuò   chǎng-   bàogào
            do   one-CLF   lecture
            'School leaders seized the opportunity to request him to give a lecture for the children.'
         b. 岳飞先派他儿子岳云领着一支精锐骑兵打先锋 (CCL)
            Yuè Fēi   xiān   pài   tā   érzǐ   Yuè Yún   lǐng-zhe
            Yue Fei   first   appoint   he   son   Yue Yun   lead-ASP
            yī-zhī   jīngruì   qíbīng   dǎ   xiānfēng
            one-CLF   picked   cavalry   fight in the van
            'Yue Fei first appointed his own son Yue Yun to lead a selected cavalry to fight in the van.'

In (4.12a), the hypo-relation realized by '抓住机遇' (seize the opportunity), '请求' (to request) and the conflated participant '他' go together to form a construction. Likewise, the hypo-relation realized by '领着' (lead) and '打先锋' (to fight in the van) is combined with the participant-conflated process '派' (appoint) in (4.12b). The secondary processes in the participant conflation tend to be non-finite; that is, 做 in (4.12a) and 领着 in (4.12b).

What is quite unique is the so-called existential clauses in English. They are, in fact, Type IV constructions because one participant in these clauses is always conflated. Usually two processes are involved in the existential clauses, the primary process being finite and the secondary non-finite. See the examples from Halliday and Matthiessen (2014: 309) in (4.13).

(4.13)   a. there was **an old woman** tossed up in a basket
         b. there's **someone** waiting at the door
         c. there's **a patient** to see you

4.5 Process as Primary Participant

Halliday and Matthiessen (2014) consider 'there was an old woman' in (4.13a) as a process and 'tossed up in a basket' as another process. Similar treatment applies to (4.13b) and (4.13c). The existential construction hence belongs to Type IV, in which the second participant in the primary process is the conflated participant. We will turn back to existential constructions in detail in Chapters 5 and 6.

4.5 Process as Primary Participant

The four types of construction discussed so far are concerned with process and process combinations. The focus may be on any of the basic roles in a typical clause. For example, the participant may be the focus. A participant is usually realized by a person, a thing or an entity, and this is the typical realization. One of the special realizations is that a clause functioning as a process is embedded to function as a participant. See Figure 4.5.

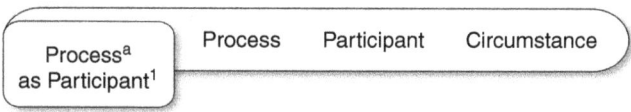

Figure 4.5 Type V: process as primary participant

In this case, the embedded clause may be either finite or non-finite, depending on the completeness of the functional roles as well as the presence of indicators (usually inflectional).

To follow the FRP (see Section 3.7), the clause may be full, intermediate or raw. 'Raw realization' refers to an embedded clause with its major functional roles (i.e. participant and process) all present. See (4.14) for examples.

(4.14) a. <u>Whoever said that</u> probably wants to take your money (NOW, 1031243)
      b. <u>我逃跑出来</u>不为别的 (BCC_FICTION)
         wǒ   táopǎo   chūlái   bù-   wéi   biéde
         I   escape   out   not-NEG   for   other things
         'That I escaped is not for anything else.'

Here in (4.14a), 'whoever said that' is a raw realization, with three basic functional roles present. With the help of 'whoever', the embedded clause keeps its original form as a clause and functions as a single participant. If 'whoever' is replaced by a specific participant like 'John', (4.14a) will be ungrammatical. The reason for this is that only one finite verb is allowed in a clause unless para-relation is involved. In other words, the LFVP is followed here. A similar phenomenon is prevalent in Chinese, but no linking devices may be used. For example, 我逃跑出来 in (4.14b) is a clause with the participant (我) and the process (逃跑) all present. There is no linking device between this process and the major process. In both cases, a clause is embedded and functions as a participant, and thus they are raw realizations. If a clause is rankshifted (compressed) into a nominal group as a full realization, then IGM will occur. See (3.5c) for full realizations (i.e. *Glass crack growth rate is associated with applied stress magnitude*). If a non-finite clause keeps its form but functions as a participant, we will have intermediate realizations. See (4.15) for examples.

(4.15)   a. <u>To see it in this state</u> must have been deeply upsetting … (NOW, 8331244)
        b. <u>少量喝酒</u>有益健康吗?(CCL)
           shǎoliàng   hējiǔ   yǒuyì   jiànkāng-ma
           a little   drink alcohol   do good   health-Q
           'Is drinking a little alcohol good for health?'

In (4.15a), the process realized by the non-finite clause (*to see it in this state*) functions as the primary participant. Similarly, 少量喝酒 as a median process functions as the primary participant in the process realized by 有益. Thus, 少量喝酒 is a non-finite clause. Three reasons for this are apparent: the adding of participant will make it unnatural, even ungrammatical; it is moodless; and it is incomplete in ideation (no primary participant is allowed). Since there is already a finite verb 有益, 喝酒 cannot be a second finite verb (see the LFVP in Chapter 3). Hence, (4.16) is not acceptable.[5]

(4.16)   *(我/你/他/张三) 少量喝酒有益健康吗?
        wǒ/nǐ/tā/Zhāng Sān shǎoliàng hējiǔ   yǒuyì   jiànkāng-ma
        I/you/he/Zhang San a little   drink alcohol do good health-Q
        *'I/You/He/Zhang San drinking a little alcohol good for health?'

Similar processes in which only the secondary participant is present occur frequently in Chinese. They read quite unnaturally if a participant is added (see 4.16). In this logic, the underlined text in (4.17) are components that are lower than typical clauses but higher than groups or prepositional phrases. They are intermediate realizations, and hence non-finite clauses.

(4.17)   a. <u>取消价格</u>就变成行政命令 (BCC_BLOG)
           qǔxiāo jiàgé   jiù   biànchéng   xíngzhèng   mìnglìng
           cancel price   just   become   administrative   order
           'Cancelling the charge becomes an administrative order.'
        b. <u>绿化江河、造福后代</u>是全体公民的义务 (BCC_NEWS)
           lǜhuà   jiāng hé   zàofú   hòudài   shì   quántǐ
           afforest   lands rivers   benefit   future generations   is   all
           gōngmín-de   yìwù
           citizen-POSS   duty
           'Making lands and rivers green and bringing benefits to future generations is a duty for all the citizens.'

---

[5] Asterisks in examples signal the ungrammaticality of the instance.

4.5 Process as Primary Participant

    c. 杀人放火都有罪 (Chao 2011 [1968]: 281)
        shārén fang huǒ dōu yǒu zuì
        kill people set fire all have guilt
        'Killing other people and setting fire to things are all guilty acts.'
    d. 老做事不休息可以把人累死 (Chao 2011 [1968]: 107)
        lǎo zuòshì bù- xiūxī kěyǐ- bǎ- rén lèisǐ
        all-time work not-NEG take rest can-MOD make-PASS man wear out
        'Doing without rests may wear one out.'
    e. 花钱做事不分你我 (BCC_SCIENCE)
        huā qián zuòshì bù- fēn nǐ wǒ
        spend money do things not-NEG differentiate you me
        'Spending money for doing things is no different for you and me.'

In (4.17), the primary process type is the relational (变成 and 是 in a. and b.) and the material (有罪, 把 ...... 累死, and 不分 in c., d. and e.), and the underlined text will be ungrammatical if participants are added to them. A difference lies in the combination of processes realized by more than one non-finite clause in (4.17b) to (4.17e). To be specific, two non-finite clauses 绿化江河 and 造福后代 in (4.17b) are used in paratactic relation. Similarly, 杀人 and 放火 in (4.17c), and 老做事 and 不休息 in (4.17d) are all non-finite clauses which are in paratactic relations. In other words, the processes realized by non-finite clauses in these instances are of equal status. (4.17e) is different from other constructions in containing two non-finite clauses in a hypotactic relation. Such hypotactic relation may be linked by '去' (meaning 'to' or 'in order to'): 花钱 去 做事. The non-finite clauses realized by this hypotactic relation function as the primary participant of the process realized by 不分.

  Non-finite clauses generally involve an 'inherent' participant, and it may be argued that the addition of a participant is possible for some clauses in English (e.g. *The president is ready to eat* and *The president is ready to eat barbecue*). More importantly, non-finite clauses in English may begin with a participant for its own (e.g. *John working so hard is something hard to believe*)[6]. Thus, the addition of a participant to the non-finite clause does not make the clause ungrammatical in English. Here the difference between *The president is ready to eat* and *The president is ready to eat barbecue* lies in the presence of the second participant 'barbecue'. In *The president is ready to eat*, the second participant is absent, and it may be filled with 'barbecue' or any other participantial component. In contrast, the basic ideational components for *John working so hard* and *John is working so hard* are the same, but it is not acceptable to say *John is working so hard is*

---

[6] The examples in this paragraph were provided by one of the anonymous reviewers who pointed out the problem in the original parameter of ideational incompleteness. I am grateful to him/her for the insightful suggestion. The third parameter has been revised accordingly.

something hard to believe. This urges us to reconsider the parameter of ideational incompleteness for determining non-finiteness in English.

To have a better understanding of the 'inherent' participant in absolute clauses that are non-finite in nature in English (Q. He & Yang 2015), we may observe several typical examples. As we can see, in *She lay for a long while, the tears falling* (BNC_FIC), *falling* cannot be replaced by *were falling*. In *All things considered, she would be better married* (BNC_FIC), *considered* cannot be replaced by *were considered*. Likewise, in *It being Ten o'clock, the debate stood adjourned* (BNC_MISC), *being* cannot be replaced by *was*. In other words, these non-finite clauses share the same ideational components with their counterpart finite clauses, but they are not interchangeable in these constructions. That is to say, incompleteness in ideation is not necessary as a parameter to determine non-finiteness in English. We assume that the major reason for this is that inflectional indicators play the decisive role in English. Therefore, only two parameters (moodlessness and clause dependency) are necessary and sufficient for determining non-finiteness in English.

Modern Chinese does not contain inflection indicators, so the three parameters (moodlessness, clause dependency and incompleteness in ideation) are all required to work simultaneously. If ideational components are added to the non-finite clauses, the expressions will be either ungrammatical or turn into embedded finite clauses. Let's consider the addition of ideational components to those in (4.17) as follows:

(4.17')   a'. 商家/市场取消价格就变成行政命令 (underlined as embedded clause)
            b'. *去年绿化江河、造福后代是全体公民的义务 (circumstance added)
            c'. *张三杀人放火都有罪 (participant added)
            d'. *昨天老做事不休息可以把人累死 (circumstance added)
            e'. 大家花钱做事不分你我 (underlined as embedded clause)

Thus, adding participants to non-finite clauses may turn them into embedded finite clauses (those underlined in (a'.) and (e'.)) or into ungrammatical expressions (c'.). The addition of circumstance usually results in ungrammaticality of the expressions ((b'.) and (d'.)). That is to say, incompleteness in ideation as one of the three parameters of the criteria is necessary for modern Chinese, which lacks inflection indicators.

4.6 Process as Secondary Participant

Not only the primary participant may be realized by a process; the secondary participant may also be realized by a process. This frequently occurs to English. See (4.18) for examples.

(4.18)   a. Some people may think <u>that a beard brings a degree of</u> ... (COCA_MAG)
          b. I assume <u>I have done something terribly wrong</u> ... (COCA_FIC)

4.6 Process as Secondary Participant

The underlined clauses in (4.18) have been discussed widely as 'subordinate clause' (Quirk et al. 1985), 'complement clause' (Huddleston & Pullum 2002) and 'projected clause' (Halliday & Matthiessen 2014). It is obvious that the underlined clauses here are the necessary components in the construction, and they cannot be reduced. The irreducibility of the clauses suggests that they should be inseparable parts of the processes realized by 'think' and 'assume'. That is to say, the underlined clauses in (4.18) function as indispensable participants, and thus the secondary process in each of the instances functions as the secondary participant. See Figure 4.6.

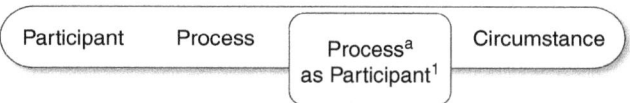

Figure 4.6 Type VI: process as secondary participant

Sometimes, there may be more than one secondary process. In other words, two or more secondary participants are realized by processes. See (4.19) for an example.

(4.19) I have heard <u>that you are a car mechanic</u> and <u>that your brother is a plumber</u>. (Quirk et al. 1985: 990)

Example (4.19) is taken as a 'complex sentence with coordinated clauses' by Quirk et al. (1985: 990). From the perspective of process relations, 'have heard' as the mental process requires two participants: Senser and Phenomenon. The Phenomenon may be composed of one or more than one fact. Here in (4.19), we have two facts (*that you are a car mechanic; that your brother is a plumber*).

Note that in behavioural processes that are to represent physiological activities realized by *cough, sigh, breathe, laugh, cry* and so on, only one participant (i.e. Behaver) is required. Thus, no other participant (realized by either a nominal or a clause) can be the secondary participant. In other words, a verb used to realize a behavioural process cannot contain a secondary participant, and it is impossible for it to be a Type VI construction.

The relation in (4.19) also applies to constructions in Chinese where processes function as secondary participants. See the underlined clauses in (4.20) for examples.

(4.20) a. 他相信<u>一个不断发展的中国将与巴西越走越近</u> (BCC_NEWS)
  tā   xiāngxìn   yí-gè   búduàn   fāzhǎnde   zhōngguó
  he   believe   one-CLF   non-stop   on-going   China
  jiāng- yǔ   bāxī   yuè   zǒu   yuè   jìn
  will-FUT with   Brazil   more   walk   more   close
  'He believes that the evolving China will walk closer and closer to Brazil.'

b. 他认为教学应为学生发展创造最近发展区 (CCL)
   tā   rènwéi jiàoxué yìng-   wéi xuéshēng fāzhǎn
   he   think   teaching should-MOD for student   develop
   chuàngzào zuìjìn   fāzhǎn   qū
   create   proximal   development zone
   'He thinks that teaching should create the zone of proximal development for students.'

c. 很多研究表明合作学习有助于学习者理解复杂的任务 (CCL)
   hěnduō yánjiū   biǎomíng hézuò   xuéxí   yǒuzhùyú
   many   research show   cooperative learning help
   xuéxízhě lǐjiě   fùzáde   rènwù
   learner   comprehend   complicated task
   'Many researches demonstrate that cooperative learning helps learners to understand complicated tasks.'

d. 我们都以为她在临时工岗位只是锻炼锻炼, 很快就会转正 (BCC_NEWS)
   women dōu yǐwéi   tā   zài línshí   gōng gǎngwèi
   we   all think   she on   temporary   work position
   zhǐshì duànliàn duànliàn, hěnkuài   jiù   huì-
   only   practice practice   very soon just will-MOD
   zhuǎnzhèng
   turn permanent
   'We all take it for granted that her temporary position is for practice only and she will get the permanent job very soon.'

The underlined clauses in (4.20) may function as individual processes, but here they act as the participants for the material process realized by 表明 (demonstrate), and participants for the mental processes realized by 相信(believe), 认为(think) and 以为(take for granted).

Though the examples in (4.20) all belong to Type VI construction, they are different in specific features. The secondary process in (4.20a) is a simple process, and the secondary process in (4.20b) contains a minor process realized by a prepositional phrase (i.e. 为学生). Example (4.20c) contains a typical nominalization (合作学习) which is an IGM, and the secondary process is realized by 有助于. Moreover, a median process is realized by a non-finite clause (理解复杂的任务), which may be linked by 去. In the process realized by 有助于, there cannot be a second process unless rankshifting or paratactic relation occurs. That explains why a median process occurs in this construction. In (4.20d), two secondary processes are in para-relation and they function as the Phenomena of the major process realized by '以为'.

4.7 Process as Circumstance

As has been shown, the basic functional roles of a clause include participant, process and circumstance. Circumstance is the functional component that helps clarify a lot of meaning elements: Time, Space, Place, Location, Manner, Cause, Degree, Matter, Accompaniment, Angle, Means and so on. The ways of representing circumstance are numerous, but here we will focus on the means by which a circumstance is expressed by a process. See Figure 4.7.

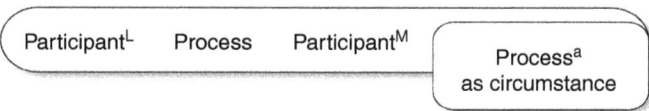

Figure 4.7 Type VII: process as circumstance

Circumstance can be realized by clauses (either finite or non-finite), phrases/groups or words. Adverbs and prepositional phrases typically function as circumstances. Non-finite clauses function as median processes, and they may be circumstances as well. In a construction where more than one process is involved, a secondary process may function as the circumstance. In this case, the secondary process may or may not be realized by a non-finite clause. See the Chinese examples in (4.21).

(4.21) a. 那姑娘特别善良，特别漂亮，<u>一双眼睛又活泼又明亮，声音像银铃一样</u> (BCC_FICTION)
nà gūniáng tèbié shànliáng, tèbié piàoliang, yī-shuāng yǎnjīng
that girl very kind very pretty one- CLF eye
yòu- huópō yòu- míngliàng, shēngyīn xiàng yínlíng
both-LNK vivid and-LNK bright voice like silver bell
yíyàng
similar
'The girl is very kind and very pretty, her eyes bright and vivid, her voice clear and sweet.'

b. 他倒愿意不睡，可是眼皮偏偏合上，<u>没有办法哟</u> (BCC_FICTION)
tā dǎo yuànyì bù- shuì, kěshì yǎnpí piānpiān
he after all want not-NEG sleep but eyelid just
héshàng, méiyǒu bànfǎ-yō
shut have no way-EXCL
'He doesn't want to sleep, but the eyelids just close, whee, he just couldn't stop that.'

The underlined text in (4.21a) is two finite clauses: 一双眼睛又活泼又明亮 and 声音像银铃一样. These two processes function as circumstances here. The underlined text in (4.21b) can be taken as a non-finite clause, because 没有办法哟 is intermediate between a clause 他没有办法哟 and a group 办法. More importantly, 没有办法哟 functions as circumstance of the primary process realized by 不睡 and 合上. Similar types of circumstance can be found in English. The position of circumstance in English is comparatively flexible: it can appear in the beginning, in the middle or at the end of a construction.

What is significant here is that a process may function as the circumstance. According to the FRP, the circumstance may be a raw realization as in (4.22a), an intermediate realization as in (4.22b), a full realization as in (4.22c), or a prepositional phrase which is a minor process as in (4.22d). Thus, the italicized clauses in (4.22) are process, median process, IGM and minor process respectively.

(4.22)   a. I bought the car *when I received my first salary*. (Quirk et al. 1985: 529)
         b. *Not liking mathematics*, he gave it up. (Quirk et al. 1985: 134)
         c. She did it without *the least hesitation*. (Quirk et al. 1985: 460)
         d. *While at Oxford*, she was active in the dramatic society. (Quirk et al. 1985: 910)

An inevitable but much-neglected topic when discussing non-finiteness is the so-called absolute clauses in English. In traditional English grammar (e.g. Quirk et al. 1985; Stump 1985), absolute constructions include free adjunct (4.23a), nominative absolute (4.23b) and augmented absolute construction (4.23c, 4.23d). See Q. He and Yang (2015) for detailed discussions on absolute clauses.

(4.23)   a. *Standing up*, she looked around the familiar room. (BNC_FIC)
         b. Racing is scheduled to start at noon Sunday, *conditions permitting*. (NOW_2521244)
         c. he's so cute, *with a twinkle in his eyes*. (COCA_FIC)
         d. Richard went ahead, *hands in pockets*. (BNC_FIC)

From the process-relation perspective, the non-finiteness in (4.23a) (*Standing up*) is a median process. In (4.23b) the non-finiteness (*conditions permitting*) may be considered as an intermediate realization functioning as circumstance. Minor process realized by prepositional phrases may also be with participants, as in *hands in pockets* in (4.23d). Sometimes, a median process may even be combined with a minor process, functioning as circumstance. See (4.24) for examples.

(4.24)   a. *With him being so bad-tempered*, I was reluctant to tell him of the car accident. (Quirk et al. 1985: 564)
         b. *Without anyone to talk to*, John felt miserable. (Quirk et al. 1985: 705)

Thus, absolute clauses in English include median process realized by non-finite clause, minor process realized by prepositional phrase and nominal

4.8 The Triple Participant

expressions. All of these function as circumstances in the constructions in which they appear.

4.8 The Triple Participant

Usually in a typical clause there are two participants and a process, with the exception of covert participants appearing in constructions like Type IV constructions (see Type I through Type VII in Sections 4.1–4.7). Apart from the types outlined here, one construction type containing three overt participants is also frequently used in both English and Chinese. See Figure 4.8.

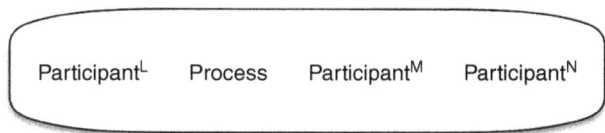

Figure 4.8 Type VIII: the triple participant in a single process

The so-called dative construction (e.g. Newman 1996; Shibatani 1999; Campbell & Tomasello 2001; Stephens 2015; Bruening 2018) is indeed a triple participant construction, because three overt participants appear in the same single process. We may find numerous examples, such as *Mary gave the visitor a glass of milk* (Quirk et al. 1985: 53) in English. It needs to be noted that some clauses look like triple participant constructions but belong to Type IV in which a participant is conflated. See (4.25) for an example.

(4.25)   Most people considered Picasso a genius. (Quirk et al. 1985: 55)

The secondary process in (4.25) is a median process realized by 'to be': *Most people considered Picasso to be a genius*. The relation between these two processes is of the conflation. By contrast, it is unacceptable to use 'to be' in *Mary gave the visitor a glass of milk*, since *Mary, the visitor* and *a glass of milk* are the participants and the construction belongs to Type VIII.

Major verbs used to realize this construction may be classified into the give-type, the throw-type and the send-type which are the most common (Levin 2008). In some languages, the dative construction may be different in form (Shibatani 1999). In English, some verbs which do not belong to the typical types mentioned here (i.e. give-, throw- and send- types) may also be used to create triple participant constructions. See (4.26) for examples.

(4.26)   a. She left Jim a card. (Quirk et al. 1985: 59)
          b. She charged me twenty dollars. (Quirk et al. 1985: 735)
          c. I paid her three pounds. (Quirk et al. 1985: 735)
          d. He got her a splendid present. (Quirk et al. 1985: 720)

The third participant may be realized by a finite clause or a non-finite clause. In other words, a process (major or median) may function as the third participant. See (4.27) for examples.

(4.27) a. They told me *that I was ill*. (Quirk et al. 1985: 1171)
　　　　b. 告诉他们<u>上了年纪该循规蹈矩</u> (BCC_FICTION)
　　　　　　gàosù tāmen shàng-le   niánjì   gāi-   xún   guī dǎo jǔ
　　　　　　tell   they   become-ASP old age should-MOD follow rule obey norm
　　　　　　'Tell them that old-aged people should follow the rules and regulations.'
　　　　c. He asked me *what time it was*. (Quirk et al. 1985: 1171)
　　　　d. 他问我<u>明天什么时候走</u> (BCC_FICTION)
　　　　　　tā   wèn   wǒ   míngtiān   shénme   shíhòu   zǒu
　　　　　　he   ask   I   tomorrow   what   time   leave
　　　　　　'He asks me what time I am going to leave.'
　　　　e. Mary showed us *what to do*. (Quirk et al. 1985: 1171)
　　　　f. 我给你看看<u>有什么</u> (BCC_FICTION)
　　　　　　wǒ   gěi   nǐ   kànkan yǒu   shénme
　　　　　　I   let   you   see   have   what
　　　　　　'I will show you what there is.'
　　　　g. I advised Mark *to see a doctor*. (Quirk et al. 1985: 1171)
　　　　h. 父亲建议我<u>去弄一根绳子</u> (BCC_FICTION)
　　　　　　fùqīn   jiànyì   wǒ   qù   nòng   yī-gēn   shéngzi
　　　　　　father advise   I   go   get   one- CLF   rope
　　　　　　'Father advised me to get a rope.'

In (4.27a) and (4.27c), two processes (*that I was ill*; *what time it was*) function as the third participant respectively. In (4.27e) and (4.27g), two median processes (*what to do*; *to see a doctor*) function as the third participant respectively. Likewise, the processes (underlined clauses) in (4.27b) and (4.27d) function as the third participant, while the median processes (underlined median clauses) in (4.27f) and (4.27h) function as the third participant. Note that (4.27h) looks very much like a construction with conflation, that is, Type IV, but the process type realized by 建议 (advise) requires the content of the process (i.e. the advice itself) rather than some causation. Thus, it is better to consider it a construction with triple participant.

Some constructions look like Type IV or Type VIII, and the adjectival phrases in these constructions are considered as verbless adverbial clauses in traditional grammar. See (4.28) for examples.

(4.28) a. They are happier *free*. (Quirk et al. 1985: 738)
　　　　b. We took a swim *naked*. (Quirk et al. 1985: 1171)
　　　　c. She ran the business *single-handed*. (Quirk et al. 1985: 1171)
　　　　d. She gave us our coffee *black*. (Quirk et al. 1985: 1171)
　　　　e. He came home *miserable*. (Quirk et al. 1985: 1171)
　　　　f. They sent him home *sober*. (Quirk et al. 1985: 1171)

4.8 The Triple Participant

From the process-relation perspective, we may say that the secondary processes in these constructions have been compressed. According to the principles proposed in Chapter 3, the constructions in (4.28) are all IGMs. For example, (4.28a) is a construction contracted from two clauses: *they are happier if / when they are free*.

The eight types of process relation help us predict non-finiteness in clauses, especially non-finiteness in Chinese clauses, which contain no morphological manifestations. In other words, these types may serve as one solution to the controversy in non-finiteness. The problem is that, in most cases, texts contain many clause combinations. In Chapter 5, therefore, we are going to consider non-finiteness in the context of clause combining.

5 Non-finiteness as the Bridge for Process Compression

Traditionally, clause combining or clause linkage, is analysed on the syntactic, semantic and prosodic levels using three parameters: 'the relation of dependency holding between the clause and the attachment site', 'properties of the attachment site' and 'properties of the attached clause'(Gast & Diessel 2012: 4). Thus, a clause is defined as 'a unit minimally consisting of a predication' (Gast & Diessel 2012: 3–4). See (5.1) from Gast and Diessel (2012: 4).

(5.1)   a. [*Bill ordered a beer*] and [*Mary ordered a wine*]. (coordination)
           b. [*I don't think* [*that he will ever change*]]. (finite complement clause)
           c. [*I asked him* [*to slow down*]]. (control infinitive)
           d. [*He risked* [*getting caught*]]. (gerund)
           e. [[*He went to the library*] [*to lend a book*]]. (adverbial infinitive)
           f. [*Walking home*], [*he met his brother-in-law*]. (adjunct participle)
           g. [*With John driving*], [*there was no need to worry*]. (absolute participle)
           h. [*Bill approached the man* [*who was drinking a Martini*]]. (relative clause)

The words in square brackets in (5.1) are all considered as clauses, and the combinations are called complex sentences in many popular grammars.

What is widely accepted today is that clause combining (Haiman & Thompson 1988a), or clause linkage (Lehmann 1988), should be understood as mechanisms of connecting clauses rather than sentences. 'Sentence' is understood as a graphological unit, while 'clause' is a grammatical unit (Halliday 1985). In this sense, it is misleading to consider all constructions in (5.1) to be complex sentences. Clause linkage strategies are usually discussed under dependency (e.g. Lyons 1968; Van Valin & LaPolla 1997), clausal embedding (e.g. Haspelmath 1995) and semantic relationship (e.g. Popjes & Popjes 1986). Different strategies are used in the constructions in (5.1).

Non-finiteness has always been a key strategy in clause linkage, but it has been much ignored and treated as a subsidiary within the literature. In order to understand the function of non-finiteness within the context of clause combining so as to answer the third research question (How does non-finiteness function for inter-clausal connectivity?), we will, in this chapter, observe how non-finiteness plays its role in clause combining from the process-relation perspective. First, a brief review of clause combining is necessary to give the background.

5.1 Clause Combining

According to Quirk et al. (1985: 1437), the relationships between parts of an English text are achieved by four types of connective features which 'not merely interact intimately but operate simultaneously', as follows: (a) pragmatic and semantic implication; (b) lexical linkage; (c) prosody and punctuation; (d) grammatical devices. Among the grammatical devices, coordination, subordination and embedding are crucial in connecting clauses. They are all fundamental to the textual organization of a written text or a spoken discourse, and should be properly addressed together with the issue of non-finiteness. Since conjunctions usually signal such clause relations, a snapshot of typical conjunctions in English and Chinese as typical examples is necessary.

5.1.1 Conjunctions in English and Chinese

According to Gleitman (1965: 260), a conjunction is traditionally defined as 'A connective or connecting particle with the special function of joining together sentences, clauses, phrases or words.' Conjunctions in English, and perhaps in many other languages if there are conjunctions at all, are usually put into two categories: coordinating conjunctions, which mark equal status between grammatical units, and subordinating conjunctions, which mark unequal status between grammatical units. See Huddleston and Pullum (2002: 22) for more explanation.

In Quirk et al. (1985: 46), we can see a detailed description of the two types of conjunctions in English, which states, 'the most common coordinating conjunctions in English are *and, or* and *but*', being used to conjoin clauses, phrases and words. Subordinating conjunctions are 'the most important formal device of subordination' (Quirk et al. 1985: 998), and may be classified as simple subordinators (e.g. *after, as, before, if, lest* ...), complex subordinators (e.g. *but that, assuming that, as long as, in case* ...) or marginal subordinators. Marginal subordinators can be further put into four types: a habitual combination of a subordinator with a preceding or following adverb (e.g. *even if, if only*), a noun phrase functioning as temporal adverbial (e.g. *the moment that, every time that*), prepositional phrases (e.g. *for the fact that*), and participle forms (e.g. *supposing that, provided that*) (Quirk et al. 1985: 1002).

What is significant to the present study is that subordinators in English are frequently used together with non-finite clauses. To-infinitive clauses are usually introduced by *as if, as though, for, in order, so as, whether* and so on.

Clauses with an -ed participle and verbless clauses are introduced by *although*, *as if*, *as soon as*, *unless*, *once*, *even if* and so on. Clauses with an -ing participle may be introduced by any of the subordinators. Bare infinitive clauses are usually introduced by *rather than*, *sooner than* and so on. See Quirk et al. (1985: 1003–6) for more examples.

Of the coordinating and subordinating conjunctions, some represent clear cases (e.g. *and* for coordinating and *if* for subordinating), and some represent an intermediate category (e.g. *for* may be either coordinating or subordinating) (Quirk et al. 1985: 90). Therefore, a coordination–subordination gradient may be drawn following the six criteria (a) through (f) (Quirk et al. 1985: 927):

(a) It is immobile in front of its clause.
(b) A clause beginning with it is sequentially fixed in relation to the previous clause, and hence cannot be moved to a position in front of that clause.
(c) It does not allow a conjunction to precede it.
(d) It links not only clauses, but predicates and other clause constituents.
(e) It can link subordinate clauses.
(f) It can link more than two clauses, and when it does so all but the final instance of the linking item can be omitted.

The coordination–conjunct–subordination gradients represented by coordinators (e.g. *and, or, but*), conjuncts (e.g. *yes, so, nor, however, therefore*) and subordinators (e.g. *for, so that, if, because*) show clearly the conjoining potentials of conjunctions in English (Quirk et al. 1985: 927). Conjunctions in some languages may not be prominent. As Mithun observes, the coordinating conjunction is absent in many languages, and if conjunctions are used, they may only be present in the written forms, and not the spoken forms (Mithun 1988).

In the case of Chinese, clause linkage may be achieved without conjunctions in both spoken and written contexts. The coordinating relationship in spoken Chinese may be signalled by the rhythm, the events and states to be described and so on. By contrast, the coordinating relationship in written Chinese may be signalled by alignment and punctuation. In both cases, no conjunction may be required.

That does not mean that conjunctions are absent in Chinese. On the one hand, almost all kinds of conjunctions can be found in both ancient and modern Chinese. On the other hand, modern Chinese has been much influenced by English through translations and other media of communication (Pang & Wang 2020), and conjunctions are used more prevalently, particularly in formal registers such as academic texts, news reports and so on.

Prepositions and conjunctions in Chinese were grouped together as joining words by L. Wang (1985 [1943]: 181). Auxiliary words were added to this categorization by S. Lü (1990 [1982]: 18). Typical auxiliary words include 之(zhī), 的(de), 所(suǒ), 者(zhě); 与(yǔ), 于(yú), 以(yǐ), 为(wéi), 把(bǎ), 被(bèi), 给(gěi),

和(hé), 而(ér), 则(zé), 因(yīn) 故(gù) and 虽(suī). Five properties of conjunctions have been identified: functioning as a joining force between words, phrases or clauses; unable to appear individually; unable to be a sentential component; not to be the head; not to be modified by others (Q. Liu 2014).

Liu, in his PhD thesis, compared five of the most influential books on conjunctions and extracted the common conjunctions; sixty-nine typical conjunctions were frequently used in these works (Q. Liu 2014: 35). Liu does not provide a categorization of the sixty-nine conjunctions, but we may here put them into four types as follows:

- **the 'and' type:** 并(bìng), 并且(bìngqiě), 不但(búdàn), 不光(bùguāng), 不仅(bùjǐn), 不论(búlùn), 此外(cǐwài), 从而(cóngér), 而且(érqiě), 跟(gēn), 和(hé), 与(yǔ), 及(jí), 以及(yǐjí)
- **the 'but' type:** 但(dàn), 但是(dànshì), 而(ér), 何况(hékuàng), 进而(jìnér), 就是(jiùshì), 可(kě), 可是(kěshì), 况且(kuàngqiě), 哪怕(nǎpà), 乃至(nǎizhì), 且(qiě), 然而(ránér), 任(rèn), 甚至(shènzhì), 虽(suī), 虽然(suīrán), 要(yào), 以(yǐ), 以免(yǐmiǎn), 以致(yǐzhì), 因而(yīnér), 于是(yúshì), 与其(yǔqí), 只是(zhǐshì)
- **the 'or' type:** 否则(fǒuzé), 还是(háishì), 或(huò), 或者(huòzhě), 不然(bùrán), 要么(yàome), 要不(yàobù), 要不然(yàoburán)
- **the circumstance type:** 除非(chúfēi), 即使(jíshǐ), 即便(jíbiàn), 既(jì), 既然(jìrán), 假使(jiǎshǐ), 因为(yīnwéi), 由于(yóuyú), 如(rú), 如果(rúguǒ), 虽说(suīshuō), 倘若(tǎngruò), 万一(wànyī), 无论(wúlùn), 要是(yàoshi), 因(yīn), 只要(zhǐyào), 只有(zhǐyǒu), 可见(kějiàn), 总之(zǒngzhī), 因此(yīncǐ), 所以(suǒyǐ).

Subordinating relationships are usually marked by conjunctions in most languages, except for situations where non-finiteness comes into play. Thus, an important question relevant to the present study is how clauses are conjoined when no conjunctions are used. For languages with inflectional indicators (e.g. English), the inflections (e.g. *-ing*, *-ed*, *to-* in English) may indicate the conjoining relationship between clauses when no conjunctions are used. For languages which lack inflectional forms (e.g. Chinese), non-finiteness has to be present as a useful strategy to perform the function of conjunctions. The difficulty is that non-finiteness in modern Chinese is not salient. '[L]inguistic items achieve categoriality through use in discourse' (Laury & Thompson 2008: ix), and they may also lose some overt features through use. Many overt features of non-finiteness in ancient Chinese and Chinese dialects are not found in modern Chinese (see Section 5.1.3).

5.1.2 *Reconsidering Coordination, Subordination and Embedding*

Coordination, subordination and embedding are traditional types of clause combining (Haiman & Thompson 1988b) or clause linkage (Lehmann 1988), and these relations are now widely understood as connecting clauses rather than sentences. As well-established grammatical terms, they are used in a variety of senses depending on the distinct theoretical contexts (Fabricius-Hansen & Ramm 2008).

'Coordination' refers to constructions in which 'two or more units of the same type are combined into a larger unit and still have the same semantic relation with other surrounding elements' (Haspelmath 2004: 34). It is 'a symmetric relation in the formal sense: if A is coordinated to B, then B is also coordinated to A' (Fabricius-Hansen & Ramm 2008: 6). In subordination, the constituent units 'form a hierarchy, the subordinate unit being a constituent of the superordinate unit' (Quirk et al. 1985: 918).

'[T]he nature of clause combining within a prosodic sentence has always been a central concern of traditional syntax' (Haiman & Thompson 1988b: ix). If no syntactic or morphological requirements are imposed, the clause linkage is more often put into hypotaxis, parataxis and embedding. Parataxis is the coordination of clauses and 'may be syndetic or asyndetic', hypotaxis is the subordination of clauses, and embedding is 'the dependency of a subordinate syntagma' (Lehmann 1988: 182).

Clause relations in SFG are described with systems of clause complexing. A recent one can be seen in Figure 5.1.

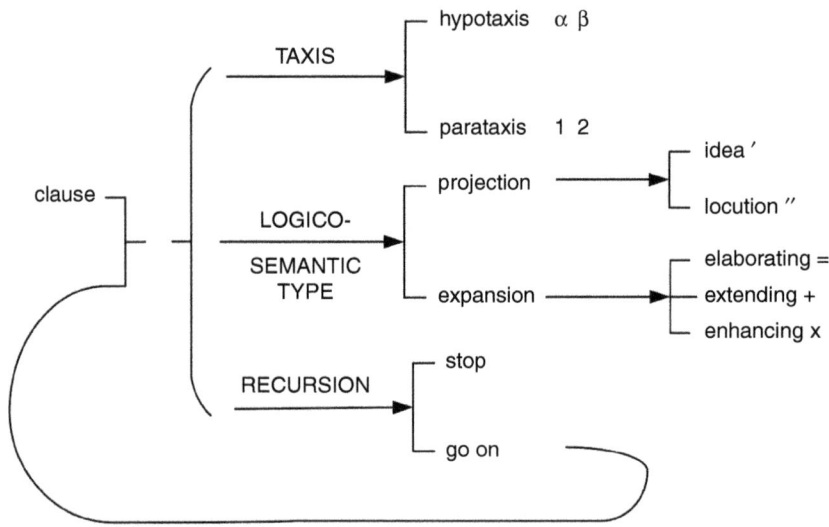

Figure 5.1 The systems of clause complexing (Halliday & Matthiessen 2014: 438)

5.1 Clause Combining

According to SFG, clause relations include hypotaxis and parataxis in terms of taxis. The logico-semantic relation of clause combining is put into two categories: expansion and projection. The expansion type includes elaborating, by which one clause expands another by elaborating on it or some portion of it; extending, by which one clause expands another by extending beyond it; and enhancing, by which one clause expands another by embellishing around it. The projection type includes two categories: locution, by which one clause is projected through another as a construction of wording; and idea, by which one clause is projected through another as a construction of meaning. See Table 5.1 for the categories with examples.

As shown in Table 5.1, the categories in SFG are different from traditional classifications of coordination and subordination in many ways. The SFG categories are meaning-based. For example, embedding in SFG is meaning-based, and classified into two types according to function: Post-modifier and Head. In other words, a clause or a phrase may be embedded to function as either Post-modifier or Head in English. See Table 5.2.

Table 5.1 *Basic types of clause complex (Halliday & Matthiessen 2014: 447)*

		(i) Paratactic	(ii) Hypotactic
(1) expansion	(a) elaboration	1 John didn't wait; =2 he ran away. 'apposition' (701 occurrences (52.5%))	α John ran away, =β which surprised everyone. 'non-defining relative' (633 occurrences (47.5%))
	(b) extension	1 John ran away, +2 and Fred stayed behind. 'coordination' (1,368 occurrences (94.2%))	α John ran away, +β whereas Fred stayed behind. (84 occurrences (5.8%))
	(c) enhancement	1 John was scared, ×2 so he ran away. (855 occurrences (32.3%))	α John ran away, ×β he was scared. 'adverbial clause' (1,799 occurrences (67.8%))
(2) projection	(a) locution	1 John said: "2 'I am running away' 'direct speech' (368 occurrences (46.2%))	α John said 'β he was running away.' 'indirect speech' (429 occurrences (53.8%))
	(b) idea	1 John thought to himself: '2 'I'll run away' (15 occurrences (2.5%))	α John thought 'β he would run away.' (580 occurrences (97.5%))

Note: The occurrences and percentages are based on results in a corpus composed of a sample of 6,832 clause nexuses in spoken and written texts from a fairly wide range of registers.

Table 5.2 *Types of embedding (Halliday & Matthiessen 2014: 492)*

Function	Class	In nominal group	In adverbial group
Postmodifier	clause: finite	the house [that Jack built]	sooner [than we had expected]
	clause: non-finite	the house [being built by Jack]	sooner [than expected]
	phrase	the house [by the bridge]	sooner [than the rest of us]
Head	clause: finite	[what Jack built]	–
	clause: non-finite	[for Jack to build a house]	–
	phrase	[by the bridge]	–

A number of papers in the volume edited by Haiman and Thompson (1988a) suggest that grammatical 'coordination and subordination arise as universal discourse structures' and they 'become conventionalized, primarily in written registers' (Haiman & Thompson 1988b: x). '[T]he distinction between subordination and coordination is not clear-cut, and takes into account the formal, semantic and pragmatic diversity of such complex sentence types' (Vajda 2008: vii). Opinions, however, vary 'as to where exactly one should draw the borderline between coordination (parataxis) and subordination (hypotaxis)' (Fabricius-Hansen & Ramm 2008: 7).

An illuminating approach is to consider the speech function of the clauses. According to Verstraete (2007: 107), the clause complex is a coordination if the secondary clause 'has a speech functional value of its own'. For example, (5.2b) allows a question for the secondary clause, so (5.2a) is a coordination. By contrast, the secondary clause in (5.3b) does not allow a question, so it is a subordination.

(5.2)   a. John offered Mary the money, but she refused it.
          b. John offered Mary the money, but didn't she refuse it?

(5.3)   a. Mary refused the money when John offered it to her.
          b. *Mary refused the money when didn't John offer it to her.

According to the 'Continuum Problem', raised by a number of linguists, even if subordinate clause types (i.e. embedded vs. non-embedded clauses) are distinguished from one another, these clause types 'will not be internally consistent as far as their morphosyntactic structure is concerned', and the distinction cannot 'account for all the clause linkage types found across the world's languages' (Cristofaro 2003: 18). Thus, the clause linkage continua proposed by Lehmann (1988) is much more persuasive for the investigation of clause relations. See Figure 5.2.

5.1 Clause Combining

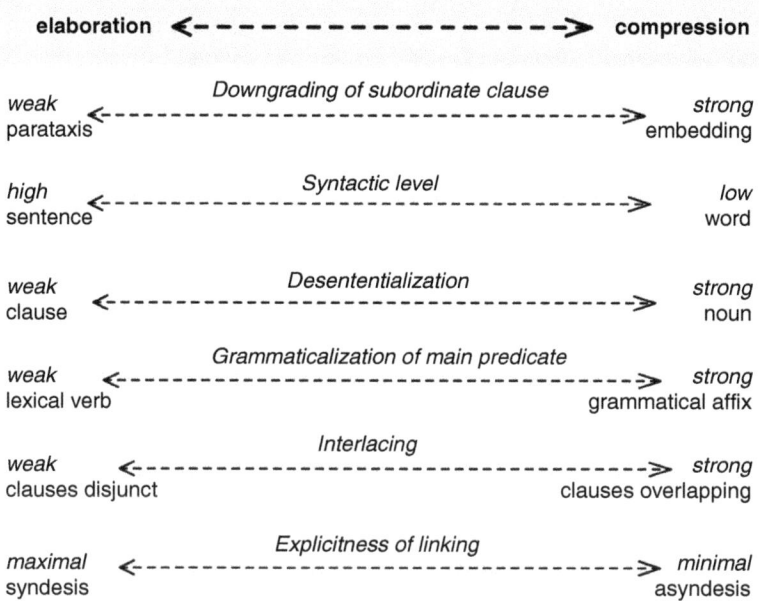

Figure 5.2 Parallelism of clause linkage continua (Lehmann 1988: 217)

As argued by Lehmann, the six parameters (downgrading of subordinate clause, syntactic level, desententialization, grammaticalization of main predicate, interlacing and explicitness of linking) of clause linkage hang together between the poles of elaboration and compression. Thus, the general tendency includes either elaboration with components (usually clauses) or compression of components (Lehmann 1988: 218). The continua are quite helpful in understanding clause relations.

Another issue is the relationship between subordination and embedding. As pointed out by Matthiessen and Thompson, '[T]here is no advantage to postulating a grammatical category of "subordinate" clause; rather the grammar of English at least, and perhaps of other languages as well, suggests that a distinction between what we have been calling "hypotaxis" and "embedding" is crucial' (Matthiessen & Thompson 1988: 317).

As these different approaches show, the widely used terms like coordination, subordination and embedding have not yet been well defined. More importantly, in the relevant discussions, non-finiteness (non-finite clauses, in particular) has not been much discussed. A general view is that 'The absence of a finite verb is itself an indicator of subordination, since nonfinite and verbless clauses are necessarily subordinate' (Quirk et al. 1985: 1006). For example:

(5.4)   *Denying any interest in politics,* she claimed that she wished to continue in forensic medicine. (Quirk et al. 1985: 1006)

Thus, one argument here is that non-finiteness as a basic category of clause conjoining can be a great help in understanding clause combining. As discussed in Section 3.7, embedding does not involve full realizations. Thus, the types of clause relation shown in Table 5.2 vary in realizations: raw, intermediate and full. The raw realizations (e.g. clause: finite) will be typical embedding when functioning as part of a construction. The intermediate realizations (e.g. clause: non-finite) are in the middle, and have to be attached to a construction.

5.1.3   Non-finite Clauses as a Basic Category of Clause Combining

If we consider clause linkage from the process-relation perspective, we will see that non-finite clauses usually function either as participant or circumstance in constructions. In other words, the conjoining of two clauses does not guarantee a construction the status of being coordinated. This is one side of the phenomenon. See (5.5) for examples.

(5.5)   a. The best thing would be *for you to tell everybody.* (Quirk et al. 1985: 993)
        b. Rather than *you do the job*, I'd prefer to finish it myself. (Quirk et al. 1985: 993)
        c. *Her aunt having left the room*, I asked Ann for some personal help. (Quirk et al. 1985: 993)

In (5.5), each of the constructions contains more than one clause, and the italicized are considered as subordinations in traditional grammar. From the process-relation perspective, they should not be regarded as subordinated clauses, but as raw realization (i.e. embedding) or full realization (i.e. rankshifting). If a clause is compressed, it is a rankshifting; if not, an embedding. Here, in (5.5), we have embeddings. The processes in (5.5a) and (5.5c) include a to-clause and an -ing clause, which are median processes. The median process *for you to tell everybody* functions as the participant (e.g. Identifier in the relational process realized by *be*) in (5.5a), and the median process *Her aunt having left the room* functions as the circumstance (e.g. in the material process realized by *ask*) in (5.5c).

The clause *you do the job* without *rather than* in (5.5b) may be considered as a major process. If we take it as a major process and reorganize the construction into (5.6), we will have a coordination, but the meaning is quite different.

(5.6)   ? *You do the job,* but I'd prefer to finish it myself.

In (5.6), we have a coordinated construction, but 'it' in the second clause does not necessarily refer back to 'the job'. The construction (5.6) is grammatically correct, but logically wrong. By contrast, in (5.5b) 'it' refers to 'the job', and the clause *Rather than you do the job* functions as the circumstance of Concession in the process realized by *prefer to finish*. Since no components are compressed in (5.5b), it is a raw realization (i.e. an embedding).

On the other hand, non-finite clauses usually do not contain conjunctions, but they themselves are able to form constructions which are traditionally called subordinations. Viewed from the process-relation perspective, non-finite clauses cannot be subordinated. They function as participant or circumstance in the constructions. (5.5a) is a typical example of the non-finite clause functioning as the participant. See more examples in (5.7).

(5.7)   a. *Leaving the room*, he tripped over the mat. (Quirk et al. 1985: 993)
        b. *With the audience turning restive*, the chairman curtailed his long introduction. (Quirk et al. 1985: 993)
        c. *Covered with confusion*, they apologized abjectly. (Quirk et al. 1985: 993)
        d. *The discussion completed*, the chairman adjourned the meeting for half an hour. (Quirk et al. 1985: 993)

The examples in (5.7) are the typical types of non-finite clauses. In our view, the non-finite clauses in (5.7) are neither coordinating nor subordinating, because they simply function as circumstances. As discussed in Section 4.7, circumstance is the functional component which helps clarify a lot of meaning elements: Time, Space, Place, Location, Manner, Cause, Degree, Matter, Accompaniment, Angle, Means and so on. The non-finite clause in (5.7a) is a circumstance of Time, meaning 'at the time of leaving the room'; those in (5.7b), (5.7c) and (5.7d) are all circumstances of Cause. These non-finite clauses can even be replaced with finite clauses together with 'because': for example, '*Because the audience turned restive,* the chairman curtailed his long introduction' for (5.7b). Adding conjunctions to the non-finite clauses does not help establish the status of such constructions as subordinations either. On the contrary, adding conjunctions foregrounds the function of non-finite constructions as circumstances. (5.7b) is a typical example of this, for the adding of 'with' foregrounds the function of the non-finite clause, being a circumstance of Cause. See (5.8) for more examples.

(5.8)   a. *With Mary being away*, John felt miserable. (Quirk et al. 1985: 705)
        b. *With no one to talk to*, John felt miserable. (Quirk et al. 1985: 705)
        c. *With Mary away*, John felt miserable. (Quirk et al. 1985: 705)
        d. *Without anyone to talk to*, John felt miserable. (Quirk et al. 1985: 705)

The key point here is that non-finite clauses, when used to combine clauses, are most likely to function as circumstances which are not obligatory in representing the core meanings of clauses. This applies to non-finite clauses introduced by other conjunctions. See (5.9).

(5.9) a. He's been getting bad headaches *since having been in the army*. (Quirk et al. 1985: 539)
b. He's been getting bad headaches *since joining the army*. (Quirk et al. 1985: 539)
c. He's been getting bad headaches *since being in the army*. (Quirk et al. 1985: 539)

When embedded to other components, non-finite clauses are usually considered as either non-restrictive post-modification (5.10) or appositive post-modification (5.11), according to Quirk et al. (1985: 1270–1).

(5.10) a. The apple tree, *swaying gently in the breeze*, was a reminder of old times.
b. The substance, *discovered almost by accident*, has revolutionized medicine.
c. This scholar, *to be found daily in the British Museum*, has devoted his life to the history of science.

(5.11) a. The appeal *to give blood* received strong support.
b. This last appeal, *to come and visit him*, was never sent.

The so-called post-modifications indeed function as qualifiers in the constructions. These qualifiers help readers understand the specific features of the Heads.

Now, we can see that non-finite clauses, as median processes, function as participant, circumstance or qualifier in English. Conjunctions are necessary when clauses are combined, unless non-finite clauses are used. In other words, non-finite clauses function as median processes on the one hand, and as a conjoining force on the other hand. The second function seems to be a by-product, but it, in fact, indicates the general tendency of non-finite clauses: to be a basic category to bridge clauses.

Chinese is morphologically distinct from English, but this does not prevent non-finite clauses from being a basic category of clause combining in Chinese as well. As we have seen in previous chapters, non-finiteness is ubiquitous in Chinese, but it is realized covertly. One piece of evidence is that inflection is an essential feature of ancient Chinese, and tradition must have left traces or marks on modern Chinese. Languages are changing, and English itself has lost many of the case systems that were similar to Latin (Mallory 1989). Likewise, many researchers have found that inflections are pervasive in ancient Chinese, dialects of Chinese, ancient Tibetan, modern Tibetan and other minority languages. See Table 5.3 for a list of the related studies.

5.1 Clause Combining

Table 5.3 *Inflections in Sino-Tibetan languages*

Languages		Studies with claims on the inflectional features
Chinese	Ancient Chinese	Karlgren (1920); Zhiyi Zhang (1987); Pan (1991); Sagart (1999); Branner (2002, 2003); Baxter & Sagart (2014)
	Chinese dialects	A. Wang (1992); R. Liu (2003); R. Liu & Zhao (2007)
Tibetan	Ancient Tibetan	B. Huang (1981); Jin (1983, 1988); A. Qu (1985)
	Tibetan	Jiang (1992); Suonan (2013)
	Tibetan dialects	Basang (1990)
Minority languages	Jingpo, Zhuang	Dai (1981); X. Li (2008)
	Miao, Yao	Yunbing Li (2006)

The inflections in ancient Chinese, and dialects of Chinese, ancient Tibetan, modern Tibetan and other minority languages (see Table 5.3) indicate that it is quite reasonable to assume there is still covert non-finiteness in modern Chinese, even though overt features have been lost in the development of Chinese. Being covert suggests that the distinction of finite and non-finite in modern Chinese should not be based on morphological features.

Another piece of evidence is that the most widely debated constructions in Chinese are identified by a good number of Chinese linguists as constructions containing non-finite clauses (see Table 2.1). We may take a quick look at the typical examples in (5.12).

(5.12) a. 吸烟危害他的身体健康 (Jinglian Li & Liu 2005: 23)
xī yān wēihài tāde shēntǐ jiànkāng
smoke cigarette harm his body health
'Smoking harms his health.'
b. 下雨了, 刮风了 (Chao 2011 [1968]: 127)
xiàyǔ-le, guāfēng-le
rain-ASP wind blow-ASP
'It is raining. It blows wind.'
c. 我没想到他忘了 (Chao 2011 [1968]: 128)
wǒ méi- xiǎngdào tā wang-le
I not-NEG think he forget-ASP
'I don't believe that he forgot it.'
d. 领导安排他在井上工作 (BCC_NEWS)
lǐngdǎo ānpái tā zàijǐngshàng gōngzuò
boss assign he above mine work
'The boss assigned him to work outside the mine.'
e. 我去书店买了一份报纸 (BCC_NEWS)
wǒ qù shūdiàn mǎi-le yī-fèn bàozhǐ
I go bookstore buy-ASP one-CLF newspaper
'I have been to the bookstore to buy a newspaper.'

The examples in (5.12) are controversial in the literature. Example (5.12a) is a simple clause, but it is also reasonable to consider it as a clause with an embedding that is a non-finite clause (i.e. 吸烟) (Jinglian Li & Liu 2005: 23). Example (5.12b) is regarded as 'a full sentence' which is 'a complex sentence of two minor sentences' (Chao 2011 [1968]: 127; Shen 2012), but the clauses here contain verbs and aspect markers (i.e. 了) only, and they tend to be non-finite clauses. Constructions such as (5.12c) are considered as 'pregnant sentences' or 'mother-and-child sentences' (Chao 2011 [1968]: 128), but it is still possible to consider the secondary clause as one participant, that is, the process 他忘了 functions as the participant of 我没想到 (see Section 4.6). Example (5.12d) may be considered either as a causative construction (L. Wang 1957) or a major clause with a non-finite clause. In other words, 他 in (5.12d) can be the participant for both processes and this participant is conflated (see Section 4.6). Example (5.12e) may be considered as SVC (Ma 1998 [1898]; Jinxi Li 2007 [1924]) or a construction with a non-finite clause, so we have Type III, in which a hypo-relation relates the two processes. See Chapter 7 for more discussion on SVC constructions.

The existence of inflectional markers in ancient Chinese and Chinese dialects, and the prevalence of non-finite clauses in the constructions listed in (5.12), suggest that non-finite clauses in Chinese should also be considered as a basic category for clause combining, a covert category without morphological indicators.

5.2 Basic Clause Relations and Non-finiteness

As outlined in Chapter 4, eight types of construction can be identified according to the functional components (process, participant and circumstance). In these types, process is the kernel component, and a process in a clause can be rankshifted or embedded in status to function as either participant or circumstance in another process. Median processes (realized by non-finite clause) and minor processes (realized by prepositional phrase) are always rankshifted or embedded. Rankshifting involves full realizations as IGMs, whereas embedding involves raw realizations as modifications. We thus agree with Matthiessen and Thompson (1988: 317) in rejecting the category of 'subordination'.

Thus, clause relations (as far as English and Chinese are concerned) can be reduced to three basic categories: paratactic relations by means of logical connectives (*and, or, but*); circumstantial relations by means of secondary clauses with conjunctions (e.g. *because, when, where* ...) in between; and participantial relations by means of process functioning as participant or qualifier. Non-finite clauses occur in all these types of relation, but they are comparatively rare in paratactic relations.

5.2 Basic Clause Relations and Non-finiteness

5.2.1 Paratactic Relations

The so-called coordinated clauses are, in general linked by logical connectives (i.e. *and*, *or* but). Since the clauses linked by *and* and *or* are equal in status, the order of the clauses linked can be reversed without changing the meaning. The relation between the clauses in such cases is paratactic, because the order of the clauses does not affect the meaning of the clauses combined. The focus may be on either of the clauses in the combination. By contrast, the focus of the clauses linked by *but* is on the clause starting with *but*. For example:

(5.13) a. (It) needs modification training, but the dog is trainable (NOW_991242)
   b. 周口市的农业结构调整已经取得一定的成效, 但科技对农业的贡献率太低 (BCC_NEWS)
   Zhōukǒushì-de   nóngyè   jiégòu   tiáozhěng   yǐjīng-
   Zhoukou City-POSS agriculture structure adjustment already-PST
   qǔdé   yídìngdé   chéngxiào,   dàn kējì   duì   nóngyède
   achieve some   effect   but S&T   to   agricultural
   gòngxiàn   lǜ   tàidī
   contribution rate too low
   'Structural adjustment of agriculture of Zhoukou City has achieved some effects, but the contribution of science and technology to agriculture is too small.'

In (5.13a), the focus is *the dog is trainable*, and the focus in (5.13b) is 科技对农业的贡献率太低, because they are clauses starting with *but* or 但. Whichever clause is in focus, the clauses in such combinations are also equal in status. In meaning conveyance, every clause in a paratactic combination is necessary and irreducible.

In some cases, neither logical connectives nor conjunctions are used between clauses, and the pragmatic and semantic implication can only be understood by their order of presentation. See (5.14) for an example:

(5.14)   Donald Cerrone wants to fight. He wants to fight you. He wants to fight me. He wants to fight everybody. He wants to fight anybody. (NOW_14291243)

The five clauses in (5.14) are linked together by their order of presentation. A logical connective 'and' can be used between the clauses without meaning alteration. In other words, (5.14) is in a paratactic relation, but this relation is implied rather than manifested. One may argue that (5.14) consists of five individual clauses graphologically separated by full stops and is not a combination of clauses. This is reasonable, if we base our thinking on punctuation. However, the process realized by 'wants to fight' repeats in every clause and it functions as a cohesive tie, and we may base our thinking on this point and regard these clauses as a combination in paratactic relation.

This phenomenon can be frequently observed in Chinese, but commas instead of periods are more often used in Chinese. See (5.15) for an example.

(5.15)　　樱花开遍了山坡，蝴蝶在花丛中自由飞翔，手持洋伞，身着各色衣服的一群日本姑娘，像无数只蝴蝶，发出愉快而又柔和的歌唱 (BCC_NEWS)

yīnghuā　　　kāibiàn-le　　shānpō,　　húdié　　zàihuācóngzhōng
cherry blossom　bloom-ASP　mountain　butterfly　among flowers
zìyóu　　fēixiáng,　shǒuchí　　yángsǎn,　shēnzhuó　gèsè　　yīfude
freely　fly　　　　handhold　umbrella　body dress　all-colour　clothes
yì-qún　　rìběn　　gūniáng,　xiàng　　wúshù-zhī　　　　húdié,
one-CLF　Japanese　girls　　like　　countless-CLF　　butterflies
fāchū　　yúkuài　　éryòu　　róuhéde　gēchàng
produce　joyful　　and　　　mellow　singing

'Cherry blossoms bloom all over the mountain, butterflies freely fly among the flowers, and a group of Japanese girls with umbrellas in hands and colourful dresses are singing joyfully and mellowly, just like countless butterflies.'

No connectives are used in (5.15) either, and the first two clauses and the clause beginning with 一群日本姑娘 are in paratactic relation. The order of the clauses can be reversed without meaning alteration. The third clause contains a circumstantial component (i.e. 像无数只小蝴蝶), which we will discuss in next section.

What is relevant to our study here is that non-finite clauses in Chinese can sometimes be used in paratactic combinations. 下雨了 and 刮风了 in (5.12b) are intermediate between a typical clause (with participant, process and circumstance present) and a typical group. They are intermediate realizations with a median process present in each. They appear here as a paratactic combination.

5.2.2   Circumstantial Relations

If two clauses are combined and one of them functions as the circumstance, the relation will be circumstantial. In (5.16a), for example, the first clause 你死了 and the second clause 我做和尚, if reversed in order, will not be acceptable in Chinese. 你死了 may follow 我做和尚, but a connective (e.g. 要是 or 一旦 or 如果) is required to indicate the circumstance of condition (i.e. 要是你死了) (5.16b). Most often, the connective may not be present but implied. This implication lies in the order of the components. This analysis also applies to (5.16c).

(5.16)　　a.　你死了，我做和尚 (L. Wang 1984: 94)
　　　　　　nǐ　　　sǐ-le,　　wǒ　zuò　　héshang
　　　　　　you　　die-ASP　I　　become　monk
　　　　　　'You die, I will become a monk.'

5.2 Basic Clause Relations and Non-finiteness

    b. 我做和尚, 要是/一旦/如果你死了
       wǒ zuò héshang, yàoshi /yídàn /rúguǒ nǐ sǐ-le
       I become monk in case that /as soon as /if you die-ASP
       'I will become a monk in the case that / as soon as /if you die.'
    c. 老太太那里有信, 你就叫我 (L. Wang 1984: 94)
       lǎotàitài nàli yǒu xìn, nǐ jiù jiào wǒ
       old lady there have message you just summon me
       'There is some message from the old lady, you just summon me.'
    d. 你叫我, 要是老太太那里有信
       nǐ jiào wǒ, yàoshi lǎotàitài nàli yǒu xìn
       you summon me in case that old lady there have message
       'You summon me in case that there arrive some messages from the old lady.'

Examples (5.16a) and (5.16c) are considered as coordinate clauses by some linguists (e.g. L. Wang 1984: 90). Coordinate clauses are paratactic, and the order of specific clauses does not affect the equal status of them. However, the examples here will have quite different meaning or even become unacceptable if the order is reversed without any connectives. See (5.17).

(5.17)   a. * 我做和尚, 你死了
       wǒ zuò héshang, nǐ sǐ-le
       I become monk you die-ASP
       'I become a monk you die'
    b. * 你就叫我, 老太太那里有信
       nǐ jiù jiào wǒ, lǎotàitài nàli yǒu xìn
       you just summon me old lady there have message
       'You just summon me, old lady got messages there.'

The combinations in (5.17) read awkwardly, because it is difficult to infer the relation between the beginning clauses and the following clauses.

  Now we can see that the morphological indicators and logical connectives determine the flexibility of clause order. The order of non-finite clauses in Chinese constructions is usually flexible if logical connectives or morphological indicators are present. Since there are usually no morphological indicators in Chinese, the order of non-finite clauses in constructions cannot be changed unless logical connectives are used. In other words, logical connectives are useful for determining whether the order of clauses can be reversed.

  If it can be deleted without altering the basic form and meaning of the major clause, a non-finite clause functions as the circumstantial component. In terms of process relations, the deletion of the median process does not change the basic function of the major process, and then the median process is used as the circumstance. See (5.18).

(5.18) 无论胜还是负，我都会向小林名人学到很多东西 (BCC_NEWS)
wúlùn   sheng   háishì   fù,   wǒ   dōu   huì-
whether win   or   lose   I   definitely   will-MOD
xiàng   Xiǎolín   míngrén   xué-dào   hěnduō   dōngxī
from   Kobayashi celebrity learn-COMPL   many   things
'I will definitely have learned a lot from the celebrity Kobayashi no matter whether I win or lose the game.'

In (5.18), the median processes realized by 胜还是负 are linked to the major process realized by 学到 through the logical connectives 无论......都会....... The deletion of the circumstance (i.e. 无论胜还是负) does not change the basic meaning of the major process realized by 学到. By contrast, the median process cannot be deleted if it does not function as the circumstance. See (5.19).

(5.19) 无论是饮食还是住宿，都让人觉得舒服 (BCC_FICTION)
wúlùn   shì   yǐnshí   háishì   zhùsù,   dōu   rang   rén   juédé   shūfu
whether being   eating   or   lodging   all   make   people   feel   good
'Eating or lodging, both make people feel good.'

In (5.19), 无论是饮食还是住宿 as a median process functions as the participant for the primary process realized by 让, so it cannot be deleted. Thus, it is not a circumstance but a participant (see Section 5.2.3).

The circumstantial relation between clauses may sometimes be implied rather than signalled. See (5.20) for an example.

(5.20)   Want the Eyeopener to cover your upcoming event? Contact us on Twitter @theeyeopener (NOW_2371244)

In (5.20), the two clauses do not have formal devices to be linked together, but the implied meaning can be better understood by adding a conjunction 'if': *If you want ..., contact us ....* . Thus, this is the implied circumstantial relation. This phenomenon can be frequently observed in Chinese.

5.2.3 Participantial Relations

A process realized by a major clause or a median clause may function as participant (see Sections 4.5 and 4.6). This has been treated as embedding or subordination in the literature. As mentioned, Wang Li (L. Wang 1984: 94) treats the combinations in (5.21a) as coordinate clauses. Such constructions, in fact, can be taken as 'process functioning as the secondary participant' from the process-relation perspective (i.e. Type VI in Section 4.6). The difference is that (5.21b) sounds more like a construction in written Chinese, while (5.21a) sounds colloquial.

(5.21) a. 想什么, 只管告诉我 (L. Wang 1984: 94)
xiǎng   shénme, zhǐguǎn   gàosù   wǒ
think   what   feel free tell   me
'Whatever you think, feel free to tell me.'
b. 只管告诉我想什么
zhǐguǎn   gàosù   wǒ   xiǎng   shénme
feel free tell   me   think   what
'Feel free to tell me what you think.'

Median process functioning as participant (either primary or secondary) can be frequently observed in both Chinese and English. See (5.22).

(5.22) a. 撂在水里不好 (L. Wang 1984: 85)
liào   zài   shuǐlǐ   bù-   hǎo
put   into   water   not-NEG good
'Putting into water is not good'
b. 我怕听见哭声 (L. Wang 1984: 85)
wǒ   pà   tīngjiàn   kūshēng
I   fear   hear   cry
'I am afraid of hearing crying.'
c. *Calling in the police* was a serious mistake. (Huddleston & Pullum 2002: 65)
d. He avoided *answering*, for he was afraid of *implicating his wife*. (Huddleston & Pullum 2002: 731)

The median processes (underlined and italicized) in (5.22) are functioning as participants. We may replace these processes with 'this' and 'that', which means that the non-finite clauses are rankshifted or embedded in these constructions. For example, *answering* is a rankshifted (components have been compressed) unit, whereas *calling the police* is an embedding.

Median processes realized by non-finite clauses may function as qualifiers. See (5.10) and (5.11) for examples in English. Here we would like to take a look at the search results in three different genres for typical qualifiers in the BCC corpus (see Table 5.4).

Table 5.4 *Qualifiers realized by rankshifted median process in three different genres of the BCC corpus*

Queries	Literature	News	Science
(a) v 的	1,012,999	8,341,169	11,799,817
受 v 的	23,105	3,009	24,728
所 v 的	35,301	343,979	506,634
为 v 的	2,929	29,012	65,902
(b) v 了的	9,012	27,830	19,919
(c) 已 v 的	1,379	24,501	29,425
(d) 要 v 的	14,239	53,995	79,649

Query (a) aims to identify clauses that are rankshifted to function as qualifiers, (b) clauses rankshifted to function as qualifiers with aspect marker 了, (c) clauses rankshifted to function as qualifiers with aspect marker 已, and (d) clauses rankshifted to function as qualifiers with modal word 要.

The search results in Table 5.4 suggest that clauses rankshifted to function as qualifiers are more often used in science than in news, and literary works do not prefer such qualifiers compared with other genres.

5.3 The Metaphoric Syndrome and Non-finite Clauses as the Bridge

As we have seen, the paratactic relation at the clause level usually involves two or more processes realized by major clauses; the circumstantial relation usually involves one major process and other processes that function as the circumstance; and the participantial relation usually involves processes being used as participants or qualifiers. When a median process realized by a non-finite clause functions as the qualifier, the construction has most often been compressed both in form and meaning.

The degree of compression can be represented by the metaphoric syndrome (see Chapter 3). Non-finite clauses in English may be nominalized, adjectivized, verbalized or adverbialized. In the scale of nominalization as shown in Figure 3.5, the non-finite clause *trying hard may make it work* acts as the intermediate between the highly compressed expression *the condition for it to work is to try hard* (typically metaphorical) and the highly loose expression *if you try hard, it might work* (typically congruent). At the two ends are the noun (i.e. *precondition*), which is demetaphorized, and the clause combination, which is typical in expressing the meaning. In this sense, we may say that non-finite clauses act as the bridge for process compression. A nominalization is usually compressed out of a clause, but before becoming nominalized, non-finite expressions may be involved. In the development of terminology in various disciplines, this bridge is critical.

As shown in Figure 3.6, non-finite clauses may be intermediate between full adjectivization and raw adjectivization, and at the two ends of adjectivization, we have a demetaphorized adjective (e.g. *simultaneous*) and a combination of two clauses which are respectively congruent in expression. In this scale, the non-finite clause (e.g. *being always angry with me*) is in the middle, playing the role of a bridge for compression. This is consistent with the clause linkage continua proposed by Lehmann (1988: 217) (see Figure 5.2).

Adverbialization (Figure 3.8) may look like adjectivization in many ways. The key point is that the metaphorical should be an adverbial group and the demetaphorized an adverb. The non-finite clause in the scale of adverbialization is positioned in much the same way as that in adjectivization. A slight difference lies in the focus of function of the clauses. In *being always angry*

5.3 The Metaphoric Syndrome and Non-finite Clauses as the Bridge   141

with me the focus is on *being*, while in *you being successful* the focus is on *you being*. The non-finite clauses link the metaphorical and the congruent just like a bridge.

In the scale of verbalization (Figure 3.7), two or more clauses are conjoined at the congruent end. When a clause is embedded into another single clause as non-finiteness, we have raw verbalization which is still congruent (e.g. *putting it in a box in order to keep it longer*). The intermediate goes to the non-finite clauses (e.g. *boxing it so as to keep it longer*). The metaphorical arrives when we use a verb to signal this relation (e.g. *boxing it causes longer preservation*). Thus, the non-finite clause again acts as the bridge between the metaphorical and the congruent.

Since there are no morphological indicators for non-finiteness in Chinese, it would be inconvenient to observe the positioning of non-finite clauses in such scales as we have for the English language. As found by Guowen Huang and many other linguists (e.g. G. Huang & Zhang 2003; M. Zhang 2015), translation equivalence between Chinese and English may be sought at different levels. Thus, we may try to observe the Chinese translations of the instances at different levels according to the scales of nominalization, adjectivization, verbalization and adverbialization. This will help reveal the positioning of non-finite clauses in Chinese. Let's take Figure 3.7 as an example and translate the English into Chinese. See Figure 5.3 for the Chinese translations and the scale of verbalization.

Figure 5.3 shows that the Chinese translations of instances in Figure 3.7 read perfectly naturally. The intermediate forms involve non-finiteness: 装盒 and 以储藏.

It is true that various choices can be used as the translations, but what is significant is that the translations in Figure 5.3 do not only reflect the meanings of the original expressions in Figure 3.7, but also re-express the constructions

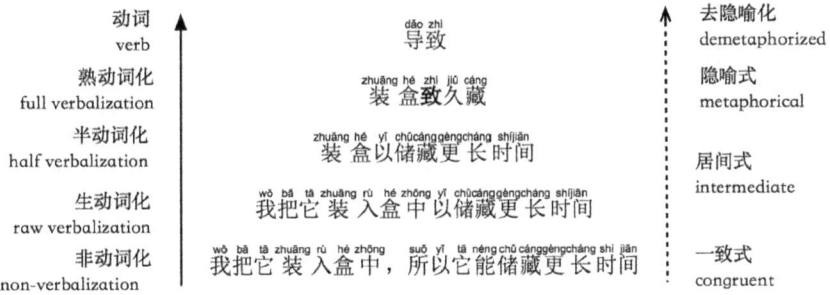

Figure 5.3 The scale of verbalization in Chinese

in Chinese, non-finiteness, in particular. In other words, non-finite clauses link the demetaphorized verb at one end and the clause combination at the other end.

Metaphor of the derivational ecosystem 'helps us to see two different facets of nominalization in English' (Lieber 2016: 9). Grammatical metaphor that focuses on the inter-relations of linguistic components also helps us to observe nominalization and many other phenomena from a brand-new perspective. In nominalization, non-finite clauses play the role of a bridge between full nominalization at one end of the scale and clause complex at the other end. Adjectivization, verbalization and adverbialization can also be conveniently observed from a similar perspective.

With the construction types depicted in Chapter 4 and the clause relations illustrated in Chapter 5, we may conclude that categories such as subordination, coordination, embedding, projection, expansion and so on are confusing in terms of clause combining, which does not help much in understanding non-finiteness. The paratactic, circumstantial and participantial relations offer a different perspective to consider clause combining, and non-finiteness may be better understood as the bridge for process compression. In Chapter 6, we will consider the controversial English constructions with non-finiteness.

6 Revisiting the Controversial English Constructions with Non-finiteness

Theoretically speaking, -ing and infinitive clauses in English can appear as any of the typical constructions. See the italicized text in (6.1) quoted from Quirk et al. (1985: 994).

(6.1) a. I expect *them to come* (Subject Verb).
       b. They wanted *us to learn economics* (Subject Verb Object).
       c. Joe supposed *the stranger to be friendly* (Subject Verb Complement).
       d. It's great *for everybody to be here* (Subject Verb Adverbial).
       e. It's best *for you to give him a call* (Subject Verb Oi Od).
       f. Paul prefers *me to make the difference clear* (Subject Verb Object Complement).
       g. He got *her to put the car in the garage* (Subject Verb Object Adverbial).

The -ed clauses can also appear in four major constructions, when not being used as modifiers. See Quirk et al. (1985: 994–5), for examples.

Moreover, some -ing and -ed forms can function both as marginal prepositions (6.2) and as conjunctions (6.3) (Quirk et al. 1985: 660–1). These should not be confused with non-finite clauses, which we focus on in (6.4).

(6.2) a. *Considering his age*, he has made excellent progress in his studies.
       b. *Given the present conditions*, I think she's done rather well.

(6.3) a. *Considering that he is rather young*, his parents have advised him not to apply.
       b. *Given that this work was produced under particularly difficult circumstance*s, the result is better than could be expected.

(6.4) a. *Considering the conditions in the office*, she thought it wise not to apply for the job.
       b. *Given the chance*, I'd do it again.

It thus seems that non-finite clauses in English can be easily identified, especially with the help of morphological indicators. The fact is that non-finite clauses such as *He stood waiting; They went hurrying; She came running* (Quirk et al. 1985: 506) are commonly used, and they are ambiguous in meaning and intermediate in construction. In this chapter, we are going to revisit the controversial constructions with non-finiteness in English according to the definition, construction types and principles proposed in Chapters 3 and 4.

6.1 Controversial Constructions with Non-finiteness in English: A Sketch

As mentioned in Section 2.7, eight types of non-finiteness are recognized in English: infinitives, free participles, gerunds (Type 1), gerunds (Type 2), reduced adverbials, reduced relatives, verb stem and with + NP (K. Brown & Miller 2016: 128–40). It is not difficult to identify non-finite clauses in clause complexes in English when conjunctions appear between them, but conjunctions 'do not usually appear in clause complexes that are composed of a finite clause and a non-finite clause' (B. Yang 2004: 238). See (2.18) through (2.20) for the controversial constructions that contain non-finiteness in English. These constructions are highly controversial in their status. For example, the construction in (2.19b), which is realized by '... *be easy to* ... ' has been heatedly discussed in generative linguistics, and an alternative explanation has been given using SFL (see G. Huang 2010). The consensus is that it is not easy to determine non-finite forms in these constructions either in meaning or in form.

Constructions in which non-finiteness plays an indispensable part may be grouped under three headings (Quirk et al. 1985): the mono-transitive, the complex transitive and the ditransitive. Mono-transitive (e.g. *They want us to help*), complex transitive (e.g. *I saw her leave the room*) and ditransitive (e.g. *I advised Mark to see a doctor*) follow a similar construction in the form: $NP_1+VP_1+NP_2+VP_2$. Similar in formal structure as they are, they are indeed different in terms of process relations and causation. The difficulty is how to identify them and what exactly the differences are.

In order to identify non-finiteness in ambiguous constructions, B. Yang (2004) proposes three criteria, one of which is related to process: the number of processes and the order of processes. We will extend it to process relations and use the construction types outlined in Chapter 3 to deal with the ambiguity. First, we shall distinguish causatives and non-causatives.

6.2 Causatives and Non-causatives

Causatives are found to be universal in world languages (Comrie 1976b; Comrie & Polinsky 1993; J. Song 2013), and 'no grammatical description can be complete without a discussion of causative constructions' (Shibatani 2001: 1). Fortunately, '[t]he grammar of causative constructions has inspired what is probably one of the most extensive literatures in modern linguistics' (Kemmer & Verhagen 1994: 115). Among the literature, works in mainstream linguistics

6.2 Causatives and Non-causatives

have provided very influential findings in this area (e.g. Comrie & Polinsky 1993; Dikken 1995; Schäfer 2008; Gilquin 2010; Tubino Blanco 2011).

As to the categories, Comrie distinguished between causatives of intransitives, causatives of transitives, and causatives of transitives with indirect object (Comrie 1976b). Yet, disputes arise in the identification of causative expressions. For example, whereas the expression *John forced/persuaded Bill to leave* is considered causative, the expression *John told Bill to leave* is not (Shibatani 2001: 3).

With the focus on the primary verbs, causatives can be categorized into four types: inactive intransitives (e.g. *show, dress, feed*); middle/ingestive verbs, including intransitive (e.g. *sit down, ascend*) and transitive (*eat, learn*); active intransitives; and transitive verbs (Shibatani 2001: 6). The hierarchy of 'inactive intransitives > active intransitives > transitives' 'reflects the degree of difficulty in bringing about a causative situation' (Shibatani 2001: 7).

Using a corpus-cognition integrated model, Gilquin looks into the causative constructions with *cause, get, have* and *make* and finds that the constructions display very different relative frequencies, among which [X cause Y $V_{to\text{-}inf}$] appears to be 'typical of scientific and technical genres' (Gilquin 2010: 277). Besides the common types of causative constructions, special and even peripheral constructions may lead to different perspectives. For example, the so-called into-causative construction, that is, 'V NP into V-ing', has 'raised intriguing questions in terms of lexical creativity as well as variation' (Kim & Davies 2019: 55). See (6.5).

(6.5)   a. Love at first sight had coerced him *into marrying a complete stranger.* (COCA_FIC)

        b. I probably pressured him *into driving around the barricades.* (COCA_FIC)

Apart from the special types like the into-causatives, one good strategy to tell causatives from non-causatives is to observe the process types (see Figure 3.4) of the major verb. As described in SFL (see Halliday & Matthiessen 2014), verbs in English can be put into six types: material, mental, relational, behavioural, verbal and existential. The typical verbs are listed in Table 6.1.

In order to check if these verbs can appear as VP_1 in $NP_1+VP_1+NP_2+VP_2$ (e.g. *I advised Mark to see a doctor*), we searched COCA for the occurrences because this corpus is evenly distributed in genre. If occurrences are found in COCA for VP_1 in $NP_1+VP_1+NP_2+VP_2$, we will use a plus to indicate it. If not, a minus. See Table 6.1.

A second point is that some $NP_1+VP_1+NP_2+VP_2$ may be causatives, and some may not. One criterion to determine if the construction is causative is to test if VP_2 is caused by NP_1. In the mono-transitive construction *They want us to help*, VP_2 (*to help*) cannot be said to be caused by NP_1 (*They*). One reason is that *us* may or may not agree to help. In the complex transitive construction

Table 6.1 *Typical verbs for the six processes in COCA and causation*

Process types	Typical verbs	VP₁+ NP₂+VP₂	As causative
Material process: doing & happening	*build, break, occur, create, make, prepare, appear, develop, burn*, etc.	+	+
Mental process: thinking & feeling	*see, hear, feel, know, think, believe, guess, imagine, like, please, want*, etc.	+	–
Relational process: being & having	*be, become, resemble, remain, represent, mean*, etc.	–	–
Behavioural process: behaving	*laugh, smile, sigh, sob, cry, breathe, cough, sneeze, look, listen*, etc.	–	–
Verbal process: saying	*say, tell, speak, talk, praise, flatter, report, ask, question, argue*, etc.	+	–
Existential process: existing	*exist, remain, arise, occur, follow, sit, stand, lie, prevail*, etc.	+	–

Note: Process types can be broken down to include more delicate types than those shown in Table 6.1, but only the six typical types are considered here, for the sake of space and representativeness.

I saw her leave the room, VP₂ (*leave the room*) cannot be said to be caused by NP₁ (*I*), because *I have done nothing but watch*. By contrast, in a construction like *The firm made the employees sign this agreement* (COCA_NEWS), VP₂ (*sign this agreement*) is caused by NP₁ (*The firm*).

Usually, the verbs used to realize material processes tend to produce causative constructions. Verbal process, mental process and existential process can also form VP₁+ NP₂+VP₂ constructions, but the verbs used to realize these processes cannot produce causatives. This echoes Shibatani's idea that *John forced Bill to leave* is causative while *John told Bill to leave* is not (Shibatani 2001: 3). The first is a typical material process and the second is a typical verbal process. The into- constructions in (6.5) are causatives because the VPs (*coerced* and *pressured*) are typical verbs used to realize material processes (Table 6.1).

6.3 COCA Distribution of Typical Verbs in (Non-)Causatives

In order to examine the specific usages of VP₁+ NP₂+VP₂ in modern English, we use two SQs (search queries) as follows to find these constructions in COCA.

6.3 COCA Distribution of Typical Verbs in (Non-)Causatives

SQ1: [nn*]|[pp*] [vv*] [nn*]|[pp*] [vvi*]
SQ2: [nn*]|[pp*] [vv*] -[v*] [nn*] [vvi*]

The first SQ helps to find any construction composed of 'any noun phrase or pronoun followed by any verb + any noun phrase or pronoun + any infinitives without *to*'. The second SQ helps to find any construction composed of 'any noun phrase or pronoun followed by any verb to be followed by any word except verbs + any noun phrase or pronoun + any infinitives without *to*'. With these SQs, 56,880 instances can be found in COCA, about 500 per million (see Table 6.2).

Table 6.2 *Query results for $NP_1 + VP_1 + NP_2 + VP_2$ in COCA*

Section	Spoken	Fiction	Magazine	Newspaper	Academic	Total
Raw freq	10,496	23,613	11,693	7,276	3,802	56,880
Per mil.	89.9	211.12	99.64	64.39	34.12	499.17

Of these instances, 1,199 constructions were excluded because they only **look** like $NP_1+VP_1+NP_2+VP_2$; for example: ... *that I need a reality check* ... (COCA_FIC).

The main verbs in the query results include *make, let, have, help, hear, feel, see* and *watch*. Table 6.3 shows the raw data for the distribution, and Table 6.4 shows the distribution per million. The occurrences of the eight words we observe show an interesting trend in different genres. See Figure 6.1.

If verbs for verbal processes (i.e. *tell, ask, say*) are taken into consideration, we see that to-infinitives usually occur as VP_2 in the construction. Here, in our observation, we exclude to-infinitives used as VP_2 for the reason that numerous purpose clauses with 'to' will be found and it will distract from the observation.

Table 6.3 *Major verbs used in the $NP_1 + VP_1 + NP_2 + VP_2$ construction in COCA*

	Spoken	Fiction	Magazine	Newspaper	Academic	Total
Make	3,234	6,022	3,683	2,447	906	16,292
Let	2,189	4,974	1,910	1,092	388	10,553
Have	143	62	85	87	80	457
Help	1,226	1,326	3,212	1,722	1,875	9,361
See	1,226	2,056	629	678	135	4,724
Hear	1,634	4,504	684	422	175	7,419
Feel	299	2,593	427	270	159	3,748
Watch	336	1,844	495	355	97	3,127
Total	10,287	23,381	11,125	7,073	3,815	55,681

Table 6.4 *Major verbs used in the $NP_1+VP_1+NP_2+VP_2$ construction in COCA (per million)*

	Spoken	Fiction	Magazine	Newspaper	Academic	Total
Make	27.70	53.85	31.38	21.65	8.13	142.71
Let	18.75	44.47	16.27	9.67	3.48	92.64
Have	1.23	0.56	0.72	0.77	0.72	4.00
Help	10.50	11.86	27.37	15.24	16.83	81.80
See	10.50	18.38	5.36	6.01	1.21	41.46
Hear	14.00	40.27	5.83	3.73	1.57	65.40
Feel	2.56	23.18	3.64	2.39	1.42	33.19
Watch	2.88	16.49	4.22	3.14	0.87	27.60
Total	88.12	209.06	94.79	62.60	34.23	488.80

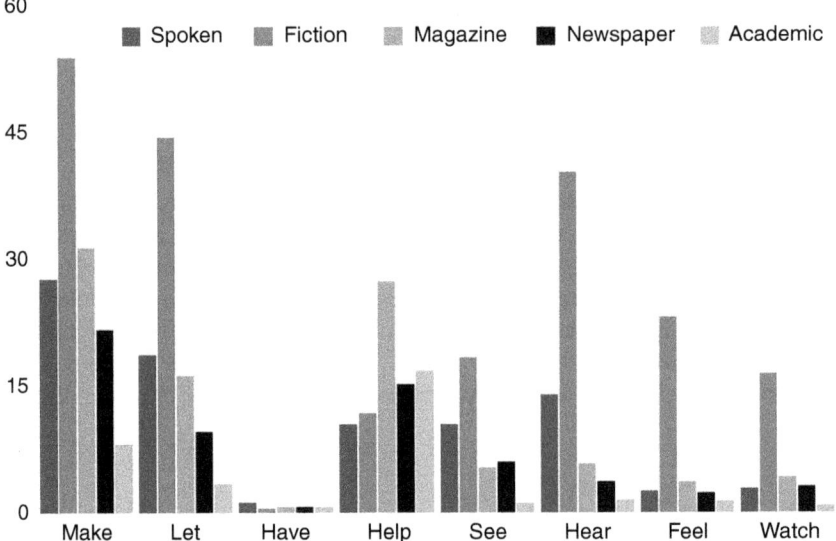

Figure 6.1 Typical verbs used as VP_1 across genres in COCA

One may argue that verbs used to realize relational processes can appear as VP_1 in the construction. See (6.6) for an example.

(6.6)   Some women **become** refugees to escape war, starvation and indignity. (COCA_MAG)

It is true that *become* in (6.6) is a relational process, but again the non-finite clause beginning with *to* is the purpose clause. (6.6), in fact, means *To escape war, starvation and indignity, some women become refugees.* This does not belong to the construction of $NP_1+VP_1+NP_2+VP_2$.

The COCA-based observation shows that VP_1 in the construction of $NP_1+VP_1+NP_2+VP_2$ are usually verbs used to realize the material processes. VP_1 can also be verbs used to realize the mental and the verbal processes, but these will not be causatives. It is debatable whether the existential process is also realized by the construction $NP_1+VP_1+NP_2+VP_2$. This will be discussed in detail in Section 6.6.

6.4 Process Relations in Typical English Constructions with Non-finiteness

It is generally believed in traditional grammar that the non-finite forms in (6.7) are all objects (Quirk et al. 1985: 1171). The difference is that the non-finite forms in (6.7a) and (6.7b) do not contain subjects while those in (6.7c) and (6.7d) do.

(6.7)   a. We've decided *to move house.* (Quirk et al. 1985: 1171)
    b. She enjoys *playing squash.* (Quirk et al. 1985: 1171)
    c. They want us *to help.* (Quirk et al. 1985: 1171)
    d. I hate the children *quarrelling.* (Quirk et al. 1985: 1171)

From the process-relation perspective, (6.7a) and (6.7b) all belong to Type III construction (Figure 4.3). Both contain more than one process, but they are in hypo-relation rather than para-relation. The hypo-relation is between the major processes (realized by *decided* and *enjoys* respectively) and the median processes (realized by *to move* and *playing*). For most such constructions, the non-finite forms will perform the conjoining power when no conjunctions are used as relators between the processes. In other words, it is not the non-finite forms that function as objects. According to Type III and the basic type (i.e. Type I), *house* and *squash* are the participants. So, we have the specific relation shown in Table 6.5.

The second process realized by the non-finite component is a median process, and it can only be secondary. The process realized by the finite component

Table 6.5 *The hypo-relation of processes with non-finiteness*

(6.7)	a.	We	've decided	to move	house
	b.	She	enjoys	playing	squash
		Participant^L	Process^A	(Hypo-relator) Median process^a	Participant^M

is always the primary. In terms of construction, this belongs to Type III. In such constructions, the hypo-relator is usually realized not by any conjunction but by the non-finiteness itself.

By contrast, the so-called mono-transitive in (6.7c) and (6.7d) are quite different from the process relation in (6.7a) and (6.7b). See Table 6.6 for the process relations.

Table 6.6 *Participant conflation in mono-transitives*

(6.7)	c. They d. I	want hate	us the children	to help quarrelling
	Participant^L	Process^A	Participant^M Participant^M	Median process^a

Here in (6.7c), *us* functions as the participants for both processes: the major process realized by *want* and the median process realized by *to help*. It is a conflation of participants. The same kind of conflation applies to (6.7d), in which the median process is realized by *quarrelling*. Both (6.7c) and (6.7d) belong to Type IV construction.

Participant conflation can also be observed in the so-called complex transitives. According to Quirk et al. (1985: 1171), constructions in (6.8) are all understood as complex transitives.

(6.8)   a. They knew him *to be a spy*. (Quirk et al. 1985: 1171)
           b. I saw her *leave the room*. (Quirk et al. 1985: 1171)
           c. I heard someone *shouting*. (Quirk et al. 1985: 1171)
           d. I got the watch *repaired*. (Quirk et al. 1985: 1171)

The first three constructions in (6.8) share the same feature with the so-called mono-transitives (see Table 6.6): the second participant being a conflation. See Table 6.7 for analysis of complex transitives.

Table 6.7 *Participant conflation in complex transitives*

(6.8)	a. They b. I	knew saw	him her	to be leave	a spy the room
	c. I Participant^L	heard Process^A	someone Participant^M Participant^M	shouting Median process^a	Participant^N

6.5 The Serial Verb Construction

The difference is that there is a third participant in (6.8a) and (6.8b) respectively. (6.8d) is again different from other constructions in containing a covert (or implied) participant. See Table 6.8.

Table 6.8 *Participant conflation and covert participant in complex transitives*

(6.8)	d. I	got	the watch	repaired	(by ...)
	Participant^L	Process^A	Participant^M		
			Participant^M	M. process^a	(Participant^N)

Now, it is apparent that some mono-transitives and complex transitives outlined in Quirk et al. (1985) may be better understood as Type IV clauses: there is always a conflation of participant, and the third participant may be implied.

Constructions in (6.9) are traditionally considered as ditransitives, because non-finite clauses in them are taken as the so-called direct objects (Quirk et al. 1985: 1171).

(6.9)   a. Mary showed us *what to do*. (Quirk et al. 1985: 1171)
        b. I advised Mark *to see a doctor*. (Quirk et al. 1985: 1171)

In terms of process relations, there is a median process in addition to the major process in each of such constructions, and the median process functions as participant. In other words, there is a third participant. Thus, they belong to the phenomenon of triple participant. See Table 6.9.

Table 6.9 *The triple participant in a process with non-finiteness*

(6.9)	a. Mary	showed	us	what to do
	b. I	advised	Mark	to see a doctor
	Participant^L	Process^A	Participant^M	Participant^N
				Median process^a

Sometimes, the third participant may be realized by a finite clause. For example, in *I ask/beg of you that you will keep this secret* and *He promised me that the debt would be repaid* (Quirk et al. 1985: 1213), the finite clause *you will keep this secret* as well as *the debt would be repaid* also function as the third participant in each of these constructions.

6.5 The Serial Verb Construction

As mentioned in Chapter 2, SVCs are 'well attested' in the major contemporary corpora of English (T. Payne 2011: 330). A significant study from the typological perspective finds that 'Verbs which form an SVC act together as a syntactic whole', and 'SVCs are often translatable as single predicates into non-serializing languages' (Aikhenvald 2006: 4). However, the 'syntactic whole' and 'the translatability' do not mean that they function in the same way as single predicates do.

SVCs in English can be grouped into two categories: those without to- and those with to- infinitives. See the examples in (6.10).

(6.10)   a. You don't just *run go play* this music ... (COCA_MAG)
          b. She promised not *to forget to arrange to collect* the key. (Huddleston & Pullum 2002: 104)
          c. She intends *to try to persuade him to help her redecorate* her flat. (Huddleston & Pullum 2002: 65).

The general impression is that SVCs are marginal in languages, and English is no exception. A corpus search using two regular expressions in COCA ([vv*] [vvi*] and [vvi*] [vv0*]) may tell us how often serial verbs are used in English. With manual exclusion of instances which contain verb + verb but are not serial verbs, we have 81,364 instances for SVCs in COCA. Note that the typical auxiliaries 'be' and 'have' are not included. See Table 6.10 for the query results of the top five serial verbs in COCA.

Table 6.10 *Query results of the top five serial verbs in COCA*

Serial verbs	Total occurrences	Example 1	Example 2	Example 3	Example 4	Example 5
help v.	53,747	help make 2,272	help keep 1,991	help prevent 1,459	help create 1,456	help build 1,165
go v.	7,497	go see 1,553	go get 1,503	go find 483	go buy 222	go take 215
let v.	5,362	let go 3,965	let stand 379	let sit 319	let slip 78	let simmer 49
come v.	2,151	come see 485	come get 356	come visit 170	come pick 103	come help 69
say v.	1,198	say thank 523	say go 61	say get 35	say let 32	say wait 27

The primary verbs in Table 6.10 mostly belong to the material process. Primary verbs can occur as any process type, with the exception of the existential process. For example:
- material process: *help make*; *go see*; *let go*
- verbal process: *claim fall*; *advise go*; *argue leave*; *say go*
- relational process: *become adapt*; *become find*; *get close*; *get hurt*
- mental process: *believe dominate*; *feel cut*; *know think*; *like see*
- behavioural process: *watch go*; *cough stop*.

6.5 The Serial Verb Construction

The process types listed in Table 6.10 show that verb combinations in series are not scarce in modern English. It is not appropriate to treat them as peripheral or unimportant in related research.

From the process-relation perspective, some serial verbs may be categorized under Type II, as shown in Section 4.2, in which a process is composed of several verbs paratactically. The verbs are equal in status, and build a combined process. Generally speaking, for the serial verb combinations that do not contain a to-infinitive, the relation may be understood as a para-relation between the verbs. Let's take (6.10a) as example for an analysis of these SVCs (Table 6.11).

Table 6.11 *Process relation in paratactic SVC*

(6.10) a.	You	don't just run go play	this music
	Participant^L	Process^{A+B+C}	Participant^M

Besides the paratactic relation, some serial verbs that contain to- infinitive are in hypo-relation. In this case, one major verb is usually followed by one or more than one to- infinitive.

In order to find SVCs with more than three verbs so that we can observe special SVCs of the hypo-relation, we use the SQ ([vv*] to [vv*] to [vv*]) in COCA for retrieving the data. The results show that there are 18,446 occurrences in total, among which 11,906 are unique. The top ten are:

going to try to get (251)
going to try to make (161)
going to want to know (83)
going to go to jail (83)
want to get to know (83)

going to try to find (74)
going to continue to work (72)
going to want to see (59)
want to try to get (58)
want to go to jail (51)

In order to see if there are instances of four or more verbs in an SVC, we used another SQ ([vv*] to [vv*] to [vv*] to [vv*]) in COCA and found 143 total occurrences, among which 139 are unique. A few examples are:

learning to read to reading to learn (3)
going to continue to try to make (2)
going to need to continue to move (2)

going to prove to show to show (1)
going to rush to try to enact (1)
going to store to store to store (1)

Some SVCs are even composed of five verbs altogether, though such constructions are seldom used. Thus, the SQ ([vv*] to [vv*] to [vv*] to [vv*] to [vv*]) returns three occurrences in COCA:

going to continue to work to try to win (1)
hoping to wait to get to jail to come (1)
need to take to continue to try to limit (1)

Specific examples can be found in different genres. For example, *So they will take the steps they need to take to continue to try to limit legalized sports gambling* in COCA_NEWS; *I was actually hoping to wait to get to jail to come out* in COCA_MAG; and *he's going to continue to work to try to win the release of hostages* in COCA_SPOK. These SVCs belong to Type III, outlined in Chapter 3. The difference is that more than one median process are involved. See Table 6.12.

Table 6.12 *Process in SVC of the hypo-relation*

(6.10)	b. She Participant^L	promised not *to forget to arrange to collect* Process^A	the key Participant^M
		Median process^a	
		Median process^b	
		Median process^c	

In some cases, one major process is used together with more than one participant, and several median processes occur in such constructions. For example, what is special to (6.10c) is that there is a hypo-relation between the major process (i.e. *intends to try to persuade*) and the median processes. Moreover, chains of participant conflation are used (i.e. *persuade him to help her redecorate her flat*). See Table 6.13.

Table 6.13 *A combination of hypo-related SVC and conflated participants*

(6.10)	c. She Participant^L	intends *to try to persuade him to help her redecorate* Process^A	her flat. Participant^M
		M. process^a	
		M. process^b	
		Conflated participant^l	
		M. process^c	
		Conflated participant^m	
		M. process^d	

As we have shown, SVC is an issue never to be ignored. The construction is also pervasive in Chinese: see Chapter 7 for details.

6.6 The Existential Construction

Existential constructions (ECs) in English were recognized to be an important linguistic phenomenon as early as the 1900s. For example, Jespersen proposed the term 'existential sentence' in 1924: 'Sentences corresponding to English

6.6 The Existential Construction

sentences with *there is* or *there are*, in which the existence of something is asserted or denied – if we want a term for them, we may call them existential sentences' (Jespersen 1924: 155).

A comprehensive work in the study of English existential sentence was carried out in 1974 as a doctoral dissertation, later published as a monograph (Milsark 2014 [1979]). In Milsark's view, existential sentences in English can be put into four categories: ontological, locational, periphrastic and verbal (which can be broken down further into inside verbal and outside verbal). In a recent study, ECs are divided into two types: those that show similarities with locatives and those which show similarities with possessives (Cruschina 2015). Because of its peculiarity, the EC has been much discussed within the generative paradigm (e.g. Hazout 2004; Šimík 2013) as well as in typological investigations (e.g. Sawyer 1973; Ziv 1982).

Quirk et al. (1985) proposed a different categorization in which the corresponding clause patterns of EC are in focus and the general rule is that the pattern of 'subject + (auxiliaries) + *be* + predication' corresponds to '*there* + (auxiliaries) + *be* + subject + predication' (Quirk et al. 1985: 1403). Thus we have the following typical ECs in English (see Quirk et al. 1985: 1404):

- There must be *something wrong*. cf. Something must be wrong. (SVC)
- Was there *anyone in the vicinity?* cf. Was anyone in the vicinity? (SVA)
- There was *no one waiting*. cf. No one was waiting. (SV)
- There are *plenty people getting promotion*. cf. Plenty of people are getting promotion. (SVO)
- There have been *two bulldozers knocking the place flat*. cf. Two bulldozers have been knocking the place flat. (SVOC)
- There is *a girl putting the kettle on*. cf. A girl is putting the kettle on. (SVOA)
- There's *something causing my friend distress*. cf. Something is causing my friend distress. (SVOO)
- There has been *a whole box stolen*. cf. A whole box has been stolen. (SVpass)
- There'll be *no shops left open*. cf. No shops will be left open. (SVpassC)

Such correspondence does not mean that the typical patterns and the ECs are the same. They are different both in meaning and in form. For example, the EC tends to describe events, so *There is a girl putting the kettle on* tells readers about one event in which a girl and a kettle are involved. By contrast, *A girl is putting the kettle on* tells readers about an activity that is happening.

Seen from the process-relation perspective, the so-called bare EC (e.g. *There arose a cult demand* [COCA_MAG]) may be realized by *be, seem, need, appear, come, go, arise*, and so on. Among such constructions, those realized by different forms of 'be' (including *has/have/had been*) are the majority. See Table 6.14.

Table 6.14 *Typical verbs used to realize existential constructions in COCA*

Verbs	be	seem	need	appear	come	go	arise
Hits	725,018	3,723	1,315	1,522	1,417	793	87

Most ECs realized by *seem*, *need* or *appear* use the expression '... to be' and may be grouped under 'be'. These constructions are used to describe states/events rather than activities. ECs realized by *come*, *go*, *arise* usually describe activities.

In terms of process relations, a large number of ECs in English follow the pattern $NP_1+VP_1+NP_2+VP_2$ in which two processes are involved. What is special is that NP_1 in these constructions is always *there*, which may be considered as 'experiential enhanced theme' in SFL (G. Huang 1996) or an 'experiential operator' (Allan 1971). VP_1 is limited to a number of verbs (Table 6.14) but VP_2 may be various. VP_1 carries the major process while VP_2 the median process. NP_2 may be any possible participant.

It is just acceptable to have a construction like '*there* VP_1+NP_2', which are referred to as bare existential clauses in traditional grammar. If there is another verb (VP_2) in the construction, the component VP_2 cannot be a finite verb. The reason for this is that two finite verbs do not occur in a single clause on the same level unless they are in paratactic relation (see the LFVP in Chapter 3). *There's a table stands in the corner* (Quirk et al. 1985: 1250), which contains two finite verbs, is acceptable in colloquial English, but the understanding of it needs 'which' in between *table* and *stand*. Moreover, ECs cannot be causative, as is shown in Table 6.1.

In order to better observe ECs, we may classify them into three types: describing a state, reporting an event or representing an activity. Bare ECs are usually used to describe states, even though nominalization occurring as NP_2 may be different. For example, *There was smoking in the corridors* may be rephrased as *They smoked in the corridors* (Quirk et al. 1985: 1067), which is an activity, but the difference between these two expressions lies in the fact that one is a state and the other is an activity. The nominalization freezes the activity and expresses it as a state.

In English, VP_2 in ECs are usually non-finite verbs. As mentioned, this is a reflection of the LFVP: only one finite verb is allowed in a single clause unless in paratactic relation. The ECs with VP_2 may be used to report an event (non-finite -ed, in particular), or to represent an activity (to- and -ing clauses in particular). Bare ECs usually describe states, but VP_2 or NP_2 may also help determine whether it is a state or an event. See (6.11).

6.6 The Existential Construction

(6.11)   a. There's a table. (Quirk et al. 1985: 1250)
         b. There is a table which stands in the corner. (Quirk et al. 1985: 1250)
         c. There's going to be an exam. (Quirk et al. 1985: 1067)

In (6.11a) and (6.11b), 'a table' as a static nominal phrase does not suggest any thing that happens. Thus it is describing a state. However, the use of 'stands' in (6.11b) suggests an activity. This means that (6.11b) tends to do more than stating. In (6.11c), 'an exam' suggests that some event happens, so it may be considered as an event rather than a state. When non-finite -ing verbs are used as VP_2 in bare existentials, the constructions also tend to report states. See (6.12).

(6.12)   a. There was shooting of prisoners. (Quirk et al. 1985: 1067)
         b. They shot the prisoners. (Quirk et al. 1985: 1067)

Similar to the 'smoking' example, the main difference between (6.12a) and (6.12b) is that the former reports a state while the latter represents an activity. The purpose of using the EC is thus to draw the readers' attention to 'shooting' instead of 'who are shooting'. Reasons may vary from trying to avoid mentioning the shooters to not knowing about the doer of shooting.

Now, we may say that the constructions in Quirk et al. (1985: 1404) listed in this section belong to one of the four types of EC: There be NP_2 (state); There be NP_2 which VP_2 ... (state/event); There be NP_2 non-finite (event); There arise/come/go NP_2 (activity). See (6.13).

(6.13)   a. There must be something wrong. (state)
         b. There is a table which stands in the corner. (state/event)
         c. There are plenty people getting promotion. (event)
         d. There arose a cult demand (COCA_MAG). (activity)

A SQ with 'there arise/go/come [nn*] [vv*]' in COCA returns no results, which means that ECs expressed by the verbs *come*, *go*, *arise* and so on, tend to be bare existentials and do not contain non-finite clauses.

From the process-relation perspective, the state-type and activity-type of ECs only contain one process each. When other clauses occur, they are usually being used as qualifiers to clarify the NPs. That is to say, only the event-type involves more than one process. The relation is similar to the conflation type: Type IV. See Table 6.15.

Table 6.15 *Process relation in the event-type existential construction*

(6.13)	c. *There*	*are*	*plenty people*	*getting*	*promotion.*
	Participant^L	Process^A	Participant^M		
			Participant^M	Median Process^b	Participant^N

6.7 The Absolute Construction

As categorized in Q. He and Yang (2015: 10–14), absolute clauses in English can be one of three types: free adjunct construction, nominative absolute construction and augmented absolute construction. Most typically, a dependent clause (i.e. non-finite clause or verbless clause) will be 'absolute'. In terms of function, these non-finite clauses function as median processes, and the verbless clauses may function as minor processes if prepositions are involved. The median and minor processes function as circumstances in the constructions in which they appear. See (6.14).

(6.14) a. *The terrain being flat*, the wind tore across scrub ... (BNC_FIC)
        b. *Dishes done*, I return home to find my bucket ... (BNC_NA)
        c. *To tell you the truth*, we are a bit at a loss. (BNC_FIC)
        d. She rushed from the shop, *hat in hand*. (BNC_ACAD)

From the process-relation perspective, absolute constructions can be considered as Type VII (see Figure 4.7), in which a process functions as circumstance. According to the LFVP, the median or minor processes in the absolute constructions can only function as circumstances. Let's observe them one by one. First, process relation in absolute construction with -ing clause can be seen in Table 6.16.

Table 6.16 *Process relation in absolute construction with -ing clause*

(6.14)	a. The terrain	being flat,	the wind	tore across	scrub
	Circumstance		Participant^L	Process^A	Participant^M
	Participant^I	Median process^a			

The major process and the median process in an absolute construction are linked by the specific constructional force, and the link is enforced by the use of non-finiteness. Thus, *The terrain being flat* in (6.14a) carries a constructional force, but it functions as the circumstance if to follow the LFVP.

In some cases, the non-finiteness appears in both the absolute clause and the major clause. Thus, more than one median process may occur in such constructions. That said, the function of the absolute clause remains as circumstance. See Table 6.17 for the process relation.

6.8 The Process Relation in Ambiguous Non-finite Constructions   159

Table 6.17 *Process relation in absolute construction with -ed clause*

(6.14)	b. *Dishes done,*		I	return home	*to find*	*my bucket*
	Circumstance^X	Participant^L		Process^A	Circumstance^Y	
	Participant^l Median process^a				Median process^b	Participant^m

Here, the non-finite clauses are the circumstantial components. A similar analysis can be applied to (6.14c), in which *To tell you the truth* is a median process which functions as circumstance. The case in (6.14d) is different, in that a prepositional phrase is used and a minor instead of a median process occurs. See Table 6.18.

Table 6.18 *Process relation in absolute construction with prepositional phrase*

(6.14)	d. She	rushed from	the shop,	hat	in hand
	Participant^L	Process^A	Participant^M	Circumstance	
				Participant^l	Minor process^a

In some cases, more than one absolute clause may appear in one construction. The principle is that the absolute clauses all function as circumstances. See Table 6.19 from the fiction genre in COCA, for example. All median clauses function as circumstance, and thus they are in a circumstantial relation with the major clause.

Table 6.19 *Process relation in multiple absolute clauses in a construction from COCA*

The noise doesn't stop –	*glass breaking,*	*wood popping,*	*everything smashing down*
Participant^L Process^A	C – – i – – r – – c – – u – – m – – s – – t – – a – – n – – c – – e		
	Participant^L M. process^a	Participant^M M. process^b	Participant^N M. process^c

In other words, the circumstance in this construction is realized by three median processes which are of equal status. The median processes realized by non-finite -ing clauses are in paratactic relation and they function as circumstances.

6.8 The Process Relation in Ambiguous Non-finite Constructions

As to the ambiguous non-finite constructions, the criteria for identification proposed by B. Yang (2004) still work here. The problem is that in B. Yang

(2004), the construction types have not been taken into consideration. Let's repeat (2.18) and (2.19) here and take them as examples.

(2.18) a. Frank sat reading the newspaper (Quirk et al. 1985: 1126).
    b. She telephoned hoping for a job (Quirk et al. 1985: 489).
    c. I hate lying (LOB).

(2.19) a. He agreed to marry Jimena Diaz (LOB).
    b. Pardao will be easy to beat (LOB).

The construction types outlined in Chapter 4 and the analysis in this chapter help to make the constructions clear, and much more generalization can consequently be made. From the process-relation perspective, (2.18a) and (2.18b) belong to Type III, in which there is a hypo-relation implied between the finite and the non-finite components. See Table 6.20.

Table 6.20 *Hypo-relation between major process and median process*

(2.18)	a. Frank	sat	reading	the newspaper
	b. She	telephoned	hoping for	a job
	Participant^L	Process^A		Participant^M
			Median process^a	

A finite form followed by a non-finite form does not necessarily indicate a hypo-relation, as shown in Table 6.20. The instance (2.18c) may be interpreted differently. Since there is no second participant in (2.18c), the status of the -ing component is not determined. There are at least three possibilities: *lying* being a nominalization; *lying* being a non-finite with a covert participant; a conflated participant being omitted; see (6.15). The process relation of (6.15b) is similar to that in Table 6.15, and that of (6.15c) is similar to that in Table 6.6. This applies to the constructions in (2.20) which may be understood as Type IV clauses: the participants (*the watch*, *John*) are conflated respectively.

(6.15) a. I hate *lying* (nominalization)
    b. I hate *lying to others* (hypo-relation)
    c. I hate other people *lying* (conflated participant)

Each of (2.19) has at least two alternative interpretations in terms of process relations. In other words, the ambiguity of (2.19) lies in more than one possible process relation. See Table 6.21.

Here, (2.19a) is ambiguous because at least two process relations are possible: *He (agreed to marry) Jimena Diaz; (In order) to marry Jimena Diaz, he agreed*. Similarly, (2.19b) is also ambiguous because at least two process relations are possible: *It is easy for Pardao to beat (someone)* or *(Someone) will find it easy to beat Pardao*.

6.8 The Process Relation in Ambiguous Non-finite Constructions   161

Table 6.21 *Ambiguous hypo-relation between major and median processes*

(2.19)	a. He	agreed	to marry	Jimena Diaz
	Participant[L]	Process[A]		Participant[M]
			Median process[a]	
(2.19)	a. He	agreed	to marry	Jimena Diaz
	Participant	Process[A]	Circumstance (Median process[a])	

In these discussions, we have seen the paratactic and circumstantial relation between major clauses and non-finite clauses. The participantial relation also applies to non-finite -ing and to-clauses. See (6.16).

(6.16) a. *Flying planes* can be dangerous. (Chomsky 1965: 21)
 b. I warned him against *driving fast*. (Quirk et al. 1985: 1065)
 c. *To be human* is *to err*. (Quirk et al. 1985: 1063)
 d. *Turn off the tap* was all I did. (Quirk et al. 1985: 1067)

English instances of constructions similar to those in (6.16) are pervasive. *Flying planes* in (6.16a) functions either as the single participant (i.e. *flying* as adjectival modifier) or as a participant realized by a median process (i.e. *flying planes*). The process relations can be seen in Table 6.22.

Table 6.22 *Process relation in* Flying planes can be dangerous

Flying planes	can be dangerous
Participant	Process
Flying planes	can be dangerous
Participant	Process[A]
Median process[a]	

Table 6.22 shows two possible interpretations of the construction: the first is a noun phrase functioning as the participant; the second is a median process realized by a non-finite clause functioning as the participant. The first belongs to Type I, while the second belongs to Type V in which a process functions as the primary participant.

In terms of non-finiteness, instances (6.16c) and (6.16d) are similar in that infinitive clauses function as participants, the difference being the omission of *to* in (6.16d) (*Turn off the tap was all I did*). See Table 6.23.

Table 6.23 *Infinitive clause functioning as participant*

(6.16)	c.	*To be human*		*is*		*to err.*
		Participant^L		Process^A		Participant^M
		Median process^a				Median process^b

Instance (6.16b) is special in that the non-finite clause functions as the participant in the minor process (i.e. prepositional phrase). The minor process as a whole functions as the circumstance (Type VII); see Table 6.24. Note that 'driving' may be considered as a nominalization or a non-finite expression, and it will be a median process if considered as non-finite.

Table 6.24 *Non-finite clause functioning as the participant in a minor process*

(6.16)	b. I		warn	him	against	*driving*	*fast.*
	Participant^L		Process^A	Participant^M	Circumstance		
					Minor process^b		
						Participant^N	
						Median process^a	

So far, we have applied what is outlined in Chapters 3 and 4 to the analysis of non-finite constructions, the controversial ones in particular. The process-relation approach to non-finite constructions in terms of function greatly helps clarify issues concerning non-finiteness in English. With the identification of major, median and minor processes and the eight types of construction, English constructions with non-finiteness can be better approached and understood. In the next chapter we will turn to similar issues in Chinese constructions with non-finiteness.

7 Revisiting the Controversial Chinese Constructions with Non-finiteness

As pointed out in Section 3.1, spoken and written languages should be distinguished because they require different grammars. A significant feature is that spoken language is full of omissions, errors and repetitions, and it is not reasonable to use grammars of written language to deal with them. For example, it is argued that 'NP+VP' cannot be applied to Chinese because a large number of expressions, such as '小王上海人(Xiǎo Wáng shànghǎi rén / Xiao Wang Shanghainese)', do not contain a verb at all (Zhu 1985).

The fact is that a large number of spoken expressions in English do not contain verbs either, for example *Irina Levshina, a New Yorker on the way* (COCA_SPOK). Here in this chapter we will not discuss omissions in English. Let's now focus on the expression '小王上海人' as a typical example. In written Chinese, the better choice is '小王是上海人(Xiǎo Wáng shì Shànghǎi rén / Xiao Wang is Shanghainese)', in which a typical verb '是(shì)' is used. In order to take a closer look at this phenomenon, we use two SQs (今天星期*; 今天是星期*) in BCC corpus to observe the actual usages (see Table 7.1).

Table 7.1 *A common Chinese expression with and without verb in the BCC corpus*

SQ / Genre	今天星期* jīntiān xīngqī today weekday	今天是星期* jīntiān shì xīngqī today is weekday
Literature	37 (19)	180
News	16 (9)	124
Blog	2,802	1,445
Science	37 (11)	96

As shown in Table 7.1, '今天是星期*' is much more frequently used in literature, news and science genres compared to '今天星期*'. The figures in the brackets indicate the number of those instances in quotation marks, which is a signal of being colloquial. For example, of the thirty-seven occurrences of

163

'今天星期*' in science, eleven are in quotation marks, suggesting that they are colloquial. The blog genre has more usages of '今天星期*', and this is quite reasonable because blogs are typically colloquial. Consequently, we may say that '今天星期*' tends to appear in spoken Chinese, while '今天是星期*' tends to appear in written Chinese. This fact tells us that research into Chinese should not be restricted to some special usages in spoken genres.

In the discussions that follow, we will focus on the controversial constructions in written Chinese.[1] This does not negate the importance of spoken Chinese. The reason for focusing on written Chinese is that we need a different grammar to deal with spoken language (see Section 3.1), which is beyond the scope of the present study. It needs to be noted that controversial construction is a broad topic, and we will restrict our discussion to those controversial constructions in which non-finiteness plays an indispensable role: the serial verb, the pivotal, the existential, and other controversial constructions, most of which are regarded as chunks in a recent study (Niu & Osborne 2019).

When discussing constructions in Chinese, we should be aware that 'any difference in form always signals a difference in meaning' (Lemmens 1998: 232). The constructions in the present chapter are centred around different verbs. Again, 'while the meanings of a verb and the construction in which it occurs can be characterized independent of each other, a specific usage will fuse them into a composite structure in which they become *interdependent*' (Lemmens 1998: 233, emphasis in original).

7.1   The Serial Verb Construction

The SVC 'can be formally described as a clause consisting of two or more predicates showing a number of properties that suggest treating them as one structural unit' (Ansaldo 2006: 260). Typical features of serialization include: a single clause describing a complex event; only one subject marked for the main predicate; no overt coordination/subordination within the construction; one or more arguments of the clause shared; a single clause in which tense, modality and aspect (TAM) and polarity markers are shared; as one intonational unit; being lexicalized or grammaticalized (Ansaldo 2006: 261).

In the 1980s, linguists found that there is a remarkable similarity in serial constructions across a wide variety of languages (e.g. Sebba 1987). Soon afterwards, Payne acknowledged, 'Serial verbs occur in all types of languages,

---

[1] It is true that, as one of the referees commented, some of the examples are speech-like, although this research intends to focus on written language. On the one hand, there is no sharp divide between many examples found in spoken and written contexts, especially in Chinese. The cline or continuum view widely accepted in linguistics today applies here. On the other hand, some speech-like examples are heatedly discussed in the literature of (non-)finiteness and cannot be ignored. What we focus on in this research is the typically written.

7.1 The Serial Verb Construction 165

but may be more common in languages that have little or no verbal morphology' (T. Payne 1997: 307). Now it is generally agreed that SVC is a cross-linguistically valid category (e.g. Aikhenvald 2006). The construction has been observed both historically (e.g. Lord 1993) and theoretically from grammatical, comparative and cognitive perspectives (e.g. Lefebvre 1991).

SVCs are also pervasive in modern Chinese, which lacks morphological indicators. The verbal groups in SVC are neither coordinated nor in modified relation, and not verb plus object either (Miao 1957). They have been found to be common in ancient Chinese (e.g. Wei 2005; Zheng 1996) and also in minority languages in China (e.g. G. Peng & Chappell 2011; D. Liu 2015). Some argue that it involves a simple juxtaposition of verbs (Jarkey 2015); others argue that serial verbs are highly related to grammaticalization and lexicalization (e.g. Gao 2006).

A quite different view is that SVC is a purpose construction: a particular relation between events in which one of the linked events 'is performed with the goal of obtaining the realization of another one' (Haspelmath et al. 2005: 506). According to this view, the SVC in Mandarin Chinese (see C. Li & Thompson 1981) 'can be regarded as a purpose clause, because this is the way Mandarin expresses the conceptual situation associated with purpose clauses in other languages' (Haspelmath et al. 2005: 506).

Regarding SVC as purpose clause seems to be radical, but is consistent with the process-relation perspective. What may be added to this view is that SVC in Chinese is more than purpose clauses. Let's start from this view with definitions of SVC.

In the context of Chinese linguistics, disputes are fierce towards the definition, classification and identification of SVCs. SVC is generally defined by Chinese linguists as a construction in which two or more verbs (or phrases) function as one single predicate (Q. Wu 1990; X. Fan 1991). Some regard the serial verb as two predicates (e.g. F. Wang 1960; Chen 1986) or complex predicate (e.g. Jiping Lü 1958; Zhigong Zhang 1982).

As for the types of SVC, the classification drawn by C. Li and Thompson (1981: 594–621) is well known: two or more separate events; one verb phrase or clause serving as the subject or direct object of another verb; pivotal constructions; and descriptive clauses. Except for the first type (i.e. two or more separate events), these are more or less concerned with the pivotal construction, which is quite different from SVC.

Two types of SVC may be identified from the process-relation perspective: one with para-relation verbs where the order of verbs can be altered without affecting the meaning, and the other with hypo-relation verbs which can be further put into strong and weak categories (i.e. explicit and implicit SVCs). The order of processes in the second type cannot be reversed, otherwise the meaning will be changed. For example, 他天天写信会客(tā tiāntiān xiěxìn huìkè / he everyday write letter meet visitor) can be reversed into 他天天会客写信(tā tiāntiān huìkè xiěxìn / he everyday meet visitor write letter) (Chao 2011 [1968]: 343) without affecting the meaning. These can be considered as verbs in para-relation, and belong to Type II. That is to say, the SVC here belongs to the para-relation type.

Based on the construction types drawn from the process-relation perspective, most SVCs in Chinese may be put into Type III (Figure 4.3), in which the hypo-relator may be present or absent. If a hypo-relator, 去(qù/in order to) or 来(lái/so as to)[2] for example, is present, and reversing the order of processes results in unacceptable expressions in written Chinese, we will have explicit SVCs; see (7.1). If a hypo-relator is not present but can be inserted between the processes, and reversing the order of processes results in different expressions, we will have implicit SVCs; see (7.2).

(7.1) a. 打水去洗澡 (Chao 2011 [1968]: 356)
 dǎ shuǐ qù- xǐzǎo
 bring water so as to-LNK bathe
 'bring water to bathe'
 b. 倒碗茶来喝 (Chao 2011 [1968]: 356)
 dǎo wǎn- chá lái- hē
 pour bowl-CLF tea in order to-LNK drink
 'pour a bowl of water in order to drink'

(7.2) a. 骑着马找马 (Chao 2011 [1968]: 357)
 qí-zhe mǎ zhǎo mǎ
 ride-ASP horse look for horse
 'riding a horse (so as to) look for the horse'
 b. 动手预备大考 (Chao 2011 [1968]: 359)
 dòngshǒu yùbèi dàkǎo
 take action prepare big exam
 'take action to get prepared for the big exam'

On the one hand, 去 or 来 as relators can be omitted in (7.1a) and (7.1b), so 打水洗澡 and 倒碗茶喝 are perfectly all right. On the other hand, the verbal groups cannot be reversed in order because 去洗澡打水 and 来喝茶倒碗 are unacceptable. Thus, (7.1a) and (7.1b) are explicit SVCs. No relators are used in (7.2a) and (7.2b), but we can insert such relators as 去 and 来 between the verbal groups: 骑着马去找马 and 动手来预备大考 are quite acceptable. Moreover, reversing the order of the processes (verbal groups) will result in

---

[2] Please note that 来 and 去 in Chinese are multi-functional. According to 现代汉语词典 (*Modern Chinese Dictionary*, 7th ed., The Commercial Press, 2020), 来 may function as a verb (e.g. 问题来了), a particle preceding (e.g. 你来念一遍) or following a verb (e.g. 我们贺喜他呢) or between verbal expressions (e.g. 你又能用什么理由来说服他呢), a noun indicating position (e.g. 两千年来), an auxiliary word (e.g. 十来天) or a suffix (e.g. 向来). Similarly, 去 may function as a verb with multiple meanings (e.g. 他去了三天; 去留两便; 去皮), a particle preceding (e.g. 自己去想办法) or following a verb (e.g. 游泳去了) or between verbal expressions (e.g. 提了一桶水去浇花), or an exclamatory adding to some adjectives (e.g. 这座楼可大了去了). The relator usage of 来 and 去 refers to their being particles in between verbal expressions.

7.1 The Serial Verb Construction

acceptable but different expressions. This absence of relators and the change of meaning depending on order make them implicit SVCs.

Now we can say that explicit SVCs usually contain relators between the processes, and the reversing of verbal groups will result in unacceptable constructions. Implicit SVCs are different in that relators are absent. What is significant is that reversing processes in explicit SVCs will result in unacceptable expressions, whereas reversing processes in implicit SVCs will bring disparity in meaning (but not ungrammaticality). See (7.3) and (7.4) for examples.

(7.3)   a. 分层、分类指导 (BCC_SCIENCE)
          fēncéng,   fēnlèi   zhǐdǎo
          stratify,   categorize instruct
    b. 分层、分类来/去指导
          fēncéng,   fēnlèi   lái-/qù-   zhǐdǎo
          stratify,   categorize so as to-LNK instruct
    c. 指导分层、分类
          zhǐdǎo   fēncéng,   fēnlèi
          instruct   stratification categorization

(7.4)   a. 进站买票 (BCC_SCIENCE)
          jìn   zhàn   mǎi   piào
          enter station buy   ticket
    b. 进站来/去买票
          jìn   zhàn   lái-/qù-   mǎi   piào
          enter station so as to-LNK buy ticket
    c. 买票进站
          mǎi   piào   jìn   zhàn
          buy   ticket enter station
          'buy ticket to enter station'

Since the reversing of verbal groups results in a significant difference in meaning, we may confirm the idea that verbal groups in SVCs of the hyporelation type cannot be reversed in order unless different meanings are required. For implicit SVCs, reversing the order is not supported in grammaticality. In other words, process relations in SVCs generally belong to Type III. See Tables 7.2 and 7.3. The order of processes in these constructions is fixed, and the processes are not parallel in status. As a result, 去洗澡 and 来喝 are better considered as median processes.

This does not mean that the relator is obligatory in explicit SVCs. As mentioned, 来 and 去 as particles may not be present in Chinese.

As we have seen, SVC are considered as a purpose construction by some linguists. One question is which clause, the major clause or the purpose clause, should be the kernel. Some believe that the second part of SVC is the kernel (e.g. Yin 1954; Zou & Zhang 2000); some suggest that the first verb should be

Table 7.2 *Process relation in explicit SVC in Chinese*

(7.1)	a. 打	水	去	洗澡
	bring	water	so as to	bathe
	b. 倒	碗茶	来	喝
	pour	bowl tea	so as to	drink
	Process^A	Participant	Relator	Median process^a

Table 7.3 *Process relation in implicit SVC in Chinese*

(7.3)	a. 分	类/层	(来/去)	指导	
		classify/stratify	(so as to)	instruct	
(7.4)	a. 进	站	(来/去)	买	票
		enter station	(so as to)	buy	ticket
	Process^A	Participant^L	(Relator)	Median process^a	Participant^l

the major verb (e.g. Zhou 1998); and some even consider the elements with stronger transitivity as the kernel (e.g. B. Zhang 2000).

As argued in Chapters 4 and 5, a non-finite clause is understood as a clause rankshifted or embedded as one expression intermediate between a clause and a group in status, which functions as participant, process or circumstance in the clause. 指导 in (7.3a) is a process, and 买票 is also a process in (7.4a). If the meanings of the constructions are to be kept, these processes cannot be reversed with the major processes 分类/层 or 进站. Moreover, the LFVP needs to be followed, and neither 指导 nor 买票 can be finite. In this sense, 指导 and 买票 serve as median processes. In other words, they are non-finite clauses.

The process relation of SVCs in Chinese is similar to that in English. What is a feature of SVCs in both languages is that the first verbal group usually determines the grammatical aspect, while the final verbal group determines the meaning: the focus of meaning is always on the purpose. In other words, the purpose part (usually the final verbal group of the SVC) should be the kernel in meaning, while the first verbal group usually carries the grammatical features. See (7.5).

(7.5) a. 他们才不会在家里吵翻了天问父母要一点小钱来享用这种东西呢
(by Can Xue)
tāmen cái   bú-   huì-   zài jiālǐ   chǎo   fān-le
they   certainly not-NEG will-MOD at   home quarrel shake-ASP

tiān wèn	fùmǔ	yào	yìdiǎn	xiǎoqián	lái
sky ask	parents	for	some	small money	so as to-LNK
xiǎngyòng	zhèzhǒng	dōngxī	ne-		
enjoy	this kind	thing	ne-EXCL		

b. (If they were eating only air,) they wouldn't *kick up such a row with their parents demanding a few pennies to enjoy this kind of thing* (translated by Karen Gernant & Zeping Chen) (quoted in D. Liu 2015: 13)

In (7.5), we have typical Chinese and English SVCs, which are multiple verbal groups in series. Multiple as the verbal groups are, the kernel meaning of (7.5a) is realized by the final verbal group (享用这种东西), while that of (7.5b) is also realized by the final verbal group (*to enjoy this kind of thing*). The grammatical change in (7.5a) is determined by the first verbal group (才不会在家里), and that in (7.5b) also by the first verbal group (*wouldn't kick up*).

In other words, the syntax of SVC is much influenced by the initial verbal group while its semantics is much influenced by the final group. Both in English and in Chinese, the verbal groups that follow the initial verbal group are likely to be non-finite clauses. This echoes one study that says that if the initial verbal group contains such verbs as 打算, 计划, 准备, 想, 开始, 要, and so on, the part that follows is very likely to be non-finite (D. Shi 2009). From the process-relation perspective, an SVC is usually composed of a major process and a median process and, unlike other constructions, the median process carries the meaning focus.

7.2 The Pivotal Construction

The construction with the form $NP_1+VP_1+NP_2+VP_2$ is called 'the pivotal construction' by the majority of Chinese linguists. The term can be traced back to F. Liu (1920: 12), who proposed '兼格代词' (merging pronoun) when discussing the grammar of '亲之欲其贵也, 爱之欲其富也' by Mencius. In Liu's view, 其 in such constructions has to be given a grammatical name because of its peculiarity. Later, in 1924, Jinxi Li (2007 [1924]: 30) considered NP_2 as 兼格 for the reason that it is used as the object and the subject simultaneously. In 1943, Wang Li (L. Wang 1985 [1943]: 92–100) proposed a new term for such constructions, 递系式 (consecutive construction), in which VP_1 is the initiating and VP_2 is the secondary. The idea was picked up by later linguists, but the term was not accepted. In 1961, Ding et al. (1999: 118–21) called the construction 兼语式, illustrating it with a number of instances from published works.

The English term 'pivotal construction' for 兼语式 was first proposed by Chao in 1968 (see Chao 2011 [1968]: 147). The core idea is that in such constructions, NP_2 is considered as the object of VP_1 and the subject of VP_2 simultaneously. 'A pivotal construction consists of a succession of a verbal expression V_1, a nominal expression, and another verbal expression V_2, with the nominal expression serving at once as object of V_1 and subject of V_2' (Chao 2011 [1968]: 147).

In English and other languages, linguists talk more about causative constructions than pivotal constructions. Pivotal syntactic arguments are sometimes discussed concerning such constructions as *She hammered the metal flat* (e.g. Van Valin & LaPolla 1997). However, there is no such term as 'pivotal construction' in English linguistics although 'pivot' is occasionally used by some linguists.

Since Chao's proposal of the term 'pivotal construction', a number of linguists in the Chinese language have used the term frequently. However, what they are actually talking about are almost causative constructions. Some linguists even categorize pivotal construction into four types as follows: implicit causatives, explicit causatives, pure causatives and causative resultatives (M. Li 2017). It is true that with contact between languages and dialects the causative construction in Chinese has been changed both in structure and meaning (C. Zhang 2014). This is why some linguists have confused causative construction and pivotal construction in Chinese linguistics. Moreover, many Chinese linguists do not distinguish between causative constructions and non-causative constructions. They refer to all constructions with the structure $VP_1+NP_2+VP_2$ as pivotal constructions. That is to say, the pivotal construction in the context of Chinese linguistics includes causative construction and non-causatives in the structure $VP_1+NP_2+VP_2$.

'The causative construction is a linguistic expression that denotes a complex situation consisting of two events': the causing event and the caused event (J. Song 2006: 265). The key words in this definition are 'causing' and 'caused'. As we can see from Table 6.1, only material processes can be causatives. In this sense, causative constructions are narrow in scope compared to pivotal constructions.

Although pivotal constructions have been found in oracle bone inscriptions (e.g. Zheng 1996) and causatives are typically pivotal, not much research has been done on causatives in the context of Chinese linguistics. It is only in recent years that types of causatives have been observed from the historical perspective and categories have been proposed (Y. He 2017). Studies of the numerous so-called pivotal construction are generally mixed up with causatives in discussions concerned, and no clear distinction has been made. For example, eleven categories of pivotal construction have been identified according to the meaning of main verbs by Yóu (2002). See Table 7.4.

Most categories in Table 7.4 are meaning-based, which is different from categorizations in studies in the literature. In current literature most studies on

7.2 The Pivotal Construction

Table 7.4 *Typical verbs used in pivotal construction in Chinese (Yóu 2002)*

Types	Typical verbs to use
urging	使(shǐ) 叫(jiào) 让(ràng) 令(lìng) 要(yào) 找(zhǎo) 导致(dǎozhì) 说服(shuōfú) 利用(lìyòng) 号召(hàozhào) 组织(zǔzhī) 发动(fādòng) 动员(dòngyuán)
ordering	命令(mìnglìng) 禁止(jìnzhǐ) 布置(bùzhì) 安排(ānpái) 分配(fēnpèi) 介绍(jièshào) 指定(zhǐdìng) 派(pài) 要求(yāoqiú)
persuading	鼓励(gǔlì) 请(qǐng) 劝告(quàngào) 嘱咐(zhǔfù) 通知(tōngzhī) 告诉(gàosù) 催(cuī) 教(jiào) 阻止(zǔzhǐ)
entrusting	委托(wěituō) 托(tuō) 拜托(bàituō) 请求(qǐngqiú) 求(qiú)
offering	留(liú) 留给(liúgěi) 供(gòng) 扶(fú) 扶植(fúzhí) 送给(sònggěi)
electing	推荐(tuījiàn) 选(xuǎn) 提名(tímíng) 调(tiáo) 叫 ... 做(jiào ... zuò) 称 ... 为(chēng ... wéi)
accompanying	送(sòng) 陪(péi)
helping	帮(bāng) 帮助(bāngzhù) 协助(xiézhù) 配合(pèihé)
following	跟随(gēnsuí) 追随(zhuīsuí) 跟从(gēncóng) 随从(suícóng)
(dis)liking	表扬(biǎoyáng) 喜欢(xǐhuan) 爱(ài) 感谢(gǎnxiè) 佩服(pèifú) 夸奖(kuājiǎng) 嫌(xián) 讨厌(tǎoyàn) 恨(hèn) 怪(guài) 气(qì) 怨(yuàn) 可怜(kělián) 笑(xiào) 骂(mà)
(not) having	有(yǒu) 没有(méiyǒu) 是(shì)

pivotal construction are form-oriented, and the most frequent idea is: two subject-predicate forms are linked as a whole, in which the object of the first clause acts as the subject of the second clause. Thus, constructions with main verbs such as 说, 喜欢 and 劝, as in (7.6), are considered to be pivotal constructions.

(7.6) a. 别人都说你是傻子 (X. Zhang 1996: 263)
       biérén dōu shuō nǐ   shì   shǎzi
       others all say   you are   fool
       'Others all say that you are dumb.'
    b. 我喜欢他老实 (X. Zhang 1996: 263)
       wǒ   xǐhuan tā   lǎoshí
       I   like   he   honest
       'I like him being honest.'
    c. 我们劝他别伤心 (X. Zhang 1996: 263)
       women quàn   tā   bié-   shāngxīn
       we   comfort he   not-NEG sad
       'We comfort him not to be sad.'

A number of special constructions are also considered as pivotal construction in Chinese. For example:

(7.7) a. 你逼得爹爹没有一点路可走了 (Y. Song 1981)
       nǐ   bī-dé   diēdiē méi-   yǒu   yìdiǎn lù   kě-   zǒu-le
       you push-COMP   Daddy   not-NEG have   a bit   way can-MOD go-EXCL
       'You push Daddy too hard to leave no way for him to go.'

b. 姑姑换给你个好东西玩 (Gong 1983, quoted in X. Zhang 1996: 264)
   gūgū   huàngěi   nǐ   gè-   hǎo   dōngxī wán
   auntie exchange you   one-CLF   good   thing play
   'Let Auntie change it for something good for you to play with.'
c. 孔乙己给小孩茴香豆吃 (Zhou 1983, quoted in X. Zhang 1996: 264)
   Kǒng Yǐjǐ   gěi   xiǎohái-   huíxiāngdòu   chī
   Kong Yiji   give   child-PL   fennel beans   eat
   'Kong Yiji gave the children some fennel beans to eat.'
d. 我买了一本旧杂志缺两页 (X. Zhang 1996: 264)
   wǒ   mǎi-le   yī   běn-   jiù zázhì   quē   liǎngyè
   I   buy-ASP   one   copy-CLF old magazine   miss two pages
   'I have bought one copy of an old magazine, two pages of which are missing.'
e. 我们队缺个大个儿打中锋 (X. Zhang 1996: 264)
   wǒmen   duì   quē   gè   dàgèer   dǎ   zhòngfēng
   we   team   lack   one   tall guy play   centre forward
   'Our team has no tall man to play the centre forward.'
f. 他有两个弟弟在北京读大学 (X. Zhang 1996: 264)
   tā   yǒu   liǎng-gè   dìdì   zài   Běijīng   dú   dàué
   he   have   two-CLF   younger brother   in   Beijing   study at   college
   'He has two brothers in Beijing who are studying at college.'
g. 大驴子被小老虎吃掉了 (Ding et al. 1999)
   dà   lǘzǐ bèi-   xiǎo   lǎohǔ   chīdiào-le
   big   donkey by-PASS small   tiger   eat up-ASP
   'The big donkey has been eaten up by a small tiger.'

Many linguists would not agree with the view that (7.7g) is a pivotal construction, because the bèi (passive indicator) construction is special in many ways and it needs special treatment. The other constructions in (7.7) are also controversial, but many linguists simply consider them as pivotal constructions.

To sum up, disputes over the property of the pivotal construction in Chinese are centred around VP_1 and VP_2. Seven major views, listed according to the chronological order of publication, can be summarized as follows.

(a) V_2 is a complement because a sentence contains only one recount (C. Shi 1954).

(b) The construction is a contracted sentence, because two clauses are combined into one (J. Zhang 1977).

(c) N_2+V_2 is an object because two predicates are not allowed in a sentence (Jiping Lü 2002 [1979]).

(d) N_2 and V_2 are double objects because N_2 identifies the target and V_2 describes the content (Fu 1980).

(e) Pivotal construction is intermediate between clause and clause complex (C. Yang 1984).

7.2 The Pivotal Construction

(f) Pivotal construction is a sub-class of consecutive predicates because V_2 is the secondary predicate (Zhu 1985).
(g) V_2 is controlled by an empty category (Y. Hu & Fan 1995).
(h) Pivotal constructions are causatives, and non-causatives cannot be included in the pivotal construction (X. Xing 2004).

Another dispute is over the types of V_2 in pivotal constructions. According to Chen (1960: 102), V_2 can be a verb (e.g. 这个问题请李华回答 zhège wèntí qǐng Lǐ Huá huídá / this question please ask Li Hua answer), an adjective (e.g. 我喜欢小刘老实 wǒ xǐhuan Xiǎo Liú lǎoshí / I like Xiao Liu honest), a noun (e.g. 喜欢那个人黄头发 xǐhuan nàgerén huáng tóufà / like that person yellow hair), or a predicate (e.g. 祝你身体健康 zhù nǐ shēntǐ jiànkāng / Wish you body healthy). Later, C. Wu and Hou (1982: 199) added a fifth class: numerical expression as V_2 (e.g. 击溃敌人一个营 jīkuì dírén yígè yíng / fight against enemy a battalion).

To resolve the disputes, it is necessary to distinguish pivotal construction in terms of process type. The reason for this is that verbs used for different process types tend to vary in causation. With the support of the BCC corpus, Yóu's (2002) types can be redrawn into six categories in terms of process type. These categories demonstrate different tendencies in pivotal construction and causation. See Table 7.5.

On one hand, the verbs used to realize relational processes (是, 成为, 像, 表示, 依旧是, etc.) cannot be used in the construction $VP_1+NP_2+VP_2$. This corresponds with findings in Yóu (2002), where they are not mentioned. On the other hand, some typical verbs in Yóu (2002) are peripheral: 送给, 帮, 帮助, 跟随, 送 and 陪. These verbs tend to be the intermediate types between material process and other processes. Semantically, they may belong to the material process because they are processes of acting. Verbs for material processes tend to be causative, but these special verbs do not necessarily bring about causation. They may be put under the category of motion verbs as a more delicate type of material process (Matthiessen 2014b). Verbs used to realize material processes may be graded in terms of degree of causation (W. He & Zhang 2017), and these verbs will have the lowest level of causation. See Table 7.8 for an analysis of a non-causative material process.

Almost all processes may be used in the form of so-called pivotal construction in Chinese. From the process-relation perspective, the type of pivotal construction depends on the process type. The verbs used in the material process form causative constructions which may be understood as Type IV (see Figure 4.4). Thus, we have the conflation of participant in these constructions. See Table 7.6 for the typical example used in the literature (see also Chao 2011 [1968]: 147; R. Peng 2013: 53).

Here in (7.8), 做代表 functions as a non-finite clause for two reasons: it is a process that shares one participant (他) with the major process, and the second

Table 7.5 *Typical verbs in pivotal constructions in Chinese*

Process types	Typical verbs	VP$_1$+NP$_2$+VP$_2$	Causative?
Material process: doing & happening	找(zhǎo / look for) 导致(dǎozhì / result in) 使(shǐ/make) 利用(lìyòng/use) 组织(zǔzhī/organize) 发动(fādòng/launch) 动员(dòngyuán/mobilize) 禁止(jìnzhǐ/forbidden) 布置(bùzhì/assign) 安排(ānpái/arrange) 分配(fēnpèi/allocate) 介绍(jièshào/introduce) 指定(zhǐdìng/appoint) 派(pài/dispatch) 教(jiào/teach) 阻止(zǔzhǐ/prevent) 委托(wěituō/entrust) 留(liú/leave) 留给(liúgěi/leave) 供(gong/supply) 扶(fú/support) 扶植(fúzhí / prop up) 推荐(tuījiàn/recommend) 选(xuǎn/select) 调(tiáo/transfer) 提名(tímíng/nominate) 命令(mìnglìng/order) 令(lìng/command) 叫(jiào/ask) 让(ràng/require) 鼓励(gǔlì/encourage)	+	+
Mental process: thinking & feeling	感谢(gǎnxiè/thank) 佩服(pèifú/admire) 讨厌(tǎoyàn/loathe) 喜欢(xǐhuan/like) 爱(ài/love) 可怜(kělián/pity) 恨(hèn/hate) 嫌(xián/dislike) 怪(guài/blame) 气(qì/anger) 怨(yuan/complain) 要(yào/want)	+	–
Relational process: being & having	是(shì/be) 意思(yìsi/mean) 表示(biǎoshì/show) 成为(chéngwéi/become) 像(xiàng/resemble) 依旧是(yījiùshì / still be)	–	–
Verbal process: saying	说服(shuōfú/persuade) 劝告(quàngào/advise) 嘱咐(zhǔfù/exhort) 通知(tōngzhī/notice) 告诉(gàosù/tell) 号召(hàozhào/recall) 说(shuō/say) 骂(mà/curse) 请(qǐng/request) 责问(zéwèn/accuse) 吹捧(chuīpěng/boost) 表扬(biǎoyáng/compliment) 夸奖(kuājiǎng/commend) 请求(qǐngqiú/request) 求(qiú/request) 要求(yāoqiú/require) 争辩(zhēngbiàn/argue) 催(cuī/urge)	+	–
Behavioural process: behaving	叹气(tànqì/sigh) 笑(xiào/laugh) 哭(kū/cry) 看(kàn/see) 听(tīng/hear)	+	–
Existential process: existing	有(yǒu/have) 没有(méiyǒu / not have) 是(shì/be)	+	–

7.2 The Pivotal Construction   175

Table 7.6 *Process relation in pivotal construction of causative*

(7.8)	我们	派	他	做	代表
	wǒmen	pài	tā	zuò	dàibiǎo
	we	appoint	him	act as	representative
	Participant^L	Process^A	Participant^M		
			Participant^M	Median process^a	Participant^N

verb 做 cannot be tensed (Yuzhi Shi 2001). Aspect/tense markers cannot come before 做, so 派他已经/将要/会做代表 are not acceptable. A BCC corpus SQ of '派n已经/将要/会做' comes out with no results. However, corpus results show that the second verb 做 can occur with aspect markers such as 了 and 过. See Table 7.7 for the SQ results of '派n做' in different genres of the BCC corpus.

Table 7.7 *Search query results for '派n做' in the BCC corpus*

	O	做 followed by aspect markers 了 or 过
Literature	3	詹石磴已派人做好了十几块木板
		Zhān Shídèng yǐ pài rén zuòhǎo-le shíjǐkuài mùbǎn
		Zhan Shideng already assign people make-ASP dozens wood board
News	26	我们派记者做了调查
		wǒmen pài jìzhě zuò-le diàochá
		we assign reporter finish-ASP survey
Blog	8	汉武帝派人做了记号
		Hànwǔdì pài rén zuò-le jìhao
		Emperor Wu of Han assign people mark-ASP sign
Science	18	乡政府为此也曾派人做过调查
		xiāng zhèngfǔ wèicǐ yě céng pài rén zuò- diào chá
		town government for this also once assign man finish-ASP survey

Key: O = occurrences

The occurrences in literature and blog genres are comparatively far fewer than those in news and science. This means that such usages are acceptable but are not used often.

As mentioned, some verbs are indeterminate in process type. They may belong to the material process but not be causatives. Causative verbs are used as material processes, but not all verbs used for material process are causatives. For example, 送给(sònggěi/give), 帮(bāng/help), 跟随(gēnsuí/follow), 送(song/see off) and 陪(péi/accompany) are not causatives. Since no causation occurs, the construction belongs to Type III, in which there is a hypo-relation between groups. See (7.9) in Table 7.8 for an example.

Table 7.8 *Process relation in non-causative material processes*

(7.9)	(他)	陪	老同志	吃	一顿饭	
	(tā	péi)	lǎo tóngzhì	chī	yīdùn-	fàn
	he	accompany	old comrades	eat	a time-CLF	meal
	Participant^L	Process^A	Participant^M	Median process^a	Participant^N	

Both causatives and non-causatives in pivotal constructions may contain non-finiteness. Most often, non-finite clauses occur in the secondary process in the construction, and relators such as 去 and 来 can be inserted between the processes. For example, in the BCC corpus, SQ '陪n去v' gives us the instances shown in (7.10).

(7.10) a. 我曾陪营长去看过地形 (BCC_FICTION)
       wǒ   céng   péi   yíngzhǎng   qù   kàn-guò   dìxíng
       I   once   accompany   battalion commander to inspect-ASP terrain
       'I once accompanied the battalion commander to inspect the terrain.'
  b. 日本朋友总愿陪客人去观赏樱花 (BCC_FICTION)
       rìběn   péngyǒu   zǒng   yuàn   péi   kèrén qù
       Japanese   friends   always   willing   accompany guests to
       guānshǎng   yīnghuā
       watch   cherry blossom
       'Japanese friends are always willing to accompany guests watching cherry blossoms.'
  c. 他三天两头陪老人去寻医、找药、检查、治疗 (BCC_NEWS)
       tā   sān   tiān   liǎng   tóu   péi   lǎorén qù xún yī,
       he   three   day   two   end   accompany elder   to visit doctor
       zhǎo   yào,   jiǎnchá,   zhìliáo
       find   medicine   physical check treat
       'He accompanies the elder almost every day to visit doctors, find medicine, do physical checks and receive treatment.'
  d. 她陪父亲去买凉鞋 (BCC_FICTION)
       tā   péi   fùqīn   qù   mǎi   liángxié
       she accompany father to   buy   sandal
       'She accompanies her father to buy a pair of sandals.'

Instances in (7.10) suggest that tense cannot be taken as a reliable indicator for identifying non-finiteness. It is the hypo-relation, that is, the irreversibility of the order of processes, that determines the non-finiteness in these constructions. Generally speaking, a material process realized by a causative verb tends to contain non-finiteness.

7.2 The Pivotal Construction

Pivotal constructions of the verbal process type are usually non-causative. Sometimes, typical verbs for verbal process may be used as material process. For example, 告诉(gàosù/tell) in (7.11a) in fact means 要求(yāoqiú/require), so it is a material process of causation. For the causative (7.11a), the process relation follows that in (7.8), and 改正(gǎizhèng/correct) may be considered as a non-finite clause.

(7.11)   a. (他)告诉工人改正 (BCC_NEWS)
           (tā)   gàosù   gōngrén   gǎizhèng
           (he)   require   workers   correct
           '(he) requires the workers to correct.'
   b. 佛教教义告诉人们要知足常乐 (BCC_NEWS)
           fójiào   jiàoyì   gàosù   rénmen   yào-   zhīzú   cháng lè
           Buddhist doctrine ask people must-MOD feel contented often happy
           'Buddhist doctrine asks people to be contented and always happy.'
   c. 告诉你们好消息 (BCC_NEWS)
           gàosù   nǐmen   hǎo   xiāoxi
           tell   you   good   news
           'tell you good news'

For the non-causative (7.11b), the process realized by 要知足常乐 functions as the secondary participant. In other words, it belongs to Type VI. Thus, we have the process relation as shown in Table 7.9.

Table 7.9 *Process relation in non-causative verbal processes*

(7.11b)	佛教教义	告诉	人们	要知足常乐
	Participant^L	Process^A	Participant^M	Participant^N Median process[a]

(7.11c) is not a pivotal construction at all, because the nominal groups 你们 and 好消息 are all participants. Thus, it belongs to Type VIII, in which triple participants are involved in a single process. See Table 7.10.

Table 7.10 *Triple participant in a single process*

(7.11c)	(我)	告诉	你们	好消息
	(Participant^L)	Process	Participant^M	Participant^N

Table 7.11 *Process relation in pivotal construction of the mental process*

(7.12)	a.	我	喜欢	小刘	老实
		wǒ	xǐhuan	Xiǎo Liú	lǎoshí
		I	like	Xiao Liu	honest
	b.	(某某)	喜欢	那个人	黄头发
		mǒumǒu	xǐhuan	nà-ge rén	huángtóufà
		(someone)	like	that-CLF man	yellow hair
	c.	(某某)	祝	你	身体健康
		mǒumǒu	zhù	nǐ	shēntǐ jiànkāng
		(someone)	wish	you	body good health
		Participant^L	Process^A	(Phenomenon)	
				Process^a as Participant^M	

Other processes may form the so-called VP$_1$+ NP$_2$+VP$_2$, but they belong to different types of organization. For the mental process, NP$_2$+VP$_2$ function as the participant, since the components in a mental process include Senser, Process and Phenomenon. Thus, the construction also belongs to Type VI; its difference from non-causative verbal process is that fewer participants are involved. See Table 7.11. The examples are from Chen (1960: 102).

We can see from Table 7.11 that in the mental process realized by 要, 喜欢, 感谢, 佩服, 讨厌, 爱, 恨, 嫌, 怪, 气, 怨, 可怜, and so on, the secondary process is often used as a participant. It belongs to Type VI, in which the secondary process functions as the secondary participant. The same applies to 他们忽然看见个和尚吊在上面(tāmen hūrán kànjiàn gèhéshang diàozài shàngmian / they suddenly see one monk hang above) (R. Peng 2016: 530), because 看见 represents a mental process.

In English, major verbs used to realize the behavioural process (e.g. *laugh*, *cry*, *listen to*, *look at*, *sigh*, etc.) cannot occur as VP$_1$ in the VP$_1$+ NP$_2$+VP$_2$ construction. It seems that major verbs used to realize the behavioural process in Chinese (e.g. 笑, 哭, 看, 听, 叹气) may occur as VP$_1$ in the VP$_1$+ NP$_2$+VP$_2$. See (7.13) for examples.

(7.13) a. 大家取笑一个人受辱 (BCC_FICTION)
　　　　　dàjiā　　　qǔxiào　　　yí-gè　　　rén　　　shòurǔ
　　　　　everybody　deride　　　one-CLF　person　get insulted
　　　　　'Everybody derides one person for being insulted.'
　　　b. 君笑总统无见识, 总统笑尔书生气啊 (BCC_NEWS)
　　　　　jūn　　　xiào　　　zǒngtǒng　wú　　　jiànshi,　zǒngtǒng　xiào　　ěr
　　　　　you　　　laugh at　president　not-NEG　insight　president　laugh at　you
　　　　　shūshēng　qì　　ā
　　　　　bookish　　air　　ah
　　　　　'You gentleman laugh at the president for having no insight, but the president laughs back at you for being bookish ah.'

c. 笑猪不会飞 (BCC_BLOG)
   xiào   zhū   bú-   huì-   fēi
   deride   pig   not-NEG   can-MOD   fly
   'deride pigs for being unable to fly'
d. 外公笑外婆像"小仙"了 (BCC_SCIENCE)
   wàigōng   xiào   wàipó   xiàng   'xiǎoxiān' -le
   Grandpa   deride   Grandma   look like   'little fairy'-EXCL
   'Grandpa derides Grandma for looking like a "little fairy"'

The process type of 笑(laugh) is behavioural, but it conveys a sense of feeling. To some extent, 笑 in (7.13) may be replaced by 取笑(joke, deride), and thus it may be included in the mental process. In this sense, the process relation for constructions in (7.13) may simply follow that in (7.12). In other words, verbs used to realize behavioural process in both English and Chinese cannot occur as VP_1 in the construction $VP_1 + NP_2 + VP_2$.

As to the verbs 有, 没(有) and 是 in Table 7.16, which may be used to realize existential process, they seem to function as VP_1 in the construction $VP_1 + NP_2 + VP_2$. We will discuss issues related to this in detail in Section 7.4.

7.3   Pivotal Construction or Grammatical Metaphor?

The so-called pivotal constructions in (7.7) are highly controversial. A number of linguists regard them as pivotal constructions, while some others do not agree with this viewpoint. For the sake of convenience, let's repeat some examples in (7.14). Note that (7.7a) is not a typical pivotal construction and (7.7g) is also better not considered as pivotal, because '被(bèi)' is an indicator for passive voice. In current literature, the constructions in (7.14) are all considered as typical pivotal constructions.[3]

(7.14)   a. 姑姑换给你个好东西玩 (Gong 1983, quoted in X. Zhang 1996: 264)
         b. 孔乙己给小孩茴香豆吃 (Zhou 1983, quoted in X. Zhang 1996: 264)
         c. 我买了一本旧杂志缺两页 (X. Zhang 1996: 264)
         d. 我们队缺个大个儿打中锋 (X. Zhang 1996: 264)
         e. 他有两个弟弟在北京读大学 (X. Zhang 1996: 264)
         f. 我单位盖了一间简易大厂房价值 30 万 (R. Peng 2016: 530)
            wǒ   dānwèi   gài-le   yī-jiān   jiǎnyì   dà   chǎngfáng   jiàzhí
            I   company   build-ASP   one-CLF   simple   big   factory house worth
            30wàn
            30wan
            'The company I work at has built a simple big factory building which is worth 300 thousand yuan.'

---

[3] Note that the notations following the Leipzig Glossing Rules for (7.14) can be seen in (7.7). All except (7.14f) are repetitions here.

From the process-relation perspective, 换给(change) and 玩(play) in (7.14a) are used to realize material processes. The relation between them is not that of a causative, because 玩 cannot result from 换给. In a typical causative pivotal construction, (7.8) for example, the second process is a result of the first process. Here in (7.14a), the two processes come consecutively. The meaning of this construction is indeed a combination of two clauses: 姑姑换给你个好东西 and 你玩(这)个好东西. In other words, two clauses are contracted into one clause. This kind of clause combining can be taken as IGM (see Chapters 3 and 5).

In (7.14b), one may argue that 孔乙己给小孩茴香豆吃 is an equivalent of 孔乙己给小孩吃茴香豆. However, 孔乙己给小孩吃茴香豆 is a typical pivotal construction of causation because 给 here is equivalent to 让, which is a causative verb. The process relation of this causative construction is the same as that of (7.8). So the question is why users bother to put the process 吃 at the end of (7.14b).

In fact, 孔乙己给小孩茴香豆吃 is different from 孔乙己给小孩吃茴香豆 in that the latter is a typical pivotal construction of causation, while the former is intended to weaken the degree of causation. In the former construction, 给 cannot be replaced by causative verbs such as 让 or 叫. The logic is that 孔乙己 (Kong Yiji) may give(给) children(小孩) fennel-flavoured beans(茴香豆), but the children(小孩) may or may not eat them. Thus, two clauses (孔乙己给小孩茴香豆 and 小孩吃茴香豆) have been put together for the purpose of avoiding causation between them.

Construction (7.14c) has the same constructional properties as (7.14a) and (7.14b), the difference being the involvement of a peripheral process: 缺(lack/be in lack of) may be either a material process or a relational process. Likewise, this construction is better understood as a contraction of two clauses: 我买了一本旧杂志 and 这本旧杂志缺两页. Similar treatment may be applied to (7.14d).

In (7.14e), the relation between the two processes is again not of causation. The construction is contracted from 他有两个弟弟 and 两个弟弟在北京读大学. IGM is the underlying mechanism. This construction is special because the EC is involved. We will discuss this in detail in Section 7.4.

The construction in (7.14f) is considered by some linguists to be a descriptive pivotal construction (see R. Peng 2016). It is in fact a contraction of two clauses from the process-relation perspective: 我单位盖了一间简易大厂房 and 这间简易大厂房价值30万. These two clauses mean the same as (7.14f), the difference being that (7.14f) is a single construction built out of two clauses. This is a typical method of clause contraction, and the mechanism is IGM.

Thus, the constructions in (7.14) all follow the principle of clause combining: two clauses are contracted into one. They all follow the principle of de-causation as well: the two processes are independent in meaning and they are in consecutive order. These constructions are IGMs, and the secondary processes may be considered to be non-finite clauses.

7.3 Pivotal Construction or Grammatical Metaphor? 181

Another typical pivotal construction is a combination of one major process (the result) and a median process (the cause). This is contrary to causative pivotal constructions in which the major process functions as the cause and the median process as the result. See (7.15).

(7.15) 张三欺负李四不识字 (R. Peng 2012: 509)
    a. Zhāng Sān   qīfù   Lǐ Sì   bù-   shí zì
       Zhang San push around Li Si not-NEG know word
       'Zhang San pushes Li Si around for his being unable to read or write.'
       (cf. 张三欺负李四, 因为李四不识字)
       Zhāng Sān qīfù   yīnwéi-   Lǐ Sì bù-   shí zì
       Zhang San push around because-LNK Li Si not-NEG know word
       'Zhang San pushes Li Si around, because Li Si is unable to read or write.'
    b. 老板要惩罚他们迟到 (R. Peng 2012: 509)
       lǎobǎn   yào-   chéngfá   tāmen   chídào
       boss   will-MOD punish   them   arrive late
       'The boss wants to punish them for arriving late.'
       (cf. 老板要惩罚他们, 因为他们迟到)
       lǎobǎn   yào   chéngfá tāmen, yīnwéi tāmen   chídào
       boss   will-MOD punish   them   because they   arrive late
       'The boss wants to punish them, because they arrive late.'
    c. 我打你不听话 (R. Peng 2012: 509)
       wǒ   dǎ   nǐ   bù-   tīnghuà
       I   beat   you   not-NEG listen
       'I beat you for not listening.'
       (cf. 我打你, 因为你不听话)
       wǒ   dǎ   nǐ,   yīnwéi   nǐ   bù-   tīnghuà
       I   beat   you   because you   not-NEG listen
       'I beat you, because you don't listen.'
    d. 别唬我没见过世面 (R. Peng 2012: 509)
       bié   hǔ   wǒ   méi-   jiàn-guò shìmiàn
       don't   scare me   not-NEG see-ASP much of life
       'Don't scare me for my not having seen much of the life.'
       (cf. 别唬我, 因为我没见过世面)
       bié   hǔ   wǒ, yīnwéi-   wǒ méi-   jiàn-guò shìmiàn
       don't scare me   because-LNK I   not-NEG see-ASP much of life
       'Don't scare me, because I have not seen much of the life.'

In (7.15a), 张三欺负李四 is the result and 李四不识字 is the cause. We may safely say that it is equivalent in meaning to the clause complex '因为李四不识字, 所以张三欺负他'. In other words, (7.15a) is a compression of two clauses. This again reflects the mechanism of IGM: two clauses as a combination are rankshifted downwards into a clause. This mechanism applies to all examples in (7.15). Thus, the so-called pivotal constructions in (7.15) are also instances of IGM.

Another important point relevant to the present research is that the secondary processes in these constructions are realized by non-finite clauses. First, they are moodless: 不识字, 迟到, 不听话 and 没见过世面 are all moodless because they cannot be preceded by '将' or other tense indicators. Second, they are clause dependent. The meaning cannot be complete unless put into a construction higher in status. Third, they are incomplete in ideation: none of them contain primary participants. Or, at least, the participants have been conflated.

In 你逼得爹爹没有一点路可走了(7.7a), 得 is used between the processes. Similar usages (see 7.16) have been noticed by a number of linguists, and they are considered to be pivotal constructions.

(7.16)   a. 那件事激动得张三留下了眼泪 (Y. He & Wang 2002: 6)
           nà   jiàn   shì   jīdòng-de Zhāng Sān liúxià-le yǎnlèi
           that   kind-CLF thing excite-COMP Zhang San shed-ASP tear
           'That thing has made Zhang San shed tears.'
           (cf. 那件事让张三激动, 所以张三留下了眼泪)
           nàjiàn   shì   rang   Zhāng Sān jīdòng, suǒyǐ- Zhāng Sān
           that   thing   make Zhang San excited, SO-LNK   Zhang San
           liúxià-le yǎnlèi
           shed-ASP tear
           'That has made Zhang San excited, so he sheds tears.'
   b. 他打得孩子到处乱跑 (Sun 1998: 32)
           tā   dǎ-dé   háizi   dàochù   luànpǎo
           he   beat-COMP   child everywhere run about
           'He beat the child so badly that the child ran everywhere.'
           (cf. 他打孩子, 所以孩子到处乱跑)
           tā   dǎ   háizi, suǒyǐ- háizi   dàochù   luànpǎo
           he   beat   child, SO-LNK child   everywhere   run about
           'He beat the child, so the child ran everywhere.'
   c. 你逼得爹爹没有一点路可走了
           nǐ   bī-dé   diēdiē   méi-   yǒu   yìdiǎn lù   kě-   zǒu-le
           you   push-COMP Daddy   not-NEG have   a bit way can-MOD go-EXCL
           'You push Daddy too hard so he finds nowhere to go.'
           (cf. 你逼爹爹, 所以爹爹没有一点路可走了)
           nǐ   bī   diēdiē, suǒyǐ diēdiē méi-   yǒu   yìdiǎn   lù
           you   push daddy, SO-LNK Daddy   not-NEG have a bit   way
           kě   zǒu-le
           can-MOD go-EXCL
           'You push Daddy, so Daddy has no way to go.'

Constructions (7.16a) and (7.16b) are again compressions of clause complexes. With 得 functioning in between, the clause of result naturally presents itself as the secondary process. Since two clauses are compressed into one, this also conforms to the mechanism of IGM. However, the use of 得, which is a complementizer, complicates the constructions in (7.16). What we are most concerned with here is the use of non-finite clauses. IGM occurs in these constructions, but non-finiteness is not involved.

7.4 The Existential Construction

Existential expressions have a long history, appearing in script on oracle bones from ancient China (J. Wang 2003). These expressions have long been noticed in modern linguistic research, and disputes arise here and there. For example, in 1898 in Ma's grammar this construction is called 'sentences with no-initializing word', or 'subjectless sentence' (Ma 1998 [1898]: 179). Linguists focus on different components of Chinese existentials, and 有 is considered by many as consisting of two basic meanings: possessing and existing (e.g. Jinxi Li 2007 [1924]: 46). Some discussions on the construction have been quite influential (e.g. F. Fan 1963; Chen 1986; L. Li 1986; Y. Song 1986).

According to the available literature, it is C. T. J. Huang's research that made Chinese existential constructions (CECs) known to the world. Huang depicts the string of CECs as ' ... (NP_1) ... V ... NP_2 ... (XP) ... ', in which the optional NP_1 is the position of the subject, NP_2 is that whose existence is being asserted, and the optional XP is an expression of predication (C. T. J. Huang 1987: 226). Based on different kinds of V, four types of CECs have been distinguished: '(a) sentences with the existential verb *yǒu* (i.e. 'have'), (b) those with a verb of appearance or disappearance, (c) those with a locative verb, and (d) those with a verb expressing the existence of an event or experience' (C. T. J. Huang 1987: 226).

Huang's classification is well known, but strong disputes have been witnessed over a number of essential issues. Some linguists believe that CECs belong to subjectless clauses, others believe that locatives in CECs can be the subjects and the typical verbs are static, and still others hold that typical verbs may be dynamic. Fan's division of CECs into three categories has been well accepted in the debates. According to F. Fan (1963), the three types of CEC are:

- **Type 1:** A (locatives) + B (verb) + C (combinations of numerals and nouns)
- **Type 2:** B (verb) + C (combinations of numerals and nouns)
- **Type 3:** A (locatives) + C (combinations of numerals and nouns).

A second debatable issue is that of (in)definiteness. The definiteness effect (i.e. the post-verbal NPs in ECs must be indefinite) proposed by Milsark (2014 [1979]) can be applied to Chinese existentials (C. T. J. Huang 1987). On some occasions, however, the effect does not work: 我们村里来了这个明星 (wǒmen cūnlǐ láile zhège míngxīng, our village come this pop star) (X. Hu 2010). This idea is supported by the data from the BCC corpus. A SQ 'f 有 这 q n' (f refers to locatives; q refers to measuring words, similar to unit words in English; and n refers to nouns) in the BCC corpus returns the results shown in Table 7.12.

Table 7.12 *Existential constructions with definite 这(zhè/this) in the BCC corpus*

Genre	Query results	Example
Fiction	16	她打得不错, 她在学校里有这门课 tā dǎ-dé búcuò, tā zài xuéxiàolǐ yǒu zhè-mén kè she play-COMP not bad, she in school have this-CLF course 我手上有这份稿子, 还有一个行李袋 wǒ shǒushàng yǒu zhè-fèn gǎozi, hái yǒu yí-gè xínglìdài I at hand have this-CLF manuscript, and have a-CLF duffel bag
News	12	殿内有这位历史伟人的大理石雕像 diàn nèi yǒu zhè-wèi lìshǐ wěirén-de dàlǐshí diāoxiàng hall inside have this-CLF history great man-POSS marble statue 俱乐部里有这部影片的详细资料 jùlèbù lǐ yǒu zhè-bù yǐngpiàn-de xiángxì zīliào club in have this-CLF movie-POSS detailed material
Blog	27	漫画里有这句台词吗 mànhuà lǐ yǒu zhè-jù táicí-ma cartoon in have this-CLF line-Q 如果你的手里有这件宝贝 rúguǒ nǐde shǒulǐ yǒu zhè-jiàn bǎobèi if your hand have this-CLF treasure
Science	29	不仅中国诗歌中有这类篇章 bùjǐn zhōngguó shīgē zhōng yǒu zhè-lèi piānzhāng not only Chinese poems among have this-CLF text 在这本书里有这段话 zài zhè-běn shū lǐ yǒu zhè-duàn huà in this-CLF book inside have this-CLF words

The query results show that CECs with definite 这 are not frequent in the four typical genres in the BCC corpus, but there is no problem with the acceptability of definite '这'. The measuring word (unit word) following 这 may be various. More importantly, a CEC like this may be embedded in other components, for example a prepositional phrase in 自她房里有这幅画后 ... ... (BCC_FICTION). Other definites such as 那, 此, 该 may also be used: 外套里有那张照片 (BCC_FICTION), for example.

As to some special constructions, disputes are also fierce. For example, the verbless CECs such as 窗前两张木桌, 三把旧椅 are considered as 'endocentric structuring as predicate', because 有 or 是 cannot be inserted between 窗前两张木桌 and 三把旧椅 (e.g. Y. Song 1982: 33). Another much-debated construction in the literature is 台上唱着寿戏 or 台上坐着主席团. Some view it as a pseudo-existential (e.g. Y. Song 1988), while others view it as a construction similar to 台上放着玫瑰花 (e.g. Jianming Lü 2009). Viewed

7.4 The Existential Construction

from the perspective of functional typology, existentials and locatives show distinct semantic distribution (Y. Wang & Xu 2013). More than semantic distribution, the process-relation perspective reveals that 台上坐着主席团 is a result of rankshifting. It is the contracted expression of two processes, that is, 这是主席台 and 主席团坐在台上. The two clauses are combined and rankshifted into a clause. In other words, it is a typical IGM (B. Yang 2019b).

The debates may go on and on. What is most interesting is the fourth type of Chinese existential in Huang's categorization: those with a verb expressing the existence of an event or experience (C. T. J. Huang 1987: 226); see (7.17).

(7.17)   a.   河边跪着两个姑娘在洗衣服 (C. T. J. Huang 1987: 228)
          hébiān   guì-zhe   liǎnggè   gūniáng   zài-   xǐ   yīfú
          riverside kneel-ASP two   girls   being-PRS wash clothes
          'On the riverside kneel two girls washing clothes.'
   b.   墙上挂着一幅画很好看 (C. T. J. Huang 1987: 229)
          qiáng   shàng   guà-zhe   yī-fú   huà   hě   hǎokàn
          wall   on   hang-ASP a-CLF picture very   beautiful
          'On the wall hangs a picture which is very beautiful.'

In order to check if these constructions can be found in real usages of Chinese, we use two SQs in the BCC corpus. The first is 'f v 着 m q n 在 v' (f: locative; v: verb; m: numeral; q: unit word), which can help find similar constructions to (7.17a). The results are shown in Table 7.13. Only eleven occurrences can be retrieved, which means they are acceptable, but seldom used in real language. Note that the BCC corpus has been updated recently and a few more occurrences can be retrieved.

Viewed from the process-relation perspective, (7.17a) is composed of two processes: an existential process and a material process. It may be reworded as two separate clauses: 河边跪着两个姑娘; 她们在洗衣服. When two clauses are combined by conjunctive devices (a semi-colon here), they form a clause nexus to realize individual processes. Here in (7.17a), the clauses are rankshifted into a clause in form, which is a typical IGM. This also applies to (7.17b), in which the second process is a relational process.

The query results from the BCC corpus show that there are only a few such constructions compared to the huge size of corpus data in four typical genres: fiction, news, blog and science. If less restricted SQs are used, more instances can be found. What is important here is that IGM can be a good theory to explain similar constructions. See Table 7.13.

Let's take one of these instances as an example for the process relation. For the sake of clarity, we will first consider a simple one; see (7.18) in Table 7.14.

The second process (在吃) cannot be an individual process for the reason that the two processes here are not in paratactic relation. To follow the LFVP,

Table 7.13 *Chinese existential construction as ideational grammatical metaphor*

Genre	Query results in BCC
Fiction	还有一个家管的, 手里拿着一个算盘在打着 hái yǒu yí-gè guǎnjiāde, shǒulǐ ná-zhe yígè suànpán zài- dǎ-zhe also have a-CLF housekeeper, in his hand hold-ASP a-CLF abacus being-PRS play-ASP 另一幅画上画着两个老头在吃西瓜 lìng yīfú huà shàng huà-zhe liǎnggè lǎotóu zài chī xīguā another picture on draw-ASP two old men being-PRS eat water melon
News	我感到和我一样, 周围竖着几十对耳朵在等待着他的回答 wǒ gǎndào hé wǒ yíyàng, zhōuwéi shù-zhe jǐshí-duì ěrduo zài- děngdài-zhe tāde huídá I feel like me the same, around stand-ASP dozens-CLF ears being-PRS wait-ASP his answer 途中看见井旁站着十多头牛在等待喝水 túzhōng kànjiàn jǐngpáng zhàn-zhe shíduō-tóu niú zài- děngdài hē shuǐ on the way see beside well stand-ASP dozens-CLF cow being-PRS wait drink water 他发现场院上站着几百名社员在看电影 tā fāxiàn chángyuàn shàng zhàn-zhe jǐbǎi-míng shèyuán zài- kàn diànyǐng he find courtyard on stand-ASP hundreds-CLF community member being-PRS watch movie
Blog	南北热炕上坐着 6 位老太太在唠家常 (2 occurrences) nán běi rèkàng shàng zuò-zhe 6-wèi lǎotàitai zài- làojiācháng south north warm brick-bed on sit-ASP 6-CLF old lady being-PRS chat 旁边坐着一个靓女在看综英 pángbiān zuò- zhe yí-gè liàngnǚ zài- kàn zōngyīng side sit-ASP a-CLF beauty being-PRS read comprehensive reading book 手里拿着一个馒头在吃 shǒulǐ ná-zhe yí-gè mántou zài- chī in the hand hold-ASP one-CLF steamed bread being-PRS eat
Science	对岸的松树下面, 坐着一只大得不合尺度的兔子竖起耳朵 duì'àn de sōngshù xiàmian, zuò-zhe yī-zhī dàdé bù- hé chǐdù de tùzǐ shùqǐ ěrduo opposite bank of pine tree under sit-ASP a-CLF big-COMP not-NEG fit size of rabbit hold up ear 如图乙: 水泥电杆上停着一只啄木鸟在捉虫子 rú túyǐ: shuǐní diàngān shàng tíng-zhe yīzhī zhuómùniǎo zài- zhuō chóngzǐ shown in figure yi: cement poles on stand-asp one-CLF woodpecker being-PRS grasp worm

Note: To save space, free translations in the tables are not provided.

7.4 The Existential Construction

Table 7.14 *Existential process combined with median process*

(7.18)	(他)	手里	拿着	一个馒头	在	吃
	tā	shǒulǐ	ná-zhe	yí-gè mántóu	zài-	chī
	he	in his hand	hold-ASP	one-CLF steamed bread	being-PRS	eat
(Participant^L)	Circumstance		Process^A	Participant^M		
						Median process[a]

there cannot be two finite verbs in a clause unless para-relation or embedding (raw realization) takes place. Thus, 在吃 here can be regarded as a non-finite clause that functions as a median process.

Similar constructions may be embedded into other clauses, but the process relation follows the same principle. See (7.19) in Table 7.15 for an example.

(7.19) is considered by some linguists as a CEC. It is reasonable to say that 井旁站着十多头牛 is an EC, and it is embedded into part of the participant of 看见. From the process-relation perspective, 看见 is a typical mental process, and all that follow 看见 should be the participant called Phenomenon.

The SQ of 'f v 着 m q n 很 a' in the BCC corpus (similar constructions to (7.17b)) returns fewer results. They are similar to 山下有一座房子很好 (shānxià yǒu yīzuò fángzi hěn hǎo / under the mountain have a house very nice) (C. T. J. Huang 1987: 230). See (7.20).

(7.20) a. 脸上透着思想很深沉 (BCC_FICTION)
    liǎnshàng   tòu-zhe   sīxiǎng   hěn   shēn chén
    on the face reflect-ASP   thinking   quite   profound
    'Thinking is reflected on the face which is quite profound.'
  b. 外面吹着大风很凉爽 (BCC_BLOG)
    wàimiàn   chuī-zhe   dàfēng   hěn   liángshuǎng
    outside   blow-ASP   strong wind   very   cool
    'Strong wind blows outside which is very cool.'
  c. 淡淡在床上吃着手指头很欢 (BCC_BLOG)
    Dàndàn   zài chuángshàng   chī-zhe   shǒuzhǐtou   hěnhuān
    Dandan   on the bed   suck-ASP   fingers   very happy
    'Dandan sucks his fingers on the bed, being very happy.'

In the same manner, each of these constructions contains more than one process. The constructions are IGMs in which two clauses are rankshifted into one clause, so one process is major and the other has to be median or minor. Thus, 很深沉, 很凉爽 and 很欢 in (7.20) are median processes.

In Chinese, constructions of 'locatives + 有 + nominals + verbs' are more frequently used as existentials. A SQ of 'f 有 [n nr nz nt ns r] v' (n: noun; nr: person name; nz: proper noun; nt: institution name; ns: place name; r: pronoun) returns a comparatively large number of results. These constructions are typical IGMs as well; see Table 7.16.

Table 7.15 *Existential process embedded as participant*

(7.19)	途中 túzhōng on the way	看见 kànjiàn see	井旁 jǐngpáng beside well	站着 zhàn-zhe stand-ASP	十多头 shíduōtóu dozens-CLF	牛 niú cow	在 zài being-PRS	等待 děngdài wait	喝 hē drink	水 shuǐ water
	Circumstance^X Process^A		Partici- Circumstance^x Process^a		Participant^1		p a n t^L Median process^b			

7.4 The Existential Construction

Table 7.16 *Typical ideational grammatical metaphors in existential constructions in the BCC corpus*

Genre	Query results	IGM example
Fiction	1,182	屋内有烛光闪烁 wūnèi yǒu zhúguāng shǎnshuò inside the house have candle light shine
News	4,226	周围有民兵掩护 zhōuwéi yǒu mínbīng yǎnhù around have militia shield
Blog	6,257	这世界上有一个人是永远等着你的 zhè shìjiè shàng yǒu yí-gè rén shì yǒngyuǎn děng-zhe nǐ in the world have one-CLF person is forever wait-ASP you
Science	7,359	下有同事可以扯皮 xià yǒu tóngshì kěyǐ- chěpí below have colleagues can-MOD wrangle

Each construction in Table 7.16 involves a compression of two clauses, 屋内有烛光 and 烛光在闪烁 for example. The clauses are rankshifted downwards and form a single clause, and this is IGM, by which the same meaning is expressed in a compressed manner.

Compared with those in other genres, there are fewest query results of CECs signalled by 有 in the genre of fiction in the BCC corpus. That does not mean that literary texts use fewer such constructions of IGM: the reason is that other indicators of existentials such as 着 are not included in the search.

The fourth type of existentials proposed by Huang includes the constructions in (7.21). These constructions are also IGMs, because they are indeed each formed out of a compression of two clauses However, they are not CECs if viewed from the process-relation perspective.

(7.21)   a. 我教过一个学生很聪明 (C. T. J. Huang 1987: 230)
         wǒ jiāo-guò yí-gè xuéshēng hěn cōngmíng
         I teach-ASP one-CLF student very smart
         'I once taught a student who was very smart.'
   b. 我爱过一个女孩很漂亮 (C. T. J. Huang 1987: 230)
         wǒ ài-guò yí-gè nǚhái hěn piàoliang
         I love-ASP one-CLF girl very beautiful
         'I once loved a girl who was very beautiful.'
   c. 我选了一门课很难懂 (C. T. J. Huang 1987: 230)
         wǒ xuǎn-le yī-mén kè hěn nán dǒng
         I select-ASP a-CLF course quite difficult understand
         'I selected a course which was very difficult to understand'

d. 他送了一本书给我很有用 (C. T. J. Huang 1987: 230)
   tā sòng-le yī-běn shū gěi wǒ hěn yǒuyòng
   he give-ASP a-CLF book to me very useful
   'He gave a book to me which is very useful.'

From the process-relation perspective, 教过, 选了 and 送了 are typical material processes, while 爱过 is a typical mental process; 过 and 了 are aspect markers, and 很聪明, 很漂亮, 很难懂 and 很有用 are all relational processes. In other words, the constructions are contracted out of clause complexes and are IGMs, and there is no existential process in these constructions at all.

7.5 Other Controversial Non-finite Constructions Revisited

As discussed, process type and construction type should be decided before non-finiteness can be identified and analysed. Such types help predict the occurrence of non-finiteness, because different types tend to contain different potentials of non-finiteness. In this section, we will apply the FRP and the LFVP to the process relation of other typical controversial instances in the literature, to show how this approach may provide insights into the controversial issues.

In defending a finite and non-finite distinction in Chinese, C. T. J. Huang argues that one criterion is that non-finite clauses cannot be used with modal verbs, so (7.22a) is acceptable, while (7.22b) is not.

(7.22) a. 我准备明天来 (C. T. J. Huang 1982: 350)[4]
          wǒ zhǔnbèi míngtiān lái
          I prepare tomorrow come
          'I prepare to come tomorrow.'
       b. *我准备明天会来 (C. T. J. Huang 1982: 351)
          wǒ zhǔnbèi míngtiān huì- lái
          I prepare tomorrow will-MOD come
          '*I prepare will come tomorrow.'
       c. *我准备我明天来 (C. T. J. Huang 1982: 351)
          wǒ zhǔnbèi wǒ míngtiān lái
          I prepare I tomorrow come
          '*I prepare I come tomorrow.'

Under the LFVP, a clause cannot contain two finite verbs unless paratactic relation or embedding is involved. Since there is no embedding in (7.22a), and 准备 and 来 are not equal in status, 来 has to be a non-finite. The problem with (7.22b) is that with the modal verb 会, the verb 会来 becomes a finite verb. In other words, two finite verbs (i.e. 准备 and 会来) are used in a single clause

---

[4] Note that C. T. J. Huang (1982) used pinyin instead of Chinese characters. For consistency in this work, we use Chinese characters with pinyin and translations.

7.5 Other Controversial Non-finite Constructions Revisited

without embedding, rankshifting or paratactic relation. This violates the LFVP. Likewise, with 我 before 明天来 in (7.22 c), 来 becomes a finite verb. Thus, two finite verbs appear in the same clause without embedding, rankshifting or paratactic relation. The expression is therefore inappropriate.

In (7.23), the construction is quite different. 劝 is a typical verbal process and the construction belongs to Type IV, in which NP_2 is a conflated participant and VP_2 is non-finite. Since verbal processes are not causatives, the construction is simply a $VP_1+ NP_2+VP_2$ construction (see Table 6.1). In such a construction, the second process is a median process realized by a non-finite clause. In other words, finite verbs are not allowed in the VP_2 position, which explains why (7.23b) and (7.23c) are inappropriate.

(7.23) a. 我劝张三不买这本书 (C. T. J. Huang 1982: 350)
    wǒ   quàn   Zhāng Sān   bù-   mǎi   zhè-běn   shū
    I   persuade   Zhang San   not-NEG   buy   this-CLF   book
    'I persuaded Zhang San not to buy this book.'
b. *我劝张三没有买这本书 (C. T. J. Huang 1982: 351)
    wǒ   quàn   Zhāng Sān   méiyǒu-   mǎi   zhè-běn   shū
    I   persuade   Zhang San   not have-NEG   buy   this-CLF   book
    '*I persuaded Zhang San not to have bought this book.'
c. *我劝张三他不买这本书 (C. T. J. Huang 1982: 351)
    wǒ   quàn   Zhāng Sān   tā   bù-   mǎi   zhè-běn   shū
    I   persuade   Zhang San   he   not-NEG   buy   this-CLF   book
    '* I persuaded Zhang San he did not buy this book.'
d. 她逼丈夫戒了烟 (Y. Huang 1994: 28)
    tā   bī   zhàngfu   jiè-le   yān
    she   force   husband   quit-ASP   cigarette
    'She forced her husband into quitting smoking.'
e. 我从前请他吃过饭 (Y. H. A. Li 1990: 19)
    wǒ   cóngqián   qǐng   tā   chī-guò   fàn
    I   beforehand   invite   him   eat-ASP   meal
    'I invited him to dinner beforehand.'
f. 我劝他坐着 (BCC_NEWS)
    wǒ   quàn   tā   zuò-zhe
    I   persuade   him   sit-ASP
    'I persuaded him to sit.'

The acceptability of (7.23d), (7.23e) and (7.23f), which are all typical $VP_1+NP_2+VP_2$ constructions, suggests that the aspect markers (着, 了 and 过)[5] cannot be a criterion for distinguishing finite from non-finite in Chinese. Similar instances, though not many, can be found in the BCC corpus. See (7.24).

---

[5] It is generally believed that tense in modern Chinese is indicated by adjuncts, and aspect is more prevalent. Thus, these are all considered as aspect markers (see Chao 2011 [1968]).

(7.24) a. 劝他们喝过汤之后 (BCC_FICTION)
quàn tāmen hē-guò tang zhīhòu
persuade them drink-ASP soup afterwards
'After persuading them to drink the soup'

b. 他劝我留着 (BCC_FICTION)
tā quàn wǒ liú-zhe
he persuade me keep-ASP
'He persuaded me to keep it.'

c. 我并非有意劝你们担着风险去学她的榜样 (BCC_FICTION)
wǒ bìngfēi yǒuyì quàn nǐmen dān-zhe fēngxiǎn
I not-NEG intend persuade you take-ASP risk
qù xué tāde bǎngyàng
to follow her example
'I didn't intend to persuade you to take risks to follow her as an example.'

d. 同志们特别是团长都劝我骑着马走 (BCC_NEWS)
tóngzhìmen tèbiéshì tuánzhǎng dōu quàn wǒ qí-zhe mǎ zǒu
comrades especially colonel all persuade me ride-ASP horse go
'The comrades, the colonel in particular, all tried to persuade me to ride the horse and go.'

e. 有人劝她领着两个孩子改嫁 (BCC_NEWS)
yǒurén quàn tā lǐng-zhe liǎng-gè háizi gǎijià
someone persuade her bring-ASP two-CLF children remarry
'Someone tried to persuade her to bring the two children and remarry.'

The constructions in (7.23) and (7.24) may be best interpreted in terms of process type as well as construction type. Two process types are involved, the first of which is a typical material process realized by 逼, and the second a verbal process realized by 劝. What is ambiguous is the meaning of 劝: advise or urge. It is a verbal process if it means 'advise' and it tends to be a material process if it means 'urge'.

When the major clause is a material process and the construction belongs to Type IV in which a participant is conflated, the secondary clause is usually non-finite. Thus, 戒了烟 in (7.23d) is non-finite. In verbal processes, the secondary clause may or may not be non-finite, depending on the major process. This explains why the clauses following 劝 may be either finite or non-finite. In (7.23a), 劝 means 'urge' because it is strong in its result: 买 or 不买. It is hence a material process. As a result, 不买这本书 and 买这本书 are non-finite. The 劝 in other constructions in (7.23) and (7.24) most likely means 'advise', and they are verbal processes. In this case, both finite and non-finite clauses are allowed in the secondary processes, but finite clauses are used more often than non-finite clauses. These secondary clauses function as Verbiage of 劝 (i.e. as participants).

Likewise, the major process in (7.25) is a verbal process. What follows 说 are all participants (Verbiage in SFL). In other words, the secondary clauses in (7.25) all function as participants. They are all embedded to function as the contents of 说.

7.5 Other Controversial Non-finite Constructions Revisited

(7.25) a. 张三说他下午会来 (C. T. J. Huang 1982: 352)
Zhāng Sān shuō tā xiàwǔ huì- lái
Zhang San say he afternoon will-MOD come
'Zhang San said that he will come in the afternoon.'
b. 张三说李四下午会来 (C. T. J. Huang 1982: 352)
Zhāng Sān shuō Lǐ Sì xiàwǔ huì- lái
Zhang San say Li Si afternoon will-MOD come
'Zhang San said that Li Si will come in the afternoon.'
c. 张三说明天不能来了 (C. T. J. Huang 1982: 353)
Zhāng Sān shuō míngtiān bù- néng- lái-le
Zhang San say tomorrow not-NEG can-MOD come-EXCL
'Zhang San said he will not be able to come tomorrow.'

A similar explanation may apply to 我预料他明天会来 (wǒ yùliào tā míngtiān huì lái / I guess he tomorrow will come) (C. T. J. Huang 1982: 351), in which the primary clause realized by 预料(guess) is a mental process and the secondary clause embedded to function as the participant (i.e. Phenomenon). Here two finite verbs occur to this construction, but one is embedded as part of a participant. The embedded clauses are raw realizations.

L. Xu (1986) argues that modal verbs can be allowed in the secondary clause in (7.22b) if 要(yào/intend) instead of 会(huì/will) is used. Thus we have (7.26).

(7.26) 我准备明天要参加一个会 (L. Xu 1986: 348)
wǒ zhǔnbèi míngtiān yào- cānjiā yí-gè huì
I prepare tomorrow must-MOD attend a-CLF meeting
'I prepare to be obliged to attend a meeting tomorrow.'

This may be intuitively understood as appropriate by native speakers of Chinese. However, a search in the BCC corpus tells us that this is not used in Chinese at all. We use the SQ 'r 准备 t 要 v' in the BCC corpus, which is supposed to find all pronouns followed by 准备 plus temporal groups plus 要 plus verbs. The result is that no instances are returned in the BCC corpus apart from the following, which are quite different in construction: 自己准备第二天要穿的衣服 / 偷偷去为她准备第二天要带的中饭. In these two constructions, 要穿的 and 要带的 are adjectivized groups and 要 is no longer a modal verb.

As for absolute construction, it seems that no one ever has considered the possibility of it existing in Chinese. However, some so-called topic-prominent constructions have the features of absolute construction in English; see (7.27).

(7.27) a. 那回大火, 幸亏消防员来得早 (Chao 2011 [1968]: 125)
nà-huí dàhuǒ, xìngkuī xiāofángyuán lái-de zǎo
that-CLF fire, fortunately fireman come-COMP early
'About that fire, it is fortunate that the firemen arrived early.'

b. 浮水你学会了没有?(Chao 2011 [1968]: 125)
   fúshuǐ   nǐ   xuéhuì-le méiyǒu
   swimming   you   learn-ASP or not
   'Speaking of swimming, have you learned it?'

On the one hand, 那回大火 and 浮水 are the 'aboutness' of what is in focus. This means they are functioning as circumstances: an exact feature of absolute clauses. On the other hand, 那回大火 is a group, and 浮水 may be considered as a median clause. In other words, it is possible to consider such expressions as absolute constructions. Since most so-called topics are nominal groups and not many instances can be found to contain non-finiteness, we will not consider this in the present research.

8 Conclusion

8.1 Overview of the Major Findings

A number of core issues related to non-finiteness in English and Chinese have been dealt with in this book, but the research is not intended to be comparative or contrastive in the strict sense. Thus, the findings should not be examined against those from contrastive linguistics. The general idea is that in-depth studies on non-finiteness are critical to the understanding of lexical and syntactic issues in the grammar as a whole. With this research, we may conclude that finiteness and non-finiteness must be a distinction not to be restricted by formal properties. Indeed, the finite/non-finite distinction is a much more abstract property in English and Chinese than is understood in current literature. The distinction signals universality of non-finiteness and urges reconsiderations of categories such as tense, aspect and modality from the process-relation perspective.

The comprehensive review of studies on non-finiteness in Chapter 2 has revealed many illuminating ideas in the literature, and a definition of non-finiteness in terms of moodlessness, clause dependency, and incompleteness in ideation (participant, process, circumstance) is possible and also beneficial. Hence, an event/state that is moodless in interpersonal meaning, dependent in clause structure and incomplete in ideational components is usually non-finite. This is true in Chinese, a language void of inflection indicators. In languages which are characterised by inflections, the inflection indicators help determine the status of being non-finite. In this case, the ideational components may be complete (e.g. absolute clauses composed of subjects and non-finites in English). However, moodlessness and clause dependency are still fundamental for determining absolute clauses.

Specifically, three parameters are basic for the finite/non-finite distinction. The first parameter is moodlessness, because a non-finite clause does not carry mood in interaction for interpersonal purposes. The second parameter is clause dependency, because the major difference between a finite clause and a non-finite clause lies in the dependency in the structure; a non-finite clause usually relies on other clauses to be meaningful. The third parameter is incompleteness in ideational components. The basic ideational components in a clause are participant, process and circumstance, among which process is the most fundamental. A non-finite clause is incomplete in ideational components, and it is usually realized by a median process. This median process may be a single non-finite element, or a non-finite element together with other components, and this applies to Chinese, which lacks inflectional indicators. In languages that carry apparent inflections for indicating non-finiteness (e.g. English), incompleteness in ideation may not be a necessary parameter.

In the study of non-finiteness, spoken and written language should be distinguished, because they require different grammars. Whatever grammar is used, cryptotype and cline are unavoidable properties of concepts, and the concept of non-finiteness is no exception. Apart from cryptotype and cline, metafunctions such as ideational, interpersonal and textual functions are universal categories, and these categories serve as the foundation for observing processes. A process is the basic semantic unit, and a clause is the basic constructional unit. The major, median and minor processes correspond with the major, median and minor clauses respectively.

According to the process-relation perspective, eight construction types can be put forward, and the types carry different potentiality for containing non-finiteness. Type III (the hypo-relation) usually contains non-finiteness. The reason for this is that the first verb in this construction already carries finiteness, and the LFVP stipulates that only one finite verb be allowed in a construction, unless embedding or a paratactic relation are involved. The second process, in Type IV, in which the participant is conflated, is always a non-finite clause. When a process functions as the participant in Type V and Type VI constructions, it may or may not be a non-finite clause, depending on the moodlessness and incompleteness in functional components. When a process functions as the circumstance (Type VII), the process again may or may not be a non-finite clause. In Type VIII, a participant may be realized by a thing, an event or a state, which may be expressed by non-finite clause.

The organization of a clause may involve compression (i.e. rankshifting) or embedding, which complicates the construction types. To observe compression in constructions, IGM may be used as a mechanism to understand how various forms are used to express a similar meaning. In this mechanism, the FRP is useful to distinguish between raw realization (embedded clause), intermediate realization (non-finite clause) and full realization (rankshifted clause as IGM). The findings serve as answers to the first and second research questions of the present research: In what way is the finite/non-finite distinction universal? And in what context can non-finiteness be positioned and identified?

Non-finiteness occupies a significant position in inter-clausal connectivity. To answer how non-finiteness functions for inter-clausal connectivity, IGM and the metaphoric syndrome are the ideal starting point, because non-finite clauses are intermediate between the metaphorical and the congruent in terms of ideational meaning. Non-finite -ing forms devoid of other components may be nominalizations, non-finite to- forms verbalizations, and non-finite -ed forms adjectivizations, all of which are manifestations of clause compression (i.e. typical IGMs). When non-finiteness is used as a clause, it tends to be intermediate between clause and group, functioning as a median process.

From the process-relation perspective, the non-finite clause is a basic category of clause combining, and three basic clause relations can be identified: paratactic relation, which is realized through logical connectives (*and, or, but*); circumstantial relation, in which secondary clauses linked by conjunctions (e.g. *because, when, where* ...) function as various circumstances; and participantial relation, in which a process functions as participant or qualifier. Non-finite clauses usually occur in the second and third types of relation, especially when no conjunctions appear. Hence, while non-finiteness acts like a bridge in a clause construction, a non-finite clause acts like a bridge in clause combining.

The controversial issues of non-finiteness in English and Chinese have been observed from the process-relation perspective. First, the difference between causative and non-causative constructions has been dealt with in terms of process types. The idea is that different process types carry different potentiality in causation. Four process types can appear in the construction of $VP_1+NP_2+VP_2$: material process of doing and happening; mental process of thinking and feeling; verbal process of saying; and existential process of existing. However, only constructions of material process can be causative. No matter whether VP_1 is causative or non-causative, VP_2 in the construction $VP_1+NP_2+VP_2$ tends to be realized by non-finiteness. Moreover, the serial verb construction, the existential construction and the absolute construction in both English and Chinese tend to contain non-finiteness.

Under the process-relation perspective, the construction types, process types, IGM, FRP, LFVP, and so on can be used to tackle the controversial issues. More importantly, this perspective helps us to find more universal rather than unique features in English and Chinese, although the focus of this study is not linguistic universality.

8.2 Limitations and Further Study

This study has its limitations. First, the definition of non-finiteness has shifted from morphology-oriented or syntax-oriented perspectives to the function-oriented perspective. Since function is too subtle to grasp, other parameters may have been skipped in the study. More crucially, the parameters have not been explored for ease of application, and possible subcategories of the parameters have not been explored.

Second, the construction types, the FRP and the LFVP all need to be verified cross-linguistically by languages other than English and Chinese. The construction types are typical both in English and Chinese, and the two principles work well for both English and Chinese, but no other languages have been testified.

Third, the special constructions in English and Chinese, ambiguous and controversial ones in particular, should be compared and contrasted in greater detail. This research was not intended to add knowledge to views on universality, but the findings do show many similar properties of English and Chinese. If universality is the concern, more research into how properties are similar in specific details need to be carried out. In addition, how various traditional categories can be understood from the process-relation perspective should be explored.

Further study could not only work for solutions to the problems mentioned here, but also cover diachronic and synchronic investigations. As a promising entry point from which many linguistic issues can be understood, non-finiteness has the potential to illuminate other topics, among which the clause, the most fundamental and the highest grammatical unit, can also be better approached diachronically.

Since the present study is aimed at written language, which requires a grammar different from that for spoken language, issues of non-finiteness specific to spoken language have not been explored. Future study may apply the findings from the present study to issues on spoken languages for verification and modification.

Theories benefit greatly from their applications, and further developments may only be possible once problems in application arise. If what is outlined in this research can be used in text segmentation, text annotation and typological studies, the subsequent developments will most probably enhance the robustness of the approach.

References

Aarts, Bas. 2011. *Oxford Modern English Grammar*. Oxford: Oxford University Press.
Aarts, Bas, Sylvia Chalker & Edmund Weiner, eds. 2014. *The Oxford Dictionary of English Grammar*. 2nd ed. Oxford: Oxford University Press.
Adger, David. 2007. 'Three Domains of Finiteness: A Minimalist Perspective'. In *Finiteness: Theoretical and Empirical Foundations*, edited by I. Nikolaeva, pp. 23–58. Oxford: Oxford University Press.
Aikhenvald, Alexandra. 2006. 'Serial Verb Constructions in a Typological Perspective'. In *Serial Verb Constructions: A Cross-Linguistic Typology*, edited by A. Aikhenvald & R. M. W. Dixon, pp. 1–68. Oxford: Oxford University Press.
Allan, Keith. 1971. 'A Note on the Source of There in Existential Sentences'. *Foundations of Language* 7(1): 1–18.
Amritavalli, Raghavachari. 2014. 'Separating Tense and Finiteness: Anchoring in Dravidian'. *Natural Language and Linguistic Theory* 32: 283–306.
Anderson, Stephen. 2002. 'Syntax and Morphology Are Different: Commentary on Jonas'. In *Syntactic Effects of Morphological Change*, edited by D. Lightfoot, pp. 271–5. Oxford: Oxford University Press.
Anderson, Stephen R. 2008. 'English Reduced Auxiliaries Really Are Simple Clitics'. *Lingue e Linguaggio* 3(1): 169–86.
Ansaldo, Umberto. 2006. 'Serial Verb Constructions'. In *Encyclopedia of Language and Linguistics*, vol. 11, edited by K. Brown, A. Anderson, L. Bauer, M. Berns, G. Hirst & J. Miller, pp. 260–4. London: Elsevier.
Aronoff, Mark. 1985. 'Orthography and Linguistic Theory'. *Language* 61: 28–72.
Austin, John Langshaw. 1962. *How to Do Things with Words*. Oxford: Clarendon.
Bache, Carl. 2008. *English Tense and Aspect in Halliday's Systemic Functional Grammar*. London: Equinox.
Banks, David. 2005. 'On the Historical Origins of Nominalized Process in Scientific Text'. *English for Specific Purposes* 24(3): 347–57.
Banks, David. 2017. *A Systemic Functional Grammar of French: A Simple Introduction*. Abingdon: Routledge.
Basang, Zhuoma. 1990. 'Batang dongci quzhe xingtai de fenxihua' [An analysis of verbal inflections in Batang]. *Minzu Yuwen* [Minority languages of China] 12(5): 76–9.
Bateman, John A. 1990. 'Finding Translation Equivalents: An Application of Grammatical Metaphor'. In *Proceedings of the 13th Conference on Computational Linguistics*, edited by H. Karlgren, pp. 13–18. Stroudsburg, PA: Association for Computational Linguistics.

Baxter, William H. & Laurent Sagart. 2014. *Old Chinese: A New Reconstruction*. Oxford: Oxford University Press.
Bergen, Benjamin & Nancy Chang. 2005. 'Embodied Construction Grammar in Simulation-Based Language Understanding'. In *Construction Grammar(s): Cognitive and Cross-Language Dimensions*, edited by J.-O. Östman & M. Fried, pp. 147–90. Amsterdam: John Benjamins.
Bhatia, Tej K. 1993. *Punjabi: A Cognitive-Descriptive Grammar*. London: Routledge.
Biber, Douglas. 1988. *Variation across Speech and Writing*. Cambridge: Cambridge University Press.
Biber, Douglas & Bethany Gray. 2016. *Grammatical Complexity in Academic English: Linguistic Change in Writing*. Cambridge: Cambridge University Press.
Biber, Douglas, Stig Johansson, Geoffrey Leech, Susan Conrad & Edward Finegan. 1999. *Longman Grammar of Spoken and Written English*. Edinburgh: Pearson Education Ltd.
Binnick, Robert I. 1991. *Time and the Verb*. Oxford: Oxford University Press.
Bisang, Walter. 1995. 'Verb Serialization and Converbs: Differences and Similarities'. In *Converbs in Cross-Linguistic Perspective*, edited by E. König & M. Haspelmath, pp. 137–88. Berlin: Mouton de Gruyter.
Bisang, Walter. 1998. 'Adverbiality: The View from the Far East'. In *Adverbial Constructions in the Languages of Europe*, edited by J. Van der Auwera & D. P. Ó. Baoill, pp. 641–812. Berlin: Mouton de Gruyter.
Bisang, Walter. 2001. 'Finite vs. Non Finite Languages'. In *Language Typology and Language Universals: An International Handbook*, edited by M. Haspelmath, E. König, W. Oesterreicher & W. Raible, pp. 1400–13. Berlin: Walter de Gruyter.
Bisang, Walter. 2007. 'Categories That Make Finiteness: Discreteness from a Functional Perspective and Some of Its Repercussions'. In *Finiteness: Theoretical and Empirical Foundations*, edited by I. Nikolaeva, pp. 115–37. Oxford: Oxford University Press.
Blom, Elma, Evelien Krikhaar & Frank Wijnen. 2001. 'Nonfinite Clauses in Dutch and English Child Language: An Experimental Approach'. In *Proceedings of the 25th Annual Boston University Conference on Language Development*, edited by H.-J. A. Do, L. Dominguez & A. Johansen, pp. 133–44. Somerville, MA: Cascadilla Press.
Bloomfield, Leonard. 1933. *Language*. London: George Allen & Unwin Ltd.
Boas, Franz. 1911. *Handbook of American Indian Languages*. Washington, DC: Government Printing Office.
Boas, Franz. 1938. *The Mind of Primitive Man*. New York: Macmillan.
Bolinger, Dwight. 1968. 'Entailment and the Meaning of Structures'. *Glossa* 2(2): 119–27.
Börjars, Kersti & Kate Burridge. 2010. *Introducing English Grammar*. 2nd ed. London: Hodder Education.
Borsley, Robert. 1996. *Modern Phrase Structure Grammar*. Oxford: Blackwell.
Bradley, Henry. 1913. *On the Relations between Spoken and Written Language with Special Reference to English*. London: Proceedings of the British Academy.
Branner, David Prager. 2002. 'Common Chinese and Early Chinese Morphology'. *Journal of the American Oriental Society* 122(4): 706–21.

Branner, David Prager. 2003. 'On Early Chinese Morphology and Its Intellectual History: Winner of the Barwis–Holliday Award for 2001'. *Journal of the Royal Asiatic Society* 13(1): 45–76.
Brown, Goold. 1851. *The Grammar of English Grammars*. New York: William Wood & Company.
Brown, Keith & Jim Miller. 2016. *A Critical Account of English Syntax: Grammar, Meaning, Text*. Edinburgh: Edinburgh University Press.
Brown, Roger. 1973. *A First Language*. Cambridge, MA: Harvard University Press.
Bruening, Benjamin. 2018. 'Double Object Constructions and Prepositional Dative Constructions Are Distinct: A Reply to Ormazabal and Romero 2012'. *Linguistic Inquiry* 49(1): 123–50.
Bühler, Karl. 2011 [1934]. *Theory of Language: The Representational Function of Language*. Amsterdam: John Benjamins.
Bullokar, William. 1906 [1586]. 'Brief Grammar for English'. In *Geschichte Der Fabeldichtung in England Bis Zu John Gay (1726)*, edited by M. Plessow, pp. 333–73. Berlin: Mayer & Müller.
Burton, Samuel Holroyd. 1984. *Mastering English Grammar*. London: Palgrave Macmillan.
Bybee, Joan. 1985. *Morphology: A Study of the Relation between Meaning and Form*. Amsterdam: John Benjamins.
Bybee, Joan & Östen Dahl. 1989. 'The Creation of Tense and Aspect Systems in the Languages of the World'. *Studies in Language* 13(1): 51–103.
Byrnes, Heidi. 2009. 'Emergent L2 German Writing Ability in a Curricular Context: A Longitudinal Study of Grammatical Metaphor'. *Linguistics and Education* 20(1): 50–66.
Caffarel, Alice. 2006. *A Systemic Functional Grammar of French: From Grammar to Discourse*. London: Continuum.
Callaway, Morgan. 1901. *The Appositive Participle in Anglo-Saxon*. Baltimore: The Modern Language Association of America.
Camacho, José A. 2013. *Null Subjects*. New York: Cambridge University Press.
Campbell, Aimee L. & Michael Tomasello. 2001. 'The Acquisition of English Dative Constructions'. *Applied Psycholinguistics* 22(2): 253–67.
Capell, Arthur. 1965. 'A Typology of Concept Domination'. *Lingua* 15: 451–62.
Carden, Guy. 1967. *Quantifiers as Higher Verbs*. IBM Boston Programming Technical Report BPC 5.
Carter, Ronald & Michael McCarthy. 2006. *Cambridge Grammar of English: A Comprehensive Guide*. Cambridge: Cambridge University Press.
Caselli, Tommaso & Rachele Sprugnoli. 2017. 'It-TimeML and the Ita-TimeBank: Language Specific Adaptations for Temporal Annotation'. In *Handbook of Linguistic Annotation*, edited by N. Ide & J. Pustejovsky, pp. 969–88. Dordrech: Springer.
Chafe, Wallace L. 1970. *Meaning and the Structure of Language*. Chicago: Chicago University Press.
Chafe, Wallace L. 1982. 'Integration and Involvement in Speaking, Writing, and Oral Literature'. In *Spoken and Written Language: Exploring Orality and Literacy*, edited by D. Tannen, pp. 35–53. Norwood, NJ: Ablex.

Chafe, Wallace L. 1994. *Discourse, Consciousness, and Time: The Flow and Displacement of Conscious Experience in Speaking and Writing*. Chicago: University of Chicago Press.

Chamoreau, Claudine & Zarina Estrada-Fernández. 2016. 'Finiteness and Nominalization: An Overview'. In *Finiteness and Nominalization*, edited by C. Chamoreau & Z. Estrada-Fernández, pp. 1–10. Amsterdam: John Benjamins.

Chao, Yuen Ren. 2011 [1968]. *A Grammar of Spoken Chinese*. Beijing: The Commercial Press.

Chelliah, Shobhana L. & Willem J. de Reuse. 2011. *Handbook of Descriptive Linguistic Fieldwork*. London: Springer.

Chen, Jianmin. 1960. 'Lun jianyushi he yixie youguan juzi fenxifa de wen' [Pivotal constructions and issues related to sentence analysis]. *Zhongguo Yuwen* [Studies of the Chinese language] 9(3): 101–6.

Chen, Jianmin. 1986. *Xiandai Hanyu juxinglun* [Sentence patterns in modern Chinese]. Beijing: Yuwen Press.

Chomsky, Noam. 1957. *Syntactic Structures*. Berlin: Walter de Gruyter.

Chomsky, Noam. 1965. *Aspects of the Theory of Syntax*. Cambridge, MA: The MIT Press.

Chomsky, Noam. 1973. 'Conditions on Transformations'. In *A Festschrift for Morris Halle*, edited by S. Anderson & P. Kiparsky, pp. 232–86. New York: Holt, Rinehart & Winston.

Chomsky, Noam. 1981. *Lectures on Government and Binding: The Pisa Lectures*. Dordrecht: Foris.

Chomsky, Noam. 1982. *Some Concepts and Consequences of the Theory of Government and Binding*. Cambridge, MA: The MIT Press.

Chomsky, Noam. 1995. *The Minimalist Program*. Cambridge, MA: The MIT Press.

Chomsky, Noam. 2000. 'Minimalist Inquiries: The Framework'. In *Step by Step: Essays on Minimalist Syntax in Honor of Howard Lasnik*, edited by R. Martin, D. Michaels & J. Uriagereka, pp. 89–155. Cambridge, MA: The MIT Press.

Chomsky, Noam & Howard Lasnik. 1993. *The Theory of Principles and Parameters*. Berlin: Walter de Gruyter.

Christie, Frances & James Robert Martin. 2007. *Language, Knowledge and Pedagogy: Functional Linguistic and Sociological Perspectives*. London: Continuum.

Clark, Eve V. & Herbert H. Clark. 1979. 'When Nouns Surface as Verbs'. *Language* 55(4): 767–811.

Classen, Ernest. 1919. *Outlines of the History of the English Language*. London: Macmillan and Co. Limited.

Cobbett, William & Alfred Ayres. 1884. *The English Grammar of William Cobbett*. New York: D. Appleton and Company.

Colombi, M. Cecilia. 2006. 'Grammatical Metaphor: Academic Language Development in Latino Students of Spanish'. In *Advanced Language Learning: The Contribution of Halliday and Vygotsky*, edited by H. Byrnes, pp. 147–63. London: Continuum.

Comrie, Bernard. 1975. 'Polite Plurals and Predicate Agreement'. *Language* 51(2): 406–18.

Comrie, Bernard. 1976a. *Aspect: An Introduction to the Study of Verbal Aspect and Related Problems*. Cambridge: Cambridge University Press.

Comrie, Bernard. 1976b. 'The Syntax of Causative Constructions: Cross-Language Similarities and Divergences'. In *The Grammar of Causative Constructions*, edited by M. Shibatani, pp. 261–312. New York: Academic Press.

Comrie, Bernard. 1985. *Tense*. Cambridge: Cambridge University Press.

Comrie, Bernard & Maria Polinsky, eds. 1993. *Causatives and Transitivity*. Philadelphia: John Benjamins.

Conrad, Bent. 1982. *Referring and Non-Referring Phrases: A Study in the Use of the Gerund and the Infinitive*. Copenhagen: Akademisk Forlag.

Cowper, Elizabeth. 2016. 'Finiteness and Pseudofiniteness'. In *Finiteness Matters: On Finiteness-Related Phenomena in Natural Languages*, edited by K. M. Eide, pp. 47–77. Amsterdam: John Benjamins.

Cristofaro, Sonia. 2003. *Subordination*. Oxford: Oxford University Press.

Cristofaro, Sonia. 2007. 'Deconstructing Categories: Finiteness in a Functional-Typological Perspective'. In *Finiteness: Theoretical and Empirical Foundations*, edited by I. Nikolaeva, pp. 91–114. Oxford: Oxford University Press.

Croft, William. 2001. *Radical Construction Grammar: Syntactic Theory in Typological Perspective*. Oxford: Oxford University Press.

Cruschina, Silvio. 2015. 'Patterns of Variation in Existential Constructions'. *Isogloss* 1(1): 33–65.

Cumming, Susanna. 1991. *Functional Change: The Case of Malay Constituent Order*. Berlin: Mouton de Gruyter.

Curme, George O. 1947. *English Grammar*. New York: Harper & Row Publishers, Inc.

Dahl, Östen. 1985. *Tense and Aspect System*. Oxford: Blackwell.

Dai, Qingxia. 1981. 'Zaiwayu shidong fanchou de xingtai bianhua' [Morphological changes in causatives in Zaiwa language]. *Minzu Yuwen* [Minority languages of China] 3(4): 36–41.

Daneš, František. 1964. 'A Three-Level Approach to Syntax'. *Travaux Linguistiques de Prague* 1: 225–40.

Daniel, Canon. 1891. *The Grammar History and Derivation of the English Language*. London: National Society's Depository.

Davidse, Kristin. 1999. *Categories of Experiential Grammar*. Clifton, Nottingham: Department of English and Media Studies, Nottingham Trent University.

Derewianka, Beverly. 1995. 'Language Development in the Transition from Childhood to Adolescence: The Role of Grammatical Metaphor'. PhD thesis, Macquarie University, Sydney.

Derewianka, Beverly. 2003. 'Grammatical Metaphor in the Transition to Adolescence'. In *Grammatical Metaphor: Views from Systemic Functional Linguistics*, edited by A.-M. Simon-Vandenbergen, M. Taverniers & L. Ravelli, pp. 185–220. Amsterdam: John Benjamins.

Devrim, Devo Y. 2015. 'Grammatical Metaphor: What Do We Mean? What Exactly Are We Researching?' *Functional Linguistics* 2(1): 1–15.

Diessel, Holger. 2004. *The Acquisition of Complex Sentences*. Cambridge: Cambridge University Press.

Dik, Simon C. 1980. *Studies in Functional Grammar*. London: Academic Press.

Dik, Simon C. 1981. *Functional Grammar*. Dordrecht: Foris.

Dik, Simon C. 1997. *The Theory of Functional Grammar: Complex and Derived Constructions*, edited by K. Hengeveld. Berlin: Mouton de Gruyter.

Dikken, Marcel den. 1995. *Particles: On the Syntax of Verb-Particle, Triadic, and Causative Constructions*. New York: Oxford University Press.
Dimroth, Christine & Ingeborg Lasser. 2002. 'Finite Options: How L1 and L2 Learners Cope with the Acquisition of Finiteness'. *Linguistics* 40(4): 647–51.
Ding, Shengshu, Shuxiang Lü, Rong Li, et al. 1999. *Xiandai Hanyu yufa jianghua* [Lectures on modern Chinese grammar]. Beijing: The Commercial Press.
Dirven, René. 1989. 'A Cognitive Perspective on Complementation'. In *Sentential Complementation and the Lexicon: Studies in Honour of Wim de Geest*, edited by D. Jaspers, W. Klooster, Y. Putseys & P. Seuren, pp. 113–39. Dordrecht: Foris.
Dirven, René & Vilém Fried, eds. 1987. *Functionalism in Linguistics*. Amsterdam: John Benjamins.
Dixon, Robert M. W. 1991. *A New Approach to English Grammar, on Semantic Principles*. Oxford: Clarendon.
Dixon, Robert M. W. 2005. *A Semantic Approach to English Grammar*. 2nd ed. Oxford: Oxford University Press.
Downing, Angela. 2015. *English Grammar: A University Course*. 3rd ed. London: Routledge.
Drieman, G. H. J. 1962. 'Differences between Written and Spoken Language: An Exploratory Study'. *Acta Psychologica* 20: 78–100.
Duffley, Patrick J. 2003. 'The Gerund and the To-Infinitive as Subject'. *Journal of English Linguistics* 31(4): 324–52.
Duffley, Patrick J. 2006. *The English Gerund-Participle: A Comparison with the Infinitive*. New York: Peter Lang.
Egan, Thomas. 2008. *Non-Finite Complementation: A Usage-Based Study of Infinitive and -ing Clauses in English*. Amsterdam: Rodopi.
Eide, Kristin Melum. 2016. 'Introduction'. In *Finiteness Matters: On Finiteness-Related Phenomena in Natural Languages*, edited by K. M. Eide, pp. 1–46. Amsterdam: John Benjamins.
Epps, Patience & Alexandre Arkhipov. 2009. 'Introduction'. In *New Challenges in Typology: Transcending the Borders and Refining the Distinctions*, edited by P. Epps & A. Arkhipov, pp. 1–9. Berlin: Walter de Gruyter.
Ernst, Thomas. 1994. 'Functional Categories and the Chinese Infl'. *Linguistics* 32: 191–212.
Evans, Nicholas. 2010. 'Semantic Typology'. In *The Oxford Handbook of Linguistic Typology*, edited by J. J. Song, pp. 504–33. Oxford: Oxford University Press.
Fabricius-Hansen, Cathrine & Wiebke Ramm. 2008. 'Editors' Introduction: Subordination and Coordination from Different Perspectives'. In *Subordination versus Coordination in Sentence and Text: A Cross-Linguistic Perspective*, edited by C. Fabricius-Hansen & W. Ramm, pp. 1–30. Amsterdam: John Benjamins.
Fan, Fanglian. 1963. 'Cunzaiju' [Existential sentence]. *Zhongguo Yuwen* [Studies of the Chinese language] 12(5): 386–95.
Fan, Xiao. 1991. *Hanyu de duanyu* [Phrases in Chinese]. Beijing: The Commercial Press.
Fang, Huaihai & Xiaomin Zhao. 2008. 'Cong mingcixing xiaoju kan Hanyu de "budingshi" jiegou' [On the infinitive structure in Chinese from the perspective of nominal clauses]. *Hanyu Xuebao* [Journal of the Chinese language] 5(2): 23–30.

Fawcett, Robin. 2008. *Invitation to Systemic Functional Linguistics through the Cardiff Grammar*. London: Equinox.
Fawcett, Robin. forthcoming. *Functional Syntax Handbook: Analyzing English at the Level of Form*. London: Equinox.
Fillmore, Charles, Paul Kay & Catherine O'Connor. 1988. 'Regularity and Idiomaticity in Grammatical Constructions: The Case of Let Alone'. *Language* 64: 501–38.
Firbas, Jan. 1964a. 'From Comparative Word-Order Studies'. *Brno Studies in English* 4: 111–28.
Firbas, Jan. 1964b. 'On Defining the Theme in Functional Sentence Analysis'. *Travaux Linguistiques de Prague* 1: 267–80.
Firbas, Jan. 1992. *Functional Sentence Perspective in Written and Spoken Communication*. Cambridge: Cambridge University Press.
Firth, John Rupert. 1957. *Papers in Linguistics 1934–1951*. London: Oxford University Press.
Firth, John Rupert. 1968. 'Descriptive Linguistics and the Study of English'. In *Selected Papers of J. R. Firth 1952–1959*, edited by F. R. Palmer, pp. 96–113. Bloomington: Indiana University Press.
Fleischhauer, Jens, Anja Latrouite & Rainer Osswald. 2016. 'Introduction.' In *Explorations of the Syntax-Semantics Interface*, edited by J. Fleischhauer, A. Latrouite & R. Osswald, pp. 7–14. Düsseldorf: Düsseldorf University Press.
Fontaine, Lise. 2012. *Analysing English Grammar: A Systemic Functional Introduction*. Cambridge: Cambridge University Press.
Fontaine, Lise. 2015. 'The Noun, Grammar and Context'. *Linguistics and the Human Sciences* 11(2–3): 178–202.
Forbes, John. 1848. *The Principles of Gaelic Grammar*. Edinburgh: Oliver & Boyd; Simpkin, Marshall, & Co.
Franks, Steven & Katarzyna Dziwirek. 1993. 'Negated Adjunct Phrases Are Really Partitive'. *Journal of Slavic Linguistics* 1(2): 208–305.
Freeborn, Dennis. 1992. *From Old English to Standard English: A Course Book in Language Variations across Time*. London: Macmillan.
Fu, Dawei. 1980. 'Cong juzi de neibu jiegou kan suowei "jianyushi"' [The so-called 'pivotal construction' from the perspective sentential inner structure]. *Journal of Liaoning University* 10(4): 90–6.
Gao, Zengxia. 2006. *Xiandai Hanyu liandongshi de yufahua shijiao* [Serial verb constructions in modern Chinese from the perspective of grammaticalization]. Beijing: China Archives Press.
Gasde, Horst-Dieter & Waltraud, Paul. 1996. 'Functional Categories, Topic Prominence, and Complex Sentences in Mandarin Chinese'. *Linguistics* 34: 263–94.
Gast, Volker & Holger Diessel. 2012. 'The Typology of Clause Linkage: Status Quo, Challenges, Prospects'. In *Clause Linkage in Cross-Linguistic Perspective: Data-Driven Approaches to Cross-Clausal Syntax*, edited by V. Gast & H. Diessel, pp. 1–36. Berlin: Mouton de Gruyter.
George, Leland & Jaklin Kornfilt. 1981. 'Finiteness and Boundedness in Turkish'. In *Binding and Filtering*, edited by F. Heny, pp. 105–27. London: Croom Helm.
Georgiou, Renos, Christos Papatzalas & Arhonto Terzi. 2016. 'A Non-Finite Period in Early Cypriot Greek'. *Modern Greek Dialects and Linguistic Theory* 6(1): 52–62.

Gilquin, Gaëtanelle. 2010. *Corpus, Cognition and Causative Constructions*. Amsterdam: John Benjamins.
Givón, Talmy. 1979. *On Understanding Grammar*. New York: Academic Press.
Givón, Talmy. 1983. 'Iconicity, Isomorphism, and Non-Arbitrary Coding in Syntax'. In *Iconicity in Syntax: Proceedings of a Symposium on Iconicity in Syntax*, edited by J. Haiman, pp. 187–220. Amsterdam: John Benjamins.
Givón, Talmy. 1990. *Syntax: A Functional-Typological Introduction*, vol. 2. Amsterdam: John Benjamins.
Givón, Talmy. 1995. *Functionalism and Grammar*. Amsterdam: John Benjamins.
Givón, Talmy. 2001. *Syntax: An Introduction*, vol. 2. Amsterdam: John Benjamins.
Givón, Talmy. 2009. *The Genesis of Syntactic Complexity: Diachrony, Ontogeny, Neuro-Cognition, Evolution*. Amsterdam: John Benjamins.
Glare, P. G. W., A. Souter, J. M. Wyllie, et al. 1968. *Oxford Latin Dictionary*. London: Oxford University Press.
Gleitman, Lila R. 1965. 'Coordinating Conjunctions in English'. *Language* 41(2): 260–93.
Goldberg, Adele E. 1995. *Constructions: A Construction Grammar Approach to Argument Structure*. Chicago: University of Chicago Press.
Goldberg, Adele E. 2003. 'Constructions: A New Theoretical Approach to Language'. *Trends in Cognitive Sciences* 7(5): 219–24.
Grano, Thomas. 2015. *Control and Restructuring*. Oxford: Oxford University Press.
Greenbaum, Sidney & Gerald Nelson. 2002. *An Introduction to English Grammar*. 2nd ed. London: Pearson Education Ltd.
Greenberg, Joseph H. 1963. 'Some Universals of Grammar with Particular Reference to the Order of Meaningful Elements'. In *Universals of Language*, edited by J. H. Greenberg, pp. 73–113. London: The MIT Press.
Gretsch, Petra & Clive Perdue. 2007. 'Finiteness in First and Second Language Acquisition'. In *Finiteness: Theoretical and Empirical Foundations*, edited by I. Nikolaeva, pp. 432–84. Oxford: Oxford University Press.
Guo, Jie. 2011. 'Xiandai Hanyu xiaoju xiandingxing shuaijian yanjiu' [A study on the attenuation of finiteness of clauses in Mandarin Chinese]. PhD thesis, Renmin University of China, Beijing.
Guo, Jie. 2013. 'Guowai xianding yu feixianding yanjiu de yanhua yu fazhan' [Overseas studies on finiteness and non-finiteness: Evolution and development]. *Dangdai Yuyanxue* [Contemporary linguistics] 15(3): 336–48.
Gwilliams, Laura & Lise Fontaine. 2015. 'Indeterminacy in Process Type Classification'. *Functional Linguistics* 2(8): 1–19.
Haiman, John & Sandra A. Thompson, eds. 1988a. *Clause Combining in Grammar and Discourse*. Amsterdam: John Benjamins.
Haiman, John & Sandra A. Thompson. 1988b. 'Introduction'. In *Clause Combining in Grammar and Discourse*, edited by J. Haiman & S. A. Thompson. Amsterdam: John Benjamins.
Halliday, Michael A. K. 1956. 'Grammatical Categories in Modern Chinese'. *Transactions of the Philosophical Society* 55(1): 177–224.
Halliday, Michael A. K. 1961. 'Categories of the Theory of Grammar'. *Word* 17(3): 241–92.

Halliday, Michael A. K. 1966a. 'Some Notes on "Deep" Grammar'. *Journal of Linguistics* 2(1): 57–67.
Halliday, Michael A. K. 1966b. 'The Concept of Rank: A Reply'. *Journal of Linguistics* 2(1): 110–18.
Halliday, Michael A. K. 1967a. 'Notes on Transitivity and Theme in English: Part I'. *Journal of Linguistics* 3(1): 37–82.
Halliday, Michael A. K. 1967b. 'Notes on Transitivity and Theme in English: Part II'. *Journal of Linguistics* 3(2): 199–244.
Halliday, Michael A. K. 1968. 'Notes on Transitivity and Theme in English: Part III'. *Journal of Linguistics* 4(2): 179–215.
Halliday, Michael A. K. 1969. 'Options and Functions in the English Clause'. *Brno Studies in English* 8: 81–8.
Halliday, Michael A. K. 1970. 'Language Structure and Language Function'. In *New Horizons in Linguistics*, edited by J. Lyons, pp. 140–65. Harmondsworth: Penguin Books.
Halliday, Michael A. K. 1975. 'Learning How to Mean: Explorations in the Development of Language'. In *Foundations of Language Development: A Multidisciplinary Perspective*, edited by E. Lenneberg & E. H. Lenneberg, pp. 239–65. London: Academic Press.
Halliday, Michael A. K. 1976. *Halliday: System and Function in Language*, edited by G. Kress. London: Oxford University Press.
Halliday, Michael A. K. 1978. *Language as Social Semiotic: The Social Interpretation of Language and Meaning*. London: Edward Arnold.
Halliday, Michael A. K. 1984. 'Grammatical Metaphor in English and Chinese'. In *New Papers on Chinese Language Use*, edited by B. Hong, pp. 9–18. Canberra: Contemporary China Centre, Australian National University.
Halliday, Michael A. K. 1985. *An Introduction to Functional Grammar*. 1st ed. London: Edward Arnold.
Halliday, Michael A. K. 1989. *Spoken and Written Language*. 2nd ed. Oxford: Oxford University Press.
Halliday, Michael A. K. 1994. *An Introduction to Functional Grammar*. 2nd ed. London: Edward Arnold.
Halliday, Michael A. K. 2002a [1992]. 'Some Lexicogrammatical Features of the *Zero Population Growth* Text'. In *The Collected Works of M. A. K. Halliday*, vol. 2: *Linguistic Studies of Text and Discourse*, edited by J. Webster, pp. 197–227. London: Continuum.
Halliday, Michael A. K. [2002b [1979]]. 'Modes of Meaning and Modes of Expression: Types of Grammatical Structure and Their Determination by Different Semantic Functions'. In *The Collected Works of M. A. K. Halliday*, vol. 1: *On Grammar*, edited by J. Webster, pp. 196–218. London: Continuum.
Halliday, Michael A. K. 2002c [1987]. 'Spoken and Written Modes of Meaning'. In *The Collected Works of M. A. K. Halliday*, vol. 1: *On Grammar*, edited by J. Webster, pp. 323–51. London: Continuum.
Halliday, Michael A. K. 2003a [1966]. 'Grammar, Society and the Noun'. In *The Collected Works of M. A. K. Halliday*, vol. 3: *On Language and Linguistics*, edited by J. Webster. pp. 50–73. London: Continuum.

Halliday, Michael A. K. 2003b [1995]. *The Collected Works of M. A. K. Halliday*, vol. 3: *On Language and Linguistics*, edited by J. Webster. London: Continuum.
Halliday, Michael A. K. 2004a [1995]. 'Language and the Reshaping of Human Experience'. In *The Collected Works of M. A. K. Halliday*, vol. 5: *The Language of Science*, edited by J. Webster, pp. 7–23. New York: Continuum.
Halliday, Michael A. K. 2004b [1998]. 'Language and Knowledge: The "Unpacking" of Text'. In *The Collected Works of M. A. K. Halliday*, vol. 5: *The Language of Science*, edited by J. Webster, pp. 24–48. New York: Continuum.
Halliday, Michael A. K. 2004c [1998]. 'Things and Relations: Regrammaticizing Experience as Technical Knowledge'. In *The Collected Works of M. A. K. Halliday*, vol. 5: *The Language of Science*, edited by J. Webster, pp. 49–101. New York: Continuum.
Halliday, Michael A. K. 2004d [1999]. 'The Grammatical Construction of Scientific Knowledge: The Framing of the English Clause'. In *The Collected Works of M. A. K. Halliday*, vol. 5: *The Language of Science*, edited by J. Webster, pp. 102–34. New York: Continuum.
Halliday, Michael A. K. 2005 [1993]. 'Quantitative Studies and Probabilities in Grammar'. In *The Collected Works of M. A. K. Halliday*, vol. 6: *Computational and Quantitative Studies*, edited by J. Webster, pp. 130–56. London: Continuum.
Halliday, Michael A. K. & Ruqaiya Hasan. 1976. *Cohesion in English*. London: Longman.
Halliday, Michael A. K. & Christian M. I. M. Matthiessen. 1999. *Construing Experience through Meaning: A Language-Based Approach to Cognition*. London: Continuum.
Halliday, Michael A. K. & Christian M. I. M. Matthiessen. 2004. *An Introduction to Functional Grammar*. 3rd ed. London: Hodder Arnold.
Halliday, Michael A. K. & Christian M. I. M. Matthiessen. 2014. *Halliday's Introduction to Functional Grammar*. 4th ed. London: Routledge.
Harris, Roy. 1998. 'Three Models of Signification'. In *Integrational Linguistics: A First Reader*, edited by R. Harris & G. Wolf, pp. 113–25. Oxford: Pergamon.
Harrison, Matthew. 1861. *Rise, Progress, and Present Structure of the English Language*. Philadelphia: E. C. and J. Biddle and Co.
Haspelmath, Martin. 1995. 'The Converb as a Cross-Linguistically Valid Category'. In *Converbs in Cross-Linguistic Perspective: Structure and Meaning of Adverbial Verb Forms – Adverbial Participles, Gerunds*, edited by M. Haspelmath & E. König, pp. 1–56. Berlin: Walter de Gruyter.
Haspelmath, Martin. 2004. 'Coordinating Constructions: An Overview'. In *Coordinating Constructions*, edited by M. Haspelmath, pp. 3–40. Amsterdam: John Benjamins.
Haspelmath, Martin, Matthew S. Dryer, David Gil & Bernard Comrie, eds. 2005. *The World Atlas of Language Structures*. Oxford: Oxford University Press.
Hazout, Ilan. 2004. 'The Syntax of Existential Constructions'. *Linguistic Inquiry* 35(3): 393–430.
He, Qingshun & Bingjun Yang. 2014. 'A Study of Transfer Directions in Grammatical Metaphor'. *Australian Journal of Linguistics* 34(3): 345–60.
He, Qingshun & Bingjun Yang. 2015. *Absolute Clauses in English from the Systemic Functional Perspective: A Corpus-Based Study*. London: Springer.

He, Wei & Minchen Wang. 2018. 'Yinghanyu "xiaoju" yufa diwei zai shenshi' [Revisiting the grammatical status of 'clause' in English and Chinese]. *Foreign Language Teaching and Research* 50(2): 195–204.

He, Wei & Ruijie Zhang. 2017. 'Hanyu shiyiju de gongneng shijiao yanjiu' [The Chinese causative clause: A functional approach]. *Waiyu Xuekan* [Foreign language research] 40(6): 53–9.

He, Yuanjian. 2017. 'Hanyu shifou cunzai hechengxing (huo fenxixing) daoxiang de leixing zhuanbian?' [How real is the syntheticity-to-analyticity shift from archaic to contemporary Chinese?]. *Yuyan Jiaoxue Yu Yanjiu* [Language teaching and linguistic studies] 39(4): 1–15.

He, Yuanjian & Lingling Wang. 2002. 'Lun Hanyu shiyiju' [The syntax of causatives in Chinese]. *Hanyu Xuexi* [Chinese language learning] 23(4): 1–9.

Hengeveld, Kees. 1992. *Non-Verbal Predication: Theory, Typology, Diachrony*. Berlin: Mouton de Gruyter.

Hengeveld, Kees & J. Lachlan Mackenzie. 2008. *Functional Discourse Grammar: A Typologically-Based Theory of Language Structure*. Oxford: Oxford University Press.

Hengeveld, Kees & J. Lachlan Mackenzie. 2010. 'Functional Discourse Grammar'. In *The Oxford Handbook of Linguistic Analysis*, edited by B. Heine & H. Narrog, pp. 367–400. Oxford: Oxford University Press.

Her, One-Soon. 2008. *Grammatical Functions and Verb Subcategorization in Mandarin Chinese*. Taipei: Crane Publishing.

Hirsh-Pasek, Kathy, Deborah G. Kemler Nelson, Peter W. Jusczyk, et al. 1987. 'Clauses Are Perceptual Units for Young Infants'. *Cognition* 26(3): 269–86.

Hita, Jorge Arús. 2018. 'A Contrastive Description of Projection in English and Spanish across Ranks: From the Clause Nexus to the Group'. In *Perspectives from Systemic Functional Linguistics*, edited by A. Sellami-Baklouti & L. Fontaine, pp. 223–45. New York: Routledge.

Hoekstra, Teun & Nina Hyams. 1998. 'Aspects of Root Infinitives'. *Lingua* 106: 81–112.

Holmberg, Anders, Urpo Nikanne, Irmeli Oraviita, Hannu Reime & Trond Trosterud. 1993. 'The Structure of INFL and the Finite Clause in Finnish'. In *Case and Other Functional Categories in Finnish Syntax*, edited by A. Holmberg & U. Nikanne, pp. 177–206. Berlin: Mouton de Gruyter.

Hopper, Paul J. & Elizabeth Traugott. 2003. *Grammaticalization*. Cambridge: Cambridge University Press.

Hornby, Albert Sydney. 1975 [1954]. *Guide to Patterns and Usage in English*. 2nd ed. Oxford: Oxford University Press.

Hornstein, Norbert. 1990. *As Time Goes By: Tense and Universal Grammar*. Cambridge, MA: The MIT Press.

Hornstein, Norbert. 1999. 'Movement and Control'. *Linguistic Inquiry* 30(1): 69–96.

House, Homer C. & Susan Emolyn Harman. 1950 [1931]. *Descriptive English Grammar*. 2nd ed. New York: Prentice-Hall, Inc.

Hu, Jianhua. 1997. 'Yinghan kongyulei de fenlei fenbu yu suozhi bijiao yanjiu' [A comparative study of the classification, distribution and reference of empty categories in Chinese and English]. *Waiguoyu* [Foreign languages] 20(5): 38–44.

Hu, Jianhua, Haihua Pan & Liejiong Xu. 2001. 'Is There a Finite vs. Nonfinite Distinction in Chinese?' *Linguistics* 39(6): 1117–48.
Hu, Xuhui. 2010. 'Chinese Existential Constructions: At the Syntax-Pragmatics Interface'. PhD thesis, Nanjing University.
Hu, Xuhui. 2018. *Encoding Events: Functional Structure and Variation*. Oxford: Oxford University Press.
Hu, Yushu & Xiao Fan, eds. 1995. *Dongci yanjiu* [On verbs]. Kaifeng: Henan University Press.
Huang, Bufan. 1981. 'Guzangyu dongci de Xingtai' [The morphology of Old Tibetan]. *Minzu Yuwen* [Minority languages of China] 3(3): 1–13.
Huang, C. T. James. 1982. 'Logical Relations in Chinese and the Theory of Grammar'. PhD thesis, Massachusetts Institute of Technology, Cambridge, MA.
Huang, C. T. James. 1983. 'A Note on the Binding Theory'. *Linguistic Inquiry* 14: 554–61.
Huang, C. T. James. 1984. 'On the Distribution and Reference of Empty Pronouns'. *Linguistic Inquiry* 15: 531–74.
Huang, C. T. James. 1987. 'Existential Sentences in Chinese and (in)Definiteness'. In *The Representation of (In)Definiteness*, edited by E. Reuland & A. G. B. ter Meulen, pp. 226–53. Cambridge, MA: The MIT Press.
Huang, C. T. James. 1989. 'Pro-Drop in Chinese: A Generalized Control Theory'. In *The Null Subject Parameter*, edited by O. A. Jaeggli & K. Safir, pp. 185–214. Dordrecht: Kluwer.
Huang, C. T. James. 1991. 'Remarks on the Status of the Null Object'. In *Principles and Parameters in Comparative Grammar*, edited by R. Freidin, pp. 56–76. Cambridge, MA: The MIT Press.
Huang, C. T. James. 1999. 'Chinese Passives in Comparative Perspective'. *Tsinghua Journal of Chinese Studies* 29: 423–509.
Huang, Guowen. 1996. 'Experiential Enhanced Theme in English'. In *Meaning and Form: Systemic Functional Interpretations*, edited by M. Berry, R. P. Fawcett, C. Butler & G. Huang, pp. 65–112. Norwood, NJ: Ablex.
Huang, Guowen. 2010. 'A Systemic Functional Analysis of "John Is Easy/Eager to Please"'. *Foreign Language Teaching and Research* 42(4): 261–7.
Huang, Guowen & Meifang Zhang. 2003. 'The Unit of Translation'. *Translation Quarterly* 30(4): 75–93.
Huang, Yan. 1989. 'Anaphora in Chinese: Toward a Pragmatic Analysis'. PhD thesis, University of Cambridge, UK.
Huang, Yan. 1991a. 'A Neo-Gricean Pragmatic Theory of Anaphora'. *Journal of Linguistics* 27: 301–35.
Huang, Yan. 1991b. 'A Pragmatic Analysis of Control in Chinese'. In *Levels of Linguistic Adaptation*, edited by J. Verschueren, pp. 113–45. Amsterdam: John Benjamins.
Huang, Yan. 1992a. 'Against Chomsky's Typology of Empty Categories'. *Journal of Pragmatics* 17(1): 1–29.
Huang, Yan. 1992b. 'Hanyu de kongfanchou' [Empty categories in Chinese]. *Zhongguo Yuwen* [Studies of the Chinese language] 31(5): 383–93.
Huang, Yan. 1994. *The Syntax and Pragmatics of Anaphora: A Study with Special Reference to Chinese*. Cambridge: Cambridge University Press.

Huang, Yan. 2000. *Anaphora: A Cross-Linguistic Approach*. Oxford: Oxford University Press.
Huang, Z. Nick. 2015. 'On Syntactic Tense in Mandarin Chinese'. In *Proceedings of the 27th North American Conference on Chinese Linguistics*, vol. 2, edited by H. Tao, Y. Lee, D. Su, et al. pp. 406–23. Los Angeles: University of California.
Huddleston, Rodney. 1969. 'Some Observations on Tense and Deixis in English'. *Language* 45(4): 777–806.
Huddleston, Rodney. 1988a. *English Grammar: An Outline*. Cambridge: Cambridge University Press.
Huddleston, Rodney. 1988b. 'Review: Constituency, Multi-functionality and Grammaticalization in Halliday's Functional Grammar'. *Journal of Linguistics* 24(1): 137–74.
Huddleston, Rodney & Geoffrey K. Pullum. 2002. *The Cambridge Grammar of the English Language*. New York: Cambridge University Press.
Hudson, Richard. 1971. *English Complex Sentences*. Amsterdam: North-Holland.
Hyams, Nina. 2011. 'Eventivity Effects in Early Grammar: The Case of Non-Finite Verbs'. *First Language* 32(1–2): 239–69.
Jakobson, Roman. 1960. 'Closing Statements: Linguistics and Poetics'. In *Style in Language*, edited by T. A. Sebeok, pp. 350–449. Cambridge, MA: The MIT Press.
Jarkey, Nerida. 2015. *Serial Verbs in White Hmong*. Leiden: Brill.
Jeffers, Robert J. 1976. 'Typological Shift and Change in Complex Sentence Structure'. In *Papers from the Parasession on Diachronic Syntax*, edited by S. B. Steever, C. A. Walker & S. S. Mufwene, pp. 136–49. Chicago: Chicago Linguistic Society.
Jespersen, Otto. 1924. *The Philosophy of Grammar*. London: George Allen & Unwin Ltd.
Jespersen, Otto. 1949. *A Modern English Grammar on Historical Principles*, vol. 1: *Syntax*. London: George Allen & Unwin Ltd.
Jiang, Di. 1992. 'Zangyu dongci quzhe xianxiang de tongji fenxi' [A statistical analysis of verbal inflections in Tibetan]. *Minzu Yuwen* [Minority languages of China] 14(4): 47–50.
Jin, Peng. 1983. 'Zangyu dongci biaosanshi de quzhe xingtai jianhua' [Two ways of simplifying the inflections for representing three tenses in Tibet]. *Yuyan Yanjiu* [Studies in language and linguistics] 3(1): 169–78.
Jin, Peng. 1988. 'Zangyu dongci quzhe xingtai xiang zhanzhe xingtai de zhuanbian' [Change from inflectional forms to affixational forms in Tibetan verbs]. *Zhongguo Zangxue* [Chinese Tibetology] 1(1): 131–9.
Johns, Alana & Carolyn Smallwood. 1999. 'On (Non-)Finiteness in Inuktitut'. *Toronto Working Papers in Linguistics* 17: 159–70.
Johnson, Samuel, ed. 1785. *A Dictionary of the English Language with a History of the Language and an English Grammar*. 6th ed. London: W. Strahan.
Joseph, Brian D. 1983. *The Synchrony and Diachrony of the Balkan Infinitive: A Study in Areal, General, and Historical Linguistics*. Cambridge: Cambridge University Press.
Kalinina, Elena J. & Nina Sumbatova. 2007. 'Clause Structure and Verbal Forms in Nakh-Daghestanian Languages'. In *Finiteness: Theoretical and Empirical Foundations*, edited by I. Nikolaeva, pp. 183–249. Oxford: Oxford University Press.

Karlgren, Bernhard. 1920. 'Le proto-Chinois, langue flexionnelle'. *Journal Asiatique* 11: 205–32.
Kemmer, Suzanne & Arie Verhagen. 1994. 'The Grammar of Causatives and the Conceptual Structure of Events'. *Cognitive Linguistics* 5(2): 115–56.
Kempson, Ruth M. & Randolph Quirk. 1971. 'Controlled Activation of Latent Contrast'. *Language* 47(3): 548–72.
Kibrik, Andrej, Olga Fedorova & Julia Nikolaeva. 2015. 'Multimodal Discourse: In Search of Units'. In *CEUR Workshop Proceedings*, edited by G. Airenti, B. G. Bara & G. Sandini, pp. 662–7. Aachen: RWTH Aachen University.
Kibrik, Andrej & Natalia Molchanova. 2013. 'Channels of Multimodal Communication: Relative Contributions to Discourse Understanding'. In *Proceedings of the 35th Annual Meeting of the Cognitive Science Society*, pp. 2704–9. New York: Curran Associates, Inc.
Kim, Jong-Bok & Mark A. Davies. 2019. 'The INTO-CAUSATIVE Construction in English: A Construction-Based Perspective'. *English Language and Linguistics* 20(1): 55–83.
Kiparsky, Paul. 1968. 'Tense and Mood in Indo-European Syntax'. *Foundations of Language* 4(1): 30–57.
Kiparsky, Paul & Carol Kiparsky. 1971. 'Fact'. In *Semantics: An Interdisciplinary Reader in Philosophy, Linguistics, and Psychology*, edited by D. D. Steinberg & L. A. Jakobovits, pp. 345–69. Cambridge: Cambridge University Press.
Klein, Wolfgang. 2006. 'On Finiteness'. In *Semantics in Acquisition*, edited by V. Van Geenhoven, pp. 245–72. Dordrecht: Springer.
Kolln, Martha J. & Robert W. Funk. 2012. *Understanding English Grammar*. 9th ed. Boston: Pearson Education.
Koptjevskaja-Tamm, Maria. 1994. 'Finiteness'. In *The Encyclopedia of Language and Linguistics*, edited by R. E. Asher, pp. 1245–8. Oxford: Pergamon.
Koptjevskaja-Tamm, Maria. 2005. 'Action Nominal Constructions'. In *The World Atlas of Language Structures*, edited by M. Haspelmath, M. S. Dryer, D. Gil & B. Comrie, pp. 254–7. Oxford: Oxford University Press.
Kornfilt, Jaklin. 2007. 'Verbal and Nominalized Finite Clauses in Turkish'. *Finiteness: Theoretical and Empirical Foundations*, edited by I. Nikolaeva, pp. 305–32. Oxford: Oxford University Press.
Kruisinga, Etsko. 1932 [1915]. *A Handbook of Present-Day English*. 5th ed. Groningen: P. Noordhoff.
Lakoff, George. 1987. *Women, Fire, and Dangerous Things: What Categories Reveal about the Mind*. Chicago: University of Chicago Press.
Lakoff, George & Mark Johnson. 1980. *Metaphors We Live By*. Chicago: University of Chicago Press.
Langacker, Ronald W. 1987. *Foundations of Cognitive Grammar: Theoretical Prerequisites*. Redwood, CA: Stanford University Press.
Langacker, Ronald W. 1991a. *Concept, Image, and Symbol: The Cognitive Basis of Grammar*. Berlin: Mouton de Gruyter.
Langacker, Ronald W. 1991b. *Foundations of Cognitive Grammar: Descriptive Application*. Redwood, CA: Stanford University Press.
Langacker, Ronald W. 1995. 'Raising and Transparency'. *Language* 71(1): 1–62.

Langacker, Ronald W. 1999. *Grammar and Conceptualization*. Berlin: Mouton de Gruyter.
Langacker, Ronald W. 2008. *Cognitive Grammar: A Basic Introduction*. Oxford: Oxford University Press.
Langacker, Ronald W. 2009. *Investigations in Cognitive Grammar*. Berlin: Mouton de Gruyter.
Langacker, Ronald W. 2013. *Essentials of Cognitive Grammar*. Oxford: Oxford University Press.
Larsson, Inger. 2013. 'Nordic Digraphia and Diglossia'. In *Spoken and Written Language: Relations between Latin and the Vernacular Languages in the Earlier Middle Ages*, edited by M. Garrison, A. P. Orbán & M. Mostert, pp. 73–86. Turnhout, Belgium: Brepols Publishers.
Lassen, Inger. 2003a. *Accessibility and Acceptability in Technical Manuals: A Survey of Style and Grammatical Metaphor*. Amsterdam: John Benjamins.
Lassen, Inger. 2003b. 'Imperative Readings of Grammatical Metaphor: A Study of Congruency in the Imperative'. In *Grammatical Metaphor: Views from Systemic Functional Linguistics*, edited by A.-M. Simon-Vandenbergen, M. Taverniers & L. Ravelli, pp. 279–308. Amsterdam: John Benjamins.
Laury, Ritva & Sandra A. Thompson. 2008. 'Introduction'. In *Studies of Clause Combining: The Multifunctionality of Conjunctions*, edited by R. Laury, pp. ix–xiv. Amsterdam: John Benjamins.
Lavid, Julia, Jorge Arús & Juan Rafael Zamorano-Mansilla. 2010. *Systemic Functional Grammar of Spanish: A Contrastive Study with English*. London: Continuum.
Ledgeway, Adam. 1998. 'Variation in the Romance Infinitive'. *Transactions of the Philological Society* 96(1): 1–61.
Ledgeway, Adam. 2007. 'Diachrony and Finiteness: Subordination in the Dialects of Southern Italy'. In *Finiteness: Theoretical and Empirical Foundations*, edited by I. Nikolaeva, pp. 335–65. Oxford: Oxford University Press.
Lee, Thomas Hun-tak. 2000. 'Finiteness and Null Arguments in Child Cantonese'. *Tsinghua Journal of Chinese Studies* 30: 365–93.
Leech, Geoffrey, Margaret Deuchar & Robert Hoogenraad. 1982. *English Grammar for Today: A New Introduction*. London: Macmillan.
Leech, Geoffrey & Jan Svartvik. 2002 [1975]. *A Communicative Grammar of English*. 3rd ed. Singapore: Longman.
Lefebvre, Claire. 1991. *Serial Verbs: Grammatical, Comparative, and Cognitive Approaches*. Amsterdam: John Benjamins.
Lehmann, Christian. 1988. 'Towards a Typology of Clause Linkage'. In *Clause Combining in Grammar and Discourse*, edited by J. Haiman & S. A. Thompson, pp. 181–225. Amsterdam: John Benjamins.
Lemmens, Maarten. 1998. *Lexical Perspectives on Transitivity and Ergativity: Causative Constructions in English*. Amsterdam: John Benjamins.
Levin, Beth. 2008. 'Dative Verbs: A Crosslinguistic Perspective'. *Lingvisticæ Investigationes* 31(2): 285–312.
Li, Charles N. & Sandra A. Thompson. 1981. *Mandarin Chinese: A Functional Reference Grammar*. Berkeley: University of California Press.
Li, Eden Sum-Hung. 2007. *A Systemic Functional Grammar of Chinese: A Text-Based Analysis*. New York: Continuum.

Li, Jinglian & Juan Liu. 2005. 'Finiteness and Non-Finiteness in Chinese'. *Hanyu Xuexi* [Chinese language learning] 26(1): 19–24.

Li, Jinxi. 2007 [1924]. *Xinzhu guowen yufa* [A new grammar of Mandarin Chinese]. Changsha: Hunan Education Press.

Li, Linding. 1986. *Xiandai Hanyu juxing* [Sentence patterns in modern Chinese]. Beijing: The Commercial Press.

Li, Ming. 2017. 'Cong "qi" tihuan "zhi" kan shanggu zhonggu Hanyu de jianyushi' [The so-called pivotal construction in old and middle Chinese: Viewed from the replacement of zhi(之) by qi(其)]. *Dangdai Yuyanxue* [Contemporary linguistics] 19(1): 1–33.

Li, Ruya. 2003. 'Shuwei biaoyin guize yu zhubin buduicheng xianxiang' [Predication indexing rule and subject-object asymmetry]. *Waiguoyu* [Foreign languages] 26(1): 22–9.

Li, Xulian. 2008. 'Douan Zhuangyu de quzhe xingtai' [Inflectional forms in the Douan Zhuang language]. *Minzu Yuwen* [Minority languages of China] 30(2): 65–7.

Li, Y. H. Audrey. 1985. 'Abstract Case in Chinese'. PhD thesis, University of Southern California, Los Angeles.

Li, Y. H. Audrey. 1990. *Order and Constituency in Mandarin Chinese*. Dordrecht: Kluwer.

Li, Yuming. 1997. 'Hanyu yufa "benwei" lunping: Jianping Xing Fuyi "xiaoju zhongshu shuo"' [Views on the 'central unit' in Chinese grammar with comments on Xing Fuyi's clause as pivot hypothesis]. *Shijie Hanyu Jiaoxue* [Chinese teaching in the world] 11(1): 16–23.

Li, Yunbing. 2006. 'Miaoyao yu de feifenxi xingtai jiqi leixingxue yiyi' [The non-synthetic forms in Miaoyao and their typological significance]. *Minzu Yuwen* [Minority languages of China] 28(2): 31–41.

Liardét, Cassi L. 2013. 'An Exploration of Chinese EFL Learner's Deployment of Grammatical Metaphor: Learning to Make Academically Valued Meanings'. *Journal of Second Language Writing* 22(2): 161–78.

Liardét, Cassi L. 2016a. 'Nominalization and Grammatical Metaphor: Elaborating the Theory'. *English for Specific Purposes* 44: 16–29.

Liardét, Cassi L. 2016b. 'Grammatical Metaphor: Distinguishing Success'. *Journal of English for Academic Purposes* 22: 109–18.

Lieber, Rochelle. 2016. *English Nouns: The Ecology of Nominalization*. Cambridge: Cambridge University Press.

Lin, Jo-Wang. 2006. 'Time in a Language without Tense: The Case of Chinese'. *Journal of Semantics* 23(1): 1–53.

Lin, Jo-Wang. 2010. 'A Tenseless Analysis of Mandarin Chinese Revisited: A Response to Sybesma'. *Linguistic Inquiry* 41(2): 305–29.

Lin, T.-H. Jonah. 2012. 'Multiple-Modal Constructions in Mandarin Chinese and Their Finiteness Properties'. *Journal of Linguistics* 48(1): 151–86.

Linell, Per. 2005. *The Written Language Bias in Linguistics: Its Nature, Origins and Transformations*. New York: Routledge.

Linn, Andrew. 2006. 'English Grammar Writing'. In *The Handbook of English Linguistics*, edited by B. Aarts & A. McMahon, pp. 72–92. Oxford: Blackwell.

Liu, Chen-Sheng. 1999. 'Anaphora in Mandarin Chinese and Binding at the Interface'. PhD thesis, University of California, Irvine.

Liu, Danqing. 2010. 'Hanyu shi yizhong dongcixing yuyan' [Chinese as a verby language]. *Shijie Hanyu Jiaoxue* [Chinese teaching in the world] 24(1): 3–17.
Liu, Danqing. 2015. 'Hanyu ji qinling yuyan liandongshi de jufa diwei he xianhedu' [The syntactic status and mightiness of serial verb constructions in Chinese and its neighboring languages]. *Minzu Yuwen* [Minority languages of China] 36(3): 3–22.
Liu, Fu. 1920. *Zhongguo wenfa tonglun* [General introduction to Chinese grammar], edited by B. Yang. Shanghai: Qunyi Books.
Liu, Qun. 2014. 'Xiandai Hanyu lianci ruogan teshulei yanjiu' [Some special types of conjunctions in modern Chinese]. PhD thesis, Wuhan University.
Liu, Ruoyun. 2003. 'Huizhouhua cinei quzhe bianhua chuyi' [On the inflectional forms in words of Huizhou dialect]. *Yuyan Yanjiu* [Studies in language and linguistics] 23(2): 110–14.
Liu, Ruoyun & Xin Zhao. 2007. 'Hanyu fangyan shengdiao quzhe de gongneng' [The function of tonic inflections in Chinese dialects]. *Fangyan* [Dialect] 29(3): 226–31.
Lord, Carol. 1993. *Historical Change in Serial Verb Constructions*. Amsterdam: John Benjamins.
Lowe, John Jeffrey. 2015. *Participles in Rigvedic Sanskrit: The Syntax and Semantics of Adjectival Verb Forms*. Oxford: Oxford University Press.
Lü, Jianming. 2009. 'Goushi yu yixiang tushi' [Construction and image schema]. *Journal of Peking University* 45(3): 103–7.
Lü, Jiping. 1958. *Fuza weiyu* [Complex predicates]. Shanghai: New Knowledge Press.
Lü, Jiping. 2002 [1979]. 'Liangge pingmian liangzhong xingzhi: Cizu he juzi de fenxi' [Two dimensions and two properties: Analysis of group and sentence]. *Xuexi Yu Tansuo* [Learning and exploring] 24(4): 80–94.
Lü, Shuxiang. 1990 [1982]. *Zhongguo wenfa yaolue* [Outlines of the grammar of Chinese]. Beijing: The Commercial Press.
Lü, Shuxiang. 2002 [1979]. *Lv Shuxiang wenji* [Collected works of Lv Shuxiang], edited by G. Huang. Changchun: Northeast China Normal University Press.
Luke, Jingguan. 2006. 'Lun xiaoju zai Hanyu yufa zhong de diwei' [On the status of clause in Chinese grammar]. *Hanyu Xuebao* [Journal of the Chinese language] 3(3): 2–14.
Luraghi, Silvia & Claudia Parodi. 2008. *Key Terms in Syntax and Syntactic Theory*. London: Continuum.
Lyons, John. 1968. *Introduction to Theoretical Linguistics*. Cambridge: Cambridge University Press.
Ma, Jianzhong. 1998 [1898]. *Mashi wentong* [Ma's Chinese grammar]. Beijing: The Commercial Press.
Maas, Utz. 2004. 'Finite and Nonfinite from a Typological Perspective'. *Linguistics* 42(2): 359–85.
Maetzner, Eduard Adolf Ferdinand. 1874. *An English Grammar*. London: John Murray.
Magnusson, Ulrika. 2013. 'Grammatical Metaphor in Swedish Monolingual and Multilingual Upper Secondary School Students' Writing'. *Functions of Language* 20(2): 250–81.
Malinowski, Bronislaw. 1946 [1923]. 'The Problem of Meaning in Primitive Languages'. In *The Meaning of Meaning*, edited by C. K. Ogden & I. A. Richards, pp. 296–336. New York: Harcourt Brace & World, Inc.

Malinowski, Bronislaw. 1935. *Coral Gardens and Their Magic: A Study of the Methods of Tilling the Soil and of Agricultural Rites in the Trobriand Islands*, vol. 2. London: George Allen & Unwin Ltd.
Mallory, James Patrick. 1989. *In Search of the Indo-Euruopeans: Language, Archaeology and Myth*. London: Thames & Hudson.
Martin, James R. 2002. 'Meaning beyond the Clause: SFL Perspectives'. *Annual Review of Applied Linguistics* 22: 52–74.
Martin, James R. 1993. 'Life as a Noun'. In *Writing Science: Literacy and Discursive Power*, edited by J. R. Martin & M. A. K. Halliday, pp. 242–93. London: Falmer Press.
Martin, Roger. 2001. 'Null Case and the Distribution of PRO'. *Linguistic Inquiry* 32(1): 141–66.
Mathesius, Vilém. 1983 [1927]. 'Functional Linguistics'. In *Praguiana: Some Basic and Less-Known Aspects of the Prague Linguistics School*, edited by J. Vachek & L. Dušková, pp. 121–42. Amsterdam: John Benjamins.
Matthews, Peter Hugoe. 1997. *The Concise Oxford Dictionary of Linguistics*. Oxford: Oxford University Press.
Matthiessen, Christian M. I. M. 2014a. 'Introduction'. In M. A. K. Halliday & C. M. I. M. Matthiessen, *Halliday's Introduction to Functional Grammar*, pp. xiii–xviii. London: Routledge.
Matthiessen, Christian M. I. M. 2014b. 'Extending the Description of Process Type within the System of Transitivity in Delicacy Based on Levinian Verb Classes'. *Functions of Language* 21(2): 139–75.
Matthiessen, Christian M. I. M., Kazuhiro Teruya & Marvin Lam. 2010. *Key Terms in Systemic Functional Linguistics*. London: Continuum.
Matthiessen, Christian M. I. M. & Sandra A. Thompson. 1988. 'The Structure of Discourse and "Subordination"'. In *Clause Combining in Grammar and Discourse*, edited by J. Haiman & S. A. Thompson, pp. 275–329. Amsterdam: John Benjamins.
McFadden, Thomas & Sandhya Sundaresan. 2014. 'Finiteness in South Asian Languages: An Introduction'. *Natural Language and Linguistic Theory* 32: 1–27.
McGregor, William B. 1997. *Semiotic Grammar*. Oxford: Clarendon.
McGregor, William B. 2002. *Verb Classification in Australian Languages*. Berlin: Mouton de Gruyter.
Mensching, Guido. 2000. *Infinitive Constructions with Specified Subjects: A Syntactic Analysis of the Romance Languages*. Oxford: Oxford University Press.
Miao, Yizhi. 1957. *Hanyu yufa jichu zhishi* [Basics in Chinese grammar]. Wuhan: Hubei People's Press.
Michaelis, Laura A. & Knud Lambrecht. 1996. 'Toward a Construction-Based Model of Language Function: The Case of Nominal Extraposition'. *Language* 72: 215–47.
Michel, Jean-Baptiste, Yuan Kui Shen, Aviva Presser Aiden, et al. 2011. 'Quantitative Analysis of Culture Using Millions of Digitized Books'. *Science* 331(6014): 176–82. https://doi.org/10.1126/science.1199644.
Miller, D. Gary. 2002. *Nonfinite Structures in Theory and Change*. Oxford: Oxford University Press.
Miller, John Ezra. 1902. 'Vergil's Use of the Infinitive'. MA thesis, University of Illinois, Chicago.

Milsark, Gary L. 2014 [1979]. *Existential Sentences in English*. New York: Garland Publishing, Inc.
Mithun, Marianne. 1988. 'The Grammaticization of Coordination'. In *Clause Combining in Grammar and Discourse*, edited by J. Haiman & S. A. Thompson, pp. 331–59. Amsterdam: John Benjamins.
Mourelatos, Alexander P. D. 1978. 'Events, Processes, and States'. *Linguistics and Philosophy* 2: 415–34.
Murray, Lindley. 1832. *A Practical Grammar of the English Language and Theory of Moods*. 3rd ed. Portland, OR: G. Hyde and Company.
Murray, Lindley. 1844 [1795]. *English Grammar*. New York: M. & S. Raynor.
Muysken, Pieter. 2008. *Functional Categories*. Cambridge: Cambridge University Press.
Nedjalkov, Vladimir P. 1995. 'Some Typological Parameters of Converbs'. In *Converbs in Cross-Linguistic Perspective: Structure and Meaning of Adverbial Verb Forms – Adverbial Participles, Gerunds*, edited by M. Haspelmath & E. König, pp. 97–136. Berlin: Mouton de Gruyter.
Nelson, Deborah G. Kemler, Kathy Hirsh-Pasek, Peter W. Jusczyk & Kimberly Wright Cassidy. 1989. 'How the Prosodic Cues in Motherese Might Assist Language Learning'. *Journal of Child Language* 16(1): 55–68.
Nelson, Gerald. 2001. *Essential English Grammar*. London: Routledge.
Nesfield, John Collinson. 1908 [1898]. *Manual of English Grammar and Composition*. London: Macmillan and Co., Ltd.
Newman, John. 1996. *Give: A Cognitive Linguistic Study*. Berlin: Mouton de Gruyter.
Newmeyer, Frederick J. 1999. 'Some Remarks on the Functionalist–Formalist Controversy in Linguistics'. In *Functionalism and Formalism in Linguistics*, vol. 1, edited by M. Darnell, E. Moravcsik, F. Newmeyer, M. Noonan & K. Wheatley, pp. 469–86. Amsterdam: John Benjamins.
Newmeyer, Frederick J. 2001. 'The Prague School and North American Functionalist Approaches to Syntax'. *Journal of Linguistics* 37: 101–26.
Nikolaeva, Irina. 2007a. 'Constructional Economy and Nonfinite Independent Clauses'. In *Finiteness: Theoretical and Empirical Foundations*, edited by I. Nikolaeva, pp. 138–80. Oxford: Oxford University Press.
Nikolaeva, Irina. 2007b. 'Introduction'. In *Finiteness: Theoretical and Empirical Foundations*, edited by I. Nikolaeva, pp. 1–19. Oxford: Oxford University Press.
Nikolaeva, Irina. 2010. 'Typology of Finiteness'. *Language and Linguistics Compass* 4(12): 1176–89.
Niu, Ruochen & Timothy Osborne. 2019. 'Chunks Are Components: A Dependency Grammar Approach to the Syntactic Structure of Mandarin'. *Lingua* 224: 60–83.
Noonan, Michael. 1985. 'Complementation'. In *Language Typology and Syntactic Description*, vol. 2: *Complex Constructions*, edited by M. Noonan, pp. 42–140. Cambridge: Cambridge University Press.
Noonan, Michael. 1992. *A Grammar of Lango*. Berlin: Mouton de Gruyter.
Nowak, Elke. 1996. *Transforming the Images: Ergativity and Transitivity in Inuktitut (Eskimo)*. Berlin: Mouton de Gruyter.
O'Donnell, Roy C. 1974. 'Syntactic Differences between Speech and Writing'. *American Speech* 49(1/2): 102–10.

O'Halloran, Kay L. 1996. 'The Discourses of Secondary School Mathematics'. PhD thesis, Murdoch University, Perth.
Onions, C. T. 1904. *An Advanced English Syntax: Based on the Principles and Requirements of the Grammatical Society*. London: Swan Sonnenschein & Co., Ltd.
Ohori, Toshio. 1992. *'Diachrony in Clause Linkage and Related Issues'*. PhD thesis, University of California at Berkeley, Berkeley.
Painter, Claire. 2003. 'The Use of a Metaphorical Mode of Meaning in Early Language Development'. In *Grammatical Metaphor: Views from Systemic Functional Linguistics*, edited by A.-M. Simon-Vandenbergen, M. Taverniers & L. Ravelli, pp. 151–68. Amsterdam: John Benjamins.
Pan, Wuyun. 1991. 'Shanggu Hanyu shidongci de quzhe xingshi' [Causative verb inflections in ancient Chinese]. *Wenzhou Shifan Xueyuan Xuebao* [Journal of Wenzhou Teachers' College] 13(2): 48–57.
Pang, Shuangzi & Kefei Wang. 2020. 'Language Contact through Translation: The Influence of Explicitness in English–Chinese Translation on Language Change in Vernacular Chinese'. *Target* 32(3): 420–55.
Payne, John R. 1985. 'Negation'. In *Language Typology and Syntactic Description*, vol. 1: *Clause Structure*, edited by T. Shopen, pp. 197–242. Cambridge: Cambridge University Press.
Payne, Thomas E. 1997. *Describing Morphosyntax*. Cambridge: Cambridge University Press.
Payne, Thomas E. 2011. *Understanding English Grammar: A Linguistic Introduction*. London: Cambridge University Press.
Peng, Guozhen & Hilary Chappell. 2011. 'Ya(33) "Give" as a Valency Increaser in Jinghpo Nuclear Serialization: From Benefactive to Malefactive'. *Studies in Language* 35(1): 128–67.
Peng, Rui. 2012. 'Suyin jianyuju de kejieshoudu he yiyi diaocha' [A survey on the acceptability and meaning judgment of cause-complement pivotal constructions]. *Zhongguo Yuwen* [Studies of the Chinese language] 62(6): 509–24.
Peng, Rui. 2013. 'A Diachronic Construction Grammar Account of the Chinese Cause-Complement Pivotal Construction'. *Language Sciences* 40: 53–79.
Peng, Rui. 2016. 'Chinese Descriptive Pivotal Construction: Taxonomy and Prototypicality'. *Language and Linguistics* 17(4): 529–73.
Peng, Xuanwei. 2011. *An Introduction to Language and Linguistics: Chinese Systemic Functional Grammar*. Beijing: Peking University Press.
Peng, Xuanwei. 2017. '"(Text as) Wording" as Wording in Text Size: Stretching Lexicogrammatical Rank Hierarchy from Clause to Text'. *Word* 63(2): 136–72.
Perlmutter, David. 2007. 'In What Ways Can Finite and Nonfinite Clauses Differ? Evidence from Russian'. In *Finiteness: Theoretical and Empirical Foundations*, edited by I. Nikolaeva, pp. 250–304. Oxford: Oxford University Press.
Pinker, Steven & Paul Bloom. 1990. 'Natural Language and Natural Selection'. *Behavioral and Brain Sciences* 13(4): 707–84.
Plag, Ingo. 1993. *Sentential Complementation in Sranan: On the Formation of an English-Based Creole Language*. Tübingen: Niemeyer.
Polinsky, Maria. 2008. 'Without Aspect'. In *Case and Grammatical Relations: Studies in honor of Bernard Comrie*, edited by G. G. Corbett & M. Noonan, pp. 263–82. Amsterdam: John Benjamins.

Popjes, Jack & Jo Popjes. 1986. 'Canela-Krahô'. In *Handbook of Amazonian Languages*, vol. 1, edited by D. C. Derbyshire & G. K. Pullum, pp. 128–99. Berlin: Mouton de Gruyter.
Postal, Paul. 2014 [1966]. 'On So-Called "Pronouns" in English'. In *An Annotated Syntax Reader: Lasting Insights and Questions*, edited by R. Kayne, T. Leu & R. Zanuttini, pp. 12–25. London: Blackwell Publishing.
Poutsma, Hendrik. 1904. *A Grammar of Late Modern English*, vol. 1. Groningen: P. Noordhoff.
Poutsma, Hendrik. 1923. *The Infinitive, the Gerund and the Participles of the English Verb*. Groningen: P. Noordhoff.
Poutsma, Hendrik. 1926. *A Grammar of Late Modern English*, vol. 2. Groningen: P. Noordhoff.
Qu, Aitang. (1985). 'Zangyu dongci quzhe xingtai de jiegou jiqi yanbian' [The structure and evolution of verbal inflections in Tibetan]. *Minzu Yuwen* [Minority languages of China] 7(1), 1–15.
Qu, Chengxi. 1996. 'Xiandai Hanyu zhong "juzi" de dingyi jiqi diwei' [The definition and status of 'sentence' in modern Chinese]. *Shijie Hanyu Jiaoxue* [Chinese teaching in the world] 10(4): 16–23.
Quirk, Randolph, Sidney Greenbaum, Geoffrey Leech & Jan Svartvik. 1972. *A Grammar of Contemporary English*. London: Longman.
Quirk, Randolph, Sidney Greenbaum, Geoffrey Leech & Jan Svartvik. 1985. *A Comprehensive Grammar of the English Language*. New York: Longman.
Radford, Andrew. 2004. *Exploring the Structure of English*. Cambridge: Cambridge University Press.
Raposo, Eduardo P. 1987. 'Case Theory and Infl-to-Comp: The Inflected Infinitive in European Portuguese'. *Linguistic Inquiry* 14: 101–36.
Ravelli, Louise. 1988. 'Grammatical Metaphor: An Initial Analysis'. In *Pragmatics, Discourse and Text: Some Systemically-Inspired Approaches*, edited by E. Steiner & R. Veltman, pp. 133–47. London: Burns & Oates.
Ravelli, Louise. 2003. 'Renewal of Connection: Integrating Theory and Practice in an Understanding of Grammatical Metaphor'. In *Grammatical Metaphor: Views from Systemic Functional Linguistics*, edited by A.-M. Simon-Vandenbergen, M. Taverniers & L. Ravelli, pp. 37–64. Amsterdam: John Benjamins.
Redeker, Gisela. 1984. 'On Differences between Spoken and Written Language'. *Discourse Processes* 7(1): 43–55.
Reed, Alonzo & Brainerd Kellogg. 1900. *A High School Grammar*. New York: Maynard, Merrill, & Co., Publishers.
Rickman, Paul & Juhani Rudanko. 2018. *Corpus-Based Studies on Non-Finite Complements in Recent English*. Cham, Switzerland: Palgrave Macmillan.
Ritter, Elizabeth & Martina Wiltschko. 2014. 'The Composition of INFL: An Exploration of Tense, Tenseless Languages, and Tenseless Constructions'. *Natural Language and Linguistic Theory* 32: 1331–86.
Rizzi, Luigi. 1982. *Issues in Italian Syntax*. Dordrecht: Foris.
Ross, Charles Hunter. 1893. *The Absolute Participle in Middle and Modern English*. Baltimore: The Modern Language Association of America.
Ross, John Robert. 1969. 'Auxiliaries as Main Verbs'. In *Studies in Philosophical Linguistics*, edited by W. Todd, pp. 77–102. Evanston, IL: Great Expectations Press.

Ross, John Robert. 1972. 'The Category Squish: Endstation Hauptwort'. In *Proceedings of the Eighth Regional Meeting of the Chicago Linguistic Society*, edited by P. M. Peranteau, J. N. Levi & G. C. Phares, pp. 316–28. Chicago: University of Chicago.

Rudanko, Juhani. 2010. 'Explaining Grammatical Variation and Change: A Case Study of Complementation in American English over Three Decades'. *Journal of English Linguistics* 38(1): 4–24.

Rudanko, Juhani. 2015. *Linking Form and Meaning: Studies on Selected Control Patterns in Recent English*. New York: Palgrave Macmillan.

Rusteberg, F. G. A. 1874. 'Historical Development of the Gerund in the English Language'. PhD thesis, University of Leipzig.

Ryshina-Pankova, Marianna. 2010. 'Toward Mastering the Discourses of Reasoning: Use of Grammatical Metaphor at Advanced Levels of Foreign Language Acquisition'. *Modern Language Journal* 94(2): 181–97.

Ryshina-Pankova, Marianna. 2015. 'A Meaning-Based Approach to the Study of Complexity in L2 Writing: The Case of Grammatical Metaphor'. *Journal of Second Language Writing* 29: 51–63.

Sagart, Laurent. 1999. *The Roots of Old Chinese*. Amsterdam: John Benjamins.

Sapir, Edward. 1921. *Language*. New York: Harcourt Brace & World.

Sapir, Edward & Morris Swadesh. 1946. 'American Indian Grammatical Categories'. *Word* 2(2): 103–12.

Sawyer, Janet. 1973. 'Existential Sentences: A Linguistic Universal?' *American Speech* 48(3): 239–45.

Schäfer, Florian. 2008. *The Syntax of (Anti-)Causatives: External Arguments in Change-of-State Contexts*. Amsterdam: John Benjamins.

Schleppegrell, Mary J. 2008. *The Language of Schooling: A Functional Linguistics Perspective*. London: Taylor & Francis.

Sebba, Mark. 1987. *The Syntax of Serial Verbs*. Amsterdam: John Benjamins.

Sells, Peter. 2007. 'Finiteness in Non-Transformational Syntactic Frameworks'. In *Finiteness: Theoretical and Empirical Foundations*, edited by I. Nikolaeva, pp. 59–88. Oxford: Oxford University Press.

Shen, Jiaxuan. 2012. '"Lingju" he "liushuiju"' ['Minor sentences' and 'flowing sentences']. *Zhongguo Yuwen* [Studies of the Chinese language] 62(5): 403–15.

Shen, Jiaxuan. 2016. *Mingci he dongci* [Nouns and verbs]. Beijing: The Commercial Press.

Shi, Cunzhi. 1954. 'Lun dixishi he jianyushi' [On consecutive and pivotal constructions]. *Zhongguo Yuwen* [Studies of the Chinese language] 3(3): 5–8.

Shi, Dingxu. 2009. 'Weicixing binyu de jufa diwei' [The syntactic status of verbal objects]. *Yuyan Kexue* [Linguistic sciences] 8(5): 493–502.

Shi, Youwei. 2017. 'The Chinese Tense and Aspect Revisited: An Approach with Le as the Focus'. *Yuyan Kexue* [Linguistic sciences] 16(2): 126–41.

Shi, Yuzhi. 1995. 'Shijian de yiweixing dui jieci yansheng de yingxiang' [The impact of one dimension of time on preposition evolution]. *Zhongguo Yuwen* [Studies of the Chinese language] 34(1): 1–10.

Shi, Yuzhi. 2001. 'Hanyu de xianding dongci he feixianding dongci zhibie' [Difference between finite verb and non-finite verb in Chinese]. *Shijie Hanyu Jiaoxue* [Chinese teaching in the world] 15(2): 23–7.

Shibatani, Masayoshi. 1999. 'Dative Subject Constructions Twenty-Two Years Later'. *Studies in the Linguistic Sciences* 29(2): 45–76.
Shibatani, Masayoshi. 2001. 'Introduction: Some Basic Issues in the Grammar of Causation'. In *The Grammar of Causation and Interpersonal Manipulation*, edited by M. Shibatani, pp. 1–22. Philadelphia: John Benjamins.
Shlonsky, Ur. 1997. *Clause Structure and Word Order in Hebrew and Arabic: An Essay in Comparative Semitic Syntax*. New York: Oxford University Press.
Sidey, Thomas K. 1909. *The Participle in Plautus, Petronius, and Apuleius*. Chicago: University of Chicago Press.
Šimík, Radek. 2013. 'The PRO-Wh Connection in Modal Existential Wh-Constructions: An Argument in Favor of Semantic Control'. *Natural Language and Linguistic Theory* 31(4): 1163–205.
Simon-Vandenbergen, Anne-Marie, Miriam Taverniers & Louise Ravelli, eds. 2003. *Grammatical Metaphor: Views from Systemic Functional Linguistics*. Amsterdam: John Benjamins.
Sinclair, John. 1991. *Corpus Concordance Collocation*. Oxford: Oxford University Press.
Smith, Carlota S. & Mary S. Erbaugh. 2005. 'Temporal Interpretation in Mandarin Chinese'. *Linguistics* 43: 713–56.
Smith, Michael & Joyce Escobedo. 2001. 'The Semantics of To-Infinitival vs. -Ing Complement Constructions in English'. In *Chicago Linguistic Society CLS 37: The Main Session*, edited by M. Andronis, C. Ball, H. Elston & S. Neuvel, pp. 549–63. Chicago: Chicago Linguistic Society.
Soames, Scott & David M. Perlmutter. 1979. *Syntactic Argumentation and the Structure of English*. Berkeley: University of California Press.
Song, Jae Jung. 2006. 'Causatives: Semantics'. In *Encyclopedia of Language and Linguistics*, vol. 2, edited by K. Brown, A. Anderson, L. Bauer, et al. pp. 265–8. London: Elsevier.
Song, Jae Jung. 2013. *Causatives and Causation: A Universal-Typological Perspective*. London: Routledge.
Song, Yuzhu. 1981. *Xiandai Hanyu yufa lunji* [Modern Chinese grammar colloquium]. Tianjin: Tianjin People's Press.
Song, Yuzhu. 1982. 'Dingxin weiyu cunzaiju' [Endocentric structuring as predicate in existential constructions]. *Yuyan Jiaoxue Yu Yanjiu* [Language teaching and linguistic studies] 4(3): 27–34.
Song, Yuzhu. 1986. *Xiandai Hanyu yufa shijiang* [Ten lectures on modern Chinese grammar]. Tianjin: Nankai University Press.
Song, Yuzhu. 1988. 'Lüetan "jia zunzaiju"' [On pseudo-existentials]). *Journal of Tianjin Normal University* 14(6): 86–9.
Sridhar, Shikaripur N. 1990. *Kannada*. London: Routledge.
Stassen, Leon. 1997. *Intransitive Predication*. Oxford: Oxford University Press.
Steiner, Erich. 2002a. 'Ideational Grammatical Metaphor: Exploring Some Implications for the Overall Model'. *Languages in Contrast* 4(1): 137–64.
Steiner, Erich. 2002b. 'Grammatical Metaphor in Translation: Some Methods for Corpus-Based Investigations'. *Language and Computers* 39(1): 213–28.
Stephens, Nola. 2015. 'Dative Constructions and Givenness in the Speech of Four-Year-Olds'. *Linguistics* 53(3): 405–42.

Stubbs, Michael. 1996. *Text and Corpus Analysis*. Oxford: Blackwell.
Stump, Gregory. 1985. *The Semantic Variability of Absolute Constructions*. Dordrecht: D. Reidel Publishing Company.
Sun, Yinxin. 1998. '"de" zi jianyuju xinlun' [Pivotal construction with 'de']. *Hanyu Xuexi* [Chinese language learning] 19(1): 32–4.
Suonan, Jiancuo. 2013. 'Zangyu dongci de nianzhuoxing ji quzhexing bianhua yanjiu' [Changes in the inflection and affixation in Tibetan verbs]. *Xizang Daxue Xuebao* [Journal of the University of Tibet] 28(1): 70–5.
Sweet, Henry. 1913. *Collected Papers of Henry Sweet*, edited by H. C. Wyld. London: Oxford University Press.
Sybesma, Rint. 2007. 'Whether We Tense-Agree Overtly or Not'. *Linguistic Inquiry* 38(3): 580–8.
Tallerman, Maggie. 1998. 'The Uniform Case-Licensing of Subjects in Welsh'. *Linguistic Review* 15(1): 69–133.
Tan, Fu. 1995. 'Hanyu zhong zhoubianxing de biaoda yiji xianding dongci he feixianding dongci de qubie' [Neighbouring expressions and the difference between finite verb and non-finite verb in Chinese]. In *The Fourth International Symposium of the Chinese Language Teaching*, pp. 337–40. Beijing: Beijing Language and Culture University Press.
Tang, Chih-Chen Jane. 1990. 'Chinese Phrase Structure and the Extended X-Bar Theory'. PhD thesis, Cornell University, New York.
Tang, Ting-Chi. 2000. 'Hanyu de xianding ziju yu feixianding ziju' [Finite and nonfinite clauses in Chinese]. *Yuyan Ji Yuyanxue* [Language and linguistics] 1(1): 191–214.
Tannen, Deborah. 1982. 'Oral and Literate Strategies in Spoken and Written Narratives'. *Language* 58(1): 1–21.
Taverniers, Miriam. 2002. 'Systemic-Functional Linguistics and the Notion of Grammatical Metaphor: A Theoretical Study and a Proposal for a Semiotic-Functional Integrative Model'. PhD thesis, Ghent University, Netherlands.
Teruya, Kazuhiro. 2007. *A Systemic Functional Grammar of Japanese*. London: Continuum.
Thompson, Sandra A. 1988. 'A Discourse Approach to the Cross-Linguistic Category "Adjective"'. In *Explaining Language Universals*, edited by J. A. Hawkins, pp. 167–85. Oxford: Basil Blackwell.
Thomson, Elizabeth & William Armour. 2008. *Systemic Functional Perspectives of Japanese: Descriptions and Applications*. London: Equinox.
Ting, Jen. 1998. 'Deriving the Bei-Construction in Mandarin Chinese'. *Journal of East Asian Linguistics* 7: 319–54.
Trask, Robert Lawrence. 1992. *A Dictionary of Grammatical Terms in Linguistics*. London: Routledge.
Trask, Robert Lawrence. 1999. *Key Concepts in Language and Linguistics*. London: Routledge.
Tubino Blanco, Mercedes. 2011. *Causatives in Minimalism*. Amsterdam: John Benjamins.
Ungerer, Friedrich. 2017. *How Grammar Links Concepts: Verb-Mediated Constructions, Attribution, Perspectivizing*. Amsterdam: John Benjamins.
Ussery, Cherlon, Lydia Ding & Yining Rebecca Liu. 2016. 'The Typology of Mandarin Infinitives'. *Proceedings of the Linguistic Society of America* 1: 1–25.

Vajda, Edward J. 2008. 'Foreword'. In *Subordination and Coordination Strategies in North Asian Languages*, edited by E. J. Vajda, pp. vii–xi. Amsterdam: John Benjamins.
Van Essen, Arthur J. 1983. *E. Kruisinga: A Chapter in the History of Linguistics in the Netherlands*. Dordrecht: Springer.
Van Valin, Robert D., ed. 1992. *Advances in Role and Reference Grammar*. Amsterdam: John Benjamins.
Van Valin, Robert Jr. & Randy LaPolla. 1997. *Syntax: Structure, Meaning and Function*. Cambridge: Cambridge University Press.
Vendler, Zeno. 1957. 'Verbs and Times'. *Philosophical Review* 66(2): 143–60.
Vendler, Zeno. 1967. *Linguistics in Philosophy*. New York: Cornell University Press.
Verspoor, Marjolijn. 1990. 'Semantic Criteria in English Complement Selection'. PhD thesis, University of Leiden.
Verspoor, Marjolijn. 1996. 'The Story of -ing: A Subjective Perspective'. In *The Construal of Space in Language and Thought*, edited by M. Pütz & R. Dirven, pp. 417–54. Berlin: Mouton de Gruyter.
Verspoor, Marjolijn. 2000. 'Iconicity in English Complement Constructions: Conceptual Distance and Cognitive Processing Levels'. In *Complementation: Cognitive and Functional Perspectives*, edited by K. Horie, pp. 199–225. Amsterdam: John Benjamins.
Verstraete, Jean-Christophe. 2007. *Rethinking the Coordinate-Subordinate Dichotomy: Interpersonal Grammar and the Analysis of Adverbial Clauses in English*. Berlin: Mouton de Gruyter.
Veselovská, Ludmila & Joseph Embley Emonds. 2015. 'The Categorial Status of Infinitives and Gerunds in English and Czech'. In *Proceedings of the Sixth International Conference on Anglophone Studies September 4–5, 2014*, edited by G. J. Bell & K. Nemčoková. Zlín, Czech Republic: Tomas Bata University.
Vincent, Nigel. 1998. 'On the Grammar of Inflected Nonfinite Forms (with Special Reference to Old Neapolitan)'. In *Clause Combining and Text Structure*, vol. 22, edited by I. Korzen & M. Herslund, pp. 135–58. Copenhagen: Samfundsliteratur.
Votaw, Clyde W. 1896. 'The Use of the Infinitive in Biblical Greek'. PhD thesis, University of Chicago, Chicago.
Vygotsky, Lev. 1986 [1934]. *Thought and Language*. Cambridge, MA: The MIT Press.
Waldenfels, Ruprecht von. 2012. *The Grammaticalization of 'Give' + Infinitive: A Comparative Study of Russian, Polish, and Czech*. Berlin: Mouton de Gruyter.
Wang, Ailu. 1992. 'Qixian fangyan dongci jieguoti de neibu quzhe' [The internal inflections of resultant verbs in Qi county dialect]. *Yuyan Yanjiu* [Studies in language and linguistics] 11(1): 26–30.
Wang, Dongmei. 2001. 'Xiandai Hanyu dongming huzhuan de renzhi yanjiu' [Nominalization and verbalization in contemporary Chinese: A cognitive linguistic enquiry]. PhD thesis, Chinese Academy of Social Sciences, Beijing.
Wang, Futing. 1960. 'Liandongshi haishi lianweishi' [Serial verb or serial predicate]. *Zhongguo Yuwen* [Studies of the Chinese language] 9(6): 281–4.
Wang, Jianjun. 2003. *Hanyu cunzaiju de lishi yanjiu* [A diachronic study of Chinese existential sentences]. Tianjin: Tianjin Classics Publishing House.
Wang, Li. 1957. *Hanyu shigao* [A history of the Chinese language]. Beijing: Zhonghua Book Company.

Wang, Li. 1984. *Zhongguo yufa lilun: Wang Li wenji diyijuan* [Theories of Chinese grammar: The collected works of Wang Li, vol. 1]. Jinan: Shangdong Education Press.

Wang, Li. 1985 [1943]. *Zhongguo xiandai yufa* [Modern Chinese grammar]. Beijing: The Commercial Press.

Wang, Yong & Jie Xu. 2013. 'A Systemic Typology of Existential and Possessive Constructions'. *Functions of Language* 20(1): 1–30.

Webster, Noah. 1828. *An American Dictionary of the English Language*. New York: S. Converse.

Webster, Noah. 1833. *An Improved Grammar of the English Language*. New Haven: Durrie & Peck.

Wei, Zhaohui. 2005. 'Zhouqin Lianghan liandongshi fazhan bianhua' [The development of serial verb construction in Zhou, Qin and Han dynasties]. PhD thesis, Huazhong University of Science and Technology, Wuhan.

Wetzer, Harrie. 1996. *The Typology of Adjectival Predication*. Berlin: Mouton de Gruyter.

Wexler, Ken. 1994. 'Optional Infinitives, Head Movement and the Economy of Derivations'. In *Verb Movement*, edited by D. Lightfoot & N. Hornstein, pp. 305–50. Cambridge: Cambridge University Press.

Wexler, Ken. 1998. 'Very Early Parameter Setting and the Unique Checking Constraint: A New Explanation of the Optional Infinitive Stage'. *Lingua* 106: 23–79.

Wexler, Ken. 2004. 'Lenneberg's Dream: Learning, Normal Language Development and Specific Language Impairment'. In *Variation and Universals in Biolinguistics*, edited by L. Jenkins, pp. 239–83. Amsterdam: Elsevier.

Whitney, William Dwight. 1886. *Essentials of English Grammar*. Boston: Ginn & Company.

Whorf, Benjamin Lee. 1945. 'Grammatical Categories'. *Language* 21(1): 1–11.

Wierzbicka, Anna. 1988. *The Semantics of Grammar*. Amsterdam: John Benjamins.

Wierzbicka, Anna. 2006. *English: Meaning and Culture*. Oxford: Oxford University Press.

Wijnen, Frank. 1997. 'Temporal Reference and Eventivity in Root Infinitives'. *MIT Occasional Papers in Linguistics* 12: 1–25.

Wijnen, Frank. 1998. 'The Interpretation of Dutch Children's Root Infinitives: The Effect of Eventivity'. *First Language* 18: 379–402.

Williams, Charles Bray. 1909. *The Participle in the Book of Acts*. Chicago: University of Chicago Press.

Winskel, Heather & Sudaporn Luksaneeyanawin. 2009. 'Obligatory Grammatical Categories and the Expression of Temporal Events'. *Journal of Child Language* 36(2): 355–80.

Wisely, John. 1907. *An English Grammar*. Chicago: Atkinson, Mentzer & Grover.

Wittgenstein, Ludwig. 1953. *Philosophical Investigations*. Oxford: Basil Blackwell.

Wood, Frederick T. 1956. 'Gerund versus Infinitive'. *ELT Journal* 11(1): 11–16.

Wu, Cunjing & Xuechao Hou. 1982. *Xiandai Hanyu jufa fenxi* [Syntactic analysis of modern Chinese]. Beijing: Peking University Press.

Wu, Qizhu. 1990. *Liandongju jianyuju* [Serial verb sentence and pivotal sentence]. Beijing: People's Education Press.

Xiao, Guozheng. 1995. '"Ju benwei" "cizu benwei" he "xiaoju zhongshu": Hanyu yufa biaoshu tixi gengdi de neizai dongli he fazhan quxiang' ['Sentence', 'group'

or 'clause' as the central unit: The inner motive and developmental trend in Chinese grammar]. *Shijie Hanyu Jiaoxue* [Chinese teaching in the world] 9(4): 5–13.
Xing, Fuyi. 1995. 'Xiaoju zhongshu shuo' [The clause-pivot theory]. *Zhongguo Yuwen* [Studies of the Chinese language] 34(6): 420–9.
Xing, Fuyi. 2017. *Modern Chinese Grammar: A Clause-Pivot Theoretical Approach*. London: Routledge.
Xing, Xin. 2004. *Xiandai Hanyu jianyushi* [Pivotal constructions in Chinese]. Beijing: Communication University of China Press.
Xu, Jie. 2010. 'Juzi yufa gongneng de xingzhi yu fanwei' [The nature and scope of grammatical function of sentence]. *Huazhong Shifan Daxue Xuebao* [Journal of Central China Normal University] 49(2): 101–6.
Xu, Liejiong. 1986. 'Towards a Lexical-Thematic Theory of Control'. *Linguistic Review* 5: 345–76.
Xu, Liejiong. 1994. 'Yu kongyulei youguan de yixie Hanyu yufa xianxiang' [Some grammatical issues related to PRO]. *Zhongguo Yuwen* [Studies of the Chinese language] 33(5): 321–9.
Xu, Liejiong. 1999. 'Chongju zhong de kongwei zhuyu' [Empty subject in subordinate clauses]. In *Gongxing yu gexing: Hanyu yuyanxue zhong de zhengyi* [Universals and specifics: Controversies in Chinese linguistics], edited by L. Xu, pp. 159–75. Beijing: Beijing Language and Culture University Press.
Yang, Bingjun. 2003. *A Study of Non-Finite Clauses in English: A Systemic Functional Approach*. Beijing: Foreign Language Teaching and Research Press.
Yang, Bingjun. 2004. 'Towards the Criteria of Non-Finite Clause Identification: A Systemic-Functional Approach'. *Language Sciences* 26(3): 233–49.
Yang, Bingjun. 2015. 'On Finiteness in Chinese from the Perspective of Cryptotype and Cline'. *Contemporary Foreign Languages Studies* 22(8): 6–10.
Yang, Bingjun. 2018. 'Textual Metaphor Revisited'. *Australian Journal of Linguistics* 38(2): 205–22.
Yang, Bingjun. 2019a. 'Interpersonal Metaphor Revisited: Identification, Categorization, and Syndrome'. *Social Semiotics* 29(2): 186–203.
Yang, Bingjun. 2019b. 'Taishang zuozhe zhuxituan de gainian yufa yinyu chanshi' [Taishang zuozhe zhuxituan in Chinese as ideational grammatical metaphor]. *Zhongguo Waiyu* [Foreign languages in China] 16(1): 48–54.
Yang, Bingjun. 2020. 'Full Realization Principle for the Identification of Ideational Grammatical Metaphor: Nominalization as Example'. *Journal of World Languages* 6(3): 161–74.
Yang, Chengkai. 1984. '"Jianyushi" cunfei zhizheng' [Arguing for and against 'pivotal construction']. *Xuexi Yu Sikao* [Learning and thinking] 2(1): 64–9.
Yang, Yanning. 2008. 'Typological Interpretation of Differences between Chinese and English in Grammatical Metaphor'. *Language Sciences* 30(4): 450–78.
Yang, Yanning. 2014. *Grammatical Metaphor in Chinese*. London: Equinox.
Yang, Yiming & Bing Cai. 2011. 'Hanyu dongci de quzhe jizhi yu xiandingxing wenti' [On the mechanism of inflection and finiteness of Chinese verbs]. *Shijie Hanyu Jiaoxue* [Chinese teaching in the world] 25(2): 159–74.
Yin, Huanxian. 1954. 'Tan liandongshi' [On serial verb construction]. *Wenshizhe* [Journal of literature, history and philosophy] 4(3): 32–3.

Yóu, Rujie. 2002. 'Xiandai Hanyu jianyuju de jufa he yuyi tezheng' [Syntactic and semantic features of V1+N+V2 in Mandarin Chinese]. *Hanyu Xuexi* [Chinese language learning] 23(6): 1–6.

Zandvoort, Reinard Willem. 1975. *A Handbook of English Grammar*. London: Longman.

Zhang, Bojiang. 2000. 'Hanyu liandongshi de jiwuxing jieshi' [Interpreting Chinese serial verb constructions with transitivity]. In *Yufa yanjiu he tansuo* [Research and exploration into grammar], vol. 9, edited by G. Shi, S. Xu, C. Rao, et al. pp. 129–41. Beijing: The Commercial Press.

Zhang, Cheng. 2014. 'Jindai Hanyu shiyiju yishi qusheng xianxiang yanjiu' [On the absence of cause in causative structures in early Mandarin: A case study of language contact]. *Zhongguo Yuwen* [Studies of the Chinese language] 64(3): 236–46.

Zhang, Jing. 1977. '"Liandongshi" he "jianyushi" yinggai quxiao' [Terms like serial and pivotal constructions to be abolished]. *Journal of Zhengzhou University* 9(4): 71–80.

Zhang, Meifang. 2015. *Functional Approaches to English-Chinese Translation*. Beijing: Foreign Languages Press.

Zhang, Ning. 1997. 'Syntactic Dependencies in Mandarin Chinese'. PhD thesis, University of Toronto.

Zhang, Xiaoshan. 1996. 'A Review of Studies on the Pivotal Construction'. In *Dongci yanjiu zongshu* [A review of studies on verbs], edited by Y. Hu & X. Fan, pp. 263–75. Taiyuan: Shanxi United Universities Press.

Zhang, Zhigong. 1982. *Xiandai Hanyu* [Modern Chinese]. Beijing: People's Education Press.

Zhang, Zhiyi. 1987. 'Hanyu quzhe bianhua de jianhua yu xiaoshi' [The simplifying and disappearing of inflections in Chinese]. *Yuwen Yanjiu* [Chinese studies] 8(3): 26–8.

Zheng, Ji'e. 1996. 'Jiaguwen zhong de liandongju he jianyuju' [Serial verb sentence and pivotal sentence in oracle bone inscriptions]. *Guhanyu Yanjiu* [Research in ancient Chinese language] 9(2): 29–31.

Zhou, Guoguang. 1998. 'Ertong yuyan zhong de lianwei jiegou he xiangguan de jufa wenti' [Predicates in series in children's language and related grammatical issues]. *Zhongguo Yuwen* [Studies of the Chinese language] 37(3): 181–8.

Zhu, Dexi. 1985. *Yufa wenda* [Answers to questions in grammar]. Beijing: The Commercial Press.

Ziv, Yael. 1982. 'On So-Called Existentials: A Typological Problem'. *Lingua* 56: 261–81.

Zou, Shaohua & Junping Zhang. 2000. 'Shilun dongci lianyong de zhongxin' [On the kernel of verbs used in series]. In *Yufa yanjiu he tansuo* [Research and exploration into grammar], vol. 9, edited by G. Shi, S. Xu, C. Rao, et al. pp. 122–8. Beijing: The Commercial Press.

Index

absolute clause, 16, 17, 63, 64, 118, 158, 194
absolute construction, 17, 63, 64, 118, 158, 159, 193, 194
accomplishment, 79
achievement, 79
activity, 62, 79, 155, 156, 157
actor–action construction, 18, 19, 84
adjectival, 11, 19, 22, 23, 65, 66, 120
adjectivization, 91, 92, 140
adverbial, 11, 16, 25, 27, 63, 120
adverbial clause, 17, 27, 63, 120
adverbialization, 94, 140, 141
agreement, 15, 20, 26, 27, 30, 31, 34, 36, 99, 107
apposition, 17
aspect marker, 29, 35, 38, 140, 175, 190, 191
asymmetry, 25, 26
atemporal construal, 39, 65
atemporal relation, 39, 65
atemporality, 39, 65

bare existential, 157
bare infinitive clause, 17
behavioural process, 81, 103, 115, 152, 178, 179

case marking, 5, 36, 38
category space, 22, 65
causative, 144, 145, 146, 149, 170, 173, 175, 176, 191
  causative construction, 144, 145, 146, 170, 173
  causative pivotal construction, 180, 181
Chinese existential, 183, 185
choreographic, 71
circumstance, 83, 91, 93, 94, 103, 117, 118, 131, 158, 194
clause, 3, 16, 17, 19, 20, 25, 26, 27, 30, 32, 33, 34, 35, 39, 40, 43, 46, 48, 49, 50, 51, 56, 60, 61, 62, 64, 70, 81, 85, 86, 87, 88, 95, 96, 97, 98, 100, 102, 104, 111, 115, 117, 122, 124, 126, 127, 143, 192, 195, 196, 197
clause combining, 41, 42, 122, 123, 126, 127, 130, 180, 197
clause complex, 46, 50, 70, 126, 127, 128
clause dependency, 6, 195
clause linkage, 42, 122, 124, 126, 129
clause linkage continua, 128, 140
  median clause, 87, 138, 159
  minor clause, 50, 87, 196
cline, 74, 102, 196
cognitive approach, 38
Cognitive Grammar, 9, 38, 44
cognitive linguistics, 44, 45
comment clause, 17
communicative performance, 68
complement clause, 30, 39, 49, 115
complement construction, 45
complex predicate, 165
complex transitive, 144, 145, 150
conceptual motivation, 44
conceptualization, 39, 44, 66
conditional clause, 17
conditional-concessive clause, 17
configurational, 87
conflation, 109, 119, 120, 150, 154
conjunction, 21, 46, 50, 106, 123, 124, 125, 132, 134, 143, 144, 197
  coordinating conjunction, 123
  subordinating conjunction, 123, 124
Construction Grammar, 45, 60
continuum hypothesis, 22, 23, 65
converb, 15, 25, 41
coordination, 38, 57, 61, 123, 124, 125, 126, 127, 128, 164
covert category, 73
cryptotype, 25, 73, 74, 102
crystalline, 71

dative construction, 119
definiteness effect, 183
deliberate semantics, 69

227

228　Index

derivational synthetic languages, 5
descriptive, 14, 26, 96, 165, 180
desententialization, 42, 44, 61, 67, 129
detachment, 70
ditransitive, 144, 151
double abstraction, 69

-ed clause, 49, 143
-ed participle, 124
elaboration, 51, 108, 129
elementary, 87
elements, 16, 38, 75, 87, 88, 117, 131
embedded construction, 58
embedding, 55, 58, 95, 97, 98, 99, 123, 125, 126, 127, 128, 129, 130, 134, 196
endocentric, 184
enhancement, 48, 51
event, 23, 26, 44, 49, 66, 69, 79, 85, 96, 100, 156, 157, 170, 195
event/state, 6, 100, 195
event-dominated, 23, 66
existential, 185, 187, 189
　existential clause, 110, 156
　existential construction, 111, 154, 157, 183, 197
　existential process, 103, 146, 190, 197
　existential sentence, 154, 155
expansion, 47, 107, 127
experiential enhanced theme, 156
experiential operator, 156
extension, 51, 96
extra-position, 17

family resemblance, 22, 27, 104
figures, 87, 88
finiteness, 4, 6, 15, 20, 21, 23, 24, 26, 29, 34, 35, 36, 37, 38, 40, 41, 43, 44, 65, 75, 83
　clausal finiteness, 60
　morphological finiteness, 5, 60
　pseudofiniteness, 25
　semantic finiteness, 5
　syntactic finiteness, 44
formalism, 78, 99
formalist, 5
form-oriented, 17, 62, 171
fragmentation, 70
full realization, 98, 112, 118, 130, 196
Full Realization Principle, 98
Functional Discourse Grammar, 57
Functional Grammar, 57, 86
functional sentence perspective, 72, 76
functionalism, 78, 99
functionalist, 5, 20
function-oriented, 62, 197

Generative Grammar, 1, 29
gerund, 12, 13, 14, 61, 62, 63
gerundial, 51
grammatical competence, 68
grammatical dependency, 40
grammatical metaphor, 6, 70, 87, 90, 96, 179
grammaticalization, 45, 129

Head-Driven Phrase Structure Grammar, 60
hypo-relation, 106, 108, 149, 154, 160, 161, 196
hypo-relator, 166
hypotactic relation, 52
hypotaxis, 70, 126, 127

iconicity meta-principle, 44
ideational, 6, 51, 77, 78, 81, 85, 100, 105, 195, 196
ideational component, 6, 100, 195
ideational metaphor, 6
imperative, 3, 10, 61
indicative, 3, 9, 10, 41
infinitive, 4, 9, 10, 11, 12, 13, 14, 16, 17, 37, 43, 45, 49, 51, 62, 124, 143
INFL, 1, 32, 34
inflection, 36, 61, 74, 75
inflectional language, 2, 28
information structure, 76
-ing clause, 49, 130, 158, 159
-ing participle, 124
integration, 44, 57, 66, 70
inter-clausal connectivity, 6, 8, 99, 196
interdependency, 48
intermediate realization, 65, 98, 99, 118, 136, 196
interpersonal, 6, 51, 52, 53, 78, 95, 100, 195
interpersonal meaning, 6, 52, 100, 195
into-causative, 145
into-causative construction, 145
intransitive, 145
involvement, 70, 180

landmark, 39, 73
language acquisition, 3, 85
Lexical-Functional Grammar, 60
lexicalization, 165
Limit of Finite Verb Principle, 98
linguistic typology, 2, 9, 22
locative, 155, 183, 185, 187
logical-semantic relation, 48
logogenesis, 89

main clausehood, 26
material process, 103, 146, 152, 173, 176, 177, 192, 197

Index

meaning potential, 46, 51
measuring word, 183, 184
median process, 154, 161
mental process, 53, 103, 115, 146, 152, 174, 178, 179, 197
metafunctions, 75, 76, 77, 78, 81, 102, 196
metaphoric syndrome, 90, 91, 93, 94, 140, 197
metaphoricity, 89
Minimalist Program, 36
modality, 38, 41, 108
mono-transitive, 144, 145, 150
mood, 3, 5, 6, 10, 11, 13, 19, 52, 53, 76
  moodless, 6, 74, 100, 195
  moodlessness, 195
motherese, 85
multifunctionality, 86

negation, 21, 23, 41
negation marker, 21, 65
nominal, 15, 17, 19, 25, 31, 39, 41, 42, 43, 51, 59, 65, 79, 84, 96, 112, 170
nominal clause, 17
nominalization, 6, 17, 21, 27, 41, 42, 79, 84, 89, 95, 96, 97, 98, 140, 142, 156, 160, 197
non-causative, 144, 173, 176, 177
  pseudo-nonfiniteness, 25
non-inflectional language, 2
noun phrase, 1
nounal verb, 14
number, 3, 5, 10, 12, 14, 15, 18, 20, 29, 37, 43, 65

object-dominated, 23, 66
obligatority, 25, 26, 27
ontogenesis, 89
optative, 3, 10, 20
Optional Infinitive stage, 27
optional infinitives, 197
overt category, 73, 134

paratactic relation, 83, 98, 134, 135, 136, 140, 159, 197
parataxis, 70, 126, 127, 129
participant, 50, 81, 82, 86, 97, 100, 102, 103, 108, 109, 111, 112, 113, 114, 115, 119, 120, 134, 138, 150, 151, 160, 161, 177, 193, 196
participant marker, 21, 65
participantial, 134, 140, 161, 197
participant-oriented, 50
participial, 46, 47, 51
participle, 11, 13, 14, 16, 39, 45, 63, 124
person, 3, 10, 12, 13, 15, 18, 20, 34, 36, 65, 79
Phenomenon, 51, 52, 81, 103, 115, 187, 193
  Macro-phenomenon, 51, 52

Meta-phenomenon, 52
phylogenesis, 89
pivotal construction, 6, 165, 169, 170, 171, 172, 173, 176, 177, 179, 180, 181, 182
polarity, 48, 66, 164
post-modification, 17
predication, 20, 39, 59, 80, 122, 155, 183
predicative function, 58
prepositional phrase, 83, 87, 104, 106, 116, 117, 118, 134, 159
prescriptive, 14
Principle of Constructional Economy, 60, 67
process, 39, 50, 52, 66, 70, 79, 80, 81, 82, 83, 84, 87, 102, 103, 104, 105, 106, 107, 108, 109, 110, 111, 112, 113, 114, 115, 116, 117, 118, 119, 120, 134, 138, 140, 144, 149, 150, 158, 167, 173, 177, 180, 192, 196, 197
  major process, 82, 87, 140, 149, 192
  median process, 82, 87, 116, 118, 120, 130, 132, 134, 137, 138, 139, 140, 150, 151, 158, 159, 187, 191, 196
  minor process, 83, 84, 87, 118, 134, 158, 162
  process types, 80, 81, 83, 104, 152, 173, 175, 190, 192, 197
process-oriented, 50
projected clause, 115
projection, 47, 108, 127
pseudo-existential, 184
purpose clause, 147, 165

qualifier, 101, 132, 139, 140
quality, 90, 91

rankshifting, 55, 56, 88, 89, 92, 94, 95, 97, 98, 99, 130, 134, 196
raw realization, 97, 98, 111, 118, 196
relational process, 81, 103, 152, 180, 185, 190
relational synthetic languages, 5
relator, 50, 91, 93, 104, 105, 106, 166, 167, 176
relator-oriented, 50
Rheme, 48
Role and Reference Grammar, 56
root infinitive, 27, 28, 29, 66

semantics, 72, 76, 88, 169
Semiotic Grammar, 55
Senser, 51, 81, 103, 115, 178
sentence-building power, 13, 18, 19, 20
sequence, 87, 88
serial verb construction, 64, 134, 151, 165, 167, 168, 169
serialization, 41, 164
simple sentence, 9, 19
situation, 49, 56, 64, 74, 79, 80, 99, 145, 170

spatial marker, 21, 65
speech, 68, 69, 70, 71, 72, 73, 80, 85
   inner speech, 69
   written speech, 69
speech production, 85
spoken language, 1, 68, 69, 70, 71, 72, 73, 163
state, 14, 44, 44, 66, 79, 80, 85, 95, 98, 100, 156, 157, 196
subject agreement, 15, 23, 34
subjectless clause, 183
subjectless sentence, 183
subjunctive, 3, 9, 10, 41
subordination, 21, 25, 38, 42, 123, 124, 125, 126, 127, 128, 129, 130, 134
subordinator, 17, 63, 123, 124
synthetic language, 5, 15, 21
Systemic Functional Grammar, 46, 47, 52, 78, 80, 81, 83, 126, 127
Systemic Functional Linguistics, 7

taxis, 48, 126, 127
temporality, 39, 65
tense, 3, 5, 10, 13, 14, 15, 18, 19, 20, 23, 26, 27, 30, 34, 35, 37, 38, 46, 47, 48, 65, 86, 99, 108, 109, 176, 195
tense–aspect, 26, 38, 66
tense marker, 35, 39, 175
tense–aspect–modality, 41, 164
text annotation, 1, 2, 198
text segmentation, 1, 2, 198
textual, 51, 52, 70, 76, 77, 85, 123, 196

Theme, 48, 51, 52, 86
to-clause, 17, 30, 49, 106, 130, 161
to-infinitive, 123
topic marker, 38
topichood, 76
topic-prominent construction, 193
traditional grammar, 14, 15, 20, 73, 89, 94, 118, 120, 130, 149, 156
trajector, 39
transitive, 145, 150
transitivity, 51, 168

verb-mediated construction, 45
verb phrase, 1
verbal group, 1, 46, 48, 81, 104, 106, 165, 166, 167, 168, 169
verbal group complex, 1, 49, 50, 83, 104, 107, 108
verbal morphology, 165
verbal noun, 11, 14, 43
verbal process, 81, 103, 146, 147, 149, 152, 177, 191, 192, 197
verbalization, 6, 89, 92, 93, 98, 141, 142, 197
Verbiage, 81, 103, 192
verbless clause, 16, 17, 49, 63, 124, 130, 158

writing, 20, 68, 69, 70, 71, 72, 80, 85, 89
written language, 6, 49, 68, 69, 70, 71, 72, 73, 85, 86, 102, 103, 163

X-bar, 2

For EU product safety concerns, contact us at Calle de José Abascal, 56–1°, 28003 Madrid, Spain or eugpsr@cambridge.org.

www.ingramcontent.com/pod-product-compliance
Ingram Content Group UK Ltd.
Pitfield, Milton Keynes, MK11 3LW, UK
UKHW020403120325
456051UK00006B/73